Tracts of the

American Revolution

1763–1776

THE AMERICAN HERITAGE SERIES

THE

American Heritage

Series

UNDER THE GENERAL EDITORSHIP OF

LEONARD W. LEVY AND ALFRED YOUNG

Tracts of the

American Revolution

1763-1776

EDITED BY

MERRILL JENSEN

Bobbs-Merrill Educational Publishing
Indianapolis

The Bobbs-Merrill Company, Inc.
4300 West 62nd Street
Indianapolis, Indiana 46268

Library of Congress Catalog Card Number 66-26805
ISBN 0-672-60046-3 (pbk)

Sixth Printing—1977

FOREWORD

This is the first volume to assemble in convenient form some of the most important tracts of the American Revolution. It is remarkable that hitherto they have been available to the general reader only in short excerpts, and to scholars in out-of-print editions or on microcard reproductions accessible only in research libraries. From 1763 to 1776 some four hundred tracts appeared in the American colonies; from these Professor Jensen has selected seventeen pamphlets and newspaper articles—a representative sampling of the total output—and presented them for the most part in their entirety.

The most famous pamphleteers are here: James Otis, John Dickinson, John Adams, Thomas Jefferson, and Thomas Paine. So are less well known ones. The various shades of American opinion are represented. For the final crisis, from 1774 to 1776, the selections permit one to examine the crucial debate over independence between Daniel Leonard and John Adams, between Thomas Paine and James Chalmers.

Inevitably readers will argue that this or that pamphlet should have been included; few, however, can fail to be interested in Professor Jensen's choices. The tracts enable the reader to study the colonists' grievances against Britain, their methods of persuasion, and the development of political thought that led to the Declaration of Independence. Inevitably these documents provide rich evidence on the still perplexing problem of the origin and nature of the American Revolution.

In his introduction Professor Jensen presents a capsule history of the events of the period and an analysis of the context of each tract. In editing each document he has modernized the original text to diminish the eccentricities of typography that present an unnecessary obstacle to contemporary readers.

This book is one of a series whose aim is to provide the

essential primary sources of the American experience, especially of American thought. The series will constitute a documentary library of American history, filling a need long felt among scholars, students, libraries, and general readers for authoritative collections of original materials. Some volumes will illuminate the thought of significant individuals, such as James Madison or Louis Brandeis; some will deal with movements, such as the Antifederalists or the Populists; others will be organized around special themes, such as Puritan political thought, or American Catholic thought on social questions. Many volumes will take up the large number of subjects traditionally studied in American history for which surprisingly there are no documentary anthologies; others will pioneer in introducing new subjects of increasing importance to scholars as to the contemporary world. The series aspires to maintain the high standards demanded of contemporary scholarship, providing authentic texts, intelligently and unobtrusively edited. It will also have the distinction of presenting documents of substantial length which give the full character and flavor of the original. When completed, the series will be the most comprehensive and authoritative of its kind.

Alfred Young
Leonard W. Levy

EDITOR'S PREFACE

Hundreds of pamphlets of all kinds were printed in America between 1763 and 1776. This volume brings together some of the more important ones, containing the basic arguments used by Americans as they opposed British measures and policies after 1763, and as they disputed the issue of independence with one another between 1774 and 1776.

The general introduction to this volume has two purposes. The first is to present a broad outline of the events between 1763 and 1776 so that the pamphlets can be placed in their political context. The second purpose is to sketch the role of the pamphlet writers in the history of the times. The brief comments on the "significance" of the pamphlets should be taken as only a general guide. Each reader doubtless will—and ought to—decide for himself what the pamphlets mean. The introductions to the individual pamphlets provide information on the circumstances surrounding their publication and circulation.

Merrill Jensen

CONTENTS

TRACTS OF THE AMERICAN REVOLUTION, 1763–1776

INTRODUCTION:
THE PAMPHLET WRITERS
AND THEIR TIMES

1. The Role of Pamphlets and Newspapers

The great debate between Britain and her American colonies, which ended with the declaration of American independence in 1776, took place on many levels, and its basic ideas were expressed in many forms. Town meetings, county meetings, and colonial legislatures adopted hundreds of resolutions and petitions. Judges, in charges to grand juries, expounded on the issues of the times as well as on matters more relevant to their duties. Poets and playwrights produced works of considerable fervor but uneven merit. Ministers of the gospel preached innumerable sermons. However, the debate was dominated and carried on most consistently by anonymous newspaper essayists and by pamphleteers who purported to be anonymous but whose identities were usually known to their contemporaries.

The eighteenth century, like the seventeenth, was a great age of political pamphleteering. The first newspapers were little more than official gazettes, and the publisher who sought to play a political role was usually suppressed or otherwise brought to heel. Hence, political writers turned to the pamphlet to criticize government policy, to demand changes in programs, or, for that matter, to defend the wielders of political power.

By 1763 American newspapers had achieved a great measure of freedom in practice, and in the years before 1776 the political essayist in the newspaper shares with the pamphleteer in the task of carrying on the debate with Britain over the nature of the British Empire and the position of the American colonies within the empire. In fact, as Moses Coit Tyler pointed out many years ago,[1] there is only a "mechanical distinction" between the newspaper essay and the pamphlet. Many newspaper essays were later printed as pamphlets, and material that first appeared in pamphlet form was often reprinted wholly or partly in the newspapers. Thus, Dickinson's vastly popular *Farmer* letters appeared in most of the colonial newspapers before they were published as a pamphlet. On the other hand, Stephen Hopkins' *The Rights of Colonies Examined* appeared first as a pamphlet and then was widely republished in the newspapers.

Did the pamphlet writers lead the debate, or did they tend to sum up ideas already prevalent and acceptable to at least a segment of American opinion? The answer is that sometimes the pamphleteers were leaders and sometimes followers. John Dickinson's *Farmer* letters in 1767–1768 were acclaimed throughout America because they offered a solution to a theoretical dilemma concerning "external" taxation. Thomas Paine's *Common Sense* was the most popular pamphlet of the age, but the ideas in it were not new. In one form or another they had been appearing in newspaper essays and paragraphs, and even in resolutions of town meetings, ever since 1765. Paine's achievement was to put those ideas into lucid, vivid prose that has as much impact today as it must have had on his readers in the eighteenth century.

On the whole, the newspapers between 1763 and 1776 were more aggressive in promoting extreme ideas than the writers of pamphlets. Certain newspapers were instruments in the hands of the men who were leading the opposition to Britain and British policies. Thus, the *Boston Gazette* was the mouthpiece of Samuel Adams, who used it to prepare the way for

---

[1] *The Literary History of the American Revolution, 1763–1783* (2 vols., New York: G. P. Putnam's Sons, 1897), I, 17.

official action by the Boston town meeting and the Massachusetts legislature. The same method was used by popular leaders in other colonies such as New York, Pennsylvania, and South Carolina. The result was that a campaign of newspaper propaganda often preceded the publication of pamphlets devoted to the discussion of similar ideas.

But whether pamphleteers led or followed is not as important as the fact that they did sum up, in extended and more permanent form, ideas that were scattered about in newspapers. It is idle to try to assign predominance to either newspapers or pamphlets: at the time, they were in fact interchangeable tools in a continuing debate.

Much of the debate revolved around the nature of the constitution of the British Empire and the role of Parliament in the empire. However, very few pamphleteers ever confined themselves exclusively to purely constitutional arguments. They were also concerned with the economic impact of British colonial policies after 1763, as were the legislatures in the hundreds of resolutions they adopted. In fact, the first significant essay of the period, Stephen Hopkins' *Essay on the Trade of the Northern Colonies,* concentrated exclusively on the economic effects of the new British enforcement policies, and when he wrote his *The Rights of Colonies Examined* less than a year later, he used both constitutional and economic arguments. So too did the pamphleteers who attacked the Stamp Act in 1765.

As time passed, more and more emphasis was placed on the constitutional issue, but even so striking a theoretical argument as *A State of the Rights of the Colonists,* adopted by the Boston town meeting in November 1772, did not ignore economic issues. And it is perfectly obvious in the *Summary View of the Rights of British America* in 1774 that Thomas Jefferson was well aware of the impact the Quebec Act would have on the expansionist policies of the Virginia planters. Thus, the pamphleteers, like the newspaper essayists, excluded no subject from consideration. Economics, politics, religion, and the "future glory" of America were all interwoven threads in the pattern of the debate over the nature of the constitutional relationship between the American colonies and the British Empire.

2. *British Policies and American Opposition, 1760–1766*

American opposition to British policies was well under way long before the crisis created by the passage of the Stamp Act in 1765. During the Seven Years' War, American and British merchants traded with the enemy, as they had done in previous wars and were to do in future ones. The attitude of most eighteenth-century merchants was summed up by Robert Morris during the war for American independence, when he declared that a merchant had no country. Britain tried in vain to stop trade with the French West Indies during the first part of the Seven Years' War, but not until after the conquest of Canada in 1760, when William Pitt ordered the British navy to stop trade with the enemy, did Britain have any success.

That success alarmed, among others, the merchants of Boston, who tried to destroy the effectiveness of the British customs service in a series of court actions. James Otis, Jr., in the first of these cases in 1761, made an eloquent speech against the use of writs of assistance by customs officers searching for smuggled goods. Otis, the merchants' lawyer, lost the case, for the Superior Court of Massachusetts, presided over by Chief Justice Thomas Hutchinson, ruled that the use of such writs was legal. Subsequent attacks against the customs service also failed in the Superior Court. Nevertheless, an investigation at the end of the war, in 1763, revealed that in most colonies the customs service was at best inefficient and at worst corrupt, and that the officers did not even collect enough money to cover their expenses.[2]

The most important law, in terms of potential revenue, was the Molasses Act of 1733. By the 1730's the British West Indies were no longer able to purchase all of the food, fish, and lumber produced in the British colonies on the mainland, nor were they able to supply the demand of those colonies for the molasses that was used for sweetening and for the production of rum. The mainland colonies therefore turned to the foreign islands in the West Indies, where there were better markets and a cheaper supply of molasses. In an effort to block this trade with the foreign islands, British owners of West Indian plantations induced Parliament to pass the Molasses Act. The law did not declare trade with the foreign islands illegal; it tried to place an economic barrier in the way by levying a duty of six pence per gallon on foreign molasses imported by the British colonies, plus duties on other foreign products such as sugar. The law was economically indefensible and was not enforced. British officials in the West Indies and on the mainland usually ignored it, and merchants in the mainland colonies evaded it when customs officials refused to co-operate. The merchants believed, with considerable justification, that trade with the foreign islands was indispensable to their prosperity. The profits from that trade helped pay for the ever greater quantity of British manufactures they imported, and which they could not pay for by shipping the products of the northern colonies to Great Britain. It was British interference with this trade to the foreign islands, first by the British navy in 1760, and then by the enforcement policies of the Grenville ministry

---

[2] For the British administrative actions and legislation affecting the colonies between 1763 and 1776 referred to in this introduction, see Merrill Jensen, ed., *American Colonial Documents to 1776* (*English Historical Documents,* IX, London: Eyre and Spotteswoode; New York: Oxford University Press, 1955).

in 1763, that set off resistance in the northern colonies. And what started as a debate over economics soon widened into a debate over the nature of the constitution of the British Empire—one that involved all the colonies, including those in the West Indies.

The first phase of the debate between Britain and America after 1763 took place against the background of the administrative policies and parliamentary legislation of the ministry headed by George Grenville, which took office as the war ended in 1763 and which fell from power in the summer of 1765. In summary, the policies were as follows:

1. Administrative reform of the customs service in America, which was inefficient and/or corrupt.

2. An act of Parliament in 1763 stationing British naval vessels in North American waters and granting their commanders the powers of land-based customs officials.

3. The stationing of regiments of the regular British army in America (a decision made before the Grenville ministry took office) to serve as frontier police, and if need be, to support British officials in the seaboard colonies.

4. The royal Proclamation of October 7, 1763, which drew a boundary line along the crest of the Appalachian Mountains and forbade settlement west of it in what amounted to an Indian reservation, and which placed land granting and regulation of the fur trade in the West in the hands of the two Indian superintendents who had been first appointed in 1755.

5. The Revenue Act ("Sugar Act") of April 5, 1764, which, in addition to imposing new duties on trade, provided for new and elaborate regulations for the shipment of goods in and out of colonial ports, established new rules for the trial of cases involving infringement of commercial laws and customs regulations, and virtually freed British customs officials from legal responsibility for their actions.

6. The establishment of an Admiralty Court at Halifax,

Nova Scotia (authorized by the Revenue Act of 1764), to which customs officials might appeal cases from admiralty and common-law courts in individual colonies, or to which they could take cases directly without first trying them in a local colonial court.

7. The Currency Act of April 19, 1764, which forbade the colonies to issue any new paper money which would be legal tender, or to reissue old paper money then in circulation.

8. The Stamp Act of March 22, 1765, which required that a wide range of legal documents, business papers, newspapers, and even advertisements be provided with stamps which had to be paid for in specie.

9. The Quartering Act of May 15, 1765, which required, when British troops were stationed in barracks belonging to the colonial governments, that those governments must provide the troops with certain supplies without charge.

The first reaction of Americans to the policies of the Grenville administration was confined to the merchants of the northern colonies, and the grounds of their opposition were entirely economic. By the end of 1763, merchants in all the northern colonies were becoming alarmed at the newly invigorated customs service and the arrival of British naval vessels in American waters. Northern newspapers urged merchants and legislators to take action to block the schemes of the "selfish" British West Indians. Americans knew that the Molasses Act of 1733, which was passed for five years at a time, would expire in 1763. However, Parliament re-enacted the law for only a year, as a temporary measure, until a comprehensive overhaul of the customs service could be completed.

The Boston merchants led the campaign against the Molasses Act and other British efforts to place obstacles in the way of American trade with the foreign West Indies. They created a formal organization early in 1763; by December they had prepared a "State of Trade," which they sent to merchants in the other northern colonies and Britain. They asked for help in defeating the "iniquitous schemes of these overgrown West Indians," and pointed out that the "State of Trade" described the peculiar problems of Massachusetts commerce and that doubtless other colonies would shape their protests to suit the character of their own commerce. There was an immediate response. In Rhode Island, Governor Stephen Hopkins wrote his widely republished *An Essay on the Trade of the Northern Colonies*[3] and the Rhode Island legislature embodied this and other documents in an official "Remonstrance" which it sent to London. The New York merchants drafted a protest which was adopted by the New York legislature as an official statement.

Hopkins' *Essay* is a far better balanced account of the trade of the colonies than the Boston "State of Trade," the Rhode Island "Remonstrance," or the petition of the New York legislature. Each of those documents emphasized the particular problems of a single colony. Hopkins took a broad view of all the colonies, including those in the South where commercial patterns were quite different from those in the North. In fact, during 1763 and early 1764 the Southerners showed no interest at all in the economic problems that agitated Americans in the northern colonies. Hopkins' particular emphasis is on the need of the northern colonies for untrammeled trade with the West Indies, both foreign and British, and his statistics are as adequate as most of those which have been brought together in the years since the eighteenth century.

If Parliament was aware of American opposition, it paid no heed, and in April 1764 it passed the Revenue Act. That act reduced the duty on foreign molasses from six pence to three pence a gallon, which Americans swore was as prohibitive a duty as the old one since molasses sold at twelve pence a gallon. For the time being they ignored the sweeping alteration of the procedures for shipping goods and for the trial of cases

---

[3] Pamphlet 1.

of customs violations. They ignored these because among the resolutions upon which the Revenue Act was based was one which declared that it would be "proper" for Parliament to levy a stamp tax on America. However, the passage of such a law was delayed for a year for the expressed purpose of giving Americans an opportunity to suggest other means of providing money to help pay a portion of Britain's expenses in the colonies.

American attention was fixed at once on this resolution. However grudgingly, most Americans conceded that Parliament had the right to levy duties in connection with the regulation of trade. But did Parliament have the right to levy taxes collectible within the colonies? Could the people in the colonies be taxed without the consent of their own legislatures? The constitutional issue thus raised was not settled until the Declaration of Independence, and the debate over it produced pamphlets, resolutions, petitions, and newspaper essays by the hundreds. American arguments were confusing and often contradictory, but between 1763 and 1765 they made it clear that they had no intention of providing money to help the British customs service pay for itself or to buy supplies for the British army.

Only a few of the pamphlets written during this first phase of the argument can be included. The first of the pamphlets written after the arrival of the news of the proposed stamp act was James Otis' *The Rights of the British Colonies Asserted and Proved.*[4]

James Otis, Jr., was the son of Colonel James Otis, a political leader in southern Massachusetts who supported the "government party" in colonial politics. In 1760 that party was led by Thomas Hutchinson. As lieutenant governor, member of the upper house of the legislature (the council), holder of two county judgeships and other minor offices, and with relatives

---

[4] Pamphlet 2.

in other official positions, Hutchinson was the political boss of the colony.

In 1760, shortly after the arrival of Francis Bernard as governor, the chief justice of the Superior Court (i.e., supreme court) died. Although a previous governor had promised Colonel Otis a place on the Superior Court when a vacancy occurred, Bernard appointed Hutchinson chief justice, in addition to his other jobs. The Otis family was outraged and joined forces with the popular leaders of Boston; thus they laid the foundation of the Popular Party, which was to lead Massachusetts into the war for independence sixteen years later. James Otis, Jr., became the darling of the populace of Boston, which elected him to the legislature in 1761. Thereafter, he usually dominated the Boston town meeting and was one of the most vocal members of the House of Representatives. He carried on a ceaseless vendetta against Governor Bernard, who was virtually driven from the colony in 1769, and against Thomas Hutchinson, who was charged with everything from authorship of the Stamp Act to a plot to destroy the liberties of Massachusetts. The opposition to British policies in Massachusetts after 1763 was led by the Popular Party, but this opposition was so intertwined with the fight against Bernard and Hutchinson that it is impossible to decide which part of the fight James Otis considered the more important. This helps to explain the confusions and contradictions in the pamphlets that he wrote during 1764 and 1765.

The Boston merchants who had been attacking British policies ever since 1761 appealed to the Massachusetts legislature for help early in 1764. The legislature responded by appointing Thomas Hutchinson as a special agent to go to England. Governor Bernard then announced that since Hutchinson was lieutenant governor he could not leave until he had permission from London. Hutchinson agreed to wait, but before the end of the legislative session, his political enemies persuaded the House of Representatives to revoke the appointment. As a result, Massachusetts, unlike Rhode Island and New York, made no official protest against renewal of the Molasses Act before the passage of the Revenue Act of 1764.

The news of the act and of the proposed stamp act reached Boston before the annual election of representatives to the legislature late in May. The town instructed its four representatives to secure a legislative petition asking for repeal of the Molasses Act and to instruct the colony's agent in London to oppose all future taxes levied by Parliament. Such taxes, declared the instructions written by Samuel Adams, would destroy the charter right of the colony to tax and govern itself.

The new legislature met for a two-week session on May 30. The house appointed a committee of six to answer letters from the house's agent in London. Three of the committee—James Otis, Oxenbridge Thacher, and Thomas Cushing—were from Boston. Meanwhile, a document called "The Rights of the British Colonies" was read to the house on June 8 and 12 and turned over to the committee. The next day the house approved a letter to the agent denouncing him for failing to do his duty, and scoffing at the delay of a stamp act as a supposed concession to the colonies. Along with the letter the house sent a copy of "The Rights of the British Colonies," written by James Otis, and soon to appear as a pamphlet.

Thomas Hutchinson denounced the house's proceedings and the Boston leaders, whose only aim, he said, was to make themselves popular. Furthermore, merchants, who were more concerned with economics than with proclamations of rights, wanted more specific action. Therefore, Governor Bernard called a special session of the legislature in October 1764 to prepare a petition to Britain. The house of representatives prepared a petition based on the "natural right" of the colony to tax itself. Hutchinson, as a member of the council, insisted that the petition be based entirely on economic grounds, and he persuaded a majority of both houses to agree with him. It is clear that the argument for "natural rights" and the other ideas in Otis' pamphlet did not represent the views of the men who dominated the government of Massachusetts in 1764.

Otis' *Rights of the British Colonies* began with a bold assertion that all government originates in the unchangeable will of God, that in every society there must be a supreme, sovereign, and uncontrollable power, and that under God comes the "power of a simple democracy." He soon abandoned this daring line of argument. He praised the British constitution as the best ever devised and asserted that Parliament had the power to legislate for the colonies and that the colonies must obey its laws. However, Americans had the same rights as their fellow subjects in Britain. He scorned colonial charters as the basis for American rights and insisted that those rights were based on the laws of God and nature, the common law, and the acts of Parliament. As he had done in his speech against writs of assistance in 1761, Otis got around his assertion of the uncontrollable power of Parliament by appealing to a "higher law." Acts of Parliament contrary to the "natural laws" of God were void. Therefore, Otis argued, "no part of his Majesty's dominions can be taxed without their own consent." Otis' solution was to establish American representation in Parliament, a solution that few Americans then or later, canny politicians that they were, found acceptable.

So far as his contemporaries could see, Otis soon reversed his position on the power of Parliament. Early in 1765 he entered into the pamphlet warfare in Rhode Island between Governor Stephen Hopkins and Martin Howard, Jr.[5] He wrote two pamphlets defending Hopkins' position and his own, but in effect he abandoned the defense of colonial rights. He asserted that Parliament had a right to "impose taxes on the colonies, internal and external, on lands as well as trade." He declared that the colonies were in fact represented in Parliament, and he refused to oppose a stamp act. Parliament was

---

[5] See Pamphlets 3 and 4.

all-powerful and must be obeyed.[6] According to some of Otis' friends, he had suffered from a "failure of nerve" when rumors reached Boston that Britain might try to punish him for his 1764 pamphlet. If he had not been attacked by a vicious piece of poetry just before the spring election of 1765, his political career might have ended then instead of a few years later.

Governor Stephen Hopkins was more consistent than Otis, although he too backed down from the position he took in *The Rights of Colonies Examined* in December 1764.[7] Hopkins was the leader of the Providence faction in Rhode Island politics. He was elected governor for the first time in 1757, and only three times between then and 1768, when both men withdrew from the race, did he lose the annual election to Samuel Ward, leader of the Newport faction.

The corruptness of Rhode Island politics during this period has seldom been equaled in all of American political history. But when Britain threatened to interfere with Rhode Island commerce or self-government, most Rhode Islanders joined forces. Thus the legislature unanimously opposed renewal of the Molasses Act in January 1764, and that fall, with the same unanimity, it adopted a petition to the king complaining of the passage of the Revenue Act of 1764 and protesting against Parliament's power to pass a stamp act. It approved, again unanimously, a pamphlet that the governor had written and ordered it printed in Britain and in the colony.

The governor's *The Rights of Colonies Examined* was published in Providence on December 22, 1764. Hopkins appealed

---

[6] Otis' *A Vindication of the British Colonies* and *Brief Remarks on the Defence of the Halifax Libel* are printed in Charles F. Mullett, ed., "Some Political Writings of James Otis," *The University of Missouri Studies*, IV (1929), 387–432. Otis' *Rights* pamphlet of 1764 and his *Vindication* of 1765 are printed in Bernard Bailyn, ed., *Pamphlets of the American Revolution*, I (Cambridge: Harvard University Press, 1965), 419–482, 554–579. Bailyn argues that there is an inner consistency in Otis' argument.

[7] Pamphlet 3.

to the history of ancient and modern colonies, and proved to his satisfaction that all colonists had always enjoyed equal rights with the citizens of their mother countries. The British colonists were no exception, and, unlike James Otis, Hopkins based much of his argument on the colonial charters. He complained about the Revenue Act of 1764, the new admiralty court established at Halifax, Nova Scotia, and the behavior of customs officers; but his main concern was the proposed stamp act. He argued that if Parliament were to levy "stamp duties and internal taxes" on the colonies "without their own consent," it would be a violation of just and long-enjoyed rights. He admitted, however, that Parliament had the right to legislate on matters of a "general nature" affecting the "whole commonwealth"—such matters as commerce, keeping the peace, and money and paper credit. But Parliament did not have the right to levy taxes on Americans because the people of England, whom Parliament represented, were not sovereign over the people of America. In effect, Hopkins was groping toward the conception of the British Empire as a commonwealth containing equal and independent legislatures, and yet one in which matters of a general nature had to be dealt with by a supreme legislature. Like others throughout history who have dealt with the problem of "federalism," Hopkins offered no clear solution.

Within a few months, Hopkins, like James Otis, retreated from his position, which was attacked by his fellow Rhode Islander, Martin Howard, Jr., of Newport, in his *Letter from a Gentleman at Halifax*[8] in February 1765. A small group of lawyers, doctors, and British officials in Newport was appalled by the "democracy" of Rhode Island and the political behavior of the majority of the people, whom they contemptuously called "the Herd." This "Newport Junto" began publishing articles in the *Newport Mercury* in 1764, attacking the colony's

---

[8] Pamphlet 4.

charter as out-of-date and insisting on the need for a general reformation of colonial government. Then sometime during the fall of 1764, the Junto sent a petition to the king asking for the revocation of the charter and the establishment of a royal government in the colony. It also sought the help of Benjamin Franklin, who had gone to England that year to lobby for the revocation of the Penn family's charter to Pennsylvania and the establishment of a royal government in that colony.[9]

Martin Howard, Jr., a lawyer, was a leading member of the Newport Junto. His pamphlet attacked both Hopkins and James Otis, and made a straightforward defense of Parliament's sovereignty over the colonies.

Although Americans such as Otis and Hopkins were ambivalent about challenging this sovereignty in 1764–1765, very few Americans indeed were willing to defend it openly, whatever they might think privately. One notable exception was Joseph Galloway, Benjamin Franklin's political ally in Pennsylvania. As "Americanus" in the *New York Gazette* on August 15 and in the *Pennsylvania Journal* on August 29, 1765, Galloway asserted that Parliament had the power to tax Americans if it chose to do so, and suggested either American representation in Parliament or the creation of an American legislature as the only solution. He thus took a position he supported consistently, a position that committed him to loyalism in 1775.

As the controversy continued, more and more Americans came to believe that the only alternative to American independence was recognition of the sovereignty of Parliament. And since some of them feared the consequences of independence, they came to the defense of that sovereignty. Thus in January 1773, Thomas Hutchinson, who had been appointed

---

[9] For a discussion of Rhode Island politics and the pamphlet warfare, see David S. Lovejoy, *Rhode Island Politics and the American Revolution, 1760–1776* (Providence, R.I.: Brown University Press, 1958).

governor of Massachusetts in 1770, defended the sovereignty of Parliament in a speech to the legislature and assured the legislators that the only alternative was American independence. The next year certain American pamphleteers took the same position as they considered the consequences of the First Continental Congress.

Martin Howard's *Letter from a Gentleman at Halifax* in February 1765 is therefore an unusual pamphlet, for it expresses what might be called the "loyalist" position very early in the debate. And temporarily, he had the better of the argument. Governor Hopkins wrote a series of articles for the *Providence Gazette* in which he insisted that he had not challenged the authority of Parliament in his pamphlet but had only given it as his opinion that internal taxation of the colonies by Parliament was contrary to British principles of government. And James Otis, in the midst of calling Howard and his allies vile names, abjectly proclaimed the absolute sovereignty of Parliament over the colonies.

Whatever satisfaction Howard derived was short-lived. He and some of his friends were forced to flee to England after the Stamp Act riots in August 1765. His flight, however, does not detract from the importance of his pamphlet, for he does express openly what other Americans were not to express until almost the end of the debate—when it was too late to alter the course of events.

The passage of the Stamp Act on March 22, 1765, presented Americans with a reality they could not escape. During the spring of that year they were also presented with a number of British pamphlets attacking the American position on taxation and asserting Parliament's right to tax them.[10] The most im-

---

[10] For a discussion of these pamphlets, see Edmund S. and Helen Morgan, *The Stamp Act Crisis: Prologue to Revolution* (Chapel Hill, N.C.: The University of North Carolina Press, 1953), Chapter VI, "Daniel Dulany: Pamphleteer."

portant of these was *The Regulations Lately Made Concerning the Colonies and the Taxes Imposed upon Them, Considered*. It was written by Thomas Whately, one of George Grenville's secretaries, and was, in effect, an official defense of the policies of the Grenville ministry; in fact, many Americans thought Grenville himself had written it. Much of the pamphlet dealt with the Revenue Act of 1764, but it concluded with an assertion of Parliament's right to levy the Stamp Tax. The pamphlet argued that the colonists were in the same situation as nine-tenths of the inhabitants of Britain, who could not vote for members of the House of Commons. Although such people were not actually represented, declared the pamphlet, they were "virtually represented," since members of the House of Commons represented all British subjects, not merely the constituents who elected them.

Most American newspaper and pamphlet writers scorned the idea of virtual representation. The most popular American pamphlet in reply was Daniel Dulany's *Considerations on the Propriety of Imposing Taxes in the British Colonies, For the Purpose of Raising a Revenue, by Act of Parliament.*[11]

Daniel Dulany (1722–1797) was a member of the proprietary "establishment" in Maryland. His father, a penniless immigrant from Ireland at the beginning of the century, had made a fortune in law and land speculation. In politics he had started out as a "popular" leader in the assembly, but by the time of his death in 1753 he was a pillar of the proprietary "party" and had been a member of the governor's council for eleven years. His son Daniel was educated at Eton, Clare Hall, Cambridge, and the Middle Temple, and when he returned to Maryland, he supported the proprietary interest from the start, first in the assembly, and after 1761, in the council. He was one of the wealthiest men in the colony and, next to the governor, its most influential political leader.

---

[11] Pamphlet 6.

Very few members of the colonial "establishment" took a bold stand against British measures after 1763, but Daniel Dulany was one of those few. In his pamphlet in 1765 he argued vigorously and effectively that Americans were not and could not be represented in Parliament, and that taxation of Americans by Parliament was contrary to the common law, the British constitution, and the colonial charters. And like other writers at the time, he urged the development of colonial manufactures as an effective method of defying British measures.

Dulany's pamphlet reflected opinion in his own colony to a remarkable degree. Prior to its publication, the assembly had elected delegates to the Stamp Act Congress and unanimously adopted resolutions declaring Maryland's charter right to tax itself, and declaring taxation by any outside power "unconstitutional." The council, of which Dulany was a member, agreed, and Governor Sharpe signed the necessary papers. Furthermore, Marylanders were as much concerned with economic problems as with constitutional issues. The colony was suffering from a depression and worried about the economic effects of a stamp tax payable in scarce and often nonexistent specie.[12] Dulany's pamphlet reflected this concern with economic problems and devoted much space to them.

Dulany's popularity was short-lived. He opposed the war for independence and became an avowed Loyalist, although unlike many others he did not flee from the country. Eventually Maryland confiscated most of his property, and he died in obscurity in 1797.

However, pamphleteers such as Dulany did not represent all of American opinion, either in theory or in action. Something far more radical was needed if the Stamp Act was to be thwarted. In May 1765 the Virginia House of Burgesses

---

[12] See Charles A. Barker, *The Background of the Revolution in Maryland* (New Haven, Conn.: Yale University Press, 1940), pp. 292–307.

adopted four of the seven resolutions presented to it by a young man who had been a member of the house 'for only ten days: Patrick Henry. The four resolutions that were adopted reiterated what the house had said before, notably in petitions to the king, Lords, and Commons in December 1764. The three rejected resolutions were far more radical. They declared that the house had the sole right and power to levy taxes in Virginia and that the attempt to vest that right in any other body was illegal and unconstitutional, that Virginians did not have to obey any laws except those passed by the House of Burgesses, and that any person who argued to the contrary was an enemy of the colony.

It mattered not that the majority of the members of the house had left for home before the resolutions were presented, or that not more than twenty-two of the 116 members had voted for any one of the four resolutions adopted. All seven resolutions soon appeared in most of the colonial newspapers as the action of the Virginia House of Burgesses.

Resolutions adopted by town and county mass meetings were even more extreme than those offered by Patrick Henry. Perhaps none were more so than those of a mass meeting at New London, Connecticut, in December 1765, which asserted that all government was based on the consent of the people, and that whenever the bounds of a constitution were ignored, the people had a right to resume their authority. The Stamp Act was unconstitutional, no obedience was due to it, and if the people could be relieved in no other way, they should "reassume their natural rights and the authority the laws of nature and of God have vested them with."

Even such striking anticipations of the Declaration of Independence could not evade the execution of the Stamp Act, which went into effect on November 1, 1765. Concrete action was necessary, and the precedent was set in the town of Boston. In August the threat of mob action forced a frightened stamp distributor to resign, and those in other colonies were forced by mobs to do likewise. As a result, on November 1, no stamp distributors could be found in office in any of the mainland colonies except Georgia. After November 1, some newspapers stopped publication; but others continued to publish as usual, and within a few months ships were sailing in and out of ports and some of the courts were functioning in open defiance of the law.

Mob violence and threats of violence, often backed by substantial citizens, and political pressure on British officials in the colonies achieved nullification of a law of Parliament. The violence and the emotion involved were reflected in the newspapers but almost never in pamphlets. But there was one publication which circulated widely in the northern colonies which did reflect popular feeling, and although not strictly a pamphlet, it is included here. New York City was one of the centers of more violent opposition to the Stamp Act and some of its newspapers contained strident articles attacking it, and even threatened independence if the act were enforced. At that, some of the articles submitted were so daring that no New York printer would publish them. However, one young man was willing.

William Goddard (1740–1817), in the course of a long career, founded three American newspapers: the *Providence Gazette* (1762), the *Pennsylvania Chronicle* (1767), and the *Maryland Journal* (1773). He was born in Connecticut, the son of a doctor who apprenticed him in 1755 to James Parker, the owner of printing shops in various colonies. Goddard finished his apprenticeship in New York in 1761, and the next year he founded the first newspaper in Providence, Rhode Island, the *Providence Gazette*. His mother financed the venture; he was supported politically by the Hopkins faction which welcomed a newspaper to help it in its fight with the Newport faction, which monopolized the *Newport Mercury*.

Despite such support, Goddard complained of "stagnation," and in May 1765 he temporarily suspended publication of the

Gazette. He left the print shop in the charge of his mother and went to New York, where he became a partner of John Holt. Holt was publishing the *New York Gazette* in a shop rented from James Parker, the former publisher, who now ran a printing shop in his home colony, New Jersey. According to Goddard, Holt told him of the pieces too daring to be printed in New York. Goddard took some of them and went to New Jersey, where he designed and printed the *Constitutional Courant*[13] in James Parker's shop. The *Courant* was not a pamphlet; it was in the guise of the first issue of a newspaper, although it was little more than a broadside.

The *Constitutional Courant* is important for at least two reasons. First, the violence of its language illustrates the popular feeling of the times as the pamphlets do not. Second, it attacks American supporters of the Stamp Act, or men who preferred to do nothing about it, and thus mirrors the internal divisions among Americans. The newspapers during these years are filled with vitriolic attacks by Americans upon fellow Americans as they disagreed with one another over what to do about British policies, or whether or not they should do anything at all. This division among Americans is not reflected in most pamphlets, at least before 1774, yet it is an integral part of the history of the times.

The repeal of the Stamp Act on March 18, 1766, ended the first crisis in the relations between Britain and the colonies, but in that same month a pamphlet was published which carried American argument to the brink of declaring the colonies independent of Great Britain, and came close to declaring that they had the right of revolution. A New London, Connecticut mass meeting had boldly asserted the right of revolution in December 1765, but pamphleteers were not so audacious. Stephen Hopkins in 1764 had fumbled with the idea that each colony was a separate part of the king's do-

---

[13] Pamphlet 5.

minions, and not subject to Parliament but only to its own
legislature; but in the end he had concluded that there were
some areas which must be controlled by parliamentary legislation.

Richard Bland (1710–1776), of Virginia, met the problem
head on, but he shrank from drawing the conclusions implicit
in his arguments. Bland was one of the most respected political leaders of Virginia and was admired for his knowledge
of the history of the colony—a knowledge reflected in his
pamphlet. He was a member of the House of Burgesses from
1742 onward and sat on its most important committees. Although he opposed Patrick Henry's Stamp Act resolutions in
1765, he went to the First Continental Congress in 1774, was
a member of the revolutionary conventions in 1775 and 1776,
and of the new state legislature until he died in October 1776.

In 1753 he had published an attack on Governor Dinwiddie
for attempting to collect a fee for each land grant he signed,
and he wrote two pamphlets denouncing Anglican clergymen
for securing a royal veto of Virginia laws converting their
salaries from tobacco into money—laws which in effect reduced their salaries at times when tobacco was higher priced
than usual. Bland therefore had had considerable experience
in the discussion of ideas concerning taxation and the rights
of legislatures before he published *An Inquiry into the Rights
of the British Colonies* in March 1766.[14]

Bland's pamphlet, like Daniel Dulany's, was in the form of
an answer to the Whately-Grenville pamphlet of 1765, *The
Regulations Lately Made,* and its argument that the colonies
were "virtually" represented in Parliament. But Bland went
much farther than Dulany. He appealed to the "law of nature"
to refute the idea of "virtual" representation, which, he declared, was no more valid for England than for the colonies.
He also appealed to the history of Virginia to demonstrate

---

[14] Pamphlet 7.

that the colonies were subject only to the Crown. He argued that from the beginning the colonies had not been a part of the realm of England, but, in effect, independent realms with independent legislatures under the Crown. He admitted that Parliament had the *power* to legislate for the colonies, a power it had exercised in the past, but he denied that Parliament could ever have the *right*, and above all the right to levy internal taxes. Furthermore, while Americans might be subjected to the *power* of Parliament, they and their sons would never lose the *right* to recover that which had been taken from them.

At this point Bland stepped back from the brink. He anticipated the Declaration of Independence but, as the author of that document wrote, many years later:

He would set out with a set of sound principles, pursue them logically till he found them leading to the precipice which he had to leap, start back alarmed, then resume his ground, go over it in another direction, be led by the correctness of his reasoning to the same place and again back about and try other processes to reconcile right and wrong but finally left his reader and himself bewildered between the steady index of the compass in their hand, and the phantasm to which it seemed to point.[15]

Bland, and Americans generally, were saved from his logic by the repeal of the Stamp Act and the temporary cessation of agitation, as Americans celebrated what they regarded as a great triumph over Parliament. The repeal had been carried out by the Rockingham ministry, which had succeeded that of George Grenville in the summer of 1765. The Rockingham ministry's hold on office was temporary at best and it had no policy to cope with the storm of protest from America that reached England in the fall of 1765. However, British merchants and manufacturers, whose principal markets were in

---

[15] Thomas Jefferson to William Wirt, August 5, 1815. In P. L. Ford, ed., *The Writings of Thomas Jefferson*, IX (New York: G. P. Putnam's Sons, 1898), 474n.

America, did have such a policy, and to these men the Rock-ingham ministry turned for support in an attempt to stay in power. The merchants and manufacturers, alarmed by the existing depression and by the threat of colonial non-importation of British goods, demanded what they called "commercial reform." Among other things, this program called for repeal of the Stamp Act and the resumption of business as usual with America. They achieved considerable success, including a revision of the Revenue Act of 1764 which reduced the duty on foreign molasses from three pence to a penny a gallon, and another law which opened up free ports in the British West Indies. However, most of this legislation was designed to suit the interests of British merchants rather than those of the Americans, who had many and bitter complaints against the Revenue Act of 1764.

But for the moment the failure to redress American commercial grievances was ignored in America because of the repeal of the Stamp Act. Ignored too was Parliament's answer to innumerable American resolutions and pamphlets asserting Americans' right to tax and govern themselves. The price of the repeal of the Stamp Act, so far as the majority in Parliament was concerned, was the passage of the Declaratory Act on the same day, an act which proclaimed that

the said colonies and plantations in America have been, are, and of right ought to be, subordinate unto and dependent upon the imperial Crown and Parliament of Great Britain, [and that Parliament] had, hath, and of right ought to have, full power and authority to make laws and statutes of sufficient force and validity to bind the colonies and people of America . . . in all cases whatsoever.

Parliament thus swept aside every American claim and argument and asserted its absolute and uncontrollable authority to legislate for Americans and for their governments. In doing so, it took a stand from which it refused to retreat, a stand that did much to bring about the war for American independence. For the moment, however, very few Americans paid any attention to the Declaratory Act in their joy over the end of the Stamp Act.

3. British Policies and American Opposition, 1767–1770

Shortly after the repeal of the Stamp Act the Rockingham ministry was replaced by that of William Pitt. The great orator, who became Lord Chatham and entered the House of Lords, was considered a friend of America. But he was ill, if not mentally deranged, and had little or no control over the ministry he headed. Occasionally he roused himself long enough to deliver rhetorical flourishes, but he offered no program, either to appease the Americans or to force them to obey.

By 1767 members of Parliament, even the "friends" of America, were increasingly irritated with American behavior. Americans showed no gratitude to Parliament for repealing the Stamp Act; they greeted repeal as the righting of a great wrong. Parliament had requested the colonial legislatures to compensate such men as Thomas Hutchinson and Cadwallader Colden for property lost during the Stamp Act riots; the legislatures either refused, or complied with ill grace and after long delays. New Yorkers and others sent petitions and letters denouncing the so-called commercial reforms of 1766 as either no reforms at all or measures designed to benefit British merchants at the expense of Americans. American merchants, and occasionally mobs, continued to make life miserable for British customs officials in the colonies, while the newspapers denounced them as greedy crooks and would-be tyrants. In every colony where British troops were stationed, the legislatures refused to obey the provisions of the Quartering Act of 1765. The most conspicuous example was New York, which was the headquarters of General Thomas Gage, commander-in-chief of the British army in America. The New York legislature did provide some supplies, but it refused to provide all those listed in the Quartering Act, and pointedly ignored the very existence of the act itself.

Meanwhile, the ministry in London was faced with an ever present financial crisis and with complaining taxpayers who demanded a reduction in the land tax. In January 1767 George Grenville told the House of Commons that the British army in America was costing the British taxpayer about £400,000 a year and that the Americans should pay a part of the expense. He then moved a twenty-five per cent reduction in the British land tax, a motion enthusiastically adopted. Charles Townshend, the chancellor of the exchequer, promised that he could collect the difference in America without arousing American opposition, as vain a promise as was ever made by an irresponsible politician.

The result was the so-called Townshend Act, the Revenue Act of June 26, 1767. Townshend declared that the American distinction between internal and external taxes was "perfect nonsense." His act therefore provided for the collection of import duties in colonial ports on glass, paper, painter's colors, red and white lead, and tea—that is, "external taxes." He estimated that the revenue would amount to £40,000 a year. Three days later Parliament passed another act to improve the effectiveness of the colonial customs service. The law created an American Board of Customs Commissioners, and the ministry, with characteristic ineptness, stationed the board in Boston, the most unruly town in America. The next year Parliament authorized the establishment of additional courts of vice-admiralty in the colonies. The one established at Halifax, Nova Scotia, in 1764 was too remote from the centers of commerce to be effective. Therefore three new courts—at Boston, Philadelphia, and Charleston—were established in addition to the one at Halifax.

However, the most striking action, and the most extraordinary interference of Parliament in the internal affairs of America, was the law of July 2, 1767, which suspended the New York assembly until it obeyed the letter of the Quartering Act of 1765, and declared that if the assembly did pass laws despite the suspension, its acts would be "null and void, and of no force or effect whatsoever."

The colonial reaction to the Townshend program was immediate. Americans of all shades of political opinion were shocked by Parliament's suspension of the New York assembly—an act without precedent since the founding of the colonies, an act with dark political and constitutional implications. (As it turned out, the New York assembly ignored the suspension and got away with it.)

The political purpose of the Revenue Act was equally disturbing. The money collected was to be paid into a special fund to be used by the ministry to pay the salaries of British civil officials in the colonies. The colonial legislatures had cherished no "right" more than the power of granting or withholding the salaries of governors and judges, and this power had been one of the weapons by which the assemblies had achieved virtual self-government by 1763. The power was perhaps more important as a symbol than as a weapon, but it was a cherished symbol indeed.

The Revenue Act was an economic threat as well, for the duties imposed, like those of the Stamp Act, had to be paid in specie. By 1767 colonial paper money was disappearing, since, according to the Currency Act of 1764, such money could not be reissued, and specie was becoming scarcer and scarcer.

Above all it was evident that the Americans' arguments in behalf of their rights had been completely ignored by Parliament. Once more Parliament was trying to tax them. Most Americans had agreed that Parliament should control the trade of the whole empire and levy duties in the course of doing so.

But the Revenue Act in 1767 was a blatant attempt to raise revenue in the guise of duties regulating trade. Strictly speaking, the duties were "external taxes," but they were taxes nonetheless. The challenge was met by John Dickinson.

Dickinson (1732–1808), one of the most distinguished lawyers in America, had received his legal training at the Middle Temple in London. He was a resident of both Delaware and Pennsylvania, and at one time or another held office in both. In Pennsylvania he was a leading supporter of the "Proprietary Party" and an opponent of Benjamin Franklin and Joseph Galloway, who were trying to secure the revocation of the proprietary charter of the Penn family and the establishment of a royal government for the colony. Dickinson was conservative by temperament and abhorred violence, but he was a consistent and outspoken opponent of British measures after 1763. He wrote powerfully against the Stamp Act and drafted the resolutions of the Stamp Act Congress, but he achieved his greatest fame as the author of *Letters from a Farmer in Pennsylvania to the Inhabitants of the British Colonies* in 1767 and 1768.[16]

The first of the twelve letters was published in a Philadelphia newspaper on December 2, 1767, and within a short time, most colonial newspapers reprinted it and the letters that followed. By March 1768 the letters were in pamphlet form. Americans had no difficulty in understanding Dickinson's argument, which was an extension of the one they had been using ever since 1764. It was true that Parliament could regulate trade and levy duties for the purpose; but when it levied duties on trade for the purpose of raising revenue, it was levying a tax—and this Parliament had no right to do. The Townshend Revenue Act was a tax on Americans, whatever its guise, and the men who wrote it admitted as much.

Dickinson achieved enormous popularity, for his identity

---

16 Pamphlet 8.

was soon known, and America rang with praise of him from one end to the other. He did not retain that popularity. As the war for independence approached, Dickinson consistently opposed violence and pleaded for reconciliation with Britain. He fought the adoption of the Declaration of Independence and refused to sign it (unlike some other opponents), but he did not become a Loyalist: he left Congress to lead troops against the British. For a time he was under a cloud, but he was back in Congress before the end of the war and was elected president of Delaware, and then of Pennsylvania.

While Dickinson challenged the right of Parliament to legislate for the colonies in particular instances, and above all the right to tax the colonies, he did not challenge the claim to absolute and uncontrollable sovereignty over the colonies which Parliament had asserted in the Declaratory Act of 1766. In fact, Dickinson consistently supported the idea that, as he said in his second *Letter,* "We are but parts of a whole; and therefore there must exist a power somewhere, to preside, and preserve the connection in due order. This power is lodged in the Parliament. . . ."

The legislation of 1767 made the meaning of the Declaratory Act clear. Dickinson refused to face the issue, but a fellow Philadelphian met it head-on. Little is known of William Hicks except that he was a supporter of the "Proprietary Party" in the 1760's. Hicks's *The Nature and Extent of Parliamentary Power Considered*[17] began as a series of newspaper essays which were soon printed as a pamphlet. The first of these essays appeared in the *Pennsylvania Journal* on January 21, 1768, and several other colonial newspapers reprinted them at the same time that they were reprinting Dickinson's *Farmer* letters. The *Boston Evening Post* even dropped Dickinson for a time to publish Hicks.

Hicks took the step that Richard Bland had refused to take

---

[17] Pamphlet 9.

in his pamphlet in 1766. His argument against the Declaratory
Act, an argument which he called "this doctrine of independence," is clear. He asserted that the "inhabitants of these new
settlements . . . totally disclaim all subordination to, and dependence upon, the two inferior estates [the House of Commons and the House of Lords] of their mother country." Unlike Dickinson, who said that Parliament must regulate the
general welfare of the empire, Hicks insisted that it could
be maintained by the "restraining power lodged in the
Crown. . . ." The idea that each of the colonies was an independent part of the empire, united only by the Crown, was
picked up during the next few years by newspaper writers,
although the pamphleteers steered clear of such daring doctrine until 1774.

American opposition to the Townshend program between
1767 and 1770 was carried on at other levels than pamphleteering. The *Boston Gazette* proposed the non-importation of British goods as soon as news of the suspension of the New York
assembly reached America. The idea was supported in virtually every colony by popular political leaders, and was opposed
by most importing merchants and by others who had been
frightened by the rise of popular leaders and mob activity
during the Stamp Act crisis. Despite such opposition, all of
the commercial cities and some colonies had adopted non-importation agreements by the middle of 1769. The agreements
varied widely in character and were enforced with varying
degrees of effectiveness. There were endless charges that the
signers of the agreements cheated and imported more goods
during its existence than before. Nevertheless, there was a
sharp reduction of British exports to the colonies.

In the spring of 1770 Parliament repealed the duties (except on tea) levied by the Townshend Revenue Act of 1767.
Repeal was followed by the collapse of the non-importation

movement in America, a collapse that left a bitter legacy of distrust between factions within colonies, and among colonies as well. Ever since 1767 the movement had been accompanied by a barrage of newspaper propaganda in which Americans charged one another with failure to live up to the agreements they had signed, and reluctant merchants were accused of being more interested in profits than in the liberties of America. And after the movement collapsed there was even more bitter recrimination. Thus, the newspapers in New York charged that the Boston merchants had cheated and lied, and the Boston newspapers replied that the New York merchants had done so.

However, there were two areas of British policy which most Americans could unite in opposing. One was the vigorous enforcement of British customs laws and regulations. The essential basis of British policy, and one not changed before 1776, was the Revenue Act of 1764. That law virtually freed customs officials from legal responsibility for their actions, and its technicalities provided greedy ones with the opportunity of lining their pockets at the expense of American merchants.

When customs officers seized vessels and/or goods, they no longer had to offer proof of fraud. It was up to the owner to prove that he was innocent, a striking reversal of a basic principle of English law. Even when the owner proved his innocence, the judge could issue a certificate stating that the customs officers had had a "probable cause" for seizure, and they could not be sued for damages.

Then there were technicalities such as the requirement that ships could not be loaded until a permit listing the cargo to be put on board was issued by a customs officer. The requirement had no relation to the way business was done. Ships often lay at docks for weeks while owners and captains advertised for cargoes; and a captain seldom knew what his final cargo would be until he was ready to sail. Reasonable customs officials ignored the law and issued the permits and necessary bonds after the cargoes were actually on board and could be listed accurately.

But customs officials could and did enforce the law to suit their own purposes. Thus the members of the American Board of Customs in Boston were irked by the contempt shown them by John Hancock, the richest young man in town. In May 1768, one of his vessels, the *Liberty,* came in from Madeira with a cargo of wine. The cargo was small, but the duties were paid and no questions were raised at the time. The *Liberty* lay at Hancock's wharf for four weeks loading a cargo for London. The Customs Board then seized it for loading without a permit, got it condemned in the Admiralty Court, and took it over as a revenue vessel—only to have it burned by the Rhode Islanders when it appeared in their colony. The Customs Board then sued Hancock for smuggling wine on the *Liberty.* He might have smuggled, but the evidence was dubious and some of it perjured; the case was finally dismissed by the Admiralty Court.

The attack on Hancock was probably the result of personal animosity. In South Carolina, greed was the motivation. The writers of the Revenue Act of 1764, ignorant of both American geography and American commerce, required that decked vessels at sea must follow all the procedures laid down by the law. Trouble came when rules designed for transoceanic commerce were applied to American coastwise trade. Most of South Carolina's coastwise trade was carried on in decked vessels too large to follow the inland waterways, and South Carolina law required them to register only once a year. In 1767, a British naval captain seized the *Active* for not carrying the required papers, although it was only sailing between two South Carolina ports. Captain James Hawker and Daniel Moore, the new collector of the port of Charleston, asked the attorney-general, Egerton Leigh, for advice. He refused, since he was also the judge of the Admiralty Court. When the case was tried, he freed the vessel but charged the owner £150 costs for a vessel not worth half that much. He also issued a certificate stating that the captain and Collector Moore had had a "probable cause" for seizure so they could not be sued for damages in the common law courts of the colony. Collector Moore then made the mistake of picking on Henry Laurens, one of the wealthiest merchants in America, and a man with friends and partners in other colonies and in England. Two of his vessels, the *Wambaw* and the *Broughton Island Packet,* were seized upon their return from his Georgia plantation because they did not carry proper bonds. Judge Leigh, who was Laurens' nephew, condemned one vessel, but because there was no evidence of fraud, allowed him to buy it back for more than it was worth, and charged him £277 costs. Leigh dismissed the charges against the other vessel as frivolous and refused to issue a certificate of "probable cause" for seizure. Laurens promptly sued the deputy collector, George Roupel, who had prosecuted, and won £1,400 in damages.

The Charleston merchants united to drive Collector Moore from the colony, but Roupel stayed behind. In the spring of 1768 he seized the ship *Ann,* owned by Laurens in partnership with merchants in Philadelphia and in Bristol, England. Laurens had secured a permit and given bond for loading a cargo of rice, and had then left for his Georgia plantation. The Captain of the *Ann* and Laurens' clerk finished loading the vessel with miscellaneous items and then went to the customs house for a permit to load and a bond for the non-enumerated goods. Roupel had cleared another vessel the day before under identical circumstances but he seized the *Ann* for not securing a permit in advance. He offered to return the vessel if Laurens would give up the damages he had won in the earlier case, but Laurens refused. Judge Leigh dismissed the case but he issued a certificate of "probable cause" for seizure so that Laurens could not sue Roupel for damages.

Laurens sent an account of these happenings to his partner in Philadelphia, who had it printed; in February 1769, Laurens published *Extracts from the Proceedings of the Court of Vice-Admiralty.*[18] Leigh, who had resigned his judgeship, then attacked his uncle in *The Man Un-Masked.* Laurens was furious and prepared a second edition, and, in advertising it in the newspapers, he described his nephew as "that POLE CAT."

American newspapers gave wide publicity to the troubles of John Hancock, Henry Laurens, and other merchants, and helped confirm Americans in the conviction that British customs officers were greedy and corrupt. It is probable that the day-to-day experience along the waterfront did as much to alienate the affections of such conservative merchants as Henry Laurens as did the erratic attempts of Britain to collect some form of revenue in the colonies. The Americans, of course, were not defenseless, and more than one hapless customs officer was covered with tar and feathers, or worse. The customs officers pictured themselves as conscientious officials who were the victims of lawbreakers and vicious mobs. And it was the fear of mobs on the part of the Customs Commissioners in Boston, and the reports they sent to England, that led to the most dramatic confrontation between Americans and Britons before the battles at Lexington and Concord—the Boston Massacre on the night of March 5, 1770.

The second area of British policy that most Americans united in opposing was the attempt to force Americans to provide supplies for the British army. The decision, toward the end of the Seven Years' War, to station regiments of the regular British army in America after the war was the source of much of the trouble between Britain and the colonies. The British government's insistence that the colonial governments should pay a part of the expense led to the Quartering Act and the Stamp Act. With a few exceptions, colonial legislatures dis-

[18] Pamphlet 10.

obeyed the Quartering Act. Georgia refused supplies at the very time it was asking for British regulars to defend it from Indians. New York was the headquarters of the British army, and although the legislature always provided some money, it ignored the letter of the law, and even its existence.

The troops had been stationed in America for the ostensible purpose of protecting the frontiers, but Americans believed, and rightly, that political motives were also involved. Most of the troops were kept near the seacoast, and during the Stamp Act crisis General Thomas Gage, commanding general in America, moved more and more of them near to the centers of population. However, Gage's instructions forbade him to use the troops unless called upon by the civil officials—that is, the colonial governors. The governors' instructions from England, in turn, forbade them to call for the help of the army unless they had the consent of their councils, and this the councils refused to give.

Mob action and the threat of mob action were more common in Boston than in any other city. Governor Francis Bernard desperately wanted troops, but he seldom had the courage to ask his council for consent, and when he did, the annually elected council always refused. The American Board of Customs Commissioners, which arrived in November 1767, wrote highly colored accounts of the dangers of life in Boston and sent them off to England. In June 1768, the ministry in London responded by ordering regiments of troops stationed in Boston.

The troops arrived in September. Thereafter, they were the object of constant newspaper propaganda; troops and the populace engaged in endless brawls on the streets and in the taverns, of which Boston had an astonishing number. Similar brawls occurred in New York City, but the climax was the Boston Massacre. The British officers and the Bostonians told such conflicting stories of the event that very few "facts" can be agreed upon. Among those few are that the "massacre" happened on the night of March 5, that it happened before the customs house, that a mob faced some soldiers, that someone yelled "Fire," that the soldiers did fire, and that five of the mob were killed. Beyond that agreement ends. When Captain Thomas Preston and eight of the soldiers were later tried for murder before the Massachusetts Superior Court, all but two soldiers were acquitted. These two were declared guilty of manslaughter, but they pleaded benefit of clergy and were freed after being branded on the hands.

The Boston Town Meeting at once prepared a pamphlet giving its version of the "massacre" and broadcast it throughout the English-speaking world.[19] The pamphlet is a vivid historical document, but it has serious limitations as history. In the years that followed, annual orations on the anniversary of what the orators called "that fatal night" provided ever more lurid descriptions of the event. Whatever the facts, the Boston Massacre and the Boston Massacre orations did much to arouse American public opinion, at least in New England, and to fix in Americans' minds that distrust of a standing army which was a part of their inheritance from England.

4. The American Debate over Independence, 1770–1776

Three years of relative calm began in 1770. In the spring of that year the new ministry of Lord North secured repeal of the import duties levied by the Revenue Act of 1767 (except that on tea) on the ground that such duties were contrary to the "principles of commerce." The North ministry had quite enough trouble at home and with Europe; it wanted to avoid trouble with America, and avoid bringing American affairs before an irritable Parliament. In America, repeal was followed by the collapse of the non-importation movement, despite the exhortations of popular leaders to continue it until

---

[19] Pamphlet 11.

the tea duty was repealed. Most American merchants and the more conservative political leaders had had enough of rioting and of interference in business and politics by the popular leaders and the common people who had supported them during the past five years. They wanted a return to peace and quiet, and an end to interference with the rule of what they liked to call "the better sort."

But some Americans continued to agitate and to seize upon every possible threat or fancied threat to American liberties as an excuse for propaganda and action. No leader was more important than Boston's Samuel Adams, who, although deserted by such former allies as John Hancock, continued to agitate. He was in a strategic position. As clerk of the House of Representatives, "boss" of the town meeting, and a principal contributor of the *Boston Gazette,* he seized upon every opportunity and made the most of it. When it was learned that Thomas Hutchinson, who had been named governor in 1770, would receive his salary from British customs revenues and not from the legislature, Adams tried to raise a storm. He failed, but in 1772, when news reached Boston that the judges of the Superior Court would be paid from British funds, Adams was successful.

The Boston town meeting asked Governor Hutchinson to call a special session of the legislature to consider this new "threat" to American liberties. The governor refused. Samuel Adams then moved the appointment of a committee of correspondence of twenty-one men to "state the rights of the colonists and of this province in particular, as men, as Christians, and as subjects; to communicate and publish the same to the several towns in this province and to the world. . . ." The town meeting agreed and thus was created a permanent grass-roots organization that became the core of the revolutionary movement in Massachusetts, and provided a measure of leadership for other colonies as well.

A State of the Rights of the Colonists[20] was both a highly skillful political platform and a strikingly radical statement of political philosophy. As a theoretical statement it differs in no essential from the basic ideas of the Declaration of Independence. It appealed to the law of nature, declared that men entered society voluntarily, and that when they were intolerably oppressed, they had the right to leave one society and join another. And like Jefferson's Declaration of Independence, this declaration of political philosophy was followed by a catalogue of grievances.

Hundreds of copies of the pamphlet were circulated throughout Massachusetts, the other colonies, and England, and by the time the Massachusetts legislature met in January 1773, more than a hundred Massachusetts towns had appointed committees of correspondence and adopted the Boston declaration or similar ones. Governor Hutchinson met the challenge in a speech to the legislature in which he asserted that the only alternative to the recognition of Parliament's sovereignty was colonial independence. In reply, the house chided the governor for raising the issue of independence, but went on to say that it was such an important question for the colonies that it could be decided only by a congress of all of them.

By the end of 1773 some American newspapers were openly asserting that America should become independent and were proposing the meeting of an American congress. Such a congress did meet in Philadelphia, in September 1774, and from then on the colonies moved steadily toward a formal declaration of American independence.

The events leading to the meeting of the First Continental Congress had their origins in London, where the ministry and Parliament had long been struggling with the tangled affairs of the East India Company. By 1773 the company was on the verge of bankruptcy, and it had vast quantities of unsold tea

---

[20] Pamphlet 12.

on hand. The Americans, who drank a great deal of tea, found it both "patriotic" and cheaper to drink smuggled Dutch tea. Parliament had tried in the past to help the East India Company compete with the Dutch in the colonies, but without success. Then in 1773 it passed what was soon known as the "Tea Act." It freed the company from the requirement that all its tea must be sold at public auction, and permitted it to send tea directly to its own agents in the colonies. The hope was that English tea could be sold more cheaply than the smuggled Dutch tea, even after paying the import duty.

Popular leaders everywhere in America at once described the "Tea Act" as another plot to tax Americans, although the import duty had been a law ever since 1767. When the tea cargoes arrived, they were sent back or stored, except in Boston, where some £10,000 worth was dumped into Boston Harbor.

The ministry and Parliament were outraged and adopted the laws the Americans at once labeled the "Intolerable Acts." Those laws (1) closed the port of Boston until the tea was paid for, (2) altered the charter of Massachusetts to give the governor more power and to provide for a royally appointed council rather than an elective one, (3) provided that British officials accused of crime in Massachusetts could be taken out of the colony for trial if a fair trial could not be obtained there, (4) further revised the Quartering Act. For a brief time, the Quebec Act was also called an "Intolerable" act. That law attached the Old Northwest to Quebec and guaranteed the Roman Catholic religion to the French inhabitants of the province. Whatever the impact on the Virginians, who claimed the Old Northwest as their own, the New Englanders at once began a vigorous campaign against the dangers of "Popery." However, they dropped that sort of propaganda as soon as the First Continental Congress appealed to the Canadians to join the colonies in the fight for "liberty."

Americans responded to the "Intolerable Acts" in various

ways, but in virtually every colony it was suggested that a continental congress should meet and agree upon common methods of opposition. As plans for the Congress got under way, the newspapers were filled with controversy. The pamphleteers, with a few exceptions, had written little since 1768. Now they began writing as never before; James Wilson in Pennsylvania, William Henry Drayton in South Carolina, and Jonathan Boucher all published pamphlets before the Congress met. But the most illuminating and far-reaching of these pamphlets was Thomas Jefferson's *A Summary View of the Rights of British America.*[21]

Jefferson's *Summary View* carried to a logical conclusion the ideas to be found in such pamphlets as Richard Bland's *Inquiry into the Rights of the British Colonies* in 1766, the Boston Town Meeting's *Rights of the Colonists* in 1772, and above all, the very explicit statements about colonial "independence" of Parliament, appearing more and more frequently in the colonial newspapers by the end of 1773. Jefferson argued that the power exercised by Parliament over the colonies was a "usurped" power, that the British Empire consisted of separate "states" with equal and independent legislatures, united only by the Crown, and that the Americans were a "free people." He also spelled out in detail, foreshadowing the charges against George III in the Declaration of Independence, the king's errors as the head of the British Empire. The style was clear, the meaning equally so, and the pamphlet placed Jefferson at the forefront of opposition. His appointment to the committee to draft a declaration of independence in June 1776 was a natural outcome.

All the thirteen colonies except Georgia sent delegates to the First Continental Congress. During the past ten years each colony had decided for itself how to oppose British measures.

---

[21] Pamphlet 13.

Now, for the first time in their history, the colonies agreed to turn policy-making over to a central body. But agreement ended there: individual colonies and groups within colonies had different ideas of what to do, or whether to do anything at all, and those disagreements were reflected within each delegation at Philadelphia. The Congress split at once into two almost evenly divided groups.

On one side were the popular leaders who had risen to prominence during the past decade as aggressive opponents of British policies; these men had been equally aggressive opponents of those Americans who occupied important positions in the colonial governments and who either supported or did not openly oppose British policies. Although most of the popular leaders had never met before, they at once formed an alliance. Thus the Lees of Virginia and the Adamses of Massachusetts were soon to be known as the "Lee-Adams junto." Such men insisted that Congress take a strong stand in declaring American rights and in stopping all trade with Britain.

The other "party" in the Congress was composed of the more conservative political leaders of the colonies, the most conspicuous being Joseph Galloway, speaker of the Pennsylvania assembly. Most of these men were opposed to British policies, but they wanted to avoid taking a stand that would prevent reconciliation with Britain. However, they were caught between the popular leaders who would accept no compromise, and a British government equally unwilling to compromise. As time passed, Britain cut the ground from under them, and the popular leaders consistently outmaneuvered them politically.

The Congress was deadlocked for weeks over a declaration of rights. The popular leaders insisted that it should be based on the "law of nature." The conservatives quite understandably opposed a foundation which had never been defined and which would allow every man to interpret its meaning for himself. They argued that American rights should be based on the colonial charters and the English constitution, which at least had the virtue of a certain amount of specific content. The outcome was a compromise. The declaration of rights finally adopted was based on the law of nature, the colonial charters, and the English constitution.

Far more crucial was the question of what concrete means of opposition were to be adopted. The popular leaders, with widespread backing throughout the colonies, demanded a complete stoppage of trade, a far more drastic measure than the non-importation agreements of 1767–1770. Many members of Congress had opposed non-importation, and they now opposed something which seemed to them far worse, but they could not prevent adoption of the Association by Congress. That agreement provided for the non-importation of all British goods beginning on December 1, 1774, and the non-exportation of all goods to Britain on September 10, 1775.

The conservatives were convinced that the decisions of the Congress would lead to disaster, and probably to war with Britain. By 1774, American leaders such as Joseph Galloway had come to the conclusion that the disputes with Britain would lead either to independence or to the absolute subjection of the colonies to Britain unless the constitutional relationship between colonies and mother country could be specifically defined. After consultation with other members of Congress, and with the backing of such New York delegates as James Duane and John Jay, Galloway offered the outlines of a written constitution. His "plan of union" provided for an American legislature or "Parliament" consisting of delegates elected by the colonial assemblies and presided over by an official appointed by the king. The American "Parliament" would have the power to legislate for all the general affairs of the colonies. In matters affecting the mutual interest of Britain and the colonies, either the British or the proposed American parliament could initiate legislation, but both bodies would have to approve of the legislation before it could become binding law.

Some time afterward Galloway wrote that all the "men of property" in Congress were for the plan, and that all the "republican party" opposed it. Galloway exaggerated, for some "men of property" opposed it as well as all of the popular leaders, some of whom were "men of property" themselves. The plan was defeated, and the record of it omitted from the journal of the Congress published after it adjourned.

The popular leaders of the colonies won a sweeping victory in the First Continental Congress. They secured the "law of nature" as one of the foundations of American rights and thus provided a flexible base from which to carry on the constitutional debate. They secured the denial of the authority of Parliament to legislate for the colonies, except for the regulation of trade, but even that was based on the consent of the colonies. They secured the tacit approval of Congress for meeting force with force if Britain used her army to impose her will. Furthermore, in the Association they secured approval for the creation of extra-legal organizations throughout the colonies. The Association called for the appointment of local committees in every community to enforce the stoppage of trade. Such committees, many of them self-appointed, sprang up everywhere, and they soon began coercing fellow Americans in political matters as one colonial legislature after the other was replaced by revolutionary congresses and conventions.

The first Congress adjourned on October 26, after resolving to meet again on May 10, 1775, unless American grievances had been redressed. The publication of the proceedings of the Congress, which astonished many Americans and terrified some, altered the nature of the pamphlet debate. For a decade the pamphleteers, with a few exceptions such as Martin Howard, Jr., had concentrated their attention on the dispute with Britain and had left it to the newspapers to carry on the political debate within America. But after the first Congress, most of the pamphlets were devoted to the central issue, that of independence, over which Americans divided bitterly. That independence was the issue was made clear at once, although the men who had shaped the outcome of the Congress denied it. However, anonymous writers showed no such restraint. On November 14, shortly after the Congress adjourned, the *Pennsylvania Packet* printed "Political Observations, without Order: addressed to the People of America." The author began by declaring that the "history of kings is nothing but the history of the folly and depravity of human nature" and that "a good king is a miracle." Congress derived its power, wisdom, and justice, not from scrolls of parchment signed by kings, "but from the people." The man who refuses to obey Congress "is a slave" and the "least deviation from the resolves of the Congress will be treason—such treason as few villains have ever had an opportunity of committing. It will be treason against the present inhabitants of the colonies—against the millions of unborn generations who are to exist hereafter in America. . . ." "Let us," exclaimed the writer, "neither think, write, speak, nor act without keeping our eyes fixed upon the period which shall dissolve our connection with Great Britain."

The piece was soon reprinted in the *New York Journal* and was at once answered by "M" in Rivington's *New York Gazetteer.* "M" declared that he was now convinced that "the republicans of North America, particularly those of New England, have long been aiming at independence . . ." and that writers in newspapers under "republican" influence made this clear, above all, the author of "Political Observations." However, unlike the "republican part of the Congress," he is acquitted of wearing "the hypocritical badge of his party." Thus the sharply divided Americans took to the newspapers and pamphlets as never before during the winter of 1774–1775, as the Association was enforced, and as the colonies began arming for war.

One of the first pamphleteers to attack the Congress was Samuel Seabury, a member of an old Connecticut family. In 1774 he was a doctor of medicine and an Anglican clergyman in Westchester County, New York. As the "Westchester Farmer" he wrote four powerful pamphlets between November 1774 and January 1775. He appealed to merchants, farmers, and the New York legislature to reject the policies of the Congress and predicted economic chaos and open war if they did not. And war would be disastrous, no matter which side won. If Britain won, as he believed it would, there would be scenes of slaughter, executions, and confiscations of property. If the Americans won they would shed still more blood in wars with one another before they could agree upon and establish a government.

Seabury was answered by a student at King's College in New York, Alexander Hamilton. Hamilton defended the Congress and reiterated American arguments against the legislative supremacy of Parliament. He displayed considerable skill in the use of invective and in the use of rhetorical flourishes, as when he proclaimed that the sacred rights of mankind "are written, as with a sun beam, in the whole volume of human nature, by the hand of divinity itself; and can never be erased or obscured by mortal power."[22]

Hamilton, like other defenders of the Congress, insisted that Americans were virtually unanimous in their support of it, and that the only opposition came from a tiny minority of self-interested "Tories." The "Whig" pamphleteers were making

---

[22] Seabury's pamphlets are reprinted in C. H. Vance, ed., *Letters of a Westchester Farmer, 1774–1775 (Publications* of the Westchester County Historical Society, VIII, White Plains, N. Y.: 1930). Hamilton's two pamphlets are reprinted in Harold C. Syrett and Jacob E. Cooke, eds., *The Papers of Alexander Hamilton,* I (New York: Columbia University Press, 1961), 45–78, 81–165.

history, not writing it. They could not afford to admit that Americans were not united and that a very large minority—probably a majority in some colonies—was opposed to the measures of the Congress, a fact made very clear indeed in the private letters of the time. However, the supporters of the Congress had a common cause and enormous enthusiasm for it, and month after month the British government took action after action that provided ample justification for that cause.

The American opposition to the Congress was intense, but it was disorganized and on the defensive during the winter of 1774–1775. Nevertheless, such writers as Samuel Seabury are significant because they represent an important segment of American thought and feeling, which must be understood if one wants to understand the history of the American Revolution. Seabury and many another American did not approve of British measures, but at the same time they placed much of the blame for the crisis on fellow Americans, whom they charged with tyranny and demagoguery.

Thus, in his final published pamphlet in January 1775, *An Alarm to the Legislature of the Province of New York*, Seabury pleaded with the New York legislature to assert its legal authority and rescue New York from the "laws" and "decrees" adopted at Philadelphia by "the enthusiastic republicans of New England and Virginia." These measures, he said, were being enforced in New York by "enthusiastic delegates and brain-sick committeemen." Seabury was convinced that New York was in the power of a "faction" which depended on a mob to carry out its measures.

It was commonly agreed at the time that several of the colonies were divided into "factions" or "parties" and had been so divided for a long time. The names commonly applied by 1774 were "Whigs" and "Tories," and neither name was usually intended as a compliment. Those whom their enemies called Tories insisted that, bad though British measures might be, one root cause of trouble was the ambition of American demagogues, whose power was based on the support of mobs and not on the votes of the electorate. Many Americans argued between 1774 and 1776 (as some had ever since 1765) that if it were not for such demagogues, reconciliation with Britain could be achieved. On the other hand, the Whigs charged that the Tories were tools of Britain and plotters against the liberties of their country. The validity of such charges and countercharges is not as relevant as the fact that men at the time believed them, acted accordingly, and thus made history.

The controversy was more virulent and incessant in Massachusetts than in any other colony. Ever since 1760 the people of Massachusetts had been filling newspapers and private letters with attacks upon one another, and the measures of the First Continental Congress provided the occasion for a unique summary of the fifteen-year-old debate. Daniel Leonard as "Massachusettensis," and John Adams as "Novanglus," delved far back into history as they debated the nature of man and government and of British policies, but the focus of their argument was the history of Massachusetts politics since 1760. They presented two quite different versions.[23]

The ancestors of Daniel Leonard (1740–1829) had settled in Massachusetts early in the seventeenth century. They founded the first successful iron works in the colony, and for a century before 1760, the Leonard family played so important a social and political role in southern Massachusetts that John Adams called it the "land of the Leonards." In 1774, Daniel Leonard, a wealthy lawyer, accepted an appointment as a member of the new royal council provided for in the Massachusetts Government Act of that year. His neighbors turned on him and drove him to seek the protection of the British army in Boston. Leonard became a Loyalist and his property was confiscated, but unlike many a Loyalist he had a long and successful career after 1776. He was chief justice of Bermuda

---

[23] Pamphlet 14.

from 1782 to 1806, and after 1816 he became one of England's more distinguished barristers.

The first of his seventeen essays signed "Massachusettensis" appeared in the *Massachusetts Gazette and Boston Post-Boy* on December 12, 1774. In it he said that Massachusetts was in a state of anarchy; he insisted that opinion in Massachusetts was not unanimous and that "a very considerable part of the men of property" were organizing to re-establish law and order in the colony. In the second essay he came to what was to be the core of the argument between him and John Adams. He wrote that "our present calamity is in great measure to be attributed to the bad policy of a popular party. . . ." He then sketched the recent history of Massachusetts from the point of view of the Hutchinson-Oliver "party," which had controlled or occupied most of the appointive offices in the colony since 1760.

The essays had an impact on public opinion. In his preface to the 1819 publication of *Massachusettensis* and *Novanglus* in a single volume, John Adams recalled that when he returned home from the first Congress he found the *Massachusetts Gazette* "teeming with political speculations, and *Massachusettensis* shining like a moon among the lesser stars." He was told that the essays "excited great exultation among the Tories and many gloomy apprehensions among the Whigs." Adams was convinced that the author was his old friend, Jonathan Sewall, onetime attorney-general of Massachusetts, and since 1768, judge of the vice-admiralty court at Halifax, Nova Scotia. Adams "instantly resolved to enter the lists with him," and his first *Novanglus* essay appeared in the popular party newspaper, the *Boston Gazette,* on January 23, 1775.

With vigor, and occasionally with venom, Adams presented the popular party's version of Massachusetts political history. The villains were Thomas Hutchinson and his allies and their tool, Governor Francis Bernard. These were the men, declared Adams, who originated the idea of parliamentary taxation of the colonies and urged it on George Grenville. They had hoped to line their pockets, said Adams, but Grenville fooled them and used the money collected to help his own political friends. Nevertheless, the Massachusetts "Tories" had continued to be the willing tools of British ministers from that time onward. As essay succeeded essay, the two men affirmed and denied the supremacy of Parliament, and argued the ability of Americans to win a war with Britain, but they always came back to the issue of which "party" in Massachusetts was responsible for the crisis of 1774–1775.

The reading of these essays, therefore, throws a good deal of light on the division among Americans. It had existed from the beginning of opposition to British policies during the closing years of the Seven Years' War, and it had grown ever sharper. By the winter of 1774–1775, Americans such as Daniel Leonard were convinced that war was inevitable if Americans continued to follow the policies laid down by the First Continental Congress. The popular leaders—or "republicans," as their opponents often called them—admitted that war might be inevitable, and they were busily preparing for it, but they insisted that it was only for the defense of colonial rights. They denied vociferously, as John Adams did in *Novanglus* on February 13, 1775, that their aim was independence; if this was their aim, and it seems likely, they were too canny to admit it. While they had the enthusiastic support of some men in virtually every community in America, they believed that many powerful as well as many lesser men would have been alienated by open admission of a desire for independence, and that organized opposition to Britain might collapse.

The popular leaders had to wait, but time was on their side, for Britain made it plain that she intended to use an army to subject the colonies to her will. Daniel Leonard was on the losing side, but that should not blind us to the equally important fact that he was just as much an American as John Adams in the course of their debate during the winter of 1774–1775, and that he represented many another American who held strongly to similar convictions. The departure from their country of perhaps 100,000 Americans who remained loyal to Britain is evidence enough on this point.

Another American opponent of independence, and one far more conspicuous than Daniel Leonard, was Joseph Galloway, long a dominating political leader of Pennsylvania. Galloway's *A Candid Examination of the Mutual Claims of Great Britain and the Colonies*[24] was perhaps the most important pamphlet published as a consequence of the First Continental Congress. Galloway (*ca.* 1731–1803), member of a wealthy Maryland family, had moved to Philadelphia, where he studied law. He was elected to the Pennsylvania legislature in 1756 and soon became one of the two leaders of the so-called Quaker or anti-proprietary party. The other leader was Benjamin Franklin. Except for one year, Galloway remained in the legislature until 1775, and from 1766 to 1775, he was its speaker and dominating figure.

Like Thomas Hutchinson in Massachusetts, Galloway was opposed to much of what Britain tried to do after 1763, and like Hutchinson he believed that Parliament did have the legal right to legislate for the colonies. By 1774 he was convinced that the disputes with Britain could be solved only if a constitutional definition of the relationship between the colonies and the mother country could be worked out. He attempted to do so in the First Continental Congress but was defeated; his plan was erased from the published journals of a body which had met in secret. He therefore published his pamphlet to present his arguments and his "plan of union" to the American people.

Galloway's pamphlet is based on the assumption that there must be one supreme legislature in every society. He presented a logical legal argument to demonstrate that Parliament was the supreme legislature of the whole British Empire, and

---

[24] Pamphlet 15.

quoted John Locke and other writers to prove his case just as aptly as other American pamphleteers had quoted them to prove the opposite. However, Galloway argued that Americans did have the right to approve or disapprove of the laws by which they were governed, and he proposed to restore that right by his plan of union between Britain and America. Galloway had argued in the first Congress that even if Americans denied all power to Parliament, they must still be united under one central government which could regulate trade, dispose of western lands, suppress internal rebellions, and the like. He predicted that the only alternative to such a central government would be anarchy and chaos.[25]

Despite the fact that Galloway became a Loyalist and was never allowed to return to the America he loved, he concerned himself with one of the main streams of American political thought. Many an American who chose to fight for American independence thought as Galloway did about the need for a central government. In a very real sense, therefore, Galloway's pamphlet serves as an introduction to *The Federalist Papers* of 1787–1788. Only the context, not the nature of the debate, was altered by the Declaration of Independence.

The shots fired at Lexington and Concord on the 19th of April, 1775, were of little military significance, but they were truly "heard round the world." Americans and Britons had spilled one another's blood in battle, and when the Second Continental Congress met on May 10, 1775, it found itself with a war to direct and with popular fervor at a peak it never again reached during the next eight years of war. Men such as Samuel and John Adams were convinced that independence was inevitable, and desirable, but they were uncertain as to

---

25 On Galloway and his plans of union, see Julian Boyd, *Anglo-American Union: Joseph Galloway's Plans to Preserve the British Empire, 1774–1788* (Philadelphia: University of Pennsylvania Press, 1941).

the amount of popular support for a public declaration of independence, and they were opposed by a formidable group of men in Congress who hoped to the end for reconciliation with Great Britain.

John Dickinson, the leader of those who wanted to stay within the British Empire, was successful in delaying consideration of independence for months. In the fall of 1775 he got the Pennsylvania legislature to instruct its delegation in Congress to vote against independence if the issue were raised, and four other colonies soon adopted similar instructions. Such men as the Adamses were infuriated by these instructions but they recognized that a declaration of independence would be futile and doomed to failure unless all thirteen colonies united behind it. Therefore, without mentioning independence by name, they persuaded Congress to take steps that were acts of independence in fact. And month by month the actions of the British government helped them to defeat the men who pleaded endlessly, if ever more hopelessly, for reconciliation with the mother country.

The members of Congress maneuvered endlessly against one another during the fall of 1775, with independence the real issue at stake. For the most part, this struggle was kept secret from the public. Then on January 9, 1776, a pamphlet presented the issue of independence to Americans as it had never been presented before, and in language that could be understood by anyone who could read. The ideas in it were not new, for they had been appearing in newspapers for years; what was new was the direct, hard-hitting prose in which those ideas were brought together in a single pamphlet. The pamphlet was *Common Sense*,[26] and its author was Thomas Paine, who had arrived in America from England late in 1774. He was the son of a poor Quaker corset-maker and was apprentice at that trade, but failed in one job after another. He had almost

---

[26] Pamphlet 16.

no formal education, yet he educated himself, absorbed the new ideas of the times, and learned to write better than most "educated" men, as did that other self-educated man, Benjamin Franklin. Somehow Paine came to Franklin's attention in London; Franklin sent him to Philadelphia, where he earned a living as a journalist and became acquainted with many of the leaders of the Second Continental Congress.

He rapidly absorbed the popular feeling of the times and put much of it into *Common Sense*. He made no money from the pamphlet nor from his other writings for the American cause; he was in fact completely indifferent to money. He was given the post of secretary to the congressional committee on foreign affairs but was forced to resign after publicly charging Silas Deane and Robert Morris with profiteering at the expense of their country. He stayed in America until 1787, when he returned to England to secure help for the building of an iron bridge he had designed. He became an ardent supporter of the French Revolution and wrote *The Rights of Man* defending it, and urging the English to overthrow the monarchy and establish a republic. The British government declared him an outlaw. He went to France, where he became a French citizen and was elected to the Assembly. When extremists got control he opposed them and they jailed him as a foreign national. In prison he began writing the greatest Deist tract of the eighteenth century, *The Age of Reason*. Many of the ideas in the book are accepted today, but orthodox religionists at the time charged that he was an "atheist," and much later, a twentieth-century President of the United States called him a "filthy little atheist."

Eventually Paine was released from prison, and in 1802 he returned to the United States. President Thomas Jefferson was glad to have him come, but most "respectable" people were horrified. He lived out the rest of his life in poverty and, according to his many enemies, as a drunkard and worse. When he died in 1809 he was denied burial in consecrated ground because of his supposed atheism. Nevertheless, his writings in behalf of the American Revolution, of the rights of man, and of the use of reason in human affairs are—or ought to be—as alive today as they were in the eighteenth century.

When Paine wrote *Common Sense* he abandoned the high-flown language of most previous pamphleteers, their concern with the legislative power of Parliament, and their professed allegiance to the British Crown. He denounced monarchy and demanded the establishment of a self-governing republic as the only fit government for free men. "The palaces of kings," wrote Paine, "are built upon the ruins of the bowers of paradise." "Of more worth is one honest man to society, and in the sight of God, than all the crowned ruffians that ever lived." As for George III, that "hardened, sullen-tempered Pharaoh" is not the father of his people, he is "the Royal Brute of Great Britain."

Paine exhorted Americans to stop talking nonsense about reconciliation and to take up arms at once and fight for independence, a fight they could win and should win, for in an independent America lay the future hope of mankind.

Every spot in the old world is overrun with oppression. Freedom hath been hunted round the Globe. Asia and Africa have long expelled her. Europe regards her like a stranger, and England hath given her warning to depart. O! receive the fugitive and prepare in time an asylum for mankind:

Common Sense went through endless printings and editions, and probably holds the record as the all-time "best seller" in American history. In 1776, the population of the colonies was about two and a half million, and of that number, a half million were Negro slaves. Paine said that 120,000 copies of *Common Sense* were sold in the first three months, and one of Paine's biographers estimates that perhaps 500,000 copies were published. Paine, clearly, had voiced the feeling and thinking of a great many of the American people.

The publication of *Common Sense* on January 9, 1776, was accompanied by an even more staggering blow to the American opponents of independence. On the same day a copy of the king's speech to Parliament in October arrived in Philadelphia. George III had declared that the "rebellious war" in the colonies was "manifestly carried on for the purpose of establishing an independent empire." At first the opponents of independence seemed unable to retaliate against *Common Sense*, although John Dickinson and his followers were able to block an open declaration of independence for another six months. But they could not block the rising agitation outside Congress and the suppression of writers opposed to independence. Thus, when a pamphlet attacking *Common Sense* was printed in New York, a "committee of mechanics" destroyed the copies before they could be sold. However, it was still possible to print such pamphlets in Philadelphia.

On March 13 the *Pennsylvania Gazette* announced the publication of *Plain Truth* by "Candidus,"[27] who attacked the ideas of government in *Common Sense* and called its author a "Political Quack." He defended monarchy and the English constitution and pictured the history of "democratical or popular" governments as one of incessant warfare, internal rebellion, and constant oppression of the rich by the poor. (Many Americans who became Patriots, as well as those who became Loyalists, believed that this was an accurate version of democracy.) "Candidus" scoffed at Paine's "glowing account of the Americans'" capacity to wage war. And if they did declare their independence, they would engage in civil war among themselves. There was some evidence for such an argument. "Candidus" appealed to the widespread distrust of New England's

---

[27] Pamphlet 17.

supposed imperial ambitions and could point to the New Englanders who claimed land in the Wyoming Valley of Pennsylvania and who were willing to shoot Pennsylvanians to maintain their claim.

The author of *Plain Truth* was James Chalmers, a Maryland landowner who eventually became a Loyalist and raised a Loyalist regiment to fight for the British. Another writer who attacked *Common Sense* was the Reverend William Smith, president of the College of Philadelphia. As "Cato" in the *Pennsylvania Gazette,* he defended the old government of Pennsylvania, urged reconciliation with Britain, and recommended *Plain Truth* to his readers. Thomas Paine, as "The Forester," answered "Cato" in the *Pennsylvania Journal* and scoffed at *Plain Truth* as "a performance which hath withered away like a sickly unnoticed weed. . . ." Most commentators since then have echoed Paine's judgment, but it is an unfair one. The colonies were in the midst of war and revolution, emotions were raw, and the behavior of many on both sides was brutal. *Plain Truth,* whatever it lacks in literary quality, matches *Common Sense* in bluntness of language, and it reflects the strong feelings of the many Americans who wished to remain a part of the British Empire.

Writers such as "Candidus" were engaged in a lost cause—the flood of events was carrying the colonies ever more rapidly in the direction of independence. On June 7, 1776, Richard Henry Lee moved that the colonies "are, and of right ought to be, free and independent states," and John Adams seconded the motion. Desperate opponents managed to delay a final vote for only three weeks. On July 2 Congress finally voted in favor of Lee's motion, and two days later, approved the final draft of the Declaration of Independence.

The pamphlet warfare with Britain over the relationship between the colonies and the empire was finished, and so was the pamphlet warfare among Americans about independence.

But Americans did not stop writing pamphlets, for they still faced the same problem they had debated with Britain: the relationship between the newly independent states and the new central government they created to take the place of the British government from which they had separated. Thus Americans continued the argument with one another in legislatures, in Congress, in the newspapers, and in pamphlets after 1776, as they debated the nature of man and of government, and made crucial decisions about the constitutions of the states and of the central government of the nation whose independence they had declared.

SELECTED BIBLIOGRAPHY

The basic guide to the materials printed in America prior to the nineteenth century is Charles Evans, *American Bibliography: A Chronological Dictionary of All Books, Pamphlets and Periodical Publications Printed in the United States from the Genesis of Printing in 1639 down to and Including the Year 1820* (12 vols., reprint, New York: Peter Smith, 1941–1942). Dr. Clifford K. Shipton, of the American Antiquarian Society, has corrected Evans' listings and published on microcards, under the title *Early American Imprints, 1639–1800,* all the items that can be found. The basic guide to the British and American pamphlets published between 1764 and 1776 is Thomas Randolph Adams, *American Independence, The Growth of an Idea: A Bibliographical Study of the American Political Pamphlets Printed Between 1764 and 1776 Dealing with the Dispute Between Great Britain and Her Colonies* (Providence, R. I.: Brown University Press, 1965).

Seventy-two of the more than 400 pamphlets published between 1750 and 1776 are now being reprinted in *Pamphlets of the American Revolution, 1750–1776* (Cambridge, Mass.: Harvard University Press, 1965–). This publication, edited by Bernard Bailyn assisted by Jane N. Garrett, will consist of four volumes. The pamphlets will be printed in their entirety and will be accompanied by editorial introductions, bibliographical references, and annotations of the texts. The first volume, published in 1965, contains fourteen pamphlets for the years 1750–1765.

The first American writer to pay careful attention to the pamphlets of the American Revolution was Moses Coit Tyler in *The Literary History of the American Revolution* (2 vols., New York: G. P. Putnam's Sons, 1897). Tyler provides an excellent description and summary of many of the important pamphlets, both Patriot and Loyalist, as well as of other forms of writing. More recent studies that make extensive use of the pamphlets of the period are Philip Davidson, *Propaganda and the American Revolution, 1763–1783* (Chapel Hill, N. C.: The University of North Carolina Press, 1941); Bruce I. Granger, *Political Satire in the American Revolution, 1763–1783* (Ithaca, N. Y.: Cornell University Press, 1960); and William H. Nelson, *The American Tory* (Oxford, England: Clarendon Press, 1961). Arthur M. Schlesinger, Sr., in *Prelude to Independence: The Newspaper War on Britain, 1764–1776* (New York: Alfred A. Knopf, 1958) discusses the role of the newspapers.

The political and constitutional ideas of the period are discussed from rather widely different points of view in Randolph F. Adams, *Political Ideas of the American Revolution* (3rd ed., New York: Barnes & Noble, 1958); Charles F. Mullett, *Fundamental Law and the American Revolution* (New York: Columbia University Press, 1933); Clinton Rossiter, *Seedtime of the Republic: The Origin of the American Tradition of Political Liberty* (New York: Harcourt Brace, 1953); and Bernard Bailyn, "The Transforming Radicalism of the American Revolution," *Pamphlets of the American Revolution, 1750–1776*, I, 3–202.

EDITOR'S NOTE

In reprinting these pamphlets, some of them for the first time since the eighteenth century, I have done a certain amount of editing. Eighteenth-century writers and printers seldom followed any common standards (even within a single publication) in spelling, punctuation, capitalization, and in the use of various kinds of type. Sometimes italic type was used for proper names, sometimes not. Italics were commonly used for emphasis, but sometimes capital letters of various sizes were used instead. Colons were often used in place of semicolons and periods, while semicolons appear in the place of commas. Commas were used with a prodigality that occasionally baffles a twentieth-century reader. Dashes and hyphens were scattered about at random, although sometimes emphasis seems intended. One suspects that printers often used whatever odds and ends of type that first came to hand.

The pamphlets printed in this volume have been edited in the following ways: (1) punctuation has been added or removed when this seemed necessary to the meaning; (2) italics used for emphasis have been retained, but random italics have been removed; (3) the original spelling and capitalization have been retained, except where noted in the introductions to individual pamphlets; (4) long quotations in the body of the pamphlets have been indented; (5) no attempt has been made to reproduce the typography of the pamphlets' title pages.

Most of the pamphlets have been reprinted in their entirety, although material has been deleted from certain of the more prolix and repetitious ones. Eighteenth-century writers were fond of lengthy quotations from past historians and political writers, even when such a display of "learning" did not advance their argument, and they occasionally wandered far from the main point they were trying to make. Where material has been omitted, the deletion has been indicated by three dots, followed by a space below. Deleted also are many of the footnotes which do not add directly to the main argument of the pamphlet. The introduction to each pamphlet indicates to what extent it has been edited.

The manuscript for this volume was based on the first or a contemporary edition of each pamphlet, with a few exceptions which were proofread against the microcard copy of the original edition to be found in Clifford K. Shipton, ed., *Early American Imprints, 1639–1800.*

Tracts of the

American Revolution

1763–1776

· 1 ·

An Essay on the Trade of
the Northern Colonies

By Stephen Hopkins

The "State of Trade" prepared by the Boston merchants was sent
to merchants in the other northern colonies at the end of 1763. The
Rhode Islanders responded at once. The merchants of Newport and
Providence were normally bitter commercial and political rivals,
but they could and did act together against any outside threat. A
committee of merchants from the two towns met in January 1764
and prepared a "Remonstrance." Governor Stephen Hopkins called
a special session of the legislature which met on January 26 and
adopted the "Remonstrance" as the official Rhode Island protest
against the renewal of the Molasses Act of 1733 and the new enforcement policies of the Grenville ministry.

Governor Hopkins wrote the *Essay* after he received a copy of
the Boston merchants' "State of Trade" and before the "Remonstrance" was adopted by the Rhode Island legislature. The *Essay*
was published in the *Providence Gazette* on January 14 and 21; it

---

From the *Newport Mercury*, February 6 and 13, 1764.

appeared in pamphlet form in London before the end of the year, although it never seems to have been issued as a pamphlet in America. The London edition purported to be a reprint of a Philadelphia edition, but it was probably copied from the *Pennsylvania Journal.* It seems clear that Hopkins spoke for the merchants in most of the northern colonies, for the *Essay* was widely reprinted in the newspapers. It appeared in the *Boston Evening Post* on January 30 and February 6, in the *New York Mercury* on February 6, in the *Newport Mercury* on February 6 and 13, and in the *Pennsylvania Journal* on March 8.

The copy that follows is from the *Newport Mercury* of February 6 and 13, 1764. The *Mercury* "modernized" capitalization in the issue of February 6, but in the issue of February 13 it capitalized about every third word, as had the *Providence Gazette* from which the *Mercury* reprinted the essay. The following text uses the *Mercury's* "modernized" capitalization throughout.

In things which concern the interest of our native country in general, every person seems to have a right to give his sentiments; or at least may be permitted, modestly to examine the subject, and propose his advice; and although the question in debate, may in general be much better managed by abler hands, yet some hints that are new, some thoughts which are useful, will be brought to light by several attempts, which had escaped the notice of the most sagacious writer. This is not only designed as an apology for the present attempt, but also to encourage others to endeavor to serve their country in the best manner they can, tho' they may not be able to do it with the same strength of delicacy as others; it being a poor excuse for not serving the public at all, because we are not able to do it so effectually as we may desire.

The commerce of the British northern colonies in America, is so peculiarly circumstanced, and from permanent causes, so

perplexed and embarrassed, that it is a business of great difficulty to investigate it, and put it in any tolerable point of light,
so that it may be understood; this perhaps may be the cause
why so little hath been attempted, and still less effected, in this
intricate tho' very interesting inquiry. That which most particularly and unhappily distinguishes most of these northern
British colonies, from all others, either British, or of any other
nation, is, that the soil and climate of them, is incapable of
producing almost any thing which will serve to send directly
home to the mother country; Yet notwithstanding this fatal
disadvantage, their situation and circumstances are such, as
to be obliged to take off, and consume greater quantities of
British manufactures, than any other colonies; their long cold
winters, call for much cloathing, but their deep and lasting
snows, make it impossible to keep sheep, and thereby procure
wool to supply that demand. Again, the same long winters
prevent the labor of slaves being of any advantage in those
colonies; this, together with the almost endless countries lying
back, yet to be settled and filled with inhabitants, makes hands
so scarce, and labor so dear, that no kind of manufactories can
be set up and supported in these colonies: And thus it appears
on one hand, that the inhabitants are obliged by necessity to
take great quantities of goods from the mother country; so on
the other, it is no less evident, that nature hath denied them
the means of returning any thing directly thither to pay for
those goods.

When these singular circumstances are fully known and duly
considered, it will easily be found what the cause is, that a
much greater number of ships and smaller vessels are employed
by the people of those colonies, than of any others in the
world: Unable to make remittances in a direct way, they are
obliged to do it by a circuity of commerce unpracticed by and
unnecessary in any other colony. The commodities shipped off
by them, are generally of such a nature, that they must be
consumed in the country where first sold, and will not bear

to be reshipped from thence to any other; from hence it happens that no one market will take off any great quantity; this obliges these people to look out for markets in every part of the world within their reach, where they can sell their goods for any tolerable price, and procure such things in return, as may serve immediately, or by several commercial exchanges, to make a remittance home.

Perhaps it may not be disagreeable to examine some branches of this commerce a little more minutely. We will begin with those colonies most to the northward, whose neighbouring seas being stored with fish, the inhabitants turn their industry to catching and curing of them; and when they are become fit to ship, all that are called merchantable are sent directly to Spain, Portugal, and Italy, and there sold for money or bills of exchange, which are sent directly to England, except a very small part returned in the ships to America, in salt, raisins, lemmons, pickles, &c. A considerable part of the fish yet remaining, which is unfit for the European markets, serves for feeding the slaves in the West-Indies; as much of this is sold in the English islands as they will purchase, and, the residue sold in the French and Dutch colonies, and in the end is turned into a remittance home. The colonies next to the southward of those we have been speaking of, export lumber, horses, pork, beef, and tobacco (of a poor and unmerchantable kind which is raised in them;) of these commodities, as much is sold in all the English West-Indies as they will purchase, the remainder is sold to the French and Dutch for molasses; this molasses is brought into these colonies, and there distilled into rum, which is sent to the coast of Africa, and there sold for gold, ivory, and slaves: the two first of these are sent directly home; the slaves are carried to the English West-Indies, and sold for money or bills of exchange, which are also remitted to England. As we still proceed further southward into the next colonies, we shall find their principal produce is wheat; which being made into flour, is exported, and brought into all the English ports in America: Yet after all these markets are supplied, a large overplus remains, which is sold to the Spaniards, French, and Dutch, as much as possible for silver and gold, which is all remitted to Great-Britain. The most southern colonies on the continent, whose produce is chiefly tobacco, naval stores and rice, find a market for their goods in the mother country, and thereby make their remittances in a more direct way, and consequently are less concerned in that tedious round of commerce to which the others are compelled to effect the same end.

Having given this brief and impartial view of the principal branches of commerce carried on by the northern British colonies, we will next endeavour to inquire, whether this commerce, taken together, or any branches of it, be detrimental to the true interests of Great-Britain, or in any degree injurious to the British sugar colonies, and shall then proceed to consider the consequences that must follow the restriction, limitation, or absolute prohibition of this commerce, or at least such part of it as is carried on with foreign nations. And first we shall acknowledge, that whatever business or commerce in any of the northern colonies interferes, or is any way detrimental to the true interest, manufactories, trade or commerce of Great-Britain, we reasonably expect will be totally prohibited. A certain illicit commerce, (not before spoken of) practised by some of the colonies directly with Holland and Hamburgh we confess to be of this kind; a like confession is due, with respect to those ships that carry on the fish trade to Spain, Italy, and Portugal, so far as they are concerned in importing any of the manufactures of these countries, directly into the colonies; tho' this is supposed to be very little, if at all practised; but in bringing raisins, lemmons, and other perishable fruits directly from those countries into the colonies, they cannot surely be liable to the same censure. For the inhabitants of the colonies must be wholly deprived of these refreshments, if they are not received in this way, their perishable nature not admitting of the round-about transportation, first to Great-Britain, and from thence to the colonies; altho' these are articles of little consequence in themselves, yet, as considerable profit is made by them, from a very small stock, this greatly encourages, and consequently increases the whole fish trade, which is a business of the utmost importance to all parts of the nation.

By some it may be supposed, that the trade from the colonies to the coast of Africa, is in some degree detrimental to the interest of Great-Britain, as it interferes with the English trade directly thither, which is carried on principally with her own manufactures; altho' this at first view appears to have some weight, yet when it is considered that in this trade from the colonies, not only the cargo sent out, but the ship's freight, mariner's wages, and all the profits of the voyage, is wholly converted into a remittance, or in other terms, into British manufactures, for the consumption in these colonies, it will be found that it is not injurious, but proves in the end beneficial to the mother country. Again, it may be said that tobacco shipped off from some of the colonies defrauds the king's revenue, and militates with the British commerce; the force of this objection will be removed, by considering that the coldness of the climate, and barrenness of the lands in the colonies where this tobacco is planted, is such, that it is impossible to produce any that will do to ship to Great-Britain; for neither the quality of it will bear the inspection of that market, nor the value come near paying the duty; Yet, this tobacco, bad as it is, finds a tolerable market among the poor slaves in the West-Indies, who are not able to purchase better; from hence it appears, the revenue could not be better'd by this tobacco being sent home; and also, that the demand for merchantable tobacco is not lessened in any degree by this being used by the negroes, who could by no means come up to the price of the other.

We now come to view the commerce of the northern colonies, as it relates to, or is any way connected with the British sugar colonies. And here we shall by no means make the same concessions, which our duty to, and dependance on the mother country, obliged us to make in discussing the former part of this question; but shall here take it for granted, that every branch of business and commerce in the northern colonies, which is beneficial to them, altho' it may in a less degree be injurious to the sugar colonies, ought notwithstanding that, to be countenanced and encouraged. What is chiefly complained of, is a trade carried on by the northern colonies, with the French and Dutch sugar colonies, and this, it is said, is injurious to the British ones; this supposed injury must happen, either by raising the price of northern produce in our West-India markets or by lessening the demand for, and consequently the price of their own: As to the first, 'tis universally known that every kind of northern produce, which finds any demand at all in our West-India markets, is continually carried thither in such quantities, as to keep the market always glutted; and, on a medium, every article is constantly sold as cheap there as the same article can be purchased in the colony where it is produced. And if all intercourse with the French and Dutch was intirely stopped, yet no greater quantities of northern produce would be sent to the British sugar islands than is now; for no body can suppose the northern people so immoderately fond of trade as to send more goods to any market than can be sold there for prime cost. Nor is there more weight in the other part of this complaint, that the sale of their own produce is hurt by this commerce; for the whole that is proposed and aimed at by the northern colonies, in this trade with the French and Dutch, is to put off their own produce for money or melasses, neither of which the British sugar colonies have to spare; except some melasses at Jamaica, the whole of which is constantly sold to the northern people by the planters, at their own extravagant price. But it is further said, that the French colonies are enriched, and the English ones impoverished by this commerce; this objection comes with a bad grace from our brethren of the West-Indies, who are constantly supplied with every sort of northern produce at fifty per cent less than the same kinds of goods are sold for to the French and Dutch, when at the same time every thing purchased in these English markets, costs fifty per cent more than the same articles are bought for amongst the French and Dutch; therefore, if one grows rich, and the other poor, it doth not arise from this commerce, but must come from other causes, which indeed could easily be pointed out, were not the task invidious. Let us pursue this reasoning a little further, and inquire, whether if all intercourse with the French and Dutch was at an end, the British sugar colonies are capable of purchasing and making use of all the northern produce now vended in the whole West-Indies? This question, the most sanguine planters, notwithstanding their good opinion of their own importance, must answer in the negative: What then is to be done with this overplus? Must the quantity of fish, flour, lumber, horses, &c. produced in the northern colonies, be lessened much more than one half, until they be made to dwindle down into the dimunitive size of these markets? Or can any succedaneum be pointed out, that will be more salutary upon the whole than the present practise? Again, upon a supposition that the whole of the northern produce could be disposed of in the British West-Indies, are they able to furnish the northern people with money, or any thing else that will enable them to make the same remittances to the mother country they now do? and which is the great and almost sole end that all their commerce aims at: or, will not this be found vastly to exceed their ability, and that the British manufactures consumed in these colonies, and the remittances made from thence annually, greatly exceed every thing produced in the sugar colonies, excepting so much of their sugar and rum as will serve for their own remittances. Upon the whole, how very unkind and ungenerous must it be, in the rich, proud, and overbearing planters of the West-Indies, to make use of all their weight and influence to limit and distress the trade, and thereby to cramp and impoverish the poorer northern colonies; when yet this conduct brings no real advantage to themselves, but only serves to shew forth a wanton display of the opulence and influence of a few overgrown West-India estates. From such a conduct, we might almost draw this untoward conclusion, that as these people are used to an arbitrary and cruel government over slaves, and have so long tasted the *sweets* of oppressing their fellow creatures, they can hardly forbear esteeming two millions of free and loyal British subjects, inhabitants of the northern colonies, in the same light; and persuading themselves, that they are only to be considered as placed there for their own use, advantage, and emolument.

The last point to be considered, is the consequences that must follow, upon the limitation, restriction, or absolute prohibition of this northern commerce. And here, if we consult experience, the surest guide to right reasoning on such subjects, we shall find, that the Act of the 6th of George the Second, commonly called the Sugar Act, laying so high a duty on all foreign sugar, melasses, and rum, imported into the British plantations, as amounts, in effect, to a prohibition, hath never in any degree increased the royal revenue, or brought any other real advantage to the mother country; Neither hath it been at all more beneficial to the British sugar colonies, at whose instance it was procured. But altho' no salutary consequences have any where followed this act, yet, many and great mischiefs and disadvantages, as well as corrupt and scandalous practices have flowed from it in all the English colonies: The merchants, unwilling to quit a trade, which was in a great measure the foundation of their whole circle of commerce, have gone into many illicit methods to cover them in still carrying it on; while the custom-house officers have made a very lucrative jobb of shutting their eyes, or at least of opening them no farther than their own private interest required. It may perhaps be thought all this may be remedied, by appointing better methods, and creating other officers, that will effectually carry this act into execution; but this will, on trial, be found a mistake: This trade may be wholly stopt; but duties as high as are laid by this act, cannot by any means whatsoever be collected, being vastly greater than the trade itself can possibly bear; therefore, any method effectual for collecting this duty, will also be effectual for putting an entire end to the whole trade. And if the design of the British legislature was, by this act, to increase the king's revenue, and not prohibit the trade, it might have answered that end much better, if, instead of sixpence, for every gallon of melasses, the duty had been a halfpenny upon each gallon, and in the same proportion for the other articles mentioned in the act; as the trade might have borne such a duty it would have been chearfully paid by the merchants, and would even at this rate, produce a far greater revenue yearly to the crown, than has ever yet been paid by all the continent, in America; and perhaps greater than any higher duty will ever produce; for the higher the duty is, the less the trade will be, and therefore it is not unreasonable to suppose a small duty will yield more than a larger one can do. And indeed, the whole exportation from these colonies, consists in articles of so great bulk, in proportion to the value, that when a ship is loaded with them, and makes a voyage, the hire of the ship mariners, wages and provisions, insurance, and other necessary charges, take so great a part of the returns, that very small profits only can be made in any branch of this trade; and therefore it is impossible it should bear any high duties.

If this matter should be pushed further, and an act of Parliament obtained for putting a total stop to all trade between the northern colonies and the Spanish, French, Dutch, and Danish settlements, in America, such an act must be absolutely ruinous to these colonies: at least for a great while, until time and necessity shall teach the people to make a thorough alteration in their whole domestic œconomy. And, if to this be added, a rigorous execution of those acts, passed long ago (tho' hitherto wisely winked at) by which the fish ships are prohibited to bring any thing but salt from Spain, Portugal, and Italy; both these measures taken together, must put an effectual end to the fishery: Being prevented by one from importing the small articles before-mentioned, in their ships from Europe, all the clear profits of these voyages will be lost; and by the other, one sixth part of their whole fish, which used to be sold in the foreign markets in America, must now perish in their hands for want of buyers; these things will fall so heavy, that all those concerned in the fish trade, must sink under their weight; and consequently the whole fishing business be lost, and in it the principal resource of remittances in several of the most considerable colonies. The case of the other colonies will not be much better, upon these measures taking place, for more than one half of their lumber, flour, horses, &c. usually exported, must now lie on hand for want of markets; and their ability to make remittances will be decreased in a much greater proportion; as it hath been by this foreign trade, and it's consequent branches, they have hitherto been enabled to make the principal part of their returns to the mother country; receiving very little in their trade with the English islands, that ever can be made to serve that great purpose. Another great mischief, fatal to many, may with certainty be pointed out: The merchants throughout the continent, who have been chiefly concerned in importing British manufactures into America, and who generally receive their goods on credit, when almost every means of making returns are taken from them, must fail in payment; and greater deficiencies must soon appear in the colonies, than we have lately heard of in Holland and Hamburgh, and the loss, in the end, fall on the manufacturers and merchants of the mother country.

It requires no great share of sagacity to perceive that all the affairs of these colonies must put on a very gloomy appearance, when twenty thousand seamen and fishermen are turned out of employ; when the shipping they used to navigate and improve, are all hauled up, and laid by as useless; when more than one half the hands, whose business it hath been to make lumber, flour, beef, pork, &c. must forsake their callings, and find out others, or starve; that these are not the wanton exaggerations of fancy, but sober and stubborn facts, with their train of melancholy consequences, that must as necessarily follow, as effects do their causes. Moreover, as the ability of these colonies to pay for British manufactures, will be two thirds taken away, the people must content themselves, and make the best they can of the one third part they are still able to purchase; and those who are taken from the sea, the fishery, and the other branches of business before-mentioned, with multitudes besides, who will not be able by any means to procure such European goods as they want, must be compelled, by mere necessity, to employ themselves in such coarse and homely manufactories, as their ability and skill will enable them; supplying their necessities in the best manner they can by their labor; having this encouragement always before them, that practice will make them more expert in their several businesses: And as all kinds of cloathing must become extremely scarce and dear, this will encourage the husbandmen, in spite of all obstacles, to keep more sheep, in order to supply this demand; so that it is very possible, the inhabitants of these colonies, in the next age, may find they are much bettered by the measures which have undone us who lived in this.

Before we leave this point, we may be permitted modestly to inquire, if any intelligent Briton, who is fully informed of all the circumstances attending this whole question, can possibly desire such limitations, restrictions, and prohibitions as have been before spoken of, should take place in these colonies? Doth not Great-Britain export to the colonies on this continent, in her own manufactures, nearly to the amount of two millions a year? Doth Great-Britain pay more than half a million a year for all the unwrought materials she purchases abroad, and which go into these manufactures she sends to America? If these premises are true, doth there not rest in her hands the immense ballance of one million and a half annually by her exportations to these colonies? And is not this a greater profit than any other kingdom on earth draws from it's colonies? Although, for want of just information, some inaccuracies be found in these calculations; yet, when those are all removed, the balance in favour of Great-Britain, by this commerce with her colonies, will be found so vastly large, that 'tis not rational to believe any of her well-inform'd sons can ever desire that this trade, or any other which enables the colonies to support and carry this on, should be any way obstructed, embarrassed, or prohibited, by any acts or laws of her own making; which, tho' they may seem on the first view, to be calculated for other and better purposes; yet, on a full and clear examination, will be found to have a direct tendency to weaken, and in the end, destroy this very beneficial intercourse between the mother country and her colonies. No advantages that can possibly accrue to the sugar colonies, and thro' them to Great-Britain, by these measures being pursued, can with justice be put in the ballance, by any reasonable and considerate man, against the real and destructive mischiefs that must fall on the northern colonies by it; and, through them, on the mother country; Nor can any supposed increase of the royal revenue, arising from burdens and duties being laid on all, or any part of the commerce in question, be any adequate compensation to Great-Britain, for the loss she must thereby sustain in the exportation of her own manufactures. For it may be depended on as an axiom, that nothing limits the consumption of British manufactures in the northern colonies, but the people's ability to pay for them; and that whatever lessens that ability, will in the same proportion, lessen the consumption. An observation or two, borrowed from a modern historian, writing about the colonies of another nation, shall conclude these remarks.

The maxim of the Spanish court has always been to make their possessions in the Indies, beneficial to the crown, rather than to the nation; and this is the true cause that they have been much less serviceable than they might have been to both. The want of a free commerce has check'd their navigation, hindered their increase of shipping, and kept them poor and weak in the midst of riches. —The only maxim therefore, that can encourage trade, is, making every thing easy to those who are disposed to engage in it, and let the profits of the government be the last thing to be considered; for which they will not be less, since the monarch of a rich people can never be poor; and the crown, where the people is poor, can never be long rich.

And, a short address to the colonies principally concerned, shall put an end to the whole. First, let them all be persuaded, not to make any dependance on eluding the force of such laws, as are already, or may hereafter be made for limiting and restraining their commerce: or rest their hope on the indulgence of the custom-house officers, whose duty it is to see these laws executed; such methods are equally unjust and ineffectual, expensive and odious; and render the colonies in which they are practised obnoxious to the resentment of the administration at home; and tend to justify an extraordinary exertion of power, employed for carrying these laws into execution, which otherwise must have been highly blameworthy. Rather let their whole expectations of relief, depend altogether on a proper application to the British legislature; in order to this, all the colonies concerned ought to unite, and appoint proper persons, who may prepare a true state of the commerce of these colonies, noting the branches which are peculiar to each; let this be sent to their several agents, and by them jointly be laid before the Lords Commissioners for Trade and Plantations, in order to be examined and corrected, as need may require; and from thence and with their recommendation, let it be brought before the Parliament, where doubtless it will be farther examined, and duly considered, and every branch of our commerce, that coincides with the general interest of the nation, be countenanced and established; and if we practice any, which are found to have a contrary tendency, they must be given up and forsaken. This, or something very like it, surely is the duty, as well as the interest of all these colonies; and if their cause be good, as most certainly it is, what have they to fear from such a procedure? Or rather, what have they not to hope, from such an application and appeal to a king who delights in doing good to all his subjects; to a peerage, wise and accurate, guided by the principles of honor and beneficence; and to a representative body, penetrating and prudent, who consider the good of the whole, and make that the measure of their public resolves.

N.B. Since the foregoing Essay came to the printer's hands, the writer has obtained accounts of the exports to North-America, and the West-India Islands, by which it appears, that there has been some increase of trade to those islands as well as to North-America, though in much less degree. The following extract from these accounts will show the reader at one view the amount of the exports to each, in two different terms of five years; the terms taken at ten years distance from each other, to show the increase, viz.

First Term, from 1744 to 1748, inclusive.

	Northern Colonies	*West-India Islands*
1744	£640,114/12/ 4	£796,112/17/ 9
1745	534,316/ 2/ 5	503,669/19/ 9
1746	754,945/ 4/ 3	472,994/19/ 7
1747	726,648/ 5/ 5	856,463/18/ 6
1748	830,243/16/ 9	734,095/15/ 3
Total	£3,486,268/ 1/ 2	£3,363,337/10/10
	Difference,	122,930/10/ 4
		£3,486,268/ 1/ 2

Second Term, from 1754 to 1758, inclusive.

	Northern Colonies	West-India Islands
1754	£1,246,615/ 1/11	£685,675/ 3/ 0
1755	1,177,848/ 6/10	694,667/13/ 3
1756	1,428,720/18/10	733,458/16/ 3
1757	1,727,924/ 2/10	776,488/ 0/ 6
1758	1,832,948/13/10	877,571/19/11
Total	£7,414,057/ 4/ 3	£3,767,841/12/11
	Difference,	3,646,215/11/ 4
		£7,414,057/ 4/ 3

In the first term, total for the West-India Islands,	£3,363,337/10/10
In the second term, ditto,	£3,767,841/12/11
Increase only,	£ 404,504/ 2/ 1

In the first term, total for the northern colonies,	£3,486,268/ 1/ 2
In the second term, ditto,	£7,414,057/ 4/ 3
Increase,	£3,927,789/ 3/ 1

By these accounts it appears, that the exports to the West-India Islands and to the northern colonies were in the first term nearly equal; the difference being only £122,936. 10s. 4d., and in the second term, the exports to those islands had only increased £404,504. 2s. 1d. Whereas the increase to the northern colonies is £3,927,789. 3s. 1d. almost four millions.

· 2 ·

The Rights of the British Colonies

Asserted and Proved

By James Otis

The Rights of the British Colonies was published in Boston on July 23, 1764.[1] It seems to have had little impact outside New England; at least it is not mentioned in the newspapers of the other colonies. In fact, Otis' retraction of the views expressed in it, in his two pamphlets the following year, almost destroyed his influence in the town of Boston. He managed to retain his hold on the populace by demagogic means until ever more frequent attacks of insanity removed him almost entirely from politics after 1769.[2]

It would seem that posterity's view of Otis as a great revolutionary leader depends almost entirely on John Adams' recollections in his old age, when he had forgotten that his own diary for the 1760's and 1770's provides evidence for the proposition that Otis was

Boston, 1764, pp. 31–40, 41–43, 47–48, 49–52, 59, 61, 64–65.

[1] *Boston Gazette*, July 23, 1764.
[2] See Ellen Brennan, "James Otis: Recreant and Patriot," *The New England Quarterly*, XII (1939), 700–711.

more of a hindrance than a help to the revolutionary movement in Massachusetts.[3]

However, since Otis' pamphlet was one of the first of those inspired by British policies after 1763, portions of it are included here. The first three sections are omitted entirely and only those parts of the final section which contain his essential arguments are printed.[4]

Otis' references in the text to "the revolution" concern the Revolution of 1688–89 in England. His references to the author of "the administration" are to Thomas Pownall and his book, *The Administration of the Colonies*, which was published in London in March, 1764. Pownall had been governor of Massachusetts from 1757 to 1760. Otis' references to Dummer's *Defence* are to Jeremiah Dummer's *Defence of the New England Charters*, published in London in 1721. Dummer was agent of Massachusetts in London from 1710 to 1730. He wrote the pamphlet in 1715 when an attempt was made to revoke all colonial charters by an act of Parliament.

OF THE POLITICAL AND CIVIL RIGHTS
OF THE BRITISH COLONISTS.

Here indeed opens to view a large field; but I must study brevity—Few people have extended their enquiries after the foundation of any of their rights, beyond a charter from the crown. There are others who think when they have got back to old *Magna Charta*, that they are at the beginning of all things. They imagine themselves on the borders of Chaos (and so indeed in some respects they are) and see creation rising out of the unformed mass, or from nothing. Hence, say they,

---

[3] See Clifford K. Shipton, "James Otis," in *Sibley's Harvard Graduates*, XI (Boston, 1960), 247–287.

[4] The entire pamphlet may be found in Bernard Bailyn, ed., *Pamphlets of the American Revolution, 1750–1776*, I (Cambridge, Mass., 1965), 419–482.

spring all the rights of men and of citizens.—— But liberty was better understood, and more fully enjoyed by our ancestors, before the coming in of the first Norman Tyrants than ever after, 'till it was found necessary, for the salvation of the kingdom, to combat the arbitrary and wicked proceedings of the Stuarts.

The present happy and most righteous establishment is justly built on the ruins, which those Princes bro't on their Family; and two of them on their own heads—The last of the name sacrificed three of the finest kingdoms in Europe, to the councils of bigotted old women, priests and more weak and wicked ministers of state: He afterward went a grazing in the fields of St. Germains, and there died in disgrace and poverty, a terrible example of God's vengeance on arbitrary princes!

The deliverance under God wrought by the prince of Orange, afterwards deservedly made King Wm. 3d. was as joyful an event to the colonies as to Great-Britain: In some of them, steps were taken in his favour as soon as in England.

They all immediately acknowledged King William and Queen Mary as their lawful Sovereign. And such has been the zeal and loyalty of the colonies ever since for that establishment, and for the protestant succession in his present Majesty's illustrious family, that I believe there is not one man in an hundred (except in Canada) who does not think himself under the best national civil constitution in the world.

Their loyalty has been abundantly proved, especially in the late war. Their affection and reverence for their mother country is unquestionable. They yield the most chearful and ready obedience to her laws, particularly to the power of that august body the parliament of Great-Britain, the supreme legislative of the kingdom and in dominions. These I declare are my own sentiments of duty and loyalty. I also hold it clear that the act of Queen Anne, which makes it high treason to deny "that the King, with and by the authority of parliament, is able to make laws and statutes of sufficient force and validity to *limit and bind* the crown, and the descent, limitation, inheritance and *government* thereof" is founded on the principles of liberty and the British constitution: And he that would palm the doctrine of unlimited passive obedience and non-resistance upon mankind, and thereby or by any other means serve the cause of the Pretender, is not only a fool and a knave, but a rebel against common sense, as well as the laws of God, of Nature, and his Country.

I also lay it down as one of the first principles from whence I intend to deduce the civil rights of the British colonies, that all of them are subject to, and dependent on Great-Britain; and that therefore as over subordinate governments, the parliament of Great-Britain has an undoubted power and lawful authority to make acts for the general good, that by naming them, shall and ought to be equally binding, as upon the subjects of Great-Britain within the realm. This principle, I presume will be readily granted on the other side of the Atlantic. It has been practiced upon for twenty years to my knowledge, in the province of the *Massachusetts-Bay;* and I have ever received it, that it has been so from the beginning, in this and the sister provinces, thro' the continent.*

I am aware, some will think it is time for me to retreat, after having expressed the power of the British parliament in quite so strong terms. But 'tis from and under this very power and its acts, and from the common law, that the political and civil rights of the Colonists are derived: And upon those grand pillars of liberty shall my defence be rested. At present therefore, the reader may suppose, that there is not one provincial charter on the continent; he may, if he pleases, imagine all taken away, without fault, without forfeiture, without tryal or notice. All this really happened to some of them in the last century. I

---

* This however was formally declared as to Ireland, but so lately as the reign of G. 1. Upon the old principles of conquest the Irish could not have so much to say for an exemption, as the unconquered Colonists.

would have the reader carry his imagination still further, and suppose a time may come, when instead of a process at common law, the parliament shall give a decisive blow to every charter in America, and declare them all void. Nay it shall also be granted, that 'tis barely possible, the time may come, when the real interest of the whole may require an act of parliament to annihilate all those charters. What could follow from all this, that would shake one of the essential, natural, civil or religious rights of the Colonists? Nothing. They would be men, citizens and british subjects after all. No act of parliament can deprive them of the liberties of such, unless any will contend that an act of parliament can make slaves not only of one, but of two millions of the commonwealth. And if so, why not of the whole? I freely own, that I can find nothing in the laws of my country, that would justify the parliament in making one slave, nor did they ever professedly undertake to make one.

Two or three innocent colony charters have been threatened with destruction an hundred and forty years past. I wish the present enemies of those harmless charters would reflect a moment, and be convinced that an act of parliament that should demolish those bugbears to the foes of liberty, would not reduce the Colonists to a state of absolute slavery. The worst enemies of the charter governments are by no means to be found in England. 'Tis a piece of justice due to Great-Britain to own, they are and have ever been natives of or residents in the colonies. A set of men in America, without honour or love to their country, have been long grasping at powers, which they think unattainable while these charters stand in the way. But they will meet with insurmountable obstacles to their project for enslaving the British colonies, should those, arising from provincial charters be removed. It would indeed seem very hard and severe, for those of the colonists, who have charters, with peculiar priviledges, to loose them. They were given to their ancestors, in consideration of their sufferings and merit, in discovering and settling America. Our fore-fathers were soon worn away in the toils of hard labour on their little plantations, and in war with the Savages. They thought they were earning a sure inheritance for their posterity. Could they imagine it would ever be tho't just to deprive them or theirs of their charter priviledges! Should this ever be the case, there are, thank God, natural, inherent and inseperable rights as men, and as citizens, that would remain after the so much wished for catastrophe, and which, whatever became of charters, can never be abolished *de jure*, if *de facto*, till the general conflagration.* Our rights as men and free born British subjects, give all the Colonists enough to make them very happy in comparison with the subjects of any other prince in the world.

Every British subject born on the continent of America, or in any other of the British dominions, is by the law of God and nature, by the common law, and by act of parliament, (exclusive of all charters from the Crown) entitled to all the natural, essential, inherent and inseparable rights of our fellow subjects in Great-Britain. Among those rights are the following, which it is humbly conceived no man or body of men, not excepting the parliament, justly, equitably and consistently with their own rights and the constitution, can take away.

1st. *That the supreme and subordinate powers of legislation should be free and sacred in the hands where the community have once rightfully placed them.*

2dly. *The supreme national legislative cannot be altered justly 'till the commonwealth is dissolved, nor a subordinate legislative taken away without forfeiture or other good cause.* Nor then can the subjects in the subordinate government be reduced to a state of slavery, and subject to the despotic rule

---

* The fine defence of the provincial charters by *Jeremy Dummer*, Esq.; the late very able and learned agent for the province of the *Massachusetts Bay*, makes it needless to go into a particular consideration of charter priviledges. That piece is unanswerable, but by power and might, and other arguments of that kind.

of others. A state has no right to make slaves of the conquered. Even when the subordinate right of legislature is forfeited, and so declared, this cannot affect the natural persons either of those who were invested with it, or the inhabitants,† so far as to deprive them of the rights of subjects and of men—The colonists will have an equitable right notwithstanding any such forfeiture of charter, to be represented in Parliament, or to have some new subordinate legislature among themselves. It would be best if they had both. Deprived however of their common rights as subjects, they cannot lawfully be, while they remain such. A representation in Parliament from the several Colonies, since they are become so large and numerous, as to be called on not to maintain provincial government, civil and military among themselves, for this they have chearfully done, but to contribute towards the support of a national standing army, by reason of the heavy national debt, when they themselves owe a large one, contracted in the common cause, can't be tho't an unreasonable thing, nor if asked, could it be called an immodest request. *Qui sentit commodum sentire debet et onus,* has been tho't a maxim of equity. But that a man should bear a burthen for other people, as well as himself, without a return, never long found a place in any law-book or decrees, but those of the most despotic princes. Besides the equity of an American representation in parliament, a thousand advantages would result from it. It would be the most effectual means of giving those of both countries a thorough knowledge of each others interests; as well as that of the whole, which are inseparable.

Were this representation allowed; instead of the scandalous memorials and depositions that have been sometimes, in days of old, privately cooked up in an inquisitorial manner, by persons of bad minds and wicked views, and sent from America

---

† See Magna Charta, the Bill of Rights. 3 Mod. 152 2. Salkeld 411. Vaughan 300.

to the several boards, persons of the first reputation among their countrymen, might be on the spot, from the several colonies, truly to represent them. Future ministers need not, like some of their predecessors, have recourse for information in American affairs, to every vagabond stroller, that has run or rid post thro' America, from his creditors, or to people of no kind of reputation from the colonies; some of whom, at the time of administring their sage advice, have been as ignorant of the state of this country, as of the regions in Jupiter and Saturn.

No representation of the Colonies in parliament alone, would however be equivalent to a subordinate legislative among themselves; nor so well answer the ends of increasing their prosperity and the commerce of Great-Britain. It would be impossible for the parliament to judge so well, of their abilities to bear taxes, impositions on trade, and other duties and burthens, or of the local laws that might be really needful, as a legislative here.

3dly. *No legislative, supreme or subordinate, has a right to make itself arbitrary.*

It would be a most manifest contradiction, for a free legislative, like that of Great-Britain, to make itself arbitrary.

4thly. *The supreme legislative cannot justly assume a power of ruling by extempore arbitrary decrees, but is bound to dispense justice by known settled rules, and by duly authorized independant judges.*

5thly. *The supreme power cannot take from any man any part of his property, without his consent in person, or by representation.*

6thly. *The legislature cannot transfer the power of making laws to any other hands.*

These are their bounds, which by God and nature are fixed, hitherto have they a right to come, and no further.

1. *To govern by stated laws.*

2. *Those laws should have no other end ultimately, but the good of the people.*

3. *Taxes are not to be laid on the people, but by their consent in person, or by deputation.*
4. *Their whole power is not transferable.**

These are the first principles of law and justice, and the great barriers of a free state, and of the British constitution in particular. I ask, I want no more—Now let it be shown how 'tis reconcileable with these principles, or to many other fundamental maxims of the British constitution, as well as the natural and civil rights, which by the laws of their country, all British subjects are intitled to, as their best inheritance and birth-right, that all the northern colonies, who are without one representative in the house of Commons, should be taxed by the British parliament.

That the colonists, black and white, born here, are free born British subjects, and entitled to all the essential civil rights of such, is a truth not only manifest from the provincial charters, from the principles of the common law, and acts of parliament; but from the British constitution, which was reestablished at the revolution, with a professed design to secure the liberties of all the subjects to all generations.†

In the 12 and 13 of Wm. cited above, the liberties of the subject are spoken of as their best birth-rights—No one ever dreamt, surely, that these liberties were confined to the realm. At that rate, no British subjects in the dominions could, without a manifest contradiction, be declared entitled to all the privileges of subjects born within the realm, to all intents and purposes, which are rightly given foreigners, by parliament, after residing seven years. These expressions of parliament, as well as of the charters, must be vain and empty sounds, unless we are allowed the essential rights of our fellow-subjects in Great-Britain.

Now can there be any liberty, where property is taken away without consent? Can it with any colour of truth, justice or

---

* See Locke on Government. B. II. C. xi.

† See the convention, and acts confirming it.

equity, be affirmed, that the northern colonies are represented in parliament? Has this whole continent of near three thousand miles in length, and in which and his other American dominions, his Majesty has, or very soon will have, some millions of as good, loyal and useful subjects, white and black, as any in the three kingdoms, the election of one member of the house of commons?

Is there the least difference, as to the consent of the Colonists, whether taxes and impositions are laid on their trade, and other property, by the crown alone, or by the parliament. As it is agreed on all hands, the Crown alone cannot impose them, we should be justifiable in refusing to pay them, but must and ought to yield obedience to an act of parliament, tho' erroneous, 'till repealed.

I can see no reason to doubt, but that the imposition of taxes, whether on trade, or on land, or houses, or ships, on real or personal, fixed or floating property, in the colonies, is absolutely irreconcileable with the rights of the Colonists, as British subjects, and as men. I say men, for in a state of nature, no man can take my property from me, without my consent: If he does, he deprives me of my liberty, and makes me a slave. If such a proceeding is a breach of the law of nature, no law of society can make it just—The very act of taxing, exercised over those who are not represented, appears to me to be depriving them of one of their most essential rights, as freemen; and if continued, seems to be in effect an entire disfranchisement of every civil right. For what one civil right is worth a rush, after a man's property is subject to be taken from him at pleasure, without his consent. If a man is not his *own assessor* in person, or by deputy, his liberty is gone, or lays intirely at the mercy of others.

I think I have heard it said, that when the Dutch are asked why they enslave their colonies, their answer is, that the liberty of Dutchmen is confined to Holland; and that it was never intended for Provincials in America, or anywhere else. A sentiment this, very worthy of modern Dutchmen; but if their brave and worthy ancestors had entertained such narrow ideas of liberty, seven poor and distressed provinces would never have asserted their rights against the whole Spanish monarchy, of which the present is but a shadow. It is to be hoped, none of our fellow subjects of Britain, great or small, have borrowed this Dutch maxim of plantation politics; if they have, they had better return it from whence it came; indeed they had. Modern Dutch or French maxims of state, never will suit with a British constitution. It is a maxim, that the King can do no wrong; and every good subject is bound to believe his King is not inclined to do any. We are blessed with a prince who has given abundant demonstrations, that in all his actions, he studies the good of his people, and the true glory of his crown, which are inseparable. It would therefore, be the highest degree of impudence and disloyalty to imagine that the King, at the head of his parliament, could have any, but the most pure and perfect intentions of justice, goodness and truth, that human nature is capable of. All this I say and believe of the King and parliament, in all their acts; even in that which so nearly affects the interest of the colonists; and that a most perfect and ready obedience is to be yielded to it, while it remains in force. I will go further, and readily admit, that the intention of the ministry was not only to promote the public good, by this act; but that Mr. Chancellor of the Exchequer had therein a particular view to the "ease, the quiet, and the good will of the Colonies," he having made this declaration more than once. Yet I hold that 'tis possible he may have erred in his kind intentions towards the Colonies, and taken away our fish, and given us a stone. With regard to the parliament, as infallability belongs not to mortals, 'tis possible *they* may have been misinformed and deceived. The power of parliament is uncontroulable, but by themselves, and we must obey. They only can repeal their own acts. There would be an end of all government, if one or a number of subjects or subordinate provinces should take upon them so far to judge of the justice of an act of parliament, as to refuse obedience to it. If there was nothing else to restrain such a step, prudence ought to do it, for forceably resisting the parliament and the King's laws, is high treason. Therefore let the parliament lay what burthens they please on us, we must, it is our duty to submit and patiently bear them, till they will be pleased to relieve us. And tis to be presumed, the wisdom and justice of that august assembly, always will afford us relief by repealing such acts, as through mistake, or other human infirmities, have been suffered to pass, if they can be convinced that their proceedings are not constitutional, or not for the common good. . . .

I have waited years in hopes to see some one friend of the colonies pleading in publick for them. I have waited in vain. One priviledge is taken away after another, and where we shall be landed, God knows, and I trust will protect and provide for us even should we be driven and persecuted into a more western wilderness, on the score of liberty, civil and religious, as many of our ancestors were, to these once inhospitable shores of America. I had formed great expectations from a gentleman,[1] who published his first volume in quarto on the rights of the colonies two years since; but, as he foresaw, the state of his health and affairs have prevented his further progress. The misfortune is, gentlemen in America, the best qualified in every respect to state the rights of the colonists, have reasons that prevent them from engaging: Some of them have good ones. There are many infinitely better able to serve this cause than I pretend to be; but from indolence, from timidity, or by necessary engagements, they are prevented. There has been a most profound, and I think shameful silence, till it seems al-

---

[1] The reference is to a pamphlet by William Bollan published in London in 1762. See Bailyn, *Pamphlets of the American Revolution*, I, 721, n. 22. [—ED.]

most too late to assert our indisputable rights as men and as citizens. What must posterity think of us. The trade of the whole continent taxed by parliament, stamps and other internal duties and taxes as they are called, talked of, and not one petition to the King and Parliament for relief.

I cannot but observe here, that if the parliament have an equitable right to tax our trade, 'tis indisputable that they have as good an one to tax the lands, and every thing else. The taxing trade furnishes one reason why the other should be taxed, or else the burdens of the province will be unequally born, upon a supposition that a tax on trade is not a tax on the whole. But take it either way, there is no foundation for the distinction some make in England, between an internal and an external tax on the colonies. By the first is meant a tax on trade, by the latter a tax on land, and the things on it. A tax on trade is either a tax of every man in the province, or 'tis not. If 'tis not a tax on the whole, 'tis unequal and unjust, that a heavy burden should be laid on the trade of the colonies, to maintain an army of soldiers, custom-house officers, and fleets of guard-ships; all which, the incomes of both trade and land would not furnish means to support so lately as the last war, when all was at stake, and the colonies were reimbursed in part by parliament. How can it be supposed that all of a sudden the trade of the colonies alone can bear all this terrible burden. The late acquisitions in America, as glorious as they have been, and as beneficial as they are to Great-Britain, are only a security to these colonies against the ravages of the French and Indians. Our trade upon the whole is not, I believe, benefited by them one groat. All the time the French Islands were in our hands, the fine sugars, &c. were all shipped home. None as I have been informed were allowed to be bro't to the colonies. They were too delicious a morsel for a North American palate. If it be said that a tax on the trade of the colonies is an equal and just tax on the whole of the inhabitants: What then becomes of the notable distinction between external and internal taxes? Why may not the parliament lay stamps, land taxes, establish tythes to the church of England, and so indefinitely. I know of no bounds. I do not mention the tythes out of any disrespect to the church of England, which I esteem by far the best *national* church, and to have had as ornaments of it many of the greatest and best men in the world. But to those colonies who in general dissent from a principle of conscience, it would seem a little hard to pay towards the support of a worship, whose modes they cannot conform to.

If an army must be kept up in America, at the expence of the colonies, it would not seem quite so hard if after the parliament had determined the sum to be raised, and apportioned it, to have allowed each colony to assess its quota, and raise it as easily to themselves as might be. But to have the whole levied and collected without our consent is extraordinary. 'Tis allowed even to *tributaries,* and those laid under *military* contribution, to assess and collect the sums demanded. The case of the provinces is certainly likely to be the hardest that can be instanced in story. Will it not equal any thing but down right military execution? Was there ever a tribute imposed even on the conquered? A fleet, an army of soldiers, and another of taxgatherers kept up, and not a single office either for securing or collecting the duty in the gift of the tributary state. . . .

To say the parliament is absolute and arbitrary, is a contradiction. The parliament cannot make 2 and 2, 5: Omnipotency cannot do it. The supreme power in a state, is *jus dicere* only: —*jus dare,* strictly speaking, belongs alone to God. Parliaments are in all cases to *declare* what is for the good of the whole; but it is not the *declaration* of parliament that makes it so: There must be in every instance, a higher authority, viz. GOD. Should an act of parliament be against any of *his* natural laws, which are *immutably* true, *their* declaration would be contrary to eternal truth, equity and justice, and consequently void: and so it would be adjudged by the parliament itself, when convinced of their mistake. Upon this great principle, parliaments repeal such acts, as soon as they find they have been mistaken, in having declared them to be for the public good, when in fact they were not so. When such mistake is evident and palpable, as in the instances in the appendix, the judges of the executive courts have declared the act "of a whole parliament void." See here the grandeur of the British constitution! See the wisdom of our ancestors! The supreme *legislative,* and the supreme *executive,* are a perpetual check and balance to each other. If the supreme executive errs, it is informed by the supreme legislative in parliament: If the supreme legislative errs, it is informed by the supreme executive in the King's courts of law. —Here, the King appears, as represented by his judges, in the highest lustre and majesty, as supreme executor of the commonwealth; and he never shines brighter, but on his Throne, at the head of the supreme legislative. This is government! This, is a constitution! to preserve which, either from foreign or domestic foes, has cost oceans of blood and treasure in every age; and the blood and the treasure have upon the whole been well spent. British America, hath been bleeding in this cause from its settlement: We have spent all we could raise, and more; for notwithstanding the parliamentary reimbursement of part, we still remain much in debt. The province of the *Massachusetts,* I believe, has expended more men and money in war since the year 1620, when a few families first landed at Plymouth, in proportion to their ability, than the three Kingdoms together. The same, I believe, may be truly affirmed, of many of the other colonies; tho' the *Massachusetts* has undoubtedly had the heaviest burthen. This may be thought incredible: but materials are collecting; and tho' some are lost, enough may remain, to demonstrate it to the world.

I have reason to hope at least, that the public will soon see such proofs exhibited, as will show, that I do not speak quite at random. . . .

The Colonies have been so remarkable for loyalty, that there never has been any instance of rebellion or treason in them. This loyalty is in very handsome terms acknowledged by the author of the administration of the colonies. "It has been often suggested that care should be taken in the administration of the plantations, lest, in some future time, these colonies should become independent of the mother country. But perhaps it may be proper on this occasion, nay, it is justice to say it, that if, by becoming independent, is meant a revolt, nothing is further from their nature, their interest, their thoughts. If a defection from the *alliance* of the mother country be suggested, it ought to be, and can be truly said, that their spirit abhors the sense of such; their attachment to the protestant succession in the house of Hanover, will ever stand unshaken; and nothing can eradicate from their hearts their natural and almost mechanical, affection to Great Britain, which they conceive under no other sense, nor call by any other name than that of *home*. Any such suggestion, therefore, is a false and unjust aspersion on their principles and affections; and can arise from nothing but an intire ignorance of their circumstances."* After all this loyalty, it is a little hard to be charged with claiming, and represented as aspiring after, independency. The inconsistency of this I leave. We have said that the loyalty of the colonies has never been suspected; this must be restricted to a just suspicion. For it seems there have long been groundless suspicions of us in the minds of individuals. And there have always been those who have endeavoured to mag-

---

* Administration, p. 25, 26. [This reference is to Thomas Pownall's *The Administration of the Colonies,* published in London in March 1764. Pownall had been governor of Massachusetts from 1757 to 1760.—ED.]

nify these chimerical fears. I find Mr. Dummer complaining of this many years since.

"There is, says he, one thing more I have heard often urged against the charter colonies, and indeed tis what one meets with from people of all conditions and qualities, tho' with due respect to their better judgments, I can see neither reason nor colour for it. 'Tis said that their increasing numbers and wealth, joined to their great distance from Britain, will give them an opportunity, in the course of some years, to throw off their dependence on the nation, and declare themselves a free state, if not curb'd in time, by being made *entirely subject to the crown.*"*

This jealousy has been so long talked of, that many seem to believe it really well grounded. Not that there is danger of a "revolt," even in the opinion of the *author of the administration,* but that the colonists will by fraud or force, avail themselves, in "fact or in deed," of an independent legislature. This, I think, would be a revolting with a vengeance. What higher revolt can there be, than for a province to assume the right of an independent legislative, or state? I must therefore think this a greater aspersion on the Colonists, than to charge them with a design to revolt, in the sense in which the Gentleman allows they have been abused: It is a more artful and dangerous way of attacking our liberties, than to charge us with being in open rebellion. That could be confuted instantly: but this seeming indirect way of charging the colonies, with a desire of throwing off their dependency, requires more pains to confute it than the other, therefore it has been recurred to. The truth is, Gentlemen have had departments in America, the functions of which they have not been fortunate in executing. The

---

* Defense. 60. [This refers to Jeremiah Dummer's *Defence of the New England Charters,* published in London in 1721. Dummer was the Massachusetts agent in London from 1710 to 1730. He wrote the pamphlet in 1715, when Parliament tried to revoke all colonial charters by an act of Parliament.—ED.]

people have by these means been rendered uneasy, at bad Provincial measures. They have been represented as factious, seditious, and inclined to democracy whenever they have refused passive obedience to provincial mandates, as arbitrary as those of a Turkish Bashaw: I say, Provincial mandates; for to the King and Parliament they have been ever submissive and obedient.

These representations of us, many of the good people of England swallow with as much ease, as they would a bottle-bubble, or any other story of a cock and a bull; and the worst of it is, among some of the most credulous, have been found Stars and Garters. However, they may all rest assured, the Colonists, who do not pretend to understand themselves so well as the people of England; tho' the author of the Administration makes them the fine compliment, to say, they "know their business much better," yet, will never think of independency. Were they inclined to it, they know the blood and the treasure it would cost, if ever effected; and when done, it would be a thousand to one if their liberties did not fall a sacrifice to the victor.

We all think ourselves happy under Great-Britain. We love, esteem and reverence our mother country, and adore our King. And could the choice of independency be offered the colonies, or subjection to Great-Britain upon any terms above absolute slavery, I am convinced they would accept the latter. The ministry, in all future generations may rely on it, that British America will never prove undutiful, till driven to it, as the last fatal resort against ministerial oppression, which will make the wisest mad, and the weakest strong.

These colonies are and always have been, "entirely subject to the crown," in the legal sense of the terms. But if any politician of "†tampering activity, of wrongheaded inexperience,

---

† Administration. 34.

misled to be meddling," means, by "curbing the colonies in time," and by "being made entirely subject to the crown;" that this subjection should be absolute, and confined to the crown, he had better have suppressed his wishes. This never will nor can be done, without making the colonists vassals of the crown. Subjects they are; their lands they hold of the crown, by common soccage, the freest feudal tennure, by which any hold their lands in England, or any where else. Would these gentlemen carry us back to the state of the Goths and Vandals, and revive all the military tenures and bondage which our fore-fathers could not bear? It may be worth noting here, that few if any instances can be given, where colonies have been disposed to forsake or disobey a tender mother: But history is full of examples, that armies stationed as guards over provinces, have seized the prey for their general, and given him a crown at the expence of his master. Are all ambitious generals dead? Will no more rise up hereafter? The danger of a standing army in remote provinces is much greater to the metropolis, than at home. Rome found the truth of this assertion, in her Sylla's, her Pompey's and Caesars; but she found it too late: Eighteen hundred years have roll'd away since her ruin. A continuation of the same liberties that have been enjoyed by the colonists since the revolution, and the same moderation of government exercised towards them, will bind them in perpetual lawful and willing subjection, obedience and love to Great-Britain: She and her colonies will both prosper and flourish: The monarchy will remain in sound health and full vigor at that blessed period, when the proud arbitrary tyrants of the continent shall either unite in the deliverance of the human race, or resign their crowns. Rescued, human nature must and will be, from the general slavery that has so long triumphed over the species. Great-Britain has done much towards it: What a Glory will it be for her to complete the work throughout the world! . . .

But to return to the subject of taxation:

I find that "the lords and commons cannot be charged with any-thing for the defence of the realm, for the safe-guard of the sea, &c. unless by their *will* in parliament."

Ld. Coke, on Magna Charta, Cap. 30.

Impositions neither in time of war, or other the greatest neces-sity or occasion, that may be, much less in the time of peace, neither upon foreign or inland commodities, of what nature soever, be they never so superfluous or unnecessary, neither upon merchants, strangers, nor denizens, may be laid by the King's absolute power, without assent of parliament, be it never for so short a time.

Viner Prerogative of the King.
Ea. 1. cites 2 Molloy. 320. Cap. 12 sec. 1.

In the reign of Edward 3, the black Prince of Wales having *Aquitain* granted to him, did lay an imposition of suage or socage a *soco*, upon his subjects of that dukedom, viz. a shilling for every fire, called hearth silver, which was of so great discontentment and odious to them, that it made them revolt. And nothing since this time has been imposed by pretext of any prerogative, upon mer-chandizes, imported into or exported out of this realm, until Queen Mary's time.   2 Inst. 61.

Nor has any thing of that kind taken place since the revo-lution. King Charles 1. his ship-money every one has heard of.

It may be said that these authorities will not serve the col-onists, because the duties laid on them are by parliament. I acknowledge the difference of fact; but cannot see the great difference in equity, while the colonists are not represented in the house of commons: And therefore with all humble defer-ence I apprehend, that 'till the colonists are so represented, the spirit of all these authorities will argue strongly in their favour. When the parliament shall think fit to allow the colonists a representation in the house of commons, the equity of their taxing the colonies, will be as clear as their power is at present of doing it without, if they please. . . .

From all which, it seems plain, that the reason why Ireland and the plantations are not bound, unless named by an Act of Parliament, is, because they are *not represented* in the British parliament. Yet, in special cases, the British parliament has an undoubted right, as well as power, to bind both by their acts. But whether this can be extended to an indefinite taxation of both, is the great question. I conceive the spirit of the British constitution must make an exception of all taxes, until it is tho't fit to unite a dominion to the realm. Such taxation must be considered either as uniting the dominions to the realm, or disfranchising them. If they are united, they will be intitled to a representation, as well as Wales; if they are so taxed without a union, or representation, they are so far disfranchised. . . .

The sum of my argument is, That civil government is of God: That the administrators of it were originally the whole people: That they might have devolved it on whom they pleased: That this devolution is fiduciary, for the good of the whole; That by the British constitution, this devolution is on the King, lords and commons, the supreme, sacred and uncontroulable legislative power, not only in the realm, but thro' the dominions: That by the abdication, the original compact was broken to pieces: That by the revolution, it was renewed, and more firmly established, and the rights and liberties of the subject in all parts of the dominions, more fully explained and confirmed: That in consequence of this establishment, and the acts of succession and union, his Majesty GEORGE III. is rightful king and sovereign, and with his parliament, the supreme legislative of Great Britain; France and Ireland, and the dominions thereto belonging: That this constitution is the most free one, and by far the best, now existing on earth: That by this constitution, every man in the dominion is a free man: That no parts of his Majesty's dominions can be taxed without their consent: That every part has a right to be represented in the supreme or some subordinate legislature: That the refusal of this, would seem to be a contradiction in practice to the theory of the constitution: That the colonies are subordinate dominions, and are now in such a state, as to make it best for the good of the whole, that they should not only be continued in the enjoyment of subordinate legislation, but be also represented in some proportion to their number and estates, in the grand legislature of the nation: That this would firmly unite all parts of the British empire, in the greatest peace and prosperity; and render it invulnerable and perpetual.

· 3 ·

The Rights of Colonies Examined

By Stephen Hopkins

Rhode Island faced the threat of a stamp tax boldly. Governor
Stephen Hopkins summoned a special session of the legislature in
November 1764 and, in his speech to it, emphasized the heavy
economic burdens imposed by the Revenue Act of 1764 and the
even worse burdens that would be imposed by the proposed stamp
act. He also told the legislature that a group of men in the colony
were appealing to the Crown for the revocation of the charter and
the establishment of a royal government.

The legislature responded by adopting a petition to the king
complaining of economic grievances and denying that Parliament
had the right to levy a stamp tax on the colonies: such a tax would
be solely for raising money and would have nothing to do with the
regulation on trade. At the same time the legislature approved a
pamphlet the governor had written, and ordered it printed in both
London and Rhode Island. On December 22, 1764, it was published
by William Goddard, printer of the *Providence Gazette,* under the
title *The Rights of Colonies Examined.* The pamphlet was widely
acclaimed. A second Providence edition appeared in 1765, and a

Providence, 1764.

London edition in 1766. Several colonial newspapers reprinted it, including the *Pennsylvania Journal* (January 12 and 24, 1765), the *New York Mercury* (January 28, 1765), and the *South Carolina Gazette* (February 9, 1765).

The text of the pamphlet printed here is based on the reprint in John R. Bartlett, ed., *Records of the Colony of Rhode Island and the Providence Plantations,* VI (Providence, 1861), 416–427. Bartlett modernized some spelling, punctuation, and capitalization and provided more paragraphs than in the original. In the following text the paragraphing and capitalization of the first edition has been restored, but Bartlett's spelling and punctuation have been retained.

> "Mid the low murmurs of submissive fear
> And mingled rage, my Hampden rais'd his voice,
> And to the laws appeal'd;——"
> *Thompson's Liberty.*

Liberty is the greatest blessing that men enjoy, and slavery the heaviest curse that human nature is capable of.—This being so, makes it a matter of the utmost importance to men, which of the two shall be their portion. Absolute liberty is, perhaps, incompatible with any kind of government.—The safety resulting from society, and the advantage of just and equal laws, hath caused men to forego some part of their natural liberty, and submit to government. This appears to be the most rational account of its beginning; although, it must be confessed, mankind have by no means been agreed about it. Some have found its origin in the divine appointment; others have thought it took its rise from power; enthusiasts have dreamed that dominion was founded in grace. Leaving these points to be settled by the descendants of Filmer, Cromwell and Venner, we will consider the British constitution, as it at present stands, on revolution principles; and from thence endeavor to find the measure of the magistrate's power and the people's obedience.

This glorious constitution, the best that ever existed among men, will be confessed by all, to be founded by compact, and established by consent of the people. By this most beneficent compact, British subjects are governed only agreeable to laws to which themselves have some way consented; and are not to be compelled to part with their property, but as it is called for by the authority of such laws. The former, is truly liberty; the latter is really to be possessed of property, and to have something that may be called one's own.

On the contrary, those who are governed at the will of another, or of others, and whose property may be taken from them by taxes, or otherwise, without their own consent, and against their will, are in the miserable condition of slaves. "For liberty solely consists in an independency upon the will of another; and by the name of slave, we understand a man who can neither dispose of his person or goods, but enjoys all at the will of his master," says Sidney, on government. These things premised, whether the British American colonies, on the continent, are justly entitled to like privileges and freedom as their fellow subjects in Great Britain are, shall be the chief point examined. In discussing this question, we shall make the colonies in New England, with whose rights we are best acquainted, the rule of our reasoning; not in the least doubting but all the others are justly entitled to like rights with them.

New England was first planted by adventurers, who left England, their native country, by permission of King Charles the First; and, at their own expense, transported themselves to America, with great risk and difficulty settled among savages, and in a very surprising manner formed new colonies in the wilderness. Before their departure, the terms of their freedom, and the relation they should stand in to the mother country, in their emigrant state, were fully settled; they were to remain subject to the King, and dependent on the kingdom of Great Britain. In return, they were to receive protection, and enjoy all the rights and privileges of free-born Englishmen.

This is abundantly proved by the charter given to the Massachusetts colony, while they were still in England, and which they received and brought over with them, as the authentic evidence of the conditions they removed upon. The colonies of Connecticut and Rhode Island, also, afterwards obtained charters from the crown, granting them the like ample privileges. By all these charters, it is in the most express and solemn manner granted, that these adventurers, and their children after them for ever, should have and enjoy all the freedom and liberty that the subjects in England enjoy; that they might make laws for their own government, suitable to their circumstances not repugnant to, but as near as might be, agreeable to the laws of England; that they might purchase lands, acquire goods, and use trade for their advantage, and have an absolute property in whatever they justly acquired. These, with many other gracious privileges, were granted them by several kings; and they were to pay, as an acknowledgment to the crown, only one-fifth part of the ore of gold and silver, that should at any time be found in the said colonies, in lieu of, and full satisfaction for, all dues and demands of the crown and kingdom of England upon them.

There is not any thing new or extraordinary in these rights granted to the British colonies; the colonies from all countries, at all times, have enjoyed equal freedom with the mother state. Indeed, there would be found very few people in the world, willing to leave their native country, and go through the fatigue and hardship of planting in a new uncultivated one, for the sake of losing their freedom. They who settle new countries, must be poor; and, in course, ought to be free. Advantages, pecuniary or agreeable, are not on the side of emigrants; and surely they must have something in their stead.

To illustrate this, permit us to examine what hath generally been the condition of colonies with respect to their freedom; we will begin with those who went out from the ancient commonwealths of Greece, which are the first, perhaps, we have any good account of. Thucidides, that grave and judicious historian, says of one of them, "they were not sent out to be slaves, but to be the equals of those who remain behind;" and again, the Corinthians gave public notice, "that a new colony was going to Epidamus, into which, all that would enter, should have equal and like privileges with those who stayed at home." This was uniformly the condition of all the Grecian colonies; they went out and settled new countries; they took such forms of government as themselves chose, though it generally nearly resembled that of the mother state, whether democratical or oligarchical. 'Tis true, they were fond to acknowledge their original, and always confessed themselves under obligation to pay a kind of honorary respect to, and show a filial dependence on, the commonwealth from whence they sprung. Thucidides again tells us, that the Corinthians complained of the Coreyreans, "from whom, though a colony of their own, they had received some contemptuous treatment; for they neither paid them the usual honor on their public solemnities, nor began with a Corinthian in the distribution of the sacrifices, which is always done by other colonies." From hence, it is plain what kind of dependence the Greek colonies were under, and what sort of acknowledgment they owed to the mother state.

If we pass from the Grecian to the Roman colonies, we shall find them not less free. But this difference may be observed between them, that the Roman colonies did not, like the Grecian, become separate states, governed by different laws, but always remained a part of the mother state; and all that were free of the colonies, were also free of Rome, and had right to an equal suffrage in making all laws, and appointing all officers for the government of the whole commonwealth. For the truth of this, we have the testimony of St. Paul, who though born at Tarsus, yet assures us he was born free of Rome. And Grotius gives us the opinion of a Roman king, concerning the freedom of colonies; King Tullius says, "For our part, we look upon it to be neither truth nor justice, that mother cities ought of necessity and by the law of nature, to rule over their colonies."

When we come down to the latter ages of the world, and consider the colonies planted in the three last centuries, in America, from several kingdoms in Europe, we shall find them, says Puffendorf, very different from the ancient colonies, and gives us an instance in those of the Spaniards. Although it be confessed, these fall greatly short of enjoying equal freedom with the ancient Greek and Roman ones; yet it will be said truly, they enjoy equal freedom with their countrymen in Spain; but as they are all under the government of an absolute monarch, they have no reason to complain that one enjoys the liberty the other is deprived of. The French colonies will be found nearly in the same condition, and for the same reason, because their fellow subjects in France, have also lost their liberty. And the question here is not whether all colonies, as compared one with another, enjoy equal liberty, but whether all enjoy as much freedom as the inhabitants of the mother state; and this will hardly be denied in the case of the Spanish, French, or other modern foreign colonies.

By this, it fully appears, that colonies, in general, both ancient and modern, have always enjoyed as much freedom as the mother state from which they went out; and will any one suppose the British colonies in America, are an exception to this general rule? Colonies that came out from a kingdom renowned for liberty; from a constitution founded on compact; from a people, of all the sons of men, the most tenacious of freedom; who left the delights of their native country, parted from their homes, and all their conveniences, searched out and subdued a foreign country, with the most amazing travail and fortitude, to the infinite advantage and emolument of the mother state; that removed on a firm reliance of a solemn compact, and royal promise and grant, that they, and their successors for ever, should be free; should be partakers and sharers in all the privileges and advantages of the then English, now British constitution.

If it were possible a doubt could yet remain, in the most unbelieving mind, that these British colonies are not every way justly and fully entitled to equal liberty and freedom with their fellow subjects in Europe, we might show, that the parliament of Great Britain, have always understood their rights in the same light.

By an act passed in the thirteenth year of the reign of his late majesty King George the second, entitled an act for naturalizing foreign protestants, &c.; and by another act passed in the twentieth year of the same reign, for nearly the same purposes, by both which it is enacted and ordained, "that all foreign protestants, who had inhabited, and resided for the space of seven years, or more, in any of his majesty's colonies, in America," might, on the conditions therein mentioned, be naturalized, and thereupon should "be deemed, adjudged and taken to be his majesty's natural born subjects of the kingdom of Great Britain, to all intents, constructions and purposes, as if they, and every one of them, had been, or were born within the same." No reasonable man will here suppose the parliament intended by these acts to put foreigners, who had been in the colonies only seven years, in a better condition than those who had been born in them, or had removed from Britain thither, but only to put these foreigners on an equality with them; and to do this, they are obliged to give them all the rights of natural born subjects of Great Britain.

From what hath been shown, it will appear beyond a doubt, that the British subjects in America, have equal rights with those in Britain; that they do not hold those rights as a privilege granted them, nor enjoy them as a grace and favor bestowed; but possess them as an inherent indefeasible right; as they, and their ancestors, were free-born subjects, justly and naturally entitled to all the rights and advantages of the British constitution.

And the British legislative and executive powers have considered the colonies as possessed of these rights, and have always heretofore, in the most tender and parental manner, treated them as their dependent, though free, condition required. The protection promised on the part of the crown, with cheerfulness and great gratitude we acknowledge, hath at all times been given to the colonies. The dependence of the colonies to Great Britain, hath been fully testified by a constant and ready obedience to all the commands of His present Majesty, and his royal predecessors; both men and money having been raised in them at all times when called for, with as much alacrity and in as large proportions as hath been done in Great Britain, the ability of each considered. It must also be confessed with thankfulness, that the first adventurers and their successors, for one hundred and thirty years, have fully enjoyed all the freedoms and immunities promised on their first removal from England. But here the scene seems to be unhappily changing. The British ministry, whether induced by a jealousy of the colonies, by false informations, or by some alteration in the system of political government, we have no information; whatever hath been the motive, this we are sure of, the parliament in their last session, passed an act, limiting, restricting and burdening the trade of these colonies, much more than had ever been done before; as also for greatly enlarging the power and jurisdiction of the courts of admiralty in the colonies; and also came to a resolution, that it might be necessary to establish stamp duties, and other internal taxes, to be collected within them. This act and this resolution, have caused great uneasiness and consternation among the British subjects on the continent of America; how much reason there is for it, we will endeavor, in the most modest and plain manner we can, to lay before our readers.

In the first place, let it be considered, that although each of the colonies hath a legislature within itself, to take care of it's interests, and provide for it's peace and internal government;

yet there are many things of a more general nature, quite out of the reach of these particular legislatures, which it is necessary should be regulated, ordered and governed. One of this kind is, the commerce of the whole British empire, taken collectively, and that of each kingdom and colony in it, as it makes a part of that whole. Indeed, every thing that concerns the proper interest and fit government of the whole commonwealth, of keeping the peace, and subordination of all the parts towards the whole, and one among another, must be considered in this light. Amongst these general concerns, perhaps, money and paper credit, those grand instruments of all commerce, will be found also to have a place. These, with all other matters of a general nature, it is absolutely necessary should have a general power to direct them; some supreme and over ruling authority, with power to make laws, and form regulations for the good of all, and to compel their execution and observation. It being necessary some such general power should exist somewhere, every man of the least knowledge of the British constitution, will be naturally led to look for, and find it in the parliament of Great Britain; that grand and august legislative body, must, from the nature of their authority, and the necessity of the thing, be justly vested with this power. Hence, it becomes the indispensable duty of every good and loyal subject, cheerfully to obey and patiently submit to all the acts, laws, orders and regulations that may be made and passed by parliament, for directing and governing all these general matters.

Here it may be urged by many, and indeed, with great appearance of reason, that the equity, justice, and beneficence of the British constitution, will require, that the separate kingdoms and distant colonies, who are to obey and be governed by these general laws and regulations, ought to be represented, some way or other, in parliament; at least whilst these general matters are under consideration. Whether the colonies will ever be admitted to have representatives in parliament,—whether it be consistent with their distant and dependent state,—and

whether if it were admitted, it would be to their advantage,—
are questions we will pass by; and observe, that these colonies
ought in justice, and for the very evident good of the whole
commonwealth, to have notice of every new measure about to
be pursued, and new act that is about to be passed, by which
their rights, liberties, or interests will be affected; they ought to
have such notice, that they may appear and be heard by their
agents, by council, or written representation, or by some other
equitable and effectual way.

The colonies are at so great a distance from England, that the
members of parliament can generally have but little knowledge
of their business, connections and interest, but what is gained
from people who have been there; the most of these, have so
slight a knowledge themselves, that the informations they can
give, are very little to be depended on, though they may pretend to determine with confidence, on matters far above their
reach. All such kind of informations are too uncertain to be
depended on, in the transacting business of so much consequence, and in which the interests of two millions of free people are so deeply concerned. There is no kind of inconveniency,
or mischief, can arise from the colonies having such notice, and
being heard in the manner abovementioned; but, on the contrary, very great mischiefs have already happened to the colonies, and always must be expected, if they are not heard, before
things of such importance are determined concerning them.

Had the colonies been fully heard, before the late act had
been passed, no reasonable man can suppose it ever would
have passed at all, in the manner it now stands; for what good
reason can possibly be given for making a law to cramp the
trade and ruin the interests of many of the colonies, and at the
same time, lessen in a prodigious manner the consumption of
the British manufactures in them? These are certainly the effects this act must produce; a duty of three pence per gallon on
foreign molasses, is well known to every man in the least
acquainted with it, to be much higher than that article can

possibly bear; and therefore must operate as an absolute prohibition. This will put a total stop to our exportation of lumber, horses, flour and fish, to the French and Dutch sugar colonies; and if any one supposes we may find a sufficient vent for these articles in the English islands in the West Indies, he only verifies what was just now observed, that he wants truer information. Putting an end to the importation of foreign molasses, at the same time puts an end to all the costly distilleries in these colonies, and to the rum trade to the coast of Africa, and throws it into the hands of the French. With the loss of the foreign molasses trade, the codfishery of the English, in America, must also be lost, and thrown also into the hands of the French. That this is the real state of the whole business, is not fancy; this, nor any part of it, is not exaggeration, but a sober and melancholy truth.

View this duty of three pence per gallon, on foreign molasses, not in the light of a prohibition, but supposing the trade to continue, and the duty to be paid. Heretofore, there hath been imported into the colony of Rhode Island only, about one million one hundred and fifty thousand gallons, annually; the duty on this quantity is £14,375, sterling, to be pair yearly, by this little colony; a larger sum than was ever in it at any one time. This money is to be sent away, and never to return; yet the payment is to be repeated every year. Can this possibly be done? Can a new colony, compelled by necessity to purchase all its clothing, furniture and utensils from England, to support the expenses of its own internal government, obliged by its duty to comply with every call from the crown to raise money on emergencies; after all this, can every man in it pay twenty-four shillings sterling, a year, for the duties of a single article, only? There is, surely, no man in his right mind, believes this possible. The charging foreign molasses with this high duty, will not affect all the colonies equally, nor any other near so much as this of Rhode Island, whose trade depended much more on foreign molasses, and on distilleries, than that of any others; this must show, that raising money for the general service of the crown, or of the colonies, by such a duty, will be extremely unequal, and therefore unjust. And now, taking either alternative; by supposing on one hand, the foreign molasses trade is stopped, and with it the opportunity or ability of the colonies to get money; or on the other, that this trade is continued, and that the colonies get money by it, but all their money is taken from them by paying the duty; can Britain be gainer by either? Is it not the chiefest interest of Britain, to dispose of and to be paid for her own manufactures? And doth she not find the greatest and best market for them in her own colonies? Will she find an advantage in disabling the colonies to continue their trade with her? Or can she possibly grow rich, by their being made poor?

Ministers have great influence, and parliaments have great power;—can either of them change the nature of things, stop all our means of getting money, and yet expect us to purchase and pay for British manufactures? The genius of the people in these colonies, is as little turned to manufacturing goods for their own use, as is possible to suppose in any people whatsoever; yet necessity will compel them, either to go naked in this cold country, or to make themselves some sort of clothing, if it be only of the skins of beasts.

By the same act of parliament, the exportation of all kinds of timber, or lumber, the most natural produce of these new colonies, is greatly encumbered and uselessly embarrassed, and the shipping it to any part of Europe, except Great Britain, prohibited. This must greatly affect the linen manufactory in Ireland, as that kingdom used to receive great quantities of flax seed from America, many cargoes, being made of that and of barrel staves, were sent thither every year; but, as the staves can no longer be exported thither, the ships carrying only flax seed casks, without the staves, which used to be intermixed among them, must lose one half of their freight, which will prevent their continuing this trade, to the great injury of Ireland, and of the plantations. And what advantage is to accrue to Great Britain, by it, must be told by those who can perceive the utility of this measure.

Enlarging the power and jurisdiction of the courts of vice admiralty in the colonies, is another part of the same act, greatly and justly complained of. Courts of admiralty have long been established in most of the colonies, whose authority were circumscribed within moderate territorial jurisdictions; and these courts have always done the business necessary to be brought before such courts for trial, in the manner it ought to be done, and in a way only moderately expensive to the subjects; and if seizures were made, or informations exhibited, without reason, or contrary to law, the informer, or seizor, was left to the justice of the common law, there to pay for his folly, or suffer for his temerity. But now, this course is quite altered; and a custom house officer may make a seizure in Georgia, of goods ever so legally imported, and carry the trial to Halifax, at fifteen hundred miles distance; and thither the owner must follow him to defend his property; and when he comes there, quite beyond the circle of his friends, acquaintance and correspondents, among total strangers, he must there give bond, and must find sureties to be bound with him in a large sum, before he shall be admitted to claim his own goods; when this is complied with, he hath a trial, and his goods acquitted. If the judge can be prevailed on, (which it is very well known may too easily be done,) to certify there was *only* probable cause for making the seizure, the unhappy owner shall not maintain any action against the illegal seizor, for damages, or obtain any other satisfaction; but he may return to Georgia quite ruined, and undone, in conformity to an act of parliament. Such unbounded encouragement and protection given to informers, must call to every one's remembrance Tacitus's account of the miserable condition of the Romans, in the reign of Tiberius, their emperor, who let loose and encouraged the informers of that age. Surely, if the colonies had been fully heard, before this had been done, the liberties and properties of the Americans would not have been so much disregarded.

The resolution of the house of commons, come into during the same session of parliament, asserting their rights to establish stamp duties, and internal taxes, to be collected in the colonies without their own consent, hath much more, and for much more reason, alarmed the British subjects in America, than any thing that had ever been done before. These resolutions, carried into execution, the colonies cannot help but consider as a manifest violation of their just and long enjoyed rights. For it must be confessed by all men, that they who are taxed at pleasure by others, cannot possibly have any property, can have nothing to be called their own; they who have no property, can have no freedom, but are indeed reduced to the most abject slavery; are in a condition far worse than countries conquered and made tributary; for these have only a fixed sum to pay, which they are left to raise among themselves, in the way that they may think most equal and easy; and having paid the stipulated sum, the debt is discharged, and what is left is their own. This is much more tolerable than to be taxed at the mere will of others, without any bounds, without any stipulation and agreement, contrary to their consent, and against their will. If we are told that those who lay these taxes upon the colonies, are men of the highest character for their wisdom, justice and integrity, and therefore cannot be supposed to deal hardly, unjustly, or unequally by any; admitting, and really believing that all this is true, it will make no alteration in the nature of the case; for one who is bound to obey the will of another, is as really a slave, though he may have a good master, as if he had a bad one; and this is stronger in politic bodies than in natural ones, as the former have perpetual succession, and remain the same; and although they may have a very good master at one time, they may have a very bad one at another. And indeed, if the people in America, are to be taxed by the representatives of the people in Britain, their malady is an increasing evil, that must always grow greater by time. Whatever burdens are laid upon the Americans, will be so much taken off the Britons; and the doing this, will soon be extremely popular; and those who put up to be members of the house of commons, must obtain the votes of the people, by promising to take more and more of the taxes off them, by putting it on the Americans. This must most assuredly be the case, and it will not be in the power even of the parliament to prevent it; the people's private interest will be concerned, and will govern them; they will have such, and only such representatives as will act agreeable to this their interest; and these taxes laid on Americans, will be always a part of the supply bill, in which the other branches of the legislature can make no alteration; and in truth, the subjects in the colonies will be taxed at the will and pleasure of their fellow subjects in Britain.—How equitable, and how just this may be, must be left to every impartial man to determine.

But it will be said, that the monies drawn from the colonies by duties, and by taxes, will be laid up and set apart to be used for their future defence. This will not at all alleviate the hardship, but serves only more strongly to mark the servile state of the people. Free people have ever thought, and always will think, that the money necessary for their defence, lies safest in their own hands, until it be wanted immediately for that purpose. To take the money of the Americans, which they want continually to use in their trade, and lay it up for their defence, at a thousand leagues distance from them, when the enemies they have to fear, are in their own neighborhood, hath not the greatest probability of friendship or of prudence.

It is not the judgment of free people only, that money for defending them, is safest in their own keeping, but it hath also been the opinion of the best and wisest kings and governors of mankind, in every age of the world, that the wealth of a state was most securely as well as most profitably deposited in the hands of their faithful subjects. Constantius, emperor of the Romans, though an absolute prince, both practised and praised this method.

Dioclesian sent persons on purpose to reproach him with his neglect of the public, and the poverty to which he was reduced by his own fault. Constantius heard these reproaches with patience; and having persuaded those who made them in Dioclesian's name, to stay a few days with him, he sent word to the most wealthy persons in the provinces, that he wanted money, and that they had now an opportunity of showing whether or no they truly loved their prince. Upon this notice, every one strove who should be foremost in carrying to the exchequer all their gold, silver and valuable effects; so that in a short time Constantius, from being the poorest, became by far the most wealthy of all the four princes. He then invited the deputies of Dioclesian to visit his treasury, desiring them to make a faithful report to their master, of the state in which they should find it. They obeyed; and, while they stood gazing on the mighty heaps of gold and silver, Constantius told them, that the wealth which they beheld with astonishment, had long since belonged to him; but that he had left it, by way of depositum, in the hands of his people; adding, the richest and surest treasure of the prince was the love of his subjects. The deputies were no sooner gone, than the generous prince sent for those who had assisted him in his exigency, commended their zeal, and returned to every one what they had so readily brought into his treasury.—*Universal Hist., Vol. XV., p. 523.*

We are not insensible, that when liberty is in danger, the liberty of complaining is dangerous; yet, a man on a wreck was never denied the liberty of roaring as loud as he could, says Dean Swift. And we believe no good reason can be given, why the colonies should not modestly and soberly inquire, what right the parliament of Great Britain have to tax them. We know such inquiries, by a late letter writer, have been branded with the little epithet of *mushroom policy;* and he insinuates, that for the colonies to pretend to claim any privileges, will draw down the resentment of the parliament on them.—Is the defence of liberty become so contemptible, and pleading for just rights so dangerous? Can the guardians of liberty be thus ludicrous? Can the patrons of freedom be so jealous and so severe? If the British house of commons are rightfully possessed of a power to tax the colonies in America, this power must be vested in them by the British constitution, as they are one branch of the great legislative body of the nation; as they are the representatives of all the people in Britain, they have, beyond doubt, all the power such a representation can possibly give; yet, great as this power is, surely it cannot exceed that of their constituents. And can it possibly be shown that the people in Britain have a sovereign authority over their fellow subjects in America? Yet such is the authority that must be exercised in taking peoples' estates from them by taxes, or otherwise, without their consent. In all aids granted to the crown, by the parliament, it is said with the greatest propriety, "We freely give unto Your Majesty;" for they give their own money, and the money of those who have entrusted them with a proper power for that purpose. But can they, with the same propriety, give away the money of the Americans, who have never given any such power? Before a thing can be justly given away, the giver must certainly have acquired a property in it; and have the people in Britain justly acquired such a property in the goods and estates of the people in these colonies, that they may give them away at pleasure?

In an imperial state, which consists of many separate governments, each of which hath peculiar privileges, and of which kind it is evident the empire of Great Britain is; no single part, though greater than another part, is by that superiority entitled to make laws for, or to tax such lesser part; but all laws, and all taxations, which bind the whole, must be made by the whole. This may be fully verified by the empire of Germany, which consists of many states; some powerful, and others weak; yet the powerful never make laws to govern or to tax the little and weak ones; neither is it done by the emperor, but only by the diet, consisting of the representatives of the whole body. Indeed, it must be absurd to suppose, that the common people of Great Britain have a sovereign and absolute authority over their fellow subjects in America, or even any sort of power whatsoever, over them; but it will be still more absurd to suppose they can give a power to their representatives, which they have not themselves. If the house of commons do not receive this authority from their constituents, it will be difficult to tell by what means they obtained it, except it be vested in them by mere superiority and power.

Should it be urged, that the money expended by the mother country, for the defence and protection of America, and especially during the late war, must justly entitle her to some retaliation from the colonies; and that the stamp duties and taxes, intended to be raised in them, are only designed for that equitable purpose; if we are permitted to examine how far this may rightfully vest the parliament with the power of taxing the colonies, we shall find this claim to have no sort of equitable foundation. In many of the colonies, especially those in New England, who were planted, as is before observed, not at the charge of the crown or kingdom of England, but at the expense of the planters themselves; and were not only planted, but also defended against the savages, and other enemies, in long and cruel wars, which continued for an hundred years, almost without intermission, solely at their own charge; and in the year 1746, when the Duke D'Anville came out from France, with the most formidable French fleet that ever was in the American seas, enraged at these colonies for the loss of Louisbourg, the year before, and with orders to make an attack on them; even in this greatest exigence, these colonies were left to the protection of Heaven and their own efforts. These colonies having thus planted and defended themselves, and removed all enemies from their borders, were in hopes to enjoy peace, and recruit their state, much exhausted by these long struggles; but they were soon called upon to raise men, and send out to the defence of other colonies, and to make conquests for the crown; they dutifully obeyed the requisition, and with ardor entered into those services, and continued in them, until all encroachments were removed, and all Canada, and even the Havana, conquered. They most cheerfully complied with every call of the crown; they rejoiced, yea, even exulted, in the prosperity and exaltation of the British empire. But these colonies, whose bounds were fixed, and whose borders were before cleared from enemies, by their own fortitude, and at their own expense, reaped no sort of advantage by these conquests; they are not enlarged, have not gained a single acre of land, have no part in the Indian or interior trade; the immense tracts of land subdued, and no less immense and profitable commerce acquired, all belong to Great Britain; and not the least share or portion to these colonies, though thousands of their men have lost their lives, and millions of their money have been expended in the purchase of them for great part of which we are yet in debt, and from which we shall not in many years be able to extricate ourselves. Hard will be the fate, yea, cruel the destiny, of these unhappy colonies, if the reward they are to receive for all this, is the loss of their freedom; better for them Canada still remained French; yea, far more eligible that it ever should remain so, than that the price of its reduction should be their slavery.

If the colonies are not taxed by parliament, are they therefore exempted from bearing their proper share in the necessary burdens of government? This by no means follows. Do they not support a regular internal government in each colony, as expensive to the people here, as the internal government of Britain is to the people there? Have not the colonies here, at all times when called upon by the crown, raised money for the public service, done it as cheerfully as the parliament have done on like occasions? Is not this the most easy, the most natural, and most constitutional way of raising money in the colonies? What occasion then to distrust the colonies? What necessity to fall on an invidious and unconstitutional method, to compel them to do what they have ever done freely? Are not the people in the colonies as loyal and dutiful subjects as any age or nation ever produced? And are they not as useful to the kingdom, in this remote quarter of the world, as their fellow subjects are who dwell in Britain? The parliament, it is confessed, have power to regulate the trade of the whole empire; and hath it not full power, by this means, to draw all the money and all the wealth of the colonies into the mother country, at pleasure? What motive, after all this, can remain, to induce the parliament to abridge the privileges, and lessen the rights of the most loyal and dutiful subjects; subjects justly entitled to ample freedom, who have long enjoyed, and not abused or forfeited their liberties; who have used them to their own advantage, in dutiful subserviency to the orders and interests of Great Britain? Why should the gentle current of tranquillity, that has so long run with peace through all the British states, and flowed with joy and with happiness in all her countries, be at last obstructed, be turned out of its true course, into unusual and winding channels, by which many of those states must be ruined; but none of them can possibly be made more rich or more happy?

Before we conclude, it may be necessary to take notice of the vast difference there is between the raising money in a country by duties, taxes or otherwise, and employing and laying out the money again in the same country; and raising the like sums of money, by the like means, and sending it away quite out of the country, where it is raised. Where the former of these is the case, although the sums raised may be very great, yet that country may support itself under them; for as fast as the money is collected together, it is again scattered abroad, to be used in commerce and every kind of business; and money is not made scarcer by this means, but rather the contrary, as this continual circulation must have a tendency to prevent, in some degree, it's being hoarded. But where the latter method is pursued, the effect will be extremely different; for here, as fast as the money can be collected, 'tis immediately sent out of the country, never to return but by a tedious round of commerce, which at best, must take up much time; here, all trade, and every kind of business depending on it, will grow dull, and must languish more and more, until it comes to a final stop at last. If the money raised in Great Britain in the three last years of the late war, and which exceeded £40,000,000, sterling, had been sent out of the kingdom, would not this have nearly ruined the trade of the nation in three years only? Think, then, what must be the condition of these miserable colonies, when all the money proposed to be raised in them, by high duties on the importation of divers kinds of goods, by the post office, by stamp duties, and other taxes, is sent quite away, as fast as it can be collected; and this to be repeated continually, and last forever! Is it possible for colonies under these circumstances, to support themselves, to have any money, any trade, or other business, carried on in them? Certainly it is not; nor is there at present, or ever was, any country under heaven, that did, or possibly could, support itself under such burdens.

We finally beg leave to assert, that the first planters of these colonies were pious christians; were faithful subjects; who, with a fortitude and perseverance little known, and less considered, settled these wild countries, by God's goodness, and their own amazing labors; thereby added a most valuable dependence to the crown of Great Britain; were ever dutifully subservient to her interests; so taught their children, that not one has been disaffected to this day; but all have honestly obeyed every royal command, and cheerfully submitted to every constitutional law; have as little inclination as they have ability, to throw off their dependency; have carefully avoided every offensive measure, and every interdicted manufacture; have risked their lives as they have been ordered, and furnished their money when it has been called for; have never been troublesome or expensive to the mother country; have kept due order, and supported a regular government; have maintained peace, and practiced christianity; and in all conditions, and in every relation, have demeaned themselves as loyal, as dutiful, and as faithful subjects ought; and that no kingdom or state hath, or ever had, colonies more quiet, more obedient, or more profitable, than these have ever been.

May the same divine goodness, that guided the first planters, protected the settlements, inspired kings to be gracious, parliaments to be tender, ever preserve, ever support our present gracious King; give great wisdom to his ministers, and much understanding to his parliaments; perpetuate the sovereignty of the British constitution, and the filial dependency and happiness of all the colonies.

P———.

Providence, in New England, November 30, 1764.

· 4 ·

A Letter From a Gentleman at Halifax

By Martin Howard, Jr.

On February 11, 1765, two days before its publication, this pamphlet was announced in the *Newport Mercury*. Its full title is *A Letter from a Gentleman at Halifax, to His Friend in Rhode Island, Containing Remarks Upon a Pamphlet Entitled The Rights of Colonies Examined.* The pamphlet was not a "letter," and it was soon known that the author was not someone at Halifax, Nova Scotia, but Martin Howard, Jr., of Newport.

As we have seen, the pamphlet forced both Governor Stephen Hopkins and James Otis to retreat from the positions they had taken in their pamphlets. Howard and some of his friends were attacked by mobs during the Stamp Act riots in August 1765, and they fled to England. They sought in vain to recover damages for lost property from the Rhode Island legislature. However, they received other compensation. Howard was given a royal appointment as chief justice of North Carolina.[1]

In reprinting the pamphlet, I have omitted the first page and a half, in which Howard attacks Hopkins' literary style, and have

Newport, 1765, pp. 5–22.

[1] Lovejoy, *Rhode Island Politics,* 49–51, 77–82.

modernized the text to the extent of omitting the random use of capital letters and italics.

. . . I would fain hope that his honour's motto is not a true portrait of the general temper and conduct of the Americans; I would rather think "the low murmurs of submissive fear, and mingled rage," delineate only a few disappointed traders. It were to be wished that some friend of the colonies would endeavour to remove any unfavourable impressions this, and other pamphlets of the like kind, may have occasioned at home; lest those in power form the general character of the colonies from such notices as these convey, and from thence be inclined to increase their dependance, rather than to emancipate them from the present supposed impositions. Depend upon it, my Friend, a people like the English, arrived to the highest pitch of glory and power, the envy and admiration of surrounding slaves, who hold the balance of Europe in their hands, and rival in arts and arms every period of ancient or modern story; a nation who, for the defence and safety of America only, staked their all in the late war; this people, I say, justly conscious of their dignity, will not patiently be dictated to by those whom they have ever considered as dependant upon them. Happy will it be for the colonies, yea happy for the honourable author, if his pamphlet should meet with nothing more than contempt and neglect; for should it catch the attention of men in power, measures may be taken to stifle in the birth "the low murmurs of submissive fear," and crush in embryo "the mingled rage," which now so prettily adorns the head of his honour's pamphlet.

However disguised, polished or softened the expression of this pamphlet may seem, yet every one must see, that its professed design is sufficiently prominent throughout, namely, to prove, *that the colonies have rights independant of, and not controulable by, the authority of parliament.* It is upon this dangerous and indiscreet position I shall communicate to you my real sentiments.

To suppose a design of enslaving the colonies by parliament, is too presumptuous; to propagate it in print, is perhaps dangerous. Perplexed between a desire of speaking all he thinks, and the fear of saying too much, the honourable author is obliged to entrench himself in obscurity and inconsistency in several parts of his performance: I shall bring one instance.

In page eleven, he says, "It is the indispensible duty of every good and loyal subject chearfully to obey, and patiently submit to, all the laws, orders, &c., that may be passed by parliament."

I do not much admire either the spirit or composition of this sentence. Is it the duty *only* of good and loyal subjects to obey? Are the wicked and disloyal subjects absolved from this obligation? else why is this passage so marvellously penned: Philolevtherus Lipsiensis would directly pronounce this a figure in rhetorick, called nonsense.—Believe me, my friend, I did not quote this passage to shew my skill in criticism, but to point out a contradiction between it, and another passage in page twenty, which runs thus: "It must be absurd to suppose, that the common people of Great Britain have a sovereign and absolute authority over their fellow subjects of America, *or even any sort of power whatsoever over them;* but it will be still more absurd to suppose, they can give a power to their representatives, which they have not themselves," &c. Here it is observable, that the first cited passage expresses a full submission to the authority of parliament; the last is as explicit a denial of that authority. The sum of his honour's argument is this: The people of Great Britain have not any sort of power over the Americans; the house of commons have no greater authority than the people of Great Britain, who are their constituents; ergo, the house of commons *have not any sort of power over the* Americans. This is indeed a curious invented syllogism, the sole merit of which is due to the first magistrate of an English colony.

I have endeavoured to investigate the true natural relation, if I may so speak, between colonies and their mother state, abstracted from compact or positive institution, but here I can find nothing satisfactory; till this relation is clearly defined upon a rational and natural principle, our reasoning upon the measure of the colonies obedience will be desultory and inconclusive. Every connection in life has its reciprocal duties; we know the relation between a parent and child, husband and wife, master and servant, and from thence are able to deduce their respective obligations; but we have no notices of any such precise natural relation between a mother state and its colonies, and therefore cannot reason with so much certainty upon the power of the one, or the duty of the others. The ancients have transmitted to us nothing that is applicable to the state of modern colonies, because the relation between these is formed by political compact; and the condition of each variant in their original, and from each other. The honourable author has not freed this subject from any of its embarrassments: Vague and diffuse talk of rights and privileges, and ringing the changes upon the words liberty and slavery, only serve to convince us, that words may affect without raising images, or affording any repose to a mind philosophically inquisitive. For my own part, I will shun the walk of metaphysicks in my enquiry, and be content to consider the colonies rights upon the footing of their charters, which are the only plain avenues, that lead to the truth of this matter.

The several New England charters ascertain, define and limit the respective rights and privileges of each colony, and I cannot conceive how it has come to pass that the colonies now claim any other or greater rights than are therein expresly granted to them. I fancy when we speak, or think of the rights of freeborn Englishmen, we confound those rights which are personal, with those which are political: There is a distinction between these, which ought always to be kept in view.

Our personal rights, comprehending those of life, liberty, and estate, are secured to us by the common law, which is every subject's birthright, whether born in Great Britain, on the ocean, or in the colonies; and it is in this sense we are said to enjoy all the rights and privileges of Englishmen. The political rights of the colonies, or the powers of government communicated to them, are more limited, and their nature, quality and extent depend altogether upon the patent or charter which first created and instituted them. As individuals, the colonists participate of every blessing the English constitution can give them: As corporations created by the crown, they are confined within the primitive views of their institution. Whether therefore their indulgence is scanty or liberal, can be no cause of complaint; for when they accepted of their charters, they tacitly submitted to the terms and conditions of them.

The colonies have no rights independant of their charters, they can claim no greater than those give them, by those the parliamentary jurisdiction over them is not taken away, neither could any grant of the king abridge that jurisdiction, because it is founded upon common law, as I shall presently shew, and was prior to any charter or grant to the colonies: Every Englishman, therefore, is subject to this jurisdiction, and it follows him wherever he goes. It is of the essence of government, that there should be a supreme head, and it would be a solecism in politicks to talk of members independant of it.

With regard to the jurisdiction of parliament, I shall endeavour to shew, that it is attached to every English subject, wherever he be: And I am led to do this from a clause in page nine of his honour's pamphlet, where he says, "That the colonies do not hold their rights, as a privilege granted them, nor enjoy them as a grace and favour bestowed; but possess them, as an inherent, indefeasible right." This postulatum cannot be true with regard to political rights, for I have already shewn, that these are derived from your charters, and are held by force of the king's grant; therefore these inherent, indefeasible rights, as his honour calls them, must be personal ones, according to the distinction already made. Permit me to say, that inherent and indefeasible as these rights may be, the jurisdiction of parliament, over every English subject, is equally as inherent and indefeasible: That both have grown out of the same stock, and that if we avail ourselves of the one, we must submit to, and acknowlege the other.

It might here be properly enough asked, Are these personal rights self-existent? Have they no original source? I answer, They are derived from the constitution of England, which is the common law; and from the same fountain is also derived the jurisdiction of parliament over us.

But to bring this argument down to the most vulgar apprehension: The common law has established it as a rule or maxim, that the plantations are bound by British acts of parliament, if particularly named: And surely no Englishman, in his senses, will deny the force of a common law maxim. One cannot but smile at the inconsistency of these inherent, indefeasible men: If one of them has a suit at law, in any part of New England, upon a question of land property, or merchandize, he appeals to the common law, to support his claim, or defeat his adversary; and yet is so profoundly stupid as to say, that an act of parliament does not bind him; when, perhaps, the same page in a law book, which points him out a remedy for a libel, or a slap in the face, would inform him that it does.—In a word, The force of an act of parliament, over the colonies, is predicated upon the common law, the origin and basis of all those inherent rights and privileges which constitute the boast and felicity of a Briton.

Can we claim the common law as an inheritance, and at the same time be at liberty to adopt one part of it, and reject the other? Indeed we cannot: The common law, pure and indivisible in its nature and essence, cleaves to us during our lives, and follows us from Nova Zembla to Cape Horn: And therefore, as the jurisdiction of parliament arises out of, and is supported by it, we may as well renounce our allegiance, or change our nature, as to be exempt from the jurisdiction of parliament: Hence, it is plain to me, that in denying this jurisdiction, we at the same time, take leave of the common law, and thereby, with equal temerity and folly, strip ourselves of every blessing we enjoy as Englishmen: A flagrant proof this, that shallow draughts in politicks and legislation confound and distract us, and that an extravagant zeal often defeats its own purposes.

I am aware that the foregoing reasoning will be opposed by the maxim, "That no Englishman can be taxed but by his own consent, or by representatives."

It is this dry maxim, taken in a literal sense, and ill understood, that, like the song of Lillibullero, has made all the mischief in the colonies: And upon this, the partizans of the colonies rights chiefly rest their cause. I don't despair, however, of convincing you, that this maxim affords but little support to their argument, when rightly examined and explained.

It is the opinion of the house of commons, and may be considered as a law of parliament, that they are the representatives of every British subject, wheresoever he be. In this view of the matter then, the aforegoing maxim is fully vindicated in practice, and the whole benefit of it, in substance and effect, extended and applied to the colonies. Indeed the maxim must be considered in this latitude, for in a literal sense or construction it ever was, and ever will be, impracticable. Let me ask, is the isle of Man, Jersey or Guernsey, represented? What is the value or amount of each man's representation in the kingdom of Scotland, which contains near two millions of people, and yet not more than three thousand have votes in the election of members of parliament? But to shew still further, that, in fact and reality, this right of representation is not of that consequence it is generally thought to be, let us take into the argument the moneyed interest of Britain, which, though immensely great, has no share in this representation; a worthless freeholder of forty shillings per annum can vote for a member of parliament, whereas a merchant, tho' worth one hundred thousand pounds sterling, if it consist only in personal effects, has no vote at all: But yet let no one suppose that the interest of the latter is not equally the object of parliamentary attention with the former.—Let me add one example more: Copyholders in England of one thousand pounds sterling per annum, whose estates in land are nominally, but not intrinsically, inferior to a freehold, cannot, by law, vote for members of parliament; yet we never hear that these people "murmur with submissive fear, and mingled rage:" They don't set up their private humour against the constitution of their country, but submit with chearfulness to those forms of government which providence, in its goodness, has placed them under.

Suppose that this Utopian privilege of representation should take place, I question if it would answer any other purpose but to bring an expence upon the colonies, unless you can suppose that a few American members could bias the deliberations of the whole British legislature. In short, this right of representation is but a phantom, and, if possessed in its full extent, would be of no real advantage to the colonies; they would, like Ixion, embrace a cloud in the shape of Juno.

In addition to this head, I could further urge the danger of innovations; every change in a constitution, in some degree, weakens its original frame; and hence it is that legislators and statesmen are cautious in admitting them: The goodly building of the British constitution will be best secured and perpetuated by adhering to its original principles. Parliaments are not of yesterday, they are as antient as our Saxon ancestors. Attendance in parliament was originally a duty arising from a tenure of lands, and grew out of the feudal system; so that the privilege of sitting in it, is territorial, and confined to Britain only. Why should the beauty and symmetry of this body be destroyed, and its purity defiled, by the unnatural mixture of representatives from every part of the British dominions. Parthians, Medes, Elamites, and the dwellers of Mesopotamia, &c. would not, in such a case, speak the same language. What a heterogeneous council would this form? what a monster in government would it be?—In truth, my friend, the matter lies here: The freedom and happiness of every British subject depends, not upon his share in elections, but upon the sense and virtue of the British parliament, and these depend reciprocally upon the sense and virtue of the whole nation. When virtue and honour are no more, the lovely frame of our constitution will be dissolved. Britain may one day be what Athens and Rome now are; but may heaven long protract the hour!

The jurisdiction of parliament being established, it will follow, that this jurisdiction cannot be apportioned; it is transcendant and entire, and may levy internal taxes as well as regulate trade; there is no essential difference in the rights: A stamp duty is confessedly the most reasonable and equitable that can be devised, yet very far am I from desiring to see it established among us, but I fear the shaft is sped, and it is now too late to prevent the blow.

The examples cited by his honour, with regard to ancient colonies, may shew his reading and erudition, but are of no authority in the present question. I am not enough skilled in the Grecian history to correct the proofs drawn from thence, though they amount to very little. If the Grecian colonies, as his honour says, "took such forms of government as themselves chose," there is no kind of similitude between them and the English colonies, and therefore to name them is nothing to the purpose. The English colonies take their forms of government from the crown; hold their privileges upon condition, that they do not abuse them; and hold their lands by the tenure of common socage, which involves in it fealty and obedience to the king: Hence it is plain, his honour's argument is not strengthened by the example of the Grecian colonies; for what likeness is there between independant colonies, as those must be, which "took such forms of government as themselves chose," and colonies like ours, which are in a manner feudatory, and holden of a superior.

With regard to the Roman colonies, I must beg leave to say, that the honourable author, either ignorantly or wilfully, mistakes the facts: A little more enquiry, or a little more candour, would have convinced him, that the Roman coloniae did not enjoy all the rights of Roman citizens; on the contrary, they only used the Roman laws and religion, and served in the legions, but had not the right of suffrage, or of bearing honours. In these respects, our English colonies exactly resemble them; we enjoy the English laws and religion, but have not the right of suffrage, or of bearing honours in Great Britain, and indeed our situation renders it impossible.

If the practice of the ancients was of any authority in this case, I could name examples to justify the enslaving of colonies. The Carthaginians were a free people, yet they, to render the Sardinians and Corsicans more dependant, forbad their planting, sowing, or doing anything of the like kind, under pain of death, so that they supplied them with necessaries from Africa: This was indeed very hard. But there is something extremely weak and inconclusive in recurring to the Grecian and Roman history for examples to illustrate any particular favourite opinion: If a deference to the ancients should direct the practice of the moderns, we might sell our children to pay our debts, and justify it by the practice of the Athenians. We might lend our wives to our friends, and justify it from the Example of Cato, among the Romans. In a word, my dear Sir, the belly of a sow, pickled, was a high dish in ancient Rome; and I imagine, as you advance in the refinements of luxury, this will become a capital part of a Rhode Island feast, so fond you seem of ancient customs and laws.

Instead of wandring in the labyrinth of ancient colonies, I would advise his honour to read the debates in parliament in the year one thousand seven hundred and thirty-three, when Mr. Partridge, your agent, petitioned the commons against the then sugar-bill; he will there find more satisfaction upon the subject of colonies, than in Thucydides's history of the Pelopennesian war. It was declared in the course of that debate, that the colonists were a part of the people of Great Britain; and, as such, fully represented in that house. The petition then presented by Mr. Partridge, was of a very different temper from those now sent home by the colonies; it was extremely modest, and only intimated that the sugar bill, if passed into a law, might be prejudicial to their charter; at the bare mention of this Sir William Yonge took fire, and said, *"It looked like aiming at an independency, and disclaiming the jurisdiction of that house, as if* (says he) *this house had not a power to tax the colonies."* Mr. Winnington, with equal warmth, added, *"I hope they have no charter which debars this house from taxing them, as well as any other subject of the nation."* Here you have the opinion of two of the most eminent members of that time; they spoke the sentiments of the whole house, and these sentiments still continue the same. And from hence you may perceive, how little prospect there is of the colonies gaining any point upon the footing of these new supposititious rights; broaching such opinions will excite the jealousy of the parliament, and you will be looked upon with an evil eye. The promoters of such doctrines are no friends to the colonies, whatever may be their pretensions. Can his honour be so vain as to imagine, that ten thousand such pamphlets as his, will influence the parliament, or that they will be persuaded, by the force of his elocution, to give up their supremacy, and right of taxing the colonies. What purpose then can be served by these pamphlets, but to embitter the minds of a simple, credulous, and hitherto loyal people, and to alienate their affections from Great Britain, their best friend, their protector, and alma mater. A different behaviour would be much more prudent and politick. If we have anything to ask, we should remember that diffidence and modesty will always obtain more from generous minds, than forwardness and impertinence.

The act of the thirteenth of his late majesty, entitled, *An act for naturalizing of foreign protestants,* had better have been omitted by his honour; for if that act is to be the measure of the colonists rights, they will be more circumscribed than he would willingly chuse. In that act, there is a proviso, that no person, who shall become a natural born subject by virtue of that act; should be of the privy council, or a member of either house of parliament, or capable of enjoying, in Great Britain or Ireland, any place of trust, civil or military, &c. This statute confirms the distinction I have set up between personal and political rights. After naturalization, foreign protestants are here admitted subjects, to all intents and purposes; that is, to the full enjoyment of those rights which are connected with the person, liberty or estate of Englishmen; but by the proviso, they are excluded from bearing offices or honours.

Enlarging the power of the court of admiralty, is much complain'd of by the honourable author. I shall open my mind to you freely on this head.

It is notorious, that smuggling, which an eminent writer calls a crime against the law of nature, had well nigh become established in some of the colonies. Acts of parliament had been uniformly dispensed with by those whose duty it was to execute them; corruption, raised upon the ruins of duty and virtue, had almost grown into a system; courts of admiralty, confined within small territorial jurisdictions, became subject to mercantile influence; and the king's revenue shamefully sacrificed to the venality and perfidiousness of courts and officers.—If, my friend, customs are due to the crown; if illicit commerce is to be put an end to, as ruinous to the welfare of the nation: —If, by reason of the interested views of traders, and the connivance of courts and custom-house officers, these ends could not be compassed or obtained in the common and ordinary way; tell me, what could the government do, but to apply a remedy desperate as the disease: There is, I own, a severity in the method of presecution, in the new established court of admiralty, under Doctor S P R Y, here; but it is a severity we have brought upon ourselves. When every mild expedient, to stop the atrocious and infamous practice of smuggling, has been try'd in vain, the government is justifiable in making laws against it, even like those of Draco, which were written in blood. The new instituted court of admiralty, and the power given to the seizer, are doubtless intended to make us more circumspect in our trade, and to confine the merchant, from motives of fear and dread, within the limits of a fair commerce. "The English constrain the merchant, but it is in favour of commerce," says the admired Secondat. This is the spirit of the new regulations, both with regard to the employing of cutters, and the enlarged power of the admiralty; and both measures are justifiable upon the same principles, as is the late act for preventing murder, which executes and dissects the murderer at surgeons-hall in twenty-four hours after conviction.

But notwithstanding the severity of this act, let me add, that no harm can accrue to the honest and fair trader, so long as the crown fills the admiralty department with an upright judge; such a one is Doctor Spry, an able civilian, and whose appointments place him above any kind of influence; yet the honourable author of the pamphlet before me, has told us to this effect; That it is very well known this judge *can be prevailed on, very easily,* to certify, upon the acquittal of a seizure, that there was a probable cause for making it.—So shamefully intemperate is his honour's zeal and opposition to every measure adopted by the government at home, that he spares not even private characters, however worthy and respectable. I fear he knows not the high value of a good name, and how dear it is to men of sentiment and honour.

> "He who filches from me my good name,
> Robs me of that, which not enriches him,
> But makes me poor indeed."   Shakespear.

To suspect the integrity of others, is not the effusion of a virtuous mind. Those who have been long used to traffick with judges and juries, are, from the depravity of their own hearts, easily led to believe others even as themselves.

This libel upon Doctor Spry, contained in a pamphlet *pub-*

lished by authority, may spread over the British dominions, and, however false and scandalous it be, yet may leave a shade upon his character which can never be effaced. With what grace, let me ask you, do such reflections as these come from the governor of a colony, where, all the world agree, the law has scarcely yet dawned, and where all your legal rights are decided by the strength of that faction which happens to be uppermost.

I am not enough skilled in trade to know whether the act, so much complained of, will do most good or most harm; and I wish others were as diffident of their knowledge in this particular. To comprehend the general trade of the British nation, much exceeds the capacity of any one man in America, how great soever he be. Trade is a vast, complicated system, and requires such a depth of genius and extent of knowledge, to understand it, that little minds, attached to their own sordid interest, and long used to the greatest licentiousness in trade, are, and must be, very incompetent judges of it. Sir Andrew Freeport is no inhabitant of Rhode-Island colony. For my own part, I am still willing to leave the management of trade with that people, who, according to the same admired author just quoted, "know better than any other people upon earth, how to value at the same time these three great advantages, religion, commerce, and liberty."

Here I would just observe, that, from the intelligence I have gained, the beloved article of melasses is now plentier and cheaper, in all New England colonies, than when it was avowedly smuggled; and so far is the linen manufacture of Ireland from being ruined, as his honour intimates, that never was a greater demand for flax-seed than during the last fall, notwithstanding the clause in the act relating to lumber. How senseless it is to imagine that the prohibiting a few dunnage staves to be carried to Ireland, will ruin the manufactures of that kingdom.

Believe me, my Friend, it gives me great pain to see so much ingratitude in the colonies to the mother country, whose arms and money so lately rescued them from a French government. I have been told, that some have gone so far as to say, that they would, as things are, prefer such a government to an English one.—Heaven knows I have but little malice in my heart, yet, for a moment, I ardently wish that these spurious, unworthy sons of Britain could feel the iron rod of a Spanish inquisitor, or a French farmer of the revenue; it would indeed be a punishment suited to their ingratitude. Here I cannot but call to mind the adder in one of the fables of Pilpay, which was preparing to sting the generous traveller who had just rescued him from the flames.

You'l easily perceive, that what I have said is upon the general design of his honour's pamphlet; if he had divided his argument with any precision, I would have followed him with somewhat more of method; The dispute between Great Britain and the colonies consists of two parts; first, the jurisdiction of parliament,—and, secondly, the exercise of that jurisdiction. His honour hath blended these together, and no where marked the division between them: The first I have principally re-marked upon: As to the second, it can only turn upon the expediency or utility of those schemes which may, from time to time, be adopted by parliament, relative to the colonies. Under this head, I readily grant, they are at full liberty to remonstrate, petition, write pamphlets and newspapers, with-out number, to prevent any improper or unreasonable imposi-tion: Nay, I would have them do all this with that spirit of freedom which Englishmen always have, and I hope ever will, exert; but let us not use our liberty for a cloak of maliciousness. Indeed I am very sure the loyalty of the colonies has ever been irreproachable; but from the pride of some, and the ignorance of others, the cry against mother country has spread from col-ony to colony; and it is to be feared, that prejudices and re-sentments are kindled among them which it will be difficult ever, thoroughly, to sooth or extinguish. It may become necessary for the supreme legislature of the nation to frame some code, and therein adjust the rights of the colonies, with precision and certainty, otherwise Great Britain will always be teazed with new claims about liberty and privileges.

I have no ambition in appearing in print, yet if you think what is here thrown together is fit for the publick eye, you are at liberty to publish it: I the more chearfully acquiesce in this, because it is with real concern I have observed, that, notwithstanding the frequent abuse poured forth in pamphlets and newspapers against the mother country, not one filial pen in America hath, as yet, been drawn, to my knowledge, in her vindication.

· 5 ·

The Constitutional Courant:

Containing Matters Interesting to Liberty,

and No Wise Repugnant to Loyalty

[By William Goddard?]

The *Courant* was probably printed at Burlington, New Jersey, to which James Parker had temporarily moved his print shop from Woodbridge, his home. Hundreds of copies spread rapidly through the northern colonies. Street hawkers sold them in New York City, and post riders carried them in their mailbags to the other northern colonies. James Parker had been secretary of the British postal organization in America ever since 1756 and must have connived; at least Lieutenant Governor Cadwallader Colden of New York was convinced that he did. Colden, then serving as governor, consulted his council, but they decided to take no action against the publication for fear that a prosecution would be used as an excuse to raise a mob in the city. Newspapers in other colonies were dis-

[Burlington, N.J.?], Sept. 21, 1765.

creet, and only a few mentioned the *Courant*. Both the *Newport Mercury* and the *Boston Evening Post* printed excerpts from it on October 7, 1765, and the *Post* said there was such a demand for it that it would be published. Although there is no further mention of it in the press, the *Courant* was obviously reprinted; several different versions exist today. Furthermore, copies soon found their way to England, and it is noteworthy that it is the only American publication mentioned in the *Annual Register* for 1765. The *Register* gives an accurate description of the *Courant*, including the snake device at the masthead.

Benjamin Franklin had first used the device in 1754; William Goddard revived it, and it was to be used by other printers later on. The device was printed below the motto JOIN OR DIE, which was placed in the center of the sheet between the words "Constitutional" and "Courant." The snake was divided into eight sections which were labeled with abbreviations for New England, New York, New Jersey, Pennsylvania, Maryland, Virginia, North Carolina, and South Carolina. Georgia was not included. No attempt has been made here to reproduce the masthead of the publication.[1]

TO THE PUBLIC.

When a new public Paper makes its appearance, the reader will naturally be curious to know from whence it came, the publisher, and the design of it. To gratify that curiosity, know reader, that the publisher having formerly acquired a competent knowledge of the Printing-business, for his amusement furnished himself with a set of proper materials;—and the authors of the following pieces having acquainted him that they applied to the printers in York, who

---

[1] For a detailed discussion of the *Courant* and the various editions, along with a copy of the original, see Albert Matthews, "The Snake Devices, 1754–1776, and the Constitutional Courant, 1765," Colonial Society of Massachusetts *Publications,* XI (1906–1907), 409–446. See also Ward L. Miner, *William Goddard, Newspaperman* (Durham, N.C., 1962).

refused to publish them in their news-papers—not because they disapproved them, or were apprehensive of danger, but purely because several of their friends had been anxious on their account, and particularly desired them to be careful not to publish any thing that might give the enemies of liberty an advantage, which they would be glad to take, over them; and as these pieces are thought to be wrote with greater freedom than any thing that has yet appeared in the public prints, they thought proper to shew so much complaisance to the advice of their friends, as to desire to be excused, and to return the copies: But I, who am under no fear of disobliging either friends or enemies, was pleased with the opportunity of turning my private amusements to the public good; I not only undertook to publish them, but now inform my countrymen, that I shall occasionally publish any thing else that falls in my way, which appears to me to be calculated to promote the cause of liberty, of virtue, of religion and my country, of love and reverence to its laws and constitution, and unshaken loyalty to the King.— And so I bid you heartily farewell.

Andrew Marvel.

At a time when our dearest privileges are torn from us, and the foundation of all our liberty subverted, every one who has the least spark of love to his country, must feel the deepest anxiety about our approaching fate. The hearts of all who have a just value for freedom, must burn within them, when they see the chains of abject slavery just ready to be riveted about our necks. It has been undeniably demonstrated, by the various authors who have dared to assert the cause of these injured colonies, that no Englishman can be taxed, agreeable to the known principles of our constitution, but by his own consent, given either by himself or his representatives,—that these colonies are not in any sense at all represented in the British parliament,—that the first adventurers into these uncultivated desarts, were, in every colony, either by royal charters, or royal concessions, in the most express terms possible, assured, that all their rights and privileges, as British subjects, should be preserved to them unimpaired,—that these original concessions have been repeatedly allowed by the crown, and have never been controverted till this *memorable period*. The arguments by which these points have been established beyond all dispute, I need not repeat; their evidence is such as must flash conviction into the minds of all but the vile minions of tyranny and arbitrary power. The tremendous conclusion, therefore, forces itself upon us, that the public faith of the nation, in which, till now, we thought we might securely confide, is violated, and we robbed of our dearest rights by the late law erecting a *stamp-office* among us.

What then is to be done? Shall we sit down quietly, while the yoke of slavery is wreathing about our necks? He that is stupid enough to plead for this, deserves to be a *slave*. Shall we not hope still that some resource is left us in the royal care and benevolence? We have the happiness to be governed by one of the best of kings, who is our common father, and must be supposed to be under no temptations to sacrifice the rights of one part of his subjects to the caprice of another.

The power of executing the laws is, by the constitution, vested in the crown. We never can suppose that our sovereign, when our state is properly represented to him, will employ that power to execute a law so evidently iniquitous and unreasonable, especially when a method of answering the same ends, (as far as they ought to be answered) perfectly agreeable to the constitution, so readily offers itself.—Let us then besiege the throne with petitions and humble remonstrances, and not doubt of a favorable issue in the result.

It must certainly give the most sensible pleasure to every American that loves this his native country, to find a proposal set on foot for all the colonies to lay before his majesty a united representation of their grievances, and pray a redress. Such a representation as this, in the name of so large and respectable a body of his subjects, must have great weight and influence in the royal councils. That so excellent a scheme is likely to be so generally complied with, raises our hopes, and demonstrates that the sons of America are not afraid nor ashamed to be her advocates against tyranny and oppression, tho' obtruding themselves under the sanction of a law. But what are we to think of a set of mushroom patriots, who have refused to concur in so noble an attempt? In what light can we view this conduct? Shall they who by *office* and *profession* engage to assert the cause of public liberty, own themselves such dastards as to be afraid to speak, when their country is injured in her most sacred rights, yea, inslaved, lest they provoke her oppressors? 'Tell it not in Gath!'—Liberty and property are necessarily connected together: He that deprives of the latter without our consent, deprives of the former. What is a slave, but one who depends upon the will of another for the enjoyment of his life and property? This surely is a very precarious tenure. He that assumes to himself a right to deprive me of any part of my estate (however small that part may be) on certain occasions, of which he is to be the sole judge, may with equal reason deprive me of the whole, when he thinks proper: And he that thinks he has a right to strip me of all my property, when he sees fit, may with equal justice deprive me of my life, when he thinks his own interest requires it. If a king, tho' invested with lawful authority, adopts these principles, none will hesitate to pronounce him a tyrant. But where is the difference between a prince who treats his subjects in this manner, and a number of fellow-subjects who usurp such a power over others? All that I can see, is, that in the former case we should groan under the oppression of one man; but in the latter, under that of a great body of men, which will generally be by far the most intolerable, as it is much better to have only one tyrant than several hundreds.

This, my countrymen, is our unhappy lot: The same principles on which the vile minions of tyranny vindicate the present tax, will vindicate the most oppressive laws conceivable. They need only boldly assert, that *we are virtually represented in the British parliament,* that *they are the properest judges of the sums necessary to be raised, and of our ability to pay them,* therefore such a tax is equitable, be it what it will, tho' it reduces nine-tenths of us to instant beggary. If we throw in petitions against them, they need only say, *'tis against the known rules of this house to admit petitions against money bills,* and so forever deny us the liberty of being heard. Was there ever a wider door opened for the entrance of arbitrary power, with all its horrors? Can the annals of Turkey produce its parallel? Even there, where tyranny has long established her gloomy throne, the subject is frequently indulged the liberty of complaining under grievances, and often uses that liberty with success. Poor America! the bootless privilege of complaining, always allowed to the vilest criminals on the rack, is denied thee!

Let none censure these free thoughts as treasonable: I know they will be called so by those who would gladly transform these flourishing colonies into the howling seats of thraldom and wretchedness; but the sentiments of such miscreants are little to be regarded. We cherish the most unfeigned loyalty to our rightful sovereign; we have a high veneration for the British parliament; we consider them as the most august assembly on earth; but the wisest of kings may be misled; some persons they must trust for the information they receive; those persons are generally such, whose interest it is to represent all things to them in false lights; so that it is rather to be admired that they are not oftener misled than they are. Parliaments also are liable to mistakes, yea, sometimes fall into capital errors, and frame laws the most oppressive to the subject, yea, sometimes take such steps, which, if persisted in, would soon unhinge the whole constitution. Our histories bear innumerable attestations to the truth of this. It cannot be treason to point out such mistakes and the consequences of them, yea to set them in the most glaring light, to alarm the subject. By acting on this principle, our ancestors have transmitted to us our privileges inviolated; let us therefore prosecute the same glorious plan. Let the British parliament be treated with all possible respect, while they treat us as fellow-subjects; but if they transgress the bounds prescribed them by the constitution, if they usurp a jurisdiction, to which they have no right; if they infringe our liberties, and pursue such measures as will infallibly end in a Turkish despotism; if they violate the public faith and destroy our confidence in the royal promises, let us boldly deny all such usurped jurisdiction; we owe them no more subjection, in this respect, than the Divan of Constantinople; to seem to acknowledge such a claim, would be to court our chains. Be assured, my countrymen, whatever spirit we manifest on this juncture, it cannot be offensive to our sovereign: *He glories in being King of freemen, and not of slaves.* To shew that we are freemen, and resolve to continue so, cannot displease, but must endear us to him. It must endear us also to all the true sons of liberty in Great-Britain, to see that we have carried over the Atlantic the genuine spirit of our ancestors. We can offend none but a set of the blackest villains, and these we must always offend, unless we will tamely suffer them to tread down our rights at pleasure. With them, liberty is always treason, and an advocate for the people's rights, a sower of sedition. Let it be our honor, let it be our boast, to be odious to these foes to human kind; let us shew them that we consider them only as beasts of prey, formed to devour; that tho' full of loyalty to the best of kings, and ready to spill the last drop of our blood in his service, yet we dare bid defiance to all who are betraying the sovereign, and sacrificing his people.

While too many to the Westward are thinking of nothing but tamely yielding their necks to the yoke, it revives the courage of all who wish well to their country, to see such a noble spirit prevailing in the eastern colonies. There the gentlemen appointed to serve as tools to enslave their countrymen, have some of them gloriously disdained the dirty employment; they have scorned to raise their own fortunes by such detestable means; they have shewn that they esteem the public good, infinitely above all private emolument; in short, they have proved themselves TRUE LOVERS OF THEIR COUNTRY. Let their names be enrolled in the annals of fame; let them be embalmed to all posterity, and serve as examples to fire the breasts of patriots yet unborn. Others, we find, have been intimidated into a resignation, by those hardy sons of liberty, and have the mortification to see all their vile schemes of enriching themselves out of the plunder of their fellow-subjects, blasted in an instant. But what name shall we give those miscreants who still resolve to keep the detested office? How hard must that heart be, which is insensible of the dearest and tenderest of all obligations? which feels no sympathy for a native country, oppressed and ruined? but can please itself with the hellish prospect of increasing private wealth by her spoils? Ye blots and stains of America! Ye vipers of human kind! Your names shall be blasted with infamy, the public execration shall pursue you while living, and your memories shall rot, when death has disabled you from propagating vassalage and misery any further: Your crimes shall haunt you like *spectres,* and take vengeance for the crimes of distressed innocence.

We cannot be enslaved without you reach out a helping hand: If you emulate the noble example of some of your fellow-officers, whose disinterestedness will endear them to generations yet unborn, the chains of thraldom cannot be put about our necks, at least the duration of our freedom will be prolonged. Dare you then bear a part in hastening its final extinction? Can you expect to escape the unseen hand of resentment, awakened by injuries like these? Assure yourselves the spirit of Brutus and Cassius is yet alive; *there are* [those] *who dare strike a blow to avenge their insulted country.* Know ye vile miscreants, we love liberty, and we fear not to shew it. We abhor slavery, and detest the remotest aiders and abettors of our bondage: but native Americans, who are diabolical enough to help forward our ruin, we execrate as the worst of parricides. Parricides! 'tis too soft a term: Murder your fathers, rip up the bowels of your mothers, dash the infants you have begotten against the stones, and be blameless;—but enslave your country! entail vassalage, that worst of all human miseries, that sum of all wretchedness, on millions! This, this is guilt, this calls for heaven's fiercest vengeance. But rouse, rouse my countrymen, let the villain that is hardy enough to persist, do it at his peril. Shew them we have resentment no less keen than our Eastern bretheren; will you tamely suffer the execution of a law that reduces you to the vile condition of slaves, and is abhorred by all the genuine sons of liberty? Let the wretch that sleeps now, be branded as an enemy to his country.

PHILOLEUTHERUS.

The late violences committed in the Eastern colonies, in resentment and opposition to the Stamp Act, and all its contrivers and abettors; whether they proceeded from the misguided zeal of those who had a strong sensibility of the injury done their country by that act, or from the villainous cunning of those who took the opportunity of the public discontent, to promote and increase the tumult, in order to perpetrate the most atrocious crimes; in either case, the true lovers of liberty and their country, who detest and abhor the Stamp Act from principle, and a certain knowledge of their rights, violated by that act, are far from countenancing, or being pleased with these violences; on the contrary, they hear of them with concern and sorrow, not only as they must necessarily involve many innocent persons in distress, who had no share in the guilt that excited the public resentment; but also as they injure a good cause, and check the spirit of opposition to an act illegally obtruded upon us, to deprive us of our most sacred rights, and change our freedom to slavery, by a legislature who have no lawful authority over us. The terrible effects of those popular tumults, are likely to startle men who have been accustomed to venerate and obey lawful authority, and who delight in peace and order; and to make them doubt the justice of the cause attended with such direful consequences. But the guilt of all these violences is most justly chargeable upon the authors and abettors of the Stamp Act. They who endeavour to destroy the foundations of the English constitution, and break thro' the fence of the laws, in order to let in a torrent of tyranny and oppression upon their fellow-subjects, ought not to be surprized if they are overwhelmed in it themselves. If they whom the people have invested with power, to be employed for the public good, pervert it to quite contrary purposes, to oppress and insult those by whom they are supported; is it not ridiculous for them to expect security from those laws which they themselves break thro' to injure their country? If they become arbitrary, and use their power against the people who give it; can they suppose that the people, in their turn, will not exert their inherent power against their oppressors, and be as arbitrary as they? When such a power is raised, as it is not under the restraint of any regular government or direction, terrible effects may generally be expected from it. But those are answerable for them, who raised the tempest.—Let no man then suffer his rights to be torn from him; for fear of the consequences of defending them,—however dreadful they may be, the guilt of them does not lie at his door. However, I would wish my countrymen to avoid such violent proceedings, if possible; but at the same time to oppose the execution of the Stamp Act, with a steady and perpetual exertion of their whole power,—and by all means, to endeavour, jointly and severally, to throw all possible obstructions in the way of its taking effect, and to treat with the utmost ignominy and detestation, all those enemies and betrayers of their country's most sacred rights, who officiously endeavour to inforce it: I would wish them never to pay one farthing of this tax, but leave the infamous officers, if they will have it, to take it by force, by way of robbery and plunder.—For the moment we submit to pay this tax, as to lawful authority, that moment we commence as errant slaves as any in Turkey, the fence of our liberty and property is broken down, and the foundation of the English constitution, with respect to us, is utterly destroyed. Let us not flatter ourselves, that we shall be happier, or treated with more lenity than our fellow slaves in Turkey: human nature is the same every where, and unlimited power is as much to be dreaded among us, as it is in the most barbarous nations upon earth: It is slavery that hath made them barbarous, and the same cause will have the same effect upon us. The inhabitants of Greece, Rome, and Constantinople, were once free and happy, and the liberal arts and sciences flourished among them; but slavery has spread ignorance, barbarism and misery over those once delightful regions, where the people are sunk into a stupid insensibility of their condition, and the spirit of liberty, after being depressed above a thousand years, seems now to be lost irrecoverably. It is better to die in defence of our rights, than to leave such a state as this to the generations that succeed us.

It cannot be possible that our sovereign, or any of our English fellow-subjects, who understand and value their own rights, can be displeased with us for asserting ours. Do we claim any but what are as clear as the noon day? Have we not by nature a right to liberty and property; as Englishmen, by laws and charters, in terms as plain as words can express? Is it not a fundamental principle of the English constitution, that no man shall be bound but by laws of his own making, nor taxed but by his own consent, given by representatives of his own choosing? And have we not a right to have all our causes tried by our peers, that is by juries, men of our own rank, indifferently chosen, and to whom we have no reasonable objection;—and does not the Stamp Act, in the most flagrant manner, violate all these rights, our liberty, our property, and trials by juries? Our liberty, in being subjected to laws that we had no share in making; our property, in being taxed without our own consent, in a parliament where we never had either the choice of a person to represent us, nor any that were qualified for the office, or interested in our welfare; and in our trials by juries, because an informer or prosecutor has it in his choice, whether to try the matter in a court of common law, or a court of admiralty:—and as these courts are immediately under the influence of the crown, and the act allows no appeal from them, except to a court of vice-admiralty, which is of the same kind, we have reason to think these courts will be as arbitrary and oppressive as ever the high commission and star chamber courts were: And as this act gives them jurisdiction over matters that have no relation to navigation or sea affairs, they may, with equal propriety, have jurisdiction in cases of life and death. This is a real representation of the slavish state we are reduced to by the Stamp Act, if we ever suffer it to take place among us. It is easy to see that the ministry design to alter and overturn the English constitution, and have invented a number of expedients to break thro' the restraints that the laws lay upon arbitrary dispositions, and are labouring to become despotic and uncontroulable.

If the English parliament can lay these burdens upon us, they can also, if they please, take our whole property from us, and order us to be sold for slaves, or put to death. But how came the English parliament by such a right over us? They are chosen by the people of Great-Britain to represent them. They have no power but what is delegated to them by their constituents; and those constituents have no power over our liberty or property. Their power (over these things at least) is purely local, and confined to the places they are chosen to represent; and it is plain they cannot represent the people of America, for that would deprive them of their most valuable rights as Englishmen, and be a contradiction to common sense.

It is a rule that no man in England shall be capable of serving as a representative in parliament, without having a considerable property in England; the reason of this rule is plain; because he will be affected in his own fortune, by the laws he is concern'd in making for the public, the good of which he will consult for his own sake:—But consider this rule with respect to America: Have all the members of parliament property there? Will they each feel part of the burdens they lay upon us?—No. But their own burdens will be lightened by laying them upon our shoulders, and all they take from us will be gains to themselves: Heaven defend us from such representatives!

Let none falsely insinuate, that this spirit of opposition to the Stamp Act, which prevails throughout the British dominions in America, has in it the least tincture of rebellion against lawful authority, or disloyalty to our king. Whoever brings such charges against us, is a slanderer and a villain. We have the highest degree of veneration for the laws and constitution of England; they are our birth-right and inheritance, and we would defend them with our lives. We have the most affectionate loyalty to our rightful sovereign George the third, and his royal house, and we are ready to risk our lives and fortunes in his and their defence. We have the highest respect and reverence for the British parliament, which we believe to be the most august and respectable body of men upon earth, and we desire that all their rights, privileges and honors may forever be preserved to them, and to every rank and order of men in the kingdom of Great-Britain, whose welfare, prosperity, and honor we sincerely wish, and should rejoice in. We consider ourselves as one people with them, and glory in the relation between us; and we desire our connection may forever continue, as it is our best security against foreign invaders, and as we may reciprocally promote the welfare and strength of each other. Such are our sentiments and affections towards our mother country. But, at the same time, we cannot yield up to her, or to any power on earth, our inherent and most valuable rights and privileges. If she would strip us of all the advantages derived to us from the English constitution, why should we desire to continue our connection? We might as well belong to France, or any other power; none could offer a greater injury to our rights and liberties than is offered by the Stamp Act. If we have delivered our sentiments of the parliament with greater freedom than they are usually mentioned with, let it be considered that it is only when they have taken upon them to deprive us of our rights, which are not under their jurisdiction: If any then take offence at the freedom with which they are treated, let them blush at the occasion given for it. Such an alarming attempt upon British liberty was never made before, nor I hope ever will again.—We have been told from England, that the Stamp Act passed without so much debate or consideration, as sometimes arose upon the most trifling bills that are brought before the house! If it had been well debated and considered, surely it never could have passed; it must astonish all concern'd in it, when they come to consider it, that ever it did pass at all, and it will doubtless be repealed as soon as ever the nature of it is fully understood.—Mean while let us never, for one moment, acknowledge that it is binding upon us, nor pay one farthing in obedience to it, for it was made by a power, that, by the fundamental laws that both they and we acknowledge, hath no jurisdiction over us.

As the ministry under whose influence this act was made, are, we have reason to hope, by this time discarded and out of place, no other I suppose will ever be found that will approve it: and it may be worth the serious consideration of those who would officiously endeavour to enslave their countrymen to enforce it, whether they will not be more likely to receive the frowns than the smiles of their superiors, for their activity in so odious an office. For if this act takes place and is established, it may be depended upon, that liberty in Great Britain will not long survive its extinction in America. PHILO PATRIÆ.

[*Since the foregoing pieces came to the Printer's hands, certain intelligence has been received from England of an universal change in the Ministry, whereby all those great officers who had rendered themselves obnoxious to the people, by their impolitic and arbitrary proceedings, are excluded from any share in the administration; and their places filled up by some of the most distinguished patriots in the nation, who it is hoped and believed will soon give a happy proof to his Majesty's subjects, in Europe and America, of their sincere love of liberty, for which they have been long contending with it's enemies, by adhering to such measures, and such only, as are consistent with the principles of the constitution. His grace the duke of Grafton, is appointed secretary of state for the Northern department, and the Rt. Hon. Henry Seymour Conway, a great friend to America, and a strong opposer of the Stamp Act, secretary for the southern. The Public is referr'd for further particulars, to the weekly papers.*]

· 6 ·

Considerations on the Propriety of Imposing Taxes in the British Colonies for the Purpose of Raising a Revenue by Act of Parliament

By Daniel Dulany

The pamphlet was published in Annapolis, Maryland, on October 14, 1765 by Jonas Green, publisher of the *Maryland Gazette*. There was no indication of this in the pamphlet itself, and the preface was dated "Virginia, August 12, 1765." Neither the place of publication nor the author remained unknown for long. The first edition sold out at once, and on October 31 the *Maryland Gazette* announced that a second edition would soon be available.

The pamphlet was the first of the period to circulate widely throughout the colonies. John Holt published an edition in New

---

New York, 1765, pp. 5–7, 9–11, 13–15, 27–28, 29–30.

York before the end of the year, and John Mein had an edition published in Boston early the next year. It was widely advertised in the newspapers: the *Newport Mercury* on February 17, the *Virginia Gazette* on March 7, and the *South Carolina Gazette* on June 2, 1766 offered the pamphlet for sale. A London edition appeared in 1766, and William Pitt, in speeches supporting repeal of the Stamp Act, used material from the pamphlet, sometimes almost word for word.

The pamphlet runs to fifty-five closely printed pages, only a few of which are reprinted here. Omitted are most of the quotations from British pamphlets which Dulany is refuting, discussions of English political history, and the detailed discussions of economic problems such as how much income Britain derived from the tobacco trade and from its monopoly of the sale of manufactures to the colonies. Omitted too is the discussion of the relative contributions of Britain and the colonies in fighting the recent war —a matter of bitter concern to most of the pamphleteers of the period, both British and American.

In preparing the pamphlet for publication, I have removed the random italics.

In the constitution of England, the three principal forms of government, monarchy, aristocracy, and democracy, are blended together in certain proportions; but each of these orders, in the exercise of the legislative authority, hath its peculiar department, from which the others are excluded. In this division, the *granting of supplies*, or *laying taxes*, is deemed to be the province of the house of commons, as the representative of the people. . . . All supplies are supposed to flow from their gift; and the other orders are permitted only to assent, or reject generally, not to propose any modification, amendment, or partial alteration of it.

This observation being considered, it will undeniably appear, that, in framing the late Stamp Act, the commons acted in the character of representative of the colonies. They assumed it as the principle of that measure, and the *propriety* of it must therefore stand, or fall, as the principle is true, or false: For the preamble sets forth, That the commons of Great Britain had resolved to *give and grant* the several rates and duties imposed by the act; but what right had the commons of Great Britain to be thus munificent at the expence of the commons of America? . . . To give property, not belonging to the giver, and without the consent of the owner, is such evident and flagrant injustice, in *ordinary cases,* that few are hardy enough to avow it; and therefore, when it really happens, the fact is disguised and varnished over by the most plausible pretences the ingenuity of the giver can suggest. . . . But it is alledged that there is a *virtual,* or *implied representation* of the colonies springing out of the constitution of the British government: And it must be confessed on all hands, that, as the representation is not actual, it is virtual, or it doth not exist at all; for no third kind of representation can be imagined. The colonies claim the privilege, which is common to all British subjects, of being taxed *only* with their own consent given by their representatives, and all the advocates for the Stamp Act admit this claim. Whether, therefore, upon the whole matter, the imposition of the Stamp Duties is a *proper* exercise of constitutional authority, or not, depends upon the single question, Whether the commons of Great Britain are *virtually* the representatives of the commons of America, or not.

The advocates for the Stamp Act admit, in express terms, that "the colonies do not choose members of parliament," "but they assert that the colonies are *virtually* represented in the same manner with the non-electors resident in Great Britain."

How have they proved this position? Where have they defined, or precisely explained what they mean by the expression, *virtual representation?* As it is the very hinge upon which the rectitude of the taxation turns, something more satisfactory than mere assertion, more solid than a form of expression, is necessary; for, how can it be seriously expected, that men, who think themselves injuriously affected in their properties and privileges, will be convinced and reconciled by a fanciful phrase, the meaning of which can't be precisely ascertained by those who use it, or properly applied to the purpose for which it hath been advanced?

They argue, that "the right of election being annexed to certain species of property, to franchises, and inhabitancy in some particular places, a very small part of the land, the property, and the people of England are comprehended in those descriptions. All landed property, not freehold, and all monied property, are *excluded.* The merchants of London, the proprietors of the public funds, the inhabitants of Leeds, Halifax, Birmingham, and Manchester, and that great corporation of the East-India company, *none of them* choose their representatives, and yet are they all represented in parliament, and the colonies being *exactly* in *their* situation, are represented in the *same manner.*"[1]

Now, this argument, which is all that their invention hath been able to supply, is totally defective; for, it consists of facts not true, and of conclusions inadmissible.

It is so far from being true, that all the persons enumerated under the character of *non-electors,* are in that predicament, that it is indubitably certain there is *no* species of property, landed, or monied, which is not possessed by *very many* of the *British electors.*

I shall undertake to disprove the supposed similarity of situation, whence the same kind of representation is deduced, of the inhabitants of the colonies, and of the British non-electors; and, if I succeed, the notion of a *virtual representation* of the colonies must fail, which, in truth, is a mere cob-web,

---

[1] Dulany is here quoting, inexactly, from *The Regulations Lately Made* . . . , a semi-official defense of the policies of the Grenville ministry published in London in 1765. For a discussion, see Morgan, *Stamp Act Crisis,* chap. VI, "Daniel Dulany, Pamphleteer." [—ED.]

spread to catch the unwary, and intangle the weak. I would be understood: I am upon a question of *propriety*, not of power; and, though some may be inclined to think it is to little purpose to discuss the one, when the other is irresistible, yet are they different considerations; and, at the same time that I invalidate the claim upon which it is founded, I may very consistently recommend a submission to the law, whilst it endures. I shall say nothing of the use I intend by the discussion; for, if it should not be perceived by the sequel, there is no use in it, and, if it should appear then, it need not be premised.

Lessees for years, copyholders, proprietors of the public funds, inhabitants of Birmingham, Leeds, Halifax, and Manchester, merchants of the city of London, or members of the corporation of the East-India company, are *as such*, under no personal incapacity to be electors; for they may acquire the right of election, and there are *actually* not only a considerable number of electors in each of the classes of lessees for years, &c. but in many of them, if not all, even members of parliament. The interests therefore of the non-electors, the electors, and the representatives, are individually the same; to say nothing of the connection among neighbours, friends, and relations. The security of the non-electors against oppression, is, that their oppression will fall also upon the electors and the representatives. The one can't be injured, and the other indemnified.

Further, if the non-electors should not be taxed by the British parliament, they would not be taxed *at all;* and it would be iniquitous as well as a solecism, in the political system, that they should partake of all the benefits resulting from the imposition, and application of taxes, and derive an immunity from the circumstance of not being qualified to vote. Under this constitution then, a double or virtual representation may be reasonably supposed. The electors, who are inseparably connected in their interests with the non-electors, may be justly deemed to be the representatives of the non-electors, at the same time they exercise their personal privilege in their right of election; and the members chosen, therefore, the representatives of both. This is the only rational explanation of the expression, *virtual representation*. None has been advanced by the assertors of it, and their meaning can only be inferred from the instances, by which they endeavour to elucidate it, and no other meaning can be stated, to which the instances apply.

It is an essential principle of the English constitution, that the subject shall not be taxed without his consent, which hath not been introduced by any particular law, but necessarily results from the nature of that mixed government; for, without it, the order of democracy could not exist. . . .

The situation of the non-electors in England—their capacity to become electors—their inseparable connection with those who are electors, and their representatives—their security against oppression resulting from this connection, and the necessity of imagining a double or virtual representation, to avoid iniquity and absurdity, have been explained—the inhabitants of the colonies are, *as such,* incapable of being electors, the privilege of election being exerciseable only in person, and therefore if *every* inhabitant of America had the requisite freehold, not *one* could vote, but upon the supposition of his ceasing to be an inhabitant of America, and becoming a resident of Great Britain, a supposition which would be impertinent, because it shifts the question—should the colonies not be taxed by *Parliamentary impositions,* their respective legislatures have a regular, adequate, and constitutional authority to tax them, and therefore there would not necessarily be an iniquitous and absurd exemption, from their not being represented by the house of commons.

There is not that intimate and inseparable relation between the electors of Great-Britain, and the Inhabitants of the colonies, which must inevitably involve both in the same taxation; on the contrary, not a single *actual* elector in England, might be immediately affected by a taxation in America, imposed by a statute which would have a general operation and effect, upon the properties of the inhabitants of the colonies. The latter might be oppressed in a thousand shapes, without any Sympathy, or exciting any alarm in the former. Moreover, even acts, oppressive and injurious to the colonies in an extreme degree, might become popular in England, from the promise or expectation, that the very measures which depressed the colonies, would give ease to the Inhabitants of Great-Britain. It is indeed true, that the interests of England and the colonies are allied, and an injury to the colonies produced into all it's consequences, will eventually affect the mother country; yet these consequences being generally remote, are not at once foreseen; they do not immediately alarm the fears, and engage the passions of the English electors; the connection between a freeholder of Great-Britain, and a British American being deducible only thro' a train of reasoning, which few will take the trouble, or can have opportunity, if they have capacity, to investigate; Wherefore the relation between the British Americans, and the English electors, is a knot too infirm to be relied on as a competent security, especially against the force of a present, counteracting expectation of relief.

If it would have been a just conclusion, that the colonies being exactly in the same situation with the non-electors of England, are therefore represented in the same manner; it ought to be allowed, that the reasoning is solid, which, after having evinced a total *dissimilarity* of situation, infers, that their representation is *different*.

If the commons of Great-Britain have no right by the constitution, to GIVE AND GRANT property *not* belonging to themselves or others, without their consent actually or virtually given; If the claim of the colonies not to be taxed *without their consent*, signified by their representatives, is well founded; if it appears that the colonies are not actually represented by the commons of Great-Britain, and that the notion of a double or virtual representation, doth not with any propriety apply to the people of America; then the principle of the stamp act, must be given up as indefensible on the point of representation, and the validity of it rested upon the *power* which they who framed it, have to carry it into execution. . . .

[*In the following section Dulany answers Thomas Pownall's assertion that the colonies are no more than common corporations and therefore no more entitled to exemption from parliamentary taxation than the citizens of London.* —ED.]

The colonies have a complete and adequate legislative authority, and are not only represented in their assemblies, but in *no other manner*. The power of making bye-laws vested in the common council is inadequate and incomplete, being bounded by a few particular subjects; and the common council are actually represented too, by having a choice of members to serve in parliament. How then can the reason of the exemption from internal parliamentary taxations, claimed by the colonies, apply to the citizens of London?

The power described in the provincial charters, is to make laws, and in the exercise of that power, the colonies are bounded by no other limitations than what result from their subordination to, and dependence upon Great Britain. The term *bye-laws* is as novel, and improper, when applied to the *assemblies,* as the expression, *acts of assembly,* would be, if applied to the parliament of Great Britain; and it is as absurd and indefensible, to call a colony a common corporation, because not an independent kingdom, and the powers of each to make laws and bye-laws, are limited, tho' not comparable in their extent, and the variety of their objects, as it would be to call lake Erie, a Duck-puddle, because not the atlantic ocean.

Should the analogy between the *colonies* and *corporations* be even admitted for a moment, in order to see what would be the consequence of the *postulatum,* it would only amount to this, The colonies are vested with as complete authority to all

intents and purposes to tax themselves, as any English corporation is to make a bye-law, in any imaginable instance for
any local purpose whatever, and the parliament doth not make
laws for corporations upon subjects, in every respect proper
for bye-laws.

But I don't rest the matter upon this, or any other circumstance, however considerable, to prove the impropriety of a
taxation by the British parliament. I rely upon the fact, that
not one inhabitant in any colony is, or can be *actually* or *virtually* represented by the British house of commons and therefore, that the Stamp duties are severely imposed.

But it has been alledged, that if the right to *give and grant*
the property of the colonies by an internal taxation is denied
by the house of commons, the subordination and dependence
of the colonies, and the superintendence of the British parliament can't be consistently establish'd. . . . That any supposed
line of distinction between the two cases, is but "a whimsical
imagination, a chimerical speculation against fact and experience.". . . Now, under favour, I conceive there is more confidence, than solidity in this assertion; and it may be satisfactorily
and easily proved, that the subordination and dependence of
the colonies may be preserved, and the *supreme authority* of
the mother country be firmly supported, and yet the principle
of representation, and the right of the British house of commons
flowing from it, to *give and grant* the property of the commons
of America, be denied.

The colonies are dependent upon Great Britain, and the
supreme authority vested in the king, lords, and commons, may
justly be exercised to secure, or preserve their dependence,
whenever necessary for that purpose. This authority results
from, and is implied in the idea of the relation subsisting
between England and her colonies; for, considering the nature
of human affections, the inferior is not to be trusted with providing regulations to prevent his rising to an equality with his
superior. But, though the right of the superior to use the

proper means for preserving the subordination of his inferior is admitted, yet it does not necessarily follow, that he has a right to seize the property of his inferior when he pleases, or to command him in every thing; since, in the degrees of it, there may very well exist a *dependence* and *inferiority*, without absolute *vassalage* and *slavery*. In what the superior may *rightfully* controul, or compel, and in what the inferior ought to be at liberty to act without controul or compulsion, depends upon the nature of the dependence, and the degree of the subordination; and, these being ascertained, the measure of obedience, and submission, and the extent of the authority and superintendence will be settled. When powers, compatible with the relation between the superior and inferior, have, by express compact, been granted to, and accepted by, the latter, and have been, after that compact, repeatedly recognized by the former —When they may be exercised effectually upon every occasion without any injury to that relation, the authority of the superior can't properly interpose; for, by the powers vested in the inferior, is the superior limited.

By their constitutions of government, the colonies are empowered to impose internal taxes. This power is compatible with their dependence, and hath been expressly recognized by British ministers and the British parliament, upon many occasions; and it may be exercised effectually without striking at, or impeaching, in any respect, the superintendence of the British parliament. May not then the line be distinctly and justly drawn between such acts as are necessary, or proper, for preserving or securing the dependence of the colonies, and such as are not necessary or proper for that very important purpose?

When the powers were conferred upon the colonies, they were conferred too as privileges and immunities, and accepted as such; or, to speak more properly, the privileges belonging necessarily to them as British subjects, were solemnly declared and confirmed by their charters, and they who settled in America under the encouragement and faith of these charters, understood, not only that They *might*, but that it was their *right* to exercise those powers without controul, or prevention. In some of the charters the distinction is expressed, and the strongest declarations made, and the most solemn assurances given, that the settlers should not have their property taxed without their own consent by their representatives; though their legislative authority is limited at the same time, by the subordination implied in their relation, and They are therefore restrained from making acts of assembly repugnant to the laws of England; and, had the distinction not been expressed, the powers given would have implied it, for, if the parliament may in any case interpose, when the authority of the colonies is adequate to the occasion, and not limited by their subordination to the mother country, it may in every case, which would make another appellation more proper to describe their condition, than the name by which their inhabitants have been usually called, and have gloried in.

Because the parliament may, when the relation between Great Britain and her colonies calls for an exertion of her superintendence, bind the colonies by statute, therefore a parliamentary interposition in every other instance, is justifiable, is an inference that may be denied. . . .

The right of exemption from all taxes *without their consent,* the colonies claim as British subjects. They derive this right from the common law, which their charters have declared and confirmed, and they conceive that when stripped of this right, whether by prerogative or by any other power, they are at the same time deprived of every privilege distinguishing free-men from slaves.

On the other hand, they acknowledge themselves to be subordinate to the mother country, and that the authority vested in the supreme council of the nation, may be justly exercised to support and preserve that subordination.

Great and just encomiums have been bestow'd upon the constitution of England, and their representative is deservedly the favourite of the inhabitants in Britain. But it is not because the supreme council is called parliament, that they boast of their constitution of government; for there is no particular magical influence from the combination of the letters which form the word; it is because they have a share in that council, that they appoint the members who constitute one branch of it, whose duty and interest it is to consult their benefit, and to assert their rights, and who are vested with an authority, to prevent any measures taking effect dangerous to their liberties, or injurious to their properties.

But the inhabitants in the colonies have no share in this great council. None of the members of it are, or can be of their appointment, or in any respect dependant upon them. There is no immediate connection, on the contrary, there may be an opposition of interest; how puerile then is the declamation "what will become of the colonies birthright, and the glorious securities which their forefathers handed down to them, if the authority of the British parliament *to impose taxes* upon them should be given up? To deny the authority of the British legislature, is to surrender all claim to a share in its councils, and if this were the tenor of their charters, a grant more insidious or replete with mischief, could not be imagined, a forfeiture of their rights would be couched under the appearance of privilege, &c."

We claim an exemption from all parliamentary impositions, that we may enjoy those securities of our rights and properties, which we are entitled to by the constitution. For those securities are derived to the subject from the principle *that he is not to be taxed without his own consent,* and an inhabitant in America can give his consent in no other manner than in assembly. It is in the councils that exist there, and there *only,* that he hath a share, and whilst he enjoys it, his rights and privileges are as well secured as any elector's in England, who hath a share in the national councils there; for the words *parliament* and *assembly* are in this respect, only different terms to express the same thing. . . .

The *English* subjects, who left their *native* country to settle in the wilderness of America, had the privileges of *other Englishmen*. They knew their value, and were desirous of having them perpetuated to their posterity. They were aware that, as their consent whilst they should reside in America, could neither be asked nor regularly given in the national legislature, and that if they were to be bound by laws without restriction, affecting the property they should earn by the utmost hazard and fatigue, they would lose every other privilege which they had enjoyed in their native country, and become meer tenants at will, dependant upon the moderation of their lords and masters, without any other security . . . that as their settlement was to be made under the protection of the English government, they knew, that in consequence of their relation to the mother country, they and their posterity would be subordinate to the supreme national council, and expected that obedience and protection would be considered as reciprocal duties.

Considering themselves, and being considered in this light, they entered into a compact with the crown, the basis of which was, *that their privileges as English subjects, should be effectually secured to themselves, and transmitted to their posterity.* As for this purpose, precise declarations and provisions formed upon the principles, and according to the spirit of the English constitution were necessary; CHARTERS were accordingly framed and conferred by the crown, and accepted by the settlers, by which all the doubts and inconveniencies which might have arisen from the application of general principles to a new subject, were prevented.

By these charters, founded upon the unalienable rights of the subject, and upon the most sacred compact, the colonies claim a right of exemption from taxes *not imposed with their consent.*—They claim it upon the principles of the constitution, as once *English,* and now *British* subjects, upon principles on which their compact with the crown was originally founded.

The origin of other governments is covered by the veil of antiquity; and is differently traced by the fancies of different men; but, of the colonies, the evidence of it is as clear and unequivocal as of any other fact.

By these declaratory charters the inhabitants of the colonies claim an exemption from *all* taxes not imposed by their own consent, and to infer from their objection to a taxation, to which their consent is not, nor can be given, *that they are setting up a right in the crown to dispense with acts of parliament, and to deprive the* British *subjects in* America *of the benefits of the common law,* is so extremely absurd, that I should be at a loss to account for the appearance of so strange an argument, were I not apprized of the unworthy arts employed by the enemies of the colonies to excite strong prejudices against them in the minds of their brethren at home, and what gross incongruities prejudiced men are wont to adopt.

· 7 ·

An Inquiry into the Rights of

the British Colonies

By Richard Bland

The full title of the pamphlet is *An Inquiry Into The Rights of the British Colonies, Intended as an Answer to The Regulations lately made concerning the Colonies, and the Taxes imposed upon them considered. In a Letter Addressed to the Author of that Pamphlet.* The pamphlet was unique in the period in that the author's name is on the title page: "By Richard Bland, of Virginia." It was published by Alexander Purdie and Company at Williamsburg, Virginia, in the week of March 7–14, 1766. Purdie's *Virginia Gazette* reprinted excerpts from the pamphlet on May 30, 1766 but no other colonial newspaper seems to have paid any attention to it. Nor was it republished elsewhere in America although it was reprinted in London in 1769.

Nevertheless, the ideas it contained are to be found in newspapers during the next few years, and the appeal to the law of nature was to be repeated and carried much farther in *A State of*

Williamsburg, Virginia, 1766, pp. 3–7, 9–15, 20–31.

the Rights of the Colonists, adopted by the Boston Town Meeting in November 1772.[1] And the final outcome of the argument of the pamphlet is to be found in the Declaration of Independence itself.

In the text that follows, all italics except those used for emphasis have been removed.

S I R,

I take the Liberty to address you, as the Author of "The Regulations lately made concerning the Colonies, and the Taxes imposed upon them considered." It is not to the Man, whoever you are, that I address myself; but it is to the Author of a Pamphlet which, according to the Light I view it in, endeavours to fix Shackles upon the American Colonies: Shackles which, however nicely polished, can by no Means sit easy upon Men who have just Sentiments of their own Rights and Liberties.

You have indeed brought this Trouble upon yourself, for you say that

many Steps have been lately taken by the Ministry to cement and perfect the necessary Connexion between the Colonies and the Mother Kingdom, which every Man who is sincerely interested in what is interesting to his Country will anxiously consider the Propriety of, will inquire into the Information, and canvas the Principles upon which they have been adopted; and will be ready to applaud what has been well done, condemn what has been done amiss, and suggest any Emendations, Improvements, or Additions which may be within his Knowledge, and occur to his Reflexion.

Encouraged therefore by so candid an Invitation, I have undertaken to examine, with an honest Plainness and Freedom, whether the Ministry, by imposing Taxes upon the Colonies by Authority of Parliament, have pursued a wise and salutary

---

[1] Pamphlet 12.

Plan of Government, or whether they have exerted pernicious and destructive Acts of Power.

I pretend not to concern myself with the Regulations lately made to encourage Population in the new Acquisitions: Time can only determine whether the Reasons upon which they have been founded are agreeable to the Maxims of Trade and sound Policy, or not. However, I will venture to observe that if the most powerful inducement towards peopling those Acquisitions is to arise from the Expectation of a Constitution to be established in them similar to the other Royal Governments in America, it must be a strong Circumstance, in my Opinion, against their being settled by Englishmen, or even by Foreigners, who do not live under the most despotick Government; since, upon your Principles of Colony Government, such a Constitution will not be worth their Acceptance.

The Question is whether the Colonies are represented in the British Parliament or not? You affirm it to be an indubitable Fact that they are represented, and from thence you infer a Right in the Parliament to impose Taxes of every Kind upon them. You do not insist upon the Power, but upon the Right of Parliament to impose Taxes upon the Colonies. This is certainly a very proper Distinction, as Right and Power have very different Meanings, and convey very different Ideas; For had you told us that the Parliament of Great Britain have Power, by the Fleets and Armies of the Kingdom, to impose Taxes and to raise Contributions upon the Colonies, I should not have presumed to dispute the Point with you; but as you insist upon the Right only, I must beg Leave to differ from you in Opinion, and shall give my Reasons for it.

But I must first recapitulate your Arguments in Support of this Right in the Parliament. You say

the Inhabitants of the Colonies do not indeed choose Members of Parliament, neither are nine Tenths of the People of Britain Electors; for the Right of Election is annexed to certain Species of Property, to peculiar Franchises, and to Inhabitancy in some particular Places.

But these Descriptions comprehend only a very small Part of the Lands, the Property and People of Britain; all Copy-Hold, all Lease-Hold Estates under the Crown, under the Church, or under private Persons, though for Terms ever so long; all landed Property in short that is not Freehold, and all monied Property whatsoever, are excluded. The Possessors of these have no Votes in the Election of Members of Parliament; Women and Persons under Age, be their Property ever so large, and all of it Freehold, have none: The Merchants of London, a numerous and respectable Body of Men, whose Opulence exceeds all that America can collect; the Proprietors of that vast Accumulation of Wealth, the Publick Funds; the Inhabitants of Leeds, of Halifax, of Birmingham, and of Manchester, Towns that are each of them larger than the largest in the Plantations; many of lesser Note, that are incorporated; and that great Corporation the East India Company, whose Rights over the Countries they possess fall very little short of Sovereignty, and whose Trade and whose Fleets are sufficient to constitute them a maritime Power, are all in the same Circumstances: And yet are they not represented in Parliament? Is their vast Property subject to Taxation without their Consent? Are they all arbitrarily bound by Laws to which they have not agreed? The Colonies are exactly in the same Situation; all British Subjects are really in the same; none are actually, all are virtually, represented in Parliament: For every Member of Parliament sits in the House not as a Representative of his own Constituents, but as one of that august Assembly by which all the Commons of Great Britain are represented.

This is the Sum of what you advance, in all the Pomp of Parliamentary Declamation, to prove that the Colonies are represented in Parliament, and therefore subject to their Taxation; but notwithstanding this Way of reasoning, I cannot comprehend how Men who are excluded from voting at the Election of Members of Parliament can be represented in that Assembly, or how those who are elected do not sit in the House as Representatives of their Constituents. These Assertions appear to me not only paradoxical, but contrary to the fundamental Principles of the English Constitution.

To illustrate this important Disquisition, I conceive we

must recur to the civil Constitution of England, and from thence deduce and ascertain the Rights and Privileges of the People at the first Establishment of the Government, and discover the Alterations that have been made in them from Time to Time; and it is from the Laws of the Kingdom, founded upon the Principles of the Law of Nature, that we are to show the Obligation every Member of the State is under to pay Obedience to its Institutions. From these Principles I shall endeavour to prove that the Inhabitants of Britain, who have no Vote in the Election of Members of Parliament, are not represented in that Assembly, and yet that they owe Obedience to the Laws of Parliament; which, as to them, are constitutional, and not arbitrary. As to the Colonies, I shall consider them afterwards.

[*Omitted here is Bland's discussion of English history, showing how many English freeholders were deprived of the right of representation.* —ED.]

Men in a State of Nature are absolutely free and independent of one another as to sovereign Jurisdiction,[2] but when they enter into a Society, and by their own Consent become Members of it, they must submit to the Laws of the Society according to which they agree to be governed; for it is evident, by the very Act of Association, that each Member subjects himself to the Authority of that Body in whom, by common Consent, the legislative Power of the State is placed: But though they must submit to the Laws, so long as they remain Members of the Society, yet they retain so much of their natural Freedom as to have a Right to retire from the Society, to renounce the Benefits of it, to enter into another Society, and to settle in

---

[2] *Vattel's Law of Nature. Locke on Civil Govern. Wollaston's Rel. of Nat.*

another Country; for their Engagements to the Society, and their Submission to the publick Authority of the State, do not oblige them to continue in it longer than they find it will conduce to their Happiness, which they have a natural Right to promote. This natural Right remains with every Man, and he cannot justly be deprived of it by any civil Authority. Every Person therefore who is denied his Share in the Legislature of the State to which he had an original Right, and every Person who from his particular Circumstances is excluded from this great Privilege, and refuses to exercise his natural Right of quitting the Country, but remains in it, and continues to exercise the Rights of a Citizen in all other Respects, must be subject to the Laws which by these Acts he *implicitly*, or to use your own Phrase, *virtually* consents to: For Men may subject themselves to Laws, by consenting to them *implicitly;* that is, by conforming to them, by adhering to the Society, and accepting the Benefits of its Constitution, as well, as *explicitly* and directly, in their own Persons, or by their Representatives substituted in their Room.[3] Thus, if a Man whose Property does not entitle him to be an Elector of Members of Parliament, and therefore cannot be represented, or have any Share in the Legislature,

inherits or takes any Thing by the Laws of the Country to which he has no indubitable Right in Nature, or which, if he has a Right to it, he cannot tell how to get or keep without the Aid of the Laws and the Advantage of Society, then, when he takes this Inheritance, or whatever it is, *with* it he takes and owns the Laws that gave it him. And since the Security he has from the Laws of the Country, in Respect of his Person and Rights, is the *Equivalent* for his Submission to them, he cannot accept *that* Security without being obliged, in Equity, to pay *this* Submission: Nay his very continuing in the Country shows that he either likes the Constitution, or likes it better, notwithstanding the Alteration made in it to his Disad-

---

[3] *Wollaston's Rel. of Nat.*

vantage, than any other; or at least thinks it better, in his Circumstances, to conform to it, than to seek any other; that is, he is content to be comprehended in it.

From hence it is evident that the Obligation of the Laws of
Parliament upon the People of Britain who have no Right to
be Electors does not arise from their being *virtually* represented, but from a quite different Principle; a Principle of the
Law of Nature, true, certain, and universal, applicable to
every Sort of Government, and not contrary to the common
Understandings of Mankind.

If what you say is a real Fact, that nine Tenths of the People of Britain are deprived of the high Privilege of being
Electors, it shows a great Defect in the present Constitution,
which has departed so much from its original Purity; but never
can prove that those People are even *virtually* represented in
Parliament. And here give me Leave to observe that it would
be a Work worthy of the best patriotick Spirits in the Nation
to effectuate an Alteration in this putrid Part of the Constitution; and, by restoring it to its pristine Perfection, prevent any
"Order or Rank of the Subjects from imposing upon or binding the rest without their Consent." But, I fear, the Gangrene
has taken too deep Hold to be eradicated in these Days of
Venality.

But if those People of Britain who are excluded from being
Electors are not represented in Parliament, the Conclusion is
much stronger against the People of the Colonies being represented; who are considered by the British Government itself, in every Instance of Parliamentary Legislation, as a distinct People. It has been determined by the Lords of the Privy
Council that "Acts of Parliament made in England without
naming the foreign Plantations will not bind them[4]." Now,
what can be the Reason of this Determination, but that the
Lords of the Privy Council are of Opinion the Colonies are a

[4] *2 Peer Williams.*

distinct People from the Inhabitants of Britain, and are not represented in Parliament. If, as you contend, the Colonies are *exactly in the same Situation* with the Subjects in Britain, the Laws will in every Instance be equally binding upon them, as upon those Subjects, unless you can discover two Species of *virtual* Representation; the one to respect the Subjects in Britain, and always existing in Time of Parliament; the other to respect the Colonies, a mere Non-Entity, if I may be allowed the Term, and never existing but when the Parliament thinks proper to produce it into Being by any particular Act in which the Colonies happen to be named. But I must examine the Case of the Colonies more distinctly.

It is in vain to search into the civil Constitution of England for Directions in fixing the proper Connexion between the Colonies and the Mother Kingdom; I mean what their reciprocal Duties to each other are, and what Obedience is due from the Children to the general Parent. The planting Colonies from Britain is but of recent Date, and nothing relative to such Plantation can be collected from the ancient Laws of the Kingdom; neither can we receive any better Information by extending our Inquiry into the History of the Colonies established by the several Nations in the more early Ages of the World. All the Colonies (except those of Georgia and Nova Scotia) formed from the English Nation, in North America, were planted in a Manner, and under a Dependence, of which there is not an Instance in all the Colonies of the Ancients; and therefore, I conceive, it must afford a good Degree of Surprise to find an English Civilian[5] giving it as his Sentiment that the English Colonies ought to be governed by the Roman Laws, and for no better Reason than because the Spanish Colonies, as he says, are governed by those Laws. The Romans established their Colonies in the Midst of vanquished Nations, upon Principles which best secured their Conquests; the Priv-

---

[5] *Strahan in his Preface to Domat.*

ileges granted to them were not always the same; their Policy in the Government of their Colonies and the conquered Nations being always directed by arbitrary Principles to the End they aimed at, the subjecting the whole Earth to their Empire. But the Colonies in North America, except those planted within the present Century, were founded by Englishmen; who, becoming private Adventurers, established themselves, without any Expense to the Nation, in this uncultivated and almost uninhabited Country; so that their Case is plainly distinguishable from that of the Roman, or any other Colonies of the ancient World.

As then we can receive no Light from the Laws of the Kingdom, or from ancient History, to direct us in our Inquiry, we must have Recourse to the Law of Nature, and those Rights of Mankind which flow from it.

I have observed before that when Subjects are deprived of their civil Rights, or are dissatisfied with the Place they hold in the Community, they have a natural Right to quit the Society of which they are Members, and to retire into another Country. Now when Men exercise this Right, and withdraw themselves from their Country, they recover their natural Freedom and Independence: The Jurisdiction and Sovereignty of the State they have quitted ceases; and if they unite, and by common Consent take Possession of a new Country, and form themselves into a political Society, they become a sovereign State, independent of the State from which they separated. If then the Subjects of England have a natural Right to relinquish their Country, and by retiring from it, and associating together, to form a new political Society and independent State, they must have a Right, by Compact with the Sovereign of the Nation, to remove into a new Country, and to form a civil Establishment upon the Terms of the Compact. In such a Case, the Terms of the Compact must be obligatory and binding upon the Parties; they must be the Magna Charta, the fundamental Principles of Government, to this new Society; and every Infringement of them must be wrong, and may be opposed. It will be necessary then to examine whether any such Compact was entered into between the Sovereign and those English Subjects who established themselves in America.

You have told us that "before the first and great Act of Navigation the Inhabitants of North America were but a few unhappy Fugitives, who had wandered thither to enjoy their civil and religious Liberties, which they were deprived of at Home." If this was true, it is evident, from what has been said upon the Law of Nature, that they have a Right to a civil independent Establishment of their own, and that Great Britain has no *Right* to interfere in it. But you have been guilty of a gross Anachronism in your Chronology, and a great Errour in your Account of the first Settlement of the Colonies in North America; for it is a notorious Fact that they were not settled by Fugitives from their native Country, but by Men who came over voluntarily, at their own Expense, and under Charters from the Crown, obtained for that Purpose, long before the first and great Act of Navigation. . . .

[*Omitted here is Bland's discussion of the various Virginia charters and the relations between the colony and England to the Restoration in 1660.* —ED.]

From this Detail of the Charters, and other Acts of the Crown, under which the first Colony in North America was established, it is evident that "the Colonists were not a few unhappy Fugitives who had wandered into a distant Part of the World to enjoy their civil and religious Liberties, which they were deprived of at home," but had a regular Government long before the first Act of Navigation, and were respected as a distinct State, independent, as to their *internal* Government, of the original Kingdom, but united with her, as to their *external* Polity, in the closest and most intimate LEAGUE AND AMITY, under the same Allegiance, and enjoying the Benefits of a reciprocal Intercourse.

But allow me to make a Reflection or two upon the preceding Account of the first Settlement of an English Colony in North America.

America was no Part of the Kingdom of England; it was possessed by a savage People, scattered through the Country, who were not subject to the English Dominion, nor owed Obedience to its Laws. This independent Country was settled by Englishmen at their own Expense, under particular Stipulations with the Crown: These Stipulations then must be the sacred Band of Union between England and her Colonies, and cannot be infringed without Injustice. But you Object that "no Power can abridge the Authority of Parliament, which has never exempted any from the Submission they owe to it; and no other Power can grant such an Exemption."

I will not dispute the Authority of the Parliament, which is without Doubt supreme within the Body of the Kingdom, and cannot be abridged by any other Power; but may not the King have Prerogatives which he has a Right to exercise without the Consent of Parliament? If he has, perhaps that of granting License to his Subjects to remove into a *new* Country, and to settle therein upon particular Conditions, may be one. If he has no such Prerogative, I cannot discover how the Royal Engagements can be made good, that "the Freedom and other Benefits of the British Constitution" shall be secured to those People who shall settle in a new Country under such Engagements; the Freedom, and other Benefits of the British Constitution, cannot be secured to a People without they are exempted from being taxed by any Authority but that of their Representatives, chosen by themselves. This is an essential Part of British Freedom; but if the King cannot grant such an Exemption, in Right of his Prerogative, the Royal Promises cannot be fulfilled; and all Charters which have been granted by our former Kings, for this Purpose, must be Deceptions upon the Subjects who accepted them, which to say would be a high Reflection upon the Honour of the Crown. But there was a Time when some Parts of England itself were exempt from the Laws of Parliament: The Inhabitants of the County Palatine of Chester were not subject to such Laws[6] *ab antiquo,* because they did not send Representatives to Parliament, but had their own *Commune Concilium;* by whose Authority, with the Consent of their Earl, their Laws were made. If this Exemption was not derived originally from the Crown, it must have arisen from that great Principle in the British Constitution by which the Freemen in the Nation are not subject to any Laws but such as are made by Representatives elected by themselves to Parliament; so that, in either Case, it is an Instance extremely applicable to the Colonies, who contend for no other Right but that of directing their *internal* Government by Laws made with their own Consent, which has been preserved to them by repeated Acts and Declarations of the Crown.

The Constitution of the Colonies, being established upon the Principles of British Liberty, has never been infringed by the immediate Act of the Crown; but the Powers of Government, agreeably to this Constitution, have been constantly declared in the King's Commissions to their Governours, which, as often as they pass the Great Seal, are *new* Declarations and Confirmations of the Rights of the Colonies. Even in the Reign of Charles the Second, a Time by no Means favourable to Liberty, these Rights of the Colonies were maintained inviolate; for when it was thought necessary to establish a permanent Revenue for the Support of Government in Virginia, the King did not apply to the English Parliament, but to the General Assembly, and sent over an Act, under the Great Seal of England, by which it was enacted "by the King's Most Excellent Majesty, by and with the Consent of the General Assembly," that two Shillings per Hogshead upon all Tobacco exported, one Shilling and Threepence per Tun upon Shipping, and Sixpence per Poll for every Person imported, not being

---

[6] *Petyt's Rights of the Commons. King's Vale Royal of England.*

actually a Mariner in Pay, were to be paid for ever as a Revenue for the Support of the Government in the Colony.

I have taken Notice of this Act, not only because it shows the proper Fountain from whence all Supplies to be raised in the Colonies ought to flow, but also as it affords an Instance that Royalty itself did not disdain formerly to be named as a Part of the Legislature of the Colony; though now, to serve a Purpose destructive of their Rights, and to introduce Principles of Despotism unknown to a free Constitution, the Legislature of the Colonies are degraded even below the Corporation of a petty Borough in England.

It must be admitted that after the Restoration the Colonies lost that Liberty of Commerce with foreign Nations they had enjoyed before that Time.

As it became a fundamental Law of the other States of Europe to prohibit all foreign Trade with their Colonies, England demanded such an exclusive Trade with her Colonies. This was effected by the Act of 25th Charles 2d, and some other subsequent Acts; which not only circumscribed the Trade of the Colonies with foreign Nations within very narrow Limits, but imposed Duties upon several Articles of their own Manufactory exported from one Colony to another. These Acts, which imposed severer Restrictions upon the Trade of the Colonies than were imposed upon the Trade of England, deprived the Colonies, so far as these Restrictions extended, of the Privileges of English Subjects, and constituted an unnatural Difference between Men under the same Allegiance, born equally free, and entitled to the same civil Rights. In this Light did the People of Virginia view the Act of 25th Charles 2d, when they sent Agents to the English Court to represent against "Taxes and Impositions being laid on the Colony by any Authority but that of their General Assembly." The Right of imposing *internal* Duties upon their Trade by Authority of Parliament was then disputed, though you say it was never called into Question; and the Agents sent from Virginia upon this Occasion obtained a Declaration from Charles 2d the 19th of April 1676, under his Privy Seal, that Impositions or "Taxes ought not be laid upon the Inhabitants and Proprietors of the Colony but by the common Consent of the General Assembly, except such Impositions as the Parliament should lay on the Commodities imported into England from the Colony:" And he ordered a Charter to be made out, and to pass the Great Seal, for securing this Right, among others, to the Colony.

But whether the Act of 25th Charles 2d, or any of the other Acts, have been complained of as Infringements of the Rights of the Colonies or not, is immaterial; for if a Man of superiour Strength takes my Coat from me, that cannot give him a Right to my Cloak, nor am I obliged to submit to be deprived of all my Estate because I may have given up some Part of it without Complaint. Besides, I have proved irrefragably that the Colonies are not represented in Parliament, and consequently, upon your own Position, that no new Law can bind them that is made without the Concurrence of their Representatives; and if so, then every Act of Parliament that imposes *internal* Taxes upon the Colonies is an Act of *Power,* and not of *Right.* I must speak freely, I am considering a Question which affects the *Rights* of above two Millions of as loyal Subjects as belong to the British Crown, and must use Terms adequate to the Importance of it; I say that *Power* abstracted from *Right* cannot give a just Title to Dominion. If a Man invades my Property, he becomes an Aggressor, and puts himself into a State of War with me: I have a Right to oppose this Invader; If I have not Strength to repel him, I must submit, but he acquires no Right to my Estate which he has usurped. Whenever I recover Strength I may renew my Claim, and attempt to regain my Possession; if I am never strong enough, my Son, or his Son, may, when able, recover the natural Right of his Ancestor which has been unjustly taken from him.

I hope I shall not be charged with Insolence, in delivering

the Sentiments of an honest Mind with Freedom: I am speaking of the *Rights* of a People; *Rights* imply *Equality* in the Instances to which they belong, and must be treated without Respect to the Dignity of the Persons concerned in them. If "the British Empire in Europe and in America is the same *Power*," if the "Subjects in both are the same People, and all equally participate in the Adversity and Prosperity of the Whole," what Distinctions can the Difference of their Situations make, and why is this Distinction made between them? Why is the Trade of the Colonies more circumscribed than the Trade of Britain? And why are Impositions laid upon the one which are not laid upon the other? If the Parliament "have a *Right* to impose Taxes of *every Kind* upon the Colonies," they ought in Justice, as the same People, to have the same Sources to raise them from: Their Commerce ought to be equally free with the Commerce of Britain, otherwise it will be loading them with Burthens at the same Time that they are deprived of Strength to sustain them; it will be forcing them to make Bricks without Straw. I acknowledge the Parliament is the sovereign legislative Power of the British Nation, and that by a full Exertion of their Power they can deprive the Colonists of the Freedom and other Benefits of the British Constitution which have been secured to them by our Kings; they can abrogate all their civil Rights and Liberties; but by what *Right* is it that the Parliament can exercise such a Power over the Colonists, who have as natural a Right to the Liberties and Privileges of Englishmen as if they were actually resident within the Kingdom? The Colonies are subordinate to the Authority of Parliament; subordinate I mean in Degree, but not absolutely so: For if by a Vote of the British Senate the Colonists were to be delivered up to the Rule of a French or Turkish Tyranny, they may refuse Obedience to such a Vote, and may oppose the Execution of it by Force. Great is the Power of Parliament, but, great as it is, it cannot, constitutionally, deprive the People of their *natural* Rights; nor, in

Virtue of the same Principle, can it deprive them of their *civil* Rights, which are founded in Compact, without their own Consent. There is, I confess, a considerable Difference between these two Cases as to the Right of Resistance: In the first, if the Colonists should be dismembered from the Nation by Act of Parliament, and abandoned to another Power, they have a natural Right to defend their Liberties by open Force, and may lawfully resist; and, if they are able, repel the Power to whose Authority they are abandoned. But in the other, if they are deprived of their civil Rights, if great and manifest Oppressions are imposed upon them by the State on which they are dependent, their Remedy is to lay their Complaints at the Foot of the Throne, and to suffer patiently rather than disturb the publick Peace, which nothing but a Denial of Justice can excuse them in breaking. But if this Justice should be denied, if the most humble and dutiful Representations should be rejected, nay not even deigned to be received, what is to be done? To such a Question Thucydides would make the Corinthians reply, that if "a decent and condescending Behaviour is shown on the Part of the Colonies, it would be base in the Mother State to press too far on such Moderation:" And he would make the Corcyreans answer, that "every Colony, whilst used in a proper Manner, ought to pay Honour and Regard to its Mother State; but, when treated with Injury and Violence, is become an Alien. They were not sent out to be the Slaves, but to be the Equals of those that remain behind."

But, according to your Scheme, the Colonies are to be prohibited from uniting in a Representation of their general Grievances to the common Sovereign. This Moment "the British Empire in Europe and in America is the same Power; its Subjects in both are the same People; each is equally important to the other, and mutual Benefits, mutual Necessities, cement their Connexion." The next Moment "the Colonies are unconnected with each other, different in their Manners, opposite in their Principles, and clash in their Interests and in their Views, from Rivalry in Trade, and the Jealousy of Neighbourhood. This happy Division, which was effected by Accident, is to be continued throughout by Design; and all Bond of Union between them" is excluded from your vast System. *Divide et impera* is your Maxim in Colony Administration, lest "an Alliance should be formed dangerous to the Mother Country." Ungenerous Insinuation! detestable Thought! abhorrent to every Native of the Colonies! who, by an Uniformity of Conduct, have ever demonstrated the deepest Loyalty to their King, as the Father of his People, and an unshaken Attachment to the Interest of Great Britain. But you must entertain a most despicable Opinion of the Understandings of the Colonists to imagine that they will allow Divisions to be fomented between them about inconsiderable Things, when the closest Union becomes necessary to maintain in a constitutional Way their dearest Interests.

Another Writer,[7] fond of his new System of placing Great Britain as the Centre of Attraction to the Colonies, says that

they must be guarded against having or forming any Principle of Coherence with each other above that whereby they cohere in the Centre; having no other Principle of Intercommunication between each other than that by which they are in joint Communication with Great Britain, as the common Centre of all. At the same Time that they are each, in their respective Parts and Subordinations, so framed as to be acted by this first Mover, they should always remain incapable of any Coherence, or of so conspiring amongst themselves as to create any other equal Force which might recoil back on this first Mover; nor is it more necessary to preserve the several Governments subordinate within their respective Orbs than it is essential to the Preservation of the Empire to keep them disconnected and independent of each other.

But how is this "Principle of Coherence," as this elegant Writer calls it, between the Colonies, to be prevented? The

---

[7] *The Administration of the Colonies by Governour Pownall.*

Colonies upon the Continent of North America lie united to each other in one Tract of Country, and are equally concerned to maintain their common Liberty. If he will attend then to the Laws of Attraction in natural as well as political Philosophy, he will find that Bodies in Contact, and cemented by mutual Interests, cohere more strongly than those which are at a Distance, and have no common Interests to preserve. But this natural Law is to be destroyed; and the Colonies, whose real Interests are the same, and therefore ought to be united in the closest Communication, are to be disjoined, and all intercommunication between them prevented. But how is this System of Administration to be established? Is it to be done by a military Force, quartered upon private Families? Is it to be done by extending the Jurisdiction of Courts of Admiralty, and thereby depriving the Colonists of legal Trials in the Courts of common Law? Or is it to be done by harassing the Colonists, and giving overbearing Taxgatherers an Opportunity of ruining Men, perhaps better Subjects than themselves, by dragging them from one Colony to another, before Prerogative Judges, exercising a despotick Sway in Inquisitorial Courts? Oppression has produced very great and unexpected Events: The Helvetick Confederacy, the States of the United Netherlands, are Instances in the Annals of Europe of the glorious Actions a petty People, in Comparision, can perform when united in the Cause of Liberty. May the Colonies ever remain under a constitutional Subordination to Great Britain! It is their Interest to live under such a Subordination; and it is their Duty, by an Exertion of all their Strength and Abilities, when called upon by their common Sovereign, to advance the Grandeur and the Glory of the Nation. May the Interests of Great Britain and her Colonies be ever united, so as that whilst they are retained in a legal and just Dependence no unnatural or unlimited Rule may be exercised over them; but that they may enjoy the Freedom, and other Benefits of the British Constitution, to the latest Page in History!

I flatter myself, by what has been said, your Position of a *virtual* Representation is sufficiently refuted; and that there is really no such Representation known in the British Constitution, and consequently that the Colonies are not subject to an *internal* Taxation by Authority of Parliament.

I could extend this Inquiry to a much greater Length, by examining into the Policy of the late Acts of Parliament, which impose heavy and severe Taxes, Duties, and Prohibitions, upon the Colonies; I could point out some very disagreeable Consequences, respecting the Trade and Manufacturers of Britain, which must necessarily result from these Acts; I could prove that the Revenues arising from the Trade of the Colonies, and the Advantage of their Exports to Great Britain in the Balance of her Trade with foreign Nations, exceed infinitely all the Expense she has been at, all the Expense she can be at, in their Protection; and perhaps I could show that the Bounties given upon some Articles exported from the Colonies were not intended, primarily, as Instances of Attention to their Interest, but arose as well from the Consideration of the disadvantageous Dependence of Great Britain upon other Nations for the principal Articles of her naval Stores, as from her losing Trade for those Articles; I could demonstrate that these Bounties are by no Means adequate to her Savings in such foreign Trade, if the Articles upon which they are given can be procured from the Colonies in Quantities sufficient to answer her Consumption; and that the Excess of these Savings is so much clear Profit to the Nation, upon the Supposition that these Bounties are drawn from it; but, as they will remain in it, and be laid out in its Manufactures and Exports, that the whole Sum which used to be paid to Foreigners for the Purchase of these Articles will be saved to the Nation. I say I could extend my Inquiry, by examining these several Matters; but as the Subject is delicate, and would carry me to a great Length, I shall leave them to the Reader's own Reflection.

· 8 ·

Letters From a Farmer in Pennsylvania to the Inhabitants of the British Colonies (1768)

By John Dickinson

The first of the twelve letters addressed to "My Dear Countrymen" and signed "A Farmer" appeared in a special issue of William Goddard's *Pennsylvania Chronicle* on December 2, 1767, and in the *Pennsylvania Gazette* the next day. The *Maryland Gazette* printed it on December 17, and Rind's *Virginia Gazette* a week later. New England newspapers began publishing the letters before the end of December, and by January 1768 they had reached the far-off *Georgia Gazette*. All but four (and two of those were in German) of the nearly thirty American newspapers published the letters. By March 1768 they were in pamphlet form. At least

First edition, Philadelphia, 1768, pp. 3–13, 18–22, 29–32, 43–57. A reprint of all the letters may be found in Forrest McDonald, ed., *Empire and Nation* (Englewood Cliffs, N. J., 1962).

seven editions were published in America, one in London, one in Dublin, and a French translation, printed in Amsterdam, circulated on the Continent.

Letters I, II, IV, VI, IX, and X are reprinted here. Of the omitted letters, the third discusses divisions among Americans and urges the avoidance of violence and the use of petitions to obtain redress. The fifth is an appeal to "history." The seventh discusses the many taxes the colonists are forced to pay. The eighth argues that the conquest of Canada and Florida benefits only Britain and that the colonies should not be taxed to pay for their defense. The eleventh is a discussion of the methods used in levying and paying taxes, particularly in the seventeenth century. The final letter is replete with rhetorical appeals to Americans to avoid "SLAVERY."

Dickinson's footnotes citing past history, classical literature, and political writers, and those elaborating points made in the text, have been omitted, as have the random italics.

LETTER I.

I am a Farmer, settled, after a variety of fortunes, near the banks of the river Delaware, in the province of Pennsylvania. I received a liberal education, and have been engaged in the busy scenes of life; but am now convinced, that a man may be as happy without bustle, as with it. My farm is small; my servants are few, and good; I have a little money at interest; I wish for no more; my employment in my own affairs is easy; and with a contented grateful mind, undisturbed by worldly hopes or fears, relating to myself, I am completing the number of days allotted to me by divine goodness.

Being generally master of my time, I spend a good deal of it in a library, which I think the most valuable part of my small estate; and being acquainted with two or three gentlemen of abilities and learning, who honour me with their friendship, I have acquired, I believe, a greater knowledge in history, and the laws and constitution of my country, than is generally attained by men of my class, many of them not being so fortunate as I have been in the opportunities of getting information.

From my infancy I was taught to love *humanity* and *liberty*. Enquiry and experience have since confirmed my reverence for the lessons then given me, by convincing me more fully of their truth and excellence. Benevolence towards mankind, excites wishes for their welfare, and such wishes endear the means of fulfilling them. *These* can be found in liberty only, and therefore her sacred cause ought to be espoused by every man, on every occasion, to the utmost of his power. As a charitable, but poor person does not withhold his *mite*, because he cannot relieve *all* the distresses of the miserable, so should not any honest man suppress his sentiments concerning freedom, however small their influence is likely to be. Perhaps he "may touch some wheel," that will have an effect greater than he could reasonably expect.

These being my sentiments, I am encouraged to offer to you, my countrymen, my thoughts on some late transactions, that appear to me to be of the utmost importance to you. Conscious of my own defects, I have waited some time, in expectation of seeing the subject treated by persons much better qualified for the task; but being therein disappointed, and apprehensive that longer delays will be injurious, I venture at length to request the attention of the public, praying, that these lines may be *read* with the same zeal for the happiness of British America with which they were *wrote*.

With a good deal of surprize I have observed, that little notice has been taken of an act of parliament, as injurious in its principle to the liberties of these colonies, as the Stamp-Act was: I mean the act for suspending the legislation of New-York.

The assembly of that government complied with a former act of parliament, requiring certain provisions to be made for the troops in America, in every particular, I think, except the articles of salt, pepper and vinegar. In my opinion they acted imprudently, considering all circumstances, in not complying so far as would have given satisfaction, as several colonies did: But my dislike of their conduct in that instance, has not blinded me so much, that I cannot plainly perceive, that they have been punished in a manner pernicious to American freedom, and justly alarming to all the colonies.

If the British parliament has a legal authority to issue an order, that we shall funish a single article for the troops here, and to compel obedience to *that* order, they have the same right to issue an order for us to supply those troops with arms, cloths, and every necessary; and to compel obedience to *that* order also; in short, to lay *any burthens* they please upon us. What is this but *taxing* us at a *certain sum,* and leaving to us only the *manner* of raising it? How is this mode more tolerable than the Stamp Act? Would that act have appeared more pleasing to Americans, if being ordered thereby to raise the sum total of the taxes, the mighty privilege had been left to them, of saying how much should be paid for an instrument of writing on paper, and how much for another on parchment?

An act of parliament, commanding us to do a certain thing, if it has any validity, is a *tax* upon us for the expence that accrues in complying with it; and for this reason, I believe, every colony on the continent, that chose to give a mark of their respect for Great-Britain, in complying with the act relating to the troops, cautiously avoided the mention of that act, lest their conduct should be attributed to its supposed obligation.

The matter being thus stated, the assembly of New-York either had, or had not, a right to refuse submission to that act. If they had, and I imagine no American will say they had not, then the parliament had *no right* to compel them to execute it. If they had not *that right,* they had *no right* to punish them for not executing it; and therefore *no right* to suspend their legislation, which is a punishment. In fact, if the people of New-York cannot be legally taxed but by their own representatives, they cannot be legally deprived of the privilege of legislation, only for insisting on that exclusive privilege of taxation. If they may be legally deprived in such a case, of the privilege of legislation, why may they not, with equal reason, be deprived of every other privilege? Or why may not every colony be treated in the same manner, when any of them shall dare to deny their assent to any impositions, that shall be directed? Or what signifies the repeal of the Stamp-Act, if these colonies are to lose their *other* privileges, by not tamely surrendering *that* of taxation?

There is one consideration arising from this suspension, which is not generally attended to, but shews its importance very clearly. It was not *necessary* that this suspension should be caused by an act of parliament. The crown might have restrained the governor of New-York, even from calling the assembly together, by its prerogative in the royal governments. This step, I suppose, would have been taken, if the conduct of the assembly of New-York had been regarded as an act of disobedience *to the crown alone;* but it is regarded as an act of "disobedience to the authority of the BRITISH LEGISLATURE." This gives the suspension a consequence vastly more affecting. It is a parliamentary assertion of the *supreme authority* of the British legislature over these colonies, in *the point of taxation,* and is intended to COMPEL New-York into a submission to that authority. It seems therefore to me as much a violation of the liberty of the people of that province, and consequently of all these colonies, as if the parliament had sent a number of regiments to be quartered upon them till they should comply. For it is evident, that the suspension is meant as a *compulsion;* and the *method* of compelling is totally indifferent. It is indeed probable, that the sight of red coats, and the hearing of drums, would have been most alarming; because people are generally more influenced by their eyes and ears, than by their reason. But whoever seriously considers the matter, must perceive that a dreadful stroke is aimed at the liberty of these colonies. I say, of these colonies; for the cause of *one* is the cause of *all.* If the parliament may lawfully deprive New-York of any of *her* rights, it may deprive any, or all the other colonies of *their* rights; and nothing can possibly so much encourage such attempts, as a mutual inattention to the interests of each other. *To divide, and thus to destroy,* is the first political maxim in attacking those, who are powerful by their union. He certainly is not a wise man, who folds his arms, and reposes himself at home, viewing, with unconcern, the flames that have invaded his neighbour's house, without using any endeavours to extinguish them. When Mr. *Hampden's* ship money cause, for *Three Shillings* and *Four-pence,* was tried, all the people of England, with anxious expectations, interested themselves in the important decision; and when the slightest point, touching the freedom of *one* colony, is agitated, I earnestly wish, that *all the rest* may, with equal ardour, support their sister. Very much may be said on this subject; but I hope, more at present is unnecessary.

With concern I have observed, that *two* assemblies of this province have sat and adjourned, without taking any notice of this act. It may perhaps be asked, what would have been proper for them to do? I am by no means fond of inflammatory measures; I detest them. I should be sorry that any thing should be done, which might justly displease our sovereign, or our mother country: But a firm, modest exertion of a free spirit, should never be wanting on public occasions. It appears to me, that it would have been sufficient for the assembly, to have ordered our agents to represent to the King's ministers, their sense of the suspending act, and to pray for its repeal. Thus we should have borne our testimony against it; and might therefore reasonably expect that, on a like occasion, we might receive the same assistance from the other colonies.

> *Concordia res parvæ crescunt.*
> Small things grow great by concord.

Nov. 5.[1]

LETTER II.

There is another late act of parliament, which appears to me to be unconstitutional, and as destructive to the liberty of these colonies, as that mentioned in my last letter; that is, the act for granting the duties on paper, glass, &c.

The parliament unquestionably possesses a legal authority to *regulate* the trade of Great-Britain, and all her colonies. Such an authority is essential to the relation between a mother country and her colonies; and necessary for the common good of all. He, who considers these provinces as states distinct from the British Empire, has very slender notions of *justice,* or of their *interests.* We are but parts of a *whole;* and therefore there must exist a power somewhere to preside, and preserve the connection in due order. This power is lodged in the parliament; and we are as much dependent on Great-Britain, as a perfectly free people can be on another.

I have looked over *every statute* relating to these colonies, from their first settlement to this time; and I find every one of them founded on this principle, till the Stamp-Act administration. *All before,* are calculated to regulate trade, and preserve or promote a mutually beneficial intercourse between the several constituent parts of the empire; and though many of them imposed duties on trade, yet those duties were always imposed *with design* to restrain the commerce of one part, that

---

[1] The day of King WILLIAM the Third's landing.

was injurious to another, and thus to promote the general welfare. The raising a revenue thereby was never intended. Thus the King, by his judges in his courts of justice, imposes fines which all together amount to a very considerable sum, and contribute to the support of government: But this is merely a consequence arising from restrictions, that only meant to keep peace, and prevent confusion; and surely a man would argue very loosely, who should conclude from hence, that the King has a right to levy money in general upon his subjects. Never did the British parliament, till the period above mentioned, think of imposing duties in America, FOR THE PURPOSE OF RAISING A REVENUE. Mr. Grenville first introduced this language, in the preamble to the 4th of *Geo.* III., Chap. 15, which has these words "And whereas it is just and necessary that A REVENUE BE RAISED IN YOUR MAJESTY'S SAID DOMINIONS IN AMERICA, *for defraying the expences of defending, protecting, and securing the same*: We your Majesty's most dutiful and loyal subjects, THE COMMONS OF GREAT-BRITAIN, in parliament assembled, being desirous to make some provision in this present session of parliament, TOWARDS RAISING SAID REVENUE IN AMERICA, have resolved to GIVE and GRANT unto your Majesty the several rates and duties herein after mentioned," &c.

A few months after came the Stamp-Act, which reciting this, proceeds in the same strange mode of expression, thus— "And whereas it is just and necessary, that provision be made FOR RAISING A FURTHER REVENUE WITHIN YOUR MAJESTY'S DOMINIONS IN AMERICA, *towards defraying the said expences*, we your Majesty's most dutiful and loyal subjects, the COMMONS OF GREAT-BRITAIN, &c. GIVE and GRANT, &c. as before.

The last act, granting duties upon paper, &c. carefully pursues these modern precedents. The preamble is, "Whereas it is expedient THAT A REVENUE SHOULD BE RAISED IN YOUR MAJESTY'S DOMINIONS IN AMERICA, *for making a more certain and adequate provision for defraying the charge of the administration of justice, and the support of civil government in such prov-*

inces, *where it shall be found necessary; and towards the further defraying the expences of defending, protecting and securing the said dominions,* we your Majesty's most dutiful and loyal subjects, the COMMONS OF GREAT-BRITAIN, *&c.* GIVE and GRANT," *&c.* as before.

Here we may observe an authority *expressly* claimed and exerted to impose duties on these colonies; not for the regulation of trade; not for the preservation or promotion of a mutually beneficial intercourse between the several constituent parts of the empire, heretofore the *sole objects* of parliamentary institutions; *but for the single purpose of levying money upon us.*

This I call an innovation; and a most dangerous innovation. It may perhaps be objected, that Great-Britain has a right to lay what duties she pleases upon her exports, and it makes no difference to us, whether they are paid here or there.

To this I answer. These colonies require many things for their use, which the laws of Great-Britain prohibit them from getting any where but from her. Such are paper and glass.

That we may legally be bound to pay any *general* duties on these commodities, relative to the regulation of trade, is granted; but we being *obliged by her laws* to take them from Great-Britain, any *special* duties imposed on their exportation *to us only, with intention to raise a revenue from us only,* are as much *taxes* upon us, as those imposed by the Stamp-Act.

What is the difference in *substance* and *right* whether the same sum is raised upon us by the rates mentioned in the Stamp-Act, on the *use* of paper, or by these duties, on the *importation* of it. It is only the edition of a former book, shifting a sentence from the *end* to the *beginning.*

Suppose the duties were made payable in Great-Britain?

It signifies nothing to us, whether they are to be paid here or there. Had the Stamp-Act directed, that all the paper should be landed at Florida, and the duties paid there, before it was brought to the British colonies, would the act have raised less money upon us, or have been less destructive of our rights? By no means: For as we were under a necessity of using the paper, we should have been under the necessity of paying the duties. Thus, in the present case, a like *necessity* will subject us, if this act continues in force, to the payment of the duties now imposed.

Why was the Stamp-Act then so pernicious to freedom? It did not enact, that every man in the colonies *should* buy a certain quantity of paper—No: It only directed, that no instrument of writing should be valid in law, if not made on stamped paper, &c.

The makers of that act knew full well, that the confusions that would arise from the disuse of writings, would COMPEL the colonies to use the stamped paper, and therefore to pay the taxes imposed. For this reason the Stamp-Act was said to be a law THAT WOULD EXECUTE ITSELF. For the very same reason, the last act of parliament, if it is granted to have any force here, WILL EXECUTE ITSELF, and will be attended with the very same consequences to American liberty.

Some persons perhaps may say, that this act lays us under no necessity to pay the duties imposed, because we may ourselves manufacture the articles on which they are laid; whereas by the Stamp-Act no instrument of writing could be good, unless made on British paper, and that too stamped.

Such an objection amounts to no more than this, that the injury resulting to these colonies, from the total disuse of British paper and glass, will not be so *afflicting* as that which would have resulted from the total disuse of writing among them; for by that means even the Stamp-Act might have been eluded. Why then was it universally detested by them as slavery itself? Because it presented to these devoted provinces nothing but a choice of calamities, imbittered by indignities, each of which it was unworthy of freemen to bear. But is no injury a violation of right but the *greatest* injury? If the eluding the payment of the taxes imposed by the Stamp-Act, would have subjected us to a more dreadful inconvenience, than the eluding the payment of those imposed by the late act; does it therefore follow, that the last is *no violation* of our rights, tho' it is calculated for the same purpose the other was, that is, *to raise money upon us,* WITHOUT OUR CONSENT?

This would be making *right* to consist, not in an exemption from *injury,* but from a certain *degree of injury.*

But the objectors may further say, that we shall suffer no injury at all by the disuse of British paper and glass. We might not, if we could make as much as we want. But can any man, acquainted with America, believe this possible? I am told there are but two or three Glass-Houses on this continent, and but very few Paper-Mills; and suppose more should be erected, a long course of years must elapse, before they can be brought to perfection. This continent is a country of planters, farmers, and fishermen; not of manufacturers. The difficulty of establishing particular manufactures in such a country, is almost insuperable. For one manufacture is connected with others in such a manner, that it may be said to be impossible to establish one or two, without establishing several others. The experience of many nations may convince us of this truth.

Inexpressible therefore must be our distresses in evading the late acts, by the disuse of British paper and glass. Nor will this be the extent of our misfortune, if we admit the legality of that act.

Great-Britain has prohibited the manufacturing iron and steel in these colonies, without any objection being made to her *right* of doing it. The *like* right she must have to prohibit any other manufacture among us. Thus she is possessed of an undisputed *precedent* on that point. This authority, she will say, is founded on the *original intention* of settling these colonies; that is, that she should manufacture for them, and that they should supply her with materials. The *equity* of this policy, she will also say, has been universally acknowledged by the colonies, who never have made the least objections to statutes for that purpose; and will further appear by the *mutual benefits* flowing from this usage ever since the settlement of these colonies.

Our great advocate, Mr. Pitt, in his speeches on the debate concerning the repeal of the Stamp-Act, acknowledged, that Great-Britain could restrain our manufactures. His words are these—"This kingdom, as the supreme governing and legislative power, has ALWAYS bound the colonies by her regulations and RESTRICTIONS in trade, in navigation, in MANUFACTURES—in every thing, *except that of taking their money out of their pockets,* WITHOUT THEIR CONSENT." Again he says, "We may bind their trade, CONFINE THEIR MANUFACTURES, and exercise every power whatever, *except that of taking their money out of their pockets,* WITHOUT THEIR CONSENT."

Here then, my dear countrymen, ROUSE yourselves, and behold the ruin hanging over your heads. If you ONCE admit, that Great-Britain may lay duties upon her exportations to us, *for the purpose of levying money on us only,* she then will have nothing to do, but to lay those duties on the articles which she prohibits us to manufacture—and the tragedy of American liberty is finished. We have been prohibited from procuring manufactures, in all cases, any where but from Great-Britain (excepting linens, which we are permitted to import directly from Ireland). We have been prohibited, in some cases, from manufacturing for ourselves; and may be prohibited in others. We are therefore exactly in the situation of a city besieged, which is surrounded by the works of the besiegers in every part *but one.* If *that* is closed up, no step can be taken, *but to surrender at discretion.* If Great-Britain can order us to come to her for necessaries we want, and can order us to pay what taxes she pleases before we take them away, or when we land them here, we are as abject slaves as France and Poland can shew in wooden shoes, and with uncombed hair.

Perhaps the nature of the *necessities* of dependent states, caused by the policy of a governing one, for her own benefit, may be elucidated by a fact mentioned in history. When the

Carthaginians were possessed of the island of Sardinia, they made a decree, that the Sardinians should not raise corn, nor get it any other way than from the Carthaginians. Then, by imposing any duties they would upon it, they drained from the miserable Sardinians any sums they pleased; and whenever that oppressed people made the least movement to assert their liberty, their tyrants starved them to death or submission. This may be called the most perfect kind of political necessity.

From what has been said, I think this uncontrovertible conclusion may be deduced, that when a ruling state obliges a dependent state to take certain commodities from her alone, it is implied in the nature of that obligation; is essentially requisite to give it the least degree of justice; and is inseparably united with it, in order to preserve any share of freedom to the dependent state; *that those commodities should never be loaded with duties,* FOR THE SOLE PURPOSE OF LEVYING MONEY ON THE DEPENDENT STATE.

Upon the whole, the single question is, whether the parliament can legally impose duties to be paid *by the people of these colonies only,* FOR THE SOLE PURPOSE OF RAISING A REVENUE, *on commodities which she obliges us to take from her alone,* or, in other words, whether the parliament can legally take money out of our pockets, without our consent. If they can, our boasted liberty is but

> *Vox et præterea nihil.*
> A sound and nothing else.

LETTER IV.

An objection, I hear, has been made against my second letter, which I would willingly clear up before I proceed. "There is," say these objectors, "a material difference between the Stamp-Act and the late Act for laying a duty on paper, &c. that justifies the conduct of those who opposed the former, and yet are willing to submit to the latter. The duties imposed by the

Stamp-Act were *internal* taxes; but the present are *external,* and therefore the parliament may have a right to impose them."

To this I answer, with a total denial of the power of parliament to lay upon these colonies any *"tax"* whatever.

This point, being so important to this, and to succeeding generations, I wish to be clearly understood.

To the word *"tax,"* I annex that meaning which the constitution and history of England require to be annexed to it; that is—that it is *an imposition on the subject, for the sole purpose of levying money.*

In the early ages of our monarchy, certain services were rendered to the crown *for the general good.* These were personal: But, in process of time, such institutions being found inconvenient, *gifts* and *grants* of their own property were made by the people, under the several names of aids, tallages, tasks, taxes and subsidies, *&c.* These were made, as may be collected even from the names, *for public service* upon "need and necessity." All these sums were levied upon the people by virtue of their voluntary gift. Their design was to support the *national honor and interest.* Some of those grants comprehended duties arising from trade; being imposts on merchandizes. These Lord Chief Justice Coke classes under "subsidies," and "parliamentary aids." They are also called "customs." But whatever the *name* was, they were always considered as *gifts of the people to the crown, to be employed for public uses.*

Commerce was at a low ebb, and surprizing instances might be produced how little it was attended to for a succession of ages. The terms that have been mentioned, and, among the rest, that of *"tax,"* had obtained a national, parliamentary meaning, drawn from the principles of the constitution, long before any Englishman thought of *imposition of duties, for the regulation of trade.*

Whenever we speak of "taxes" among Englishmen, let us therefore speak of them with reference to the *principles* on which, and the *intentions* with which they have been established. This will give certainty to our expression, and safety to our conduct: But if, when we have in view the liberty of these colonies, we proceed in any other course, we pursue a Juno indeed, but shall only catch a cloud.

In the national, parliamentary sense insisted on, the word "tax" was certainly understood by the congress at New-York, whose resolves may be said to form the American "bill of rights."

The third, fourth, fifth, and sixth resolves, are thus expressed.

III. "That it is *inseparably essential to the freedom of a people,* and the *undoubted right* of *Englishmen,* that NO TAX be imposed on them, *but with their own consent,* given personally, or by their representatives."

IV. "That the people of the colonies are not, and from their local circumstances, cannot be represented in the house of commons in Great-Britain."

V. "That the only representatives of the people of the colonies, are the persons chosen therein by themselves; and that NO TAXES ever have been, or can be constitutionally imposed on them, but by their respective legislatures."

VI. "That all *supplies to the crown,* being free gifts of the people, it is *unreasonable, and inconsistent with the principles and spirit of the* British *constitution,* for the people of Great-Britain to grant to his Majesty *the property of the colonies.*"

Here is no distinction made between *internal* and *external* taxes. It is evident from the short reasoning thrown into these resolves, that every imposition "to grant to his Majesty *the property of the colonies,*" was thought a "tax;" and that every such imposition, if laid any other way than "with their consent, given personally, or by their representatives," was not only "unreasonable, and inconsistent with the principles and spirit of the British constitution," but destructive "to the freedom of a people."

This language is clear and important. A "TAX" means an imposition to raise money. Such persons therefore as speak of *internal* and *external* "TAXES," I pray may pardon me, if I object to that expression, as applied to the privileges and interests of these colonies. There may be *internal* and *external* IMPOSITIONS, founded on *different principles,* and having *different tendencies;* every "tax" being an imposition, tho' every imposition is not a "tax." But *all taxes* are founded on the *same principles;* and have the *same tendency.*

External impositions, for the regulation of our trade, do not "grant to his Majesty *the property of the colonies.*" They only *prevent the colonies acquiring property,* in things not necessary, in a manner judged to be injurious to the welfare of the whole empire. But the last statute respecting us, "grants to his Majesty *the property of the colonies,*" by laying duties on the manufactures of Great-Britain which they MUST take, and which she settled them, on purpose that they SHOULD take.

What *tax* can be more *internal* than this? Here is money drawn, *without their consent,* from a society, who have constantly enjoyed a constitutional mode of raising all money among themselves. The payment of this *tax* they have no possible method of avoiding; as they cannot do without the commodities on which it is laid, and they cannot manufacture these commodities themselves. Besides, if this unhappy country should be so lucky as to elude this act, by getting parchment enough, in the place of paper, or by reviving the antient method of writing on wax and bark, and by inventing something to serve instead of glass, her ingenuity would stand her in little stead; for then the parliament would have nothing to do but to prohibit such manufactures, or to lay a tax on *hats* and *woollen cloths,* which they have already prohibited the colonies *from supplying each other with;* or on instruments, and tools of *steel* and *iron,* which they have prohibited the provincials *from manufacturing at all:* And then, what little gold and silver they have, must be torn from their hands, or they will not be able, in a short time, to get an ax, for cutting their firewood, nor a plough, for raising their food. In what respect, therefore, I beg leave to ask, is the late act preferable to the Stamp-Act, or more consistent with the liberties of the colonies? For my own part, I regard them both with equal apprehensions; and think they ought to be in the same manner opposed.

Habemus quidem senatus consultum,—tanquam gladium in vagina repositum.

We have a statute, laid up for future use, like a sword in the scabbard.

LETTER VI.

It may perhaps be objected against the arguments that have been offered to the public, concerning the legal power of the parliament, "that it has always exercised the power of imposing duties, for the purposes of raising a revenue on the productions of these colonies carried to Great-Britain, which may be called a tax on them." To this objection I answer, that this is no violation of the rights of the colonies, it being implied in the relation between them and Great-Britain, that they should not carry such commodities to other nations, as should enable them to interfere with the mother country. The imposition of duties on these commodities, when brought to her, is only a consequence of her parental right; and if the point is thoroughly examined, the duties will be found to be laid on the people of the mother country. Whatever they are, they must proportionably raise the price of the goods, and consequently must be paid by the consumers. In this light they were considered by the parliament in the 25th Charles II. Chap. 7, Sect. 2, which says, that the productions of the plantations were carried from one to another free from all customs, "while the subjects of this your kingdom of *England* have paid *great customs and impositions for what of them have been* SPENT HERE," *&c.*

Besides, if Great-Britain exports these commodities again, the duties will injure her own trade, so that she cannot hurt us, without plainly and immediately hurting herself; and this is our check against her acting arbitrarily in this respect.

It may be perhaps further objected, "that it being granted that statutes made for regulating trade, are binding upon us, it will be difficult for any person, but the makers of the laws, to determine, which of them are made for the regulating of trade, and which for raising a revenue; and that from hence may arise confusion."

To this I answer, that the objection is of no force in the present case, or such as resemble it; because the act now in question, is formed *expressly* FOR THE SOLE PURPOSE OF RAISING A REVENUE.

However, supposing the design of parliament had not been *expressed*, the objection seems to me of no weight, with regard to the influence which those who may make it, might expect it ought to have on the conduct of these colonies.

It is true, that *impositions for raising a revenue,* may be hereafter called *regulations of trade:* But names will not change the nature of things. Indeed we ought firmly to believe, what is an undoubted truth, confirmed by the unhappy experience of many states heretofore free, that UNLESS THE MOST WATCHFUL ATTENTION BE EXERTED, A NEW SERVITUDE MAY BE SLIPPED UPON US, UNDER THE SANCTION OF USUAL AND RESPECTABLE TERMS.

Thus the Cæsars ruined the Roman liberty, under the titles of *tribunical* and *dictatorial* authorities, old and venerable dignities, known in the most flourishing times of freedom. In imitation of the same policy, James II. when he *meant* to establish popery, *talked* of liberty of conscience, the most sacred of all liberties; and had thereby almost deceived the Dissenters into destruction.

All artful rulers, who strive to extend their power beyond its just limits, endeavor to give to their attempts as much semblance of legality as possible. Those who succeed them may venture to go a little further; for each new encroachment will be strengthened by a former. "That which is now supported by examples, growing old, will become an example itself," and thus support fresh usurpations.

A free people therefore can never be too quick in observing, nor too firm in opposing the beginnings of *alteration* either in *form* or *reality*, respecting institutions formed for their security. The first kind of alteration leads to the last: Yet, on the other hand, nothing is more certain, than that the *forms* of liberty may be retained, when the *substance* is gone. In government, as well as in religion, "The *letter* killeth, but the *spirit* giveth life."

I will beg leave to enforce this remark by a few instances. The crown, by the constitution, has the prerogative of creating peers. The existence of that order, in due number and dignity, is essential to the constitution; and if the crown did not exercise that prerogative, the peerage must have long since decreased so much as to have lost its proper influence. Suppose a prince, for some unjust purposes, should, from time to time, advance so many needy, profligate wretches to that rank, that all the independence of the house of lords should be destroyed; there would then be a manifest violation of the constitution, *under the appearance of using legal prerogative.*

The house of commons claims the privilege of forming all money bills, and will not suffer either of the other branches of the legislature to add to, or alter them; contending that their power simply extends to an acceptance or rejection of them. This privilege appears to be just: but under pretence of this just privilege, the house of commons has claimed a licence of tacking to money bills, clauses relating to things of a totally different kind, and thus forcing them in a manner on the king and lords. This seems to be an abuse of that privilege, and it may be vastly more abused. Suppose a future house, influenced by some displaced, discontented demagogues—in a time of danger, should tack to a money bill, something so injurious to the king and peers, that they would not assent to it, and yet the commons should obstinately insist on it; the whole kingdom would be exposed to ruin by them, *under the appearance of maintaining a valuable privilege.*

In these cases it might be difficult for a while to determine, whether the king intended to exercise his prerogative in a constitutional manner or not; or whether the commons insisted on their demand factiously, or for the public good: But surely the conduct of the crown or of the house, would in time sufficiently explain itself.

Ought not the PEOPLE therefore to watch? to observe facts? to search into causes? to investigate designs? And have they not a right of JUDGING from the evidence before them, on no slighter points than their *liberty* and *happiness?* It would be less than trifling, wherever a British government is established, to make use of any arguments to prove such a right. It is sufficient to remind the reader of the day, on the anniversary of which the first of these letters is dated.

I will now apply what has been said to the present question.

The *nature* of any impositions laid by parliament on these colonies, must determine the *design* in laying them. It may not be easy in every instance to discover that design. Wherever it is doubtful, I think submission cannot be dangerous; nay, it must be right; for, in my opinion, there is no privilege these colonies claim, which they ought in *duty* and *prudence* more earnestly to maintain and defend, than the authority of the British parliament to regulate the trade of all her dominions. Without this authority, the benefits she enjoys from our commerce, must be lost to her: The blessings we enjoy from our dependence upon her, must be lost to us. Her strength must decay; her glory vanish; and she cannot suffer without our partaking in her misfortune. *Let us therefore cherish her interests as our own, and give her every thing, that it becomes* FREEMEN *to give or to receive.*

The *nature* of any impositions she may lay upon us may, in general, be known, by considering how far they relate to the preserving, in due order, the connection between the several parts of the British empire. One thing we may be assured of, which is this—Whenever she imposes duties on commodities, to be paid only upon their exportation from Great-Britain to these colonies, it is not a regulation of trade, but a design to raise a revenue upon us. Other instances may happen, which it may not be necessary at present to dwell on. I hope these colonies will never, to their latest existence, want understanding sufficient to discover the intentions of those who rule over them, nor the resolution necessary for asserting their interests. They will always have the same rights, that all free states have, of judging when their privileges are invaded, and of using all prudent measures for preserving them.

> *Quocirca vivite fortes,*
> *Fortiaque adversis opponite pectora rebus.*
> Wherefore keep up your spirits, and gallantly oppose this
> adverse course of affairs.

LETTER IX.

I have made some observations on the PURPOSES for which money is to be levied upon us by the late act of parliament. I shall now offer to your consideration some further reflections on that subject: And, unless I am greatly mistaken, if these purposes are accomplished according to the *expressed* intention of the act, they will be found effectually to *supersede* that authority in our respective assemblies, which is essential to liberty. The question is not, whether some branches shall be lopt off—The axe is laid to the root of the tree; and the whole body must infallibly perish, if we remain idle spectators of the work.

No free people ever existed, or can ever exist, without keeping, to use a common, but strong expression, "the purse strings," in their own hands. Where this is the case, *they* have a *constitutional check* upon the administration, which may thereby be brought into order *without violence:* But where such a power is not lodged in the *people,* oppression proceeds uncontrouled in its career, till the governed, transported into rage, seek redress in the midst of blood and confusion.

The elegant and ingenious Mr. Hume, speaking of the Anglo Norman government, says—"Princes and Ministers were too ignorant, to be themselves sensible of the advantage attending an equitable administration, and there was no established council or *assembly,* WHICH COULD PROTECT THE PEOPLE, and BY WITHDRAWING SUPPLIES, regularly and PEACEABLY admonish the king of his duty, and ENSURE THE EXECUTION OF THE LAWS."

Thus this great man, whose political reflections are so much admired, makes *this power* one of the foundations of liberty.

The English history abounds with instances, proving that *this* is the proper and successful way to obtain redress of grievances. How often have kings and ministers endeavoured to throw off this legal curb upon them, by attempting to raise money by a variety of inventions, under pretence of law, without having recourse to parliament? And how often have they been brought to reason, and peaceably obliged to do justice, by the exertion of this constitutional authority of the people, vested in their representatives?

The inhabitants of these colonies have, on numberless occasions, reaped the benefit of this authority *lodged in their assemblies.*

It has been for a long time, and now is, a constant instruction to all governors, *to obtain a* PERMANENT *support for the offices of government.* But as the author of "the administration of the colonies" says, "this order of the crown is generally, if not universally, rejected by the legislatures of the colonies."

They perfectly know *how much* their grievances would be regarded, if they had *no other* method of engaging attention, than by *complaining.* Those who rule, are extremely apt to think well of the constructions made by themselves in support of their own power. *These* are frequently erroneous, and pernicious to those they govern. Dry remonstrances, to shew that such constructions are wrong and oppressive, carry very little weight with them, in the opinions of persons who gratify their own inclinations in making these constructions. *They* CANNOT understand the reasoning that opposes *their* power and desires. But let it be made *their interest* to understand such reasoning—and a *wonderful light* is instantly thrown upon the matter; and then, rejected remonstrances become as clear as "proofs of holy writ."

The three most important articles that our assemblies, or any legislatures can provide for, are, First—the defence of the society: Secondly—the administration of justice: And thirdly—the support of civil government.

Nothing can properly regulate the expence of making provision for these occasions, but the *necessities* of the society; its *abilities;* the *conveniency* of the modes of levying money in it; the *manner* in which the laws have been executed; and the *conduct* of the officers of government: *All which* are circumstances, that *cannot* possibly be properly *known,* but by the society itself; or if they should be known, *will not* probably be properly *considered* but by that society.

If money be raised upon us by *others,* without our consent, for our "defence," those who are the judges in *levying* it, must also be the judges in *applying* it. Of consequence the money *said* to be taken from us for our defence, *may be employed* to our injury. We may be chained in by a line of fortifications—obliged to pay for the building and maintaining them—and be told, that they are for our defence. With what face can we dispute the fact, after having granted that those who *apply* the money, had a right to *levy* it? For surely, it is much easier for their wisdom to understand how to apply it in the best manner, than how to levy it in the best manner. Besides, the *right of levying* is of infinitely more consequence, than *that of applying.* The people of England, who would burst out into fury, if the crown should attempt to *levy* money by its own authority, have always assigned to the crown the *application* of money.

As to "the administration of justice"—the judges ought, in a well regulated state, to be equally independent of the executive and legislative powers. Thus in England, judges hold their commissions from the crown *"during good behaviour,"* and have salaries, suitable to their dignity, *settled* on them by parliament. The purity of the courts of law since this establishment, is a proof of the wisdom with which it was made.

But in these colonies, how fruitless has been every attempt to have the judges appointed *"during good behaviour?"* Yet whoever considers the matter will soon perceive, that *such commissions* are beyond all comparison more necessary in these colonies, than they were in England.

The chief danger to the subject *there,* arose from the arbitrary *designs of the crown;* but *here,* the time may come, when we may have to contend with the *designs of the crown, and of a mighty kingdom.* What then must be our chance, when the laws of life and death are to be spoken by judges totally dependent on *that crown,* and *that kingdom*—sent over perhaps *from thence*—filled with *British prejudices*—and *backed by a* STANDING *army*—supported out of OUR OWN pockets, to "assert and maintain" OUR OWN "dependence and obedience."

But supposing that through the extreme lenity that will prevail in the government *through all future ages,* these colonies will never behold any thing like the campaign of chief justice Jeffereys, yet what innumerable acts of injustice may be committed, and how fatally may the principles of liberty be sapped, by a succession of judges *utterly independent of the people?* Before such judges the supple wretches, who cheerfully join in avowing sentiments inconsistent with freedom, will always meet with smiles; while the honest and brave men, who disdain to sacrifice their native land to their own advantage, but on every occasion boldly vindicate her cause, will constantly be regarded with frowns.

There are two other considerations relating to this head, that deserve the most serious attention.

By the late act, the officers of the customs are "impowered to enter into any HOUSE, warehouse, shop, cellar, or other place, in the British colonies or plantations in America, to search for or seize prohibited or unaccustomed [uncustomed] goods," &c. on "writs granted by the superior or supreme court of justice, having jurisdiction within such colony or plantation respectively."

If we only reflect that the judges of these courts are to be *during pleasure*—that they are to have *"adequate provision"* made for them, which is to continue *during their complaisant behaviour*—that they may be *strangers* to these colonies— what an engine of oppression may this authority be in such hands?

I am well aware, that writs of this kind may be granted at home, under the seal of the court of exchequer: But I know also, that the greatest asserters of the rights of Englishmen have always strenuously contended, that *such a power* was dangerous to freedom, and expressly contrary to the common law, which ever regarded a man's *house* as his castle, or a place of perfect security.

If such power was in the least degree dangerous *there*, it must be utterly destructive to liberty *here*. For the people there have two securities against the undue exercise of this power by the crown, which are wanting with us, if the late act takes place. In the first place, if any injustice is done *there*, the person injured may bring his action against the offender, and have it tried before INDEPENDENT JUDGES, who are NO PARTIES IN COMMITTING THE INJURY. *Here* he must have it tried before DEPENDENT JUDGES, being the men WHO GRANTED THE WRIT.

To say, that the cause is to be tried by a jury, can never reconcile men who have any idea of freedom, to *such a power*. For we know that sheriffs in almost every colony on this continent, are totally dependent on the crown; and packing of juries has been frequently practised even in the capital of the British empire. Even if juries are well inclined, we have too many instances of the influence of over-bearing unjust judges upon them. The brave and wise men who accomplished the revolution, thought the *independency of judges* essential to freedom.

The other security which the people have at home, but which we shall want here, is this.

If this power is abused *there,* the parliament, the grand resource of the oppressed people, is ready to afford relief. Redress of grievances must precede grants of money. But what regard can *we* expect to have paid to our assemblies, when they will not hold even the puny privilege of French parliaments—that of registering, before they are put in execution, the edicts that take away our money.

The second consideration above hinted at, is this. There is a *confusion* in our laws, that is quite unknown in Great-Britain. As this cannot be described in a more clear or exact manner, than has been done by the ingenious author of the history of New-York, I beg leave to use his words. "The state of our laws opens a door to much controversy. The *uncertainty,* with respect to them, RENDERS PROPERTY PRECARIOUS, and GREATLY EXPOSES US TO THE ARBITRARY DECISION OF BAD JUDGES. The common law of England is generally received, together with such statutes as were enacted before we had a legislature of our own; but our courts EXERCISE A SOVEREIGN AUTHORITY, in determining *what parts of the common and statute law* ought to be extended: For it must be admitted, that the *difference of circumstances* necessarily requires us, in some cases *to* REJECT *the determination of both.* In many instances, they have also extended even acts of parliament, passed since we had a distinct legislature, *which is greatly adding to our confusion.* The practice of our courts is no less *uncertain* than the law. Some of the English rules are adopted, others rejected. Two things therefore seem to be ABSOLUTELY NECESSARY for the PUBLIC SECURITY. First, the passing an act for settling the extent of the English laws. Secondly, that the courts ordain a general sett of rules for the regulation of the practice."

How easy it will be, under this "state of our laws," for an

artful judge, to act in the most arbitrary manner, and yet cover his conduct under specious pretences; and how difficult it will be for the injured people to obtain relief, may be readily perceived. We may take a voyage of 3000 miles to complain; and after the trouble and hazard we have undergone, we may be told, that the collection of the revenue, and maintenance of the prerogative, must not be discouraged—and if the misbehavior is so gross as to admit of no justification, it may be said, that it was an error in judgment only, arising from the confusion of our laws, and the zeal of the King's servants to do their duty.

If the commissions of judges are *during the pleasure of the crown,* yet if their salaries are *during the pleasure of the people,* there will be *some check* upon their conduct. Few men will consent to draw on themselves the hatred and contempt of those among whom they live, for the empty honor of being judges. It is the sordid love of gain, that tempts men to turn their backs on virtue, and pay their homage where they ought not.

As to the third particular, "the support of civil government,"—few words will be sufficient. Every man of the least understanding must know, that the *executive* power may be exercised in a manner so disagreeable and harassing to the people, that it is absolutely requisite, that *they* should be enabled by the gentlest method which human policy has yet been ingenious enough to invent, that is, *by shutting their hands,* to "ADMONISH" (as Mr. Hume says) certain persons "OF THEIR DUTY."

What shall we now think when, upon looking into the late act, we find the assemblies of these provinces thereby stript of their authority *on these several heads?* The *declared* intention of the act is, "that a revenue should be raised IN HIS MAJ-ESTY's DOMINIONS IN AMERICA, for making a more certain and adequate provision *for defraying the charge of* THE AD-MINISTRATION OF JUSTICE, and *the support of* CIVIL GOVERN-

MENT in such provinces where it shall be found necessary, and *towards further defraying the expences of* DEFENDING, PROTECTING AND SECURING THE SAID DOMINIONS."

Let the reader pause here one moment—and reflect—whether the colony in which *he* lives, has not made such "certain and adequate provision" *for these purposes, as is by the colony judged suitable to its abilities, and all other circumstances.* Then let him reflect—whether if this act takes place, money is not to be raised on *that* colony *without its consent,* to make "provision" *for these purposes,* which *it does not judge to be suitable to its abilities, and all other circumstances.* Lastly, let him reflect—whether the people of that country are not in a state of the most abject slavery, *whose property may be taken from them* under the notion of right, *when they have refused to give it.*

For my part, I think I have good reason for vindicating the honor of the assemblies on this continent, by publicly asserting, that THEY *have made as "certain and adequate provision" for the purposes abovementioned, as they ought to have made,* and that it should not be presumed, that they will not do it hereafter. Why then should *these most important trusts* be wrested out of their hands? Why should they not now be permitted to enjoy that authority, which they have exercised from the first settlement of these colonies? Why should they be scandalized by this innovation, when their respective provinces are now, and will be, for several years, labouring under loads of debt, imposed on them for the very purpose now spoken of? Why should all the inhabitants of these colonies be, with the utmost indignity, treated as a herd of despicable stupid wretches, so utterly void of common sense, that they will not even make "adequate provision" for "the administration of justice, and the support of civil government" among them, or for their own "defence"—though without such "provision" every people must inevitably be overwhelmed with anarchy and destruction? Is it possible to form an idea of a slavery more *compleat,* more *miserable,* more *disgraceful,* than that of a people, where *justice is administered, government exercised,* and a *standing army maintained,* AT THE EXPENCE OF THE PEOPLE, and yet WITHOUT THE LEAST DEPENDENCE UPON THEM? If we can find no relief from this infamous situation, it will be fortunate for us, if Mr. Greenville, setting his fertile fancy again at work, can, as by one exertion of it he has stript us of our *property* and *liberty,* by another deprive us of so much of our *understanding;* that, unconscious of what we *have been* or *are,* and ungoaded by tormenting reflections, we may bow down our necks, with all the stupid serenity of servitude, to any drudgery, which our lords and masters shall please to command.

When the charges of the "administration of justice," the "support of civil government," and the expences of "defending, protecting and securing" us, are provided for, I should be glad to know, upon *what occasions* the crown will ever call our assemblies together. Some few of them may meet of their own accord, by virtue of their charters. But what will they have to do, when they are met? To what shadows will they be reduced? The men, whose deliberations heretofore had an influence on every matter relating to the *liberty* and *happiness* of themselves and their constituents, and whose authority in domestic affairs at least, might well be compared to that of Roman senators, will *now* find their deliberations of no more consequence, than those of *constables.* They may *perhaps* be allowed to make laws *for the yoking of hogs,* or *the pounding of stray cattle.* Their influence will hardly be permitted to extend *so high,* as the *keeping roads in repair,* as *that business* may more properly be executed by those who receive the public cash.

One most memorable example in history is so applicable to the point now insisted on, that it will form a just conclusion of the observations that have been made.

Spain was once *free.* Their Cortes resembled our parliaments. No *money* could be raised on the subject, *without their consent.* One of their Kings having received a grant from them, to maintain a war against the Moors, desired, that if the sum which they had given, should not be sufficient, he might be allowed, *for that emergency only,* to raise more money *without assembling the Cortes.* The request was violently opposed by the best and wisest men in the assembly. It was, however, complied with by the votes of a majority; and this single concession was a PRECEDENT for other concessions of the like kind, until at last the crown obtained a general power of raising money, in cases of necessity. From that period the Cortes ceased to be *useful,*—the *people* ceased to be *free.*

> *Venienti occurite morbo.*
> Oppose a disease at its beginning.

LETTER X.

The consequences, mentioned in the last letter, will not be the utmost limits of our *misery* and *infamy,* if the late act is acknowledged to be binding upon us. We feel too sensibly, that *any ministerial measures* relating to these colonies, are soon carried successfully through the parliament. Certain prejudices operate there so strongly against us, that it may be justly questioned, whether *all* the provinces united, will ever be able effectually to call to an account before the parliament, any minister who shall abuse the power by the late act given to the crown in America. He may divide the spoils torn from us in what manner he pleases, *and we shall have no way of making him responsible.* If he should order, that every *governor* shall have a yearly salary of 5000 l. sterling; every *chief justice* of 3000 l.; every inferior officer in proportion; and should then reward the most profligate, ignorant, or needy dependents on himself or his friends, with places of the greatest trust, because they were of the greatest profit, this would be called an arrangement in consequence of the "adequate provision for defraying the charge of the administration of justice, and the support of the civil government:" And if the taxes should prove at any time insufficient to answer all the expences of the numberless offices, which ministers may please to create, surely the members of the house of commons will be so *"modest,"* as not to "contradict a minister" who shall tell them, it is become necessary to lay a new tax upon the colonies, for the laudable purposes of defraying the charges of the "administration of justice, and support of civil government," among them. Thus, in fact, we shall be taxed by ministers. In short, it will be in their power to settle upon us any CIVIL, ECCLESIASTICAL, or MILITARY establishment, which they choose.

We may perceive, by the example of Ireland, how eager ministers are to seize upon any settled revenue, and apply it in supporting their own power. Happy are the men, and *happy the people who grow wise by the misfortunes of others.* Earnestly, my dear countrymen, do I beseech the author of all good gifts, that you may grow wise in this manner; and if I may be allowed to take such a liberty, I beg leave to recommend to you in general, as the best method of attaining this wisdom, diligently to study the histories of other countries. You will there find all the arts, that can possibly be practiced by cunning rulers, or false patriots among yourselves, so fully delineated, that, changing names, the account would serve for your own times.

It is pretty well known on this continent, that Ireland has, with a regular consistency of injustice, been cruelly treated by ministers in the article of *pensions;* but there are some alarming circumstances relating to that subject, which I wish to have better known among us.

The revenue of the crown there arises principally from the Excise granted *"for pay of the army and defraying other* PUBLIC *charges, in defence and preservation of the kingdom"*—from the tonnage and additional poundage granted *"for protecting the trade of the kingdom at sea, and augmenting the* PUBLIC *revenue"*—from the hearth money granted—as a "PUB-

LIC *revenue, for a* PUBLIC *charge and expences.*" There are some other branches of the revenue, concerning which there is not any *express* appropriation of them for PUBLIC *service,* but which were plainly *so intended.*

Of *these* branches of the revenue the crown is only *trustee* for the public. They are unalienable. They are inapplicable to any other purposes, but those for which they were established; and therefore are not *legally* chargeable with pensions.

There is another kind of revenue, which is a private revenue. This is not limited to any public uses; but the crown has the same property in it, that any person has in his estate. This does not amount, at the most, to Fifteen Thousand Pounds a year, probably not to Seven, and is the only revenue, that can be *legally* charged with pensions.

If ministers were accustomed to regard the rights or happiness of the people, the pensions in Ireland would not exceed the sum just mentioned: But long since have they exceeded that limit; and in December 1765, a motion was made in the house of commons in that kingdom, to address his Majesty on the great increase of pensions on the Irish establishment, amounting to the sum of 158,685 l.—in the last two years.

Attempts have been made to gloss over these gross encroachments, by this specious argument—"That expending a competent part of the PUBLIC REVENUE in pensions, from a principle of charity or generosity, adds to the dignity of the crown; and is *therefore* useful to the PUBLIC." To give this argument any weight, it must appear, that the pensions proceed from "*charity or generosity* only"—and that it "adds to the dignity of the crown," *to act directly contrary to law.*

From this conduct towards Ireland, in open violation of law, we may easily foresee what *we* may expect, when a minister will have the *whole revenue* of America in his own hands, to be disposed of at his own pleasure: For *all* the monies raised by the late act are to be "*applied* by virtue of warrants under the sign manual, countersigned by the high treasurer, or any three of the commissioners of the treasury." The "RESIDUE" indeed is to be "paid into the receipt of the exchequer, and to be disposed of by parliament." So that a minister will have nothing to do, but to take care, that there shall be no "residue," and he is superior to all controul.

Besides the burden of *pensions* in Ireland, which have enormously encreased within these few years, almost all the *offices* in that poor kingdom, have been, since the commencement of the present century, and now are bestowed upon *strangers*. For tho' the merit of persons born there, justly raises them to places of high trust when they go abroad, as all Europe can witness, yet he is an uncommonly lucky Irishman, who can get a good post *in his* NATIVE *country*.

When I consider the manner in which that island has been uniformly depressed for so many years past, with this pernicious particularity *of their parliament continuing as long as the crown pleases,* I am astonished to observe *such a love of liberty* still animating that LOYAL and GENEROUS nation; and nothing can raise higher my idea of the INTEGRITY and PUBLIC SPIRIT of a people, who have preserved the sacred fire of freedom from being extinguished, tho' the altar on which it burnt, has been overturned.

In the same manner shall we unquestionably be treated, as soon as the late taxes laid upon us, shall make posts in the "government," and the "administration of justice" *here,* worth the attention of persons of influence in Great-Britain. We know enough already to satisfy us of this truth. But this will not be the worst part of our case.

The *principals,* in all great offices, will reside in England, making some paltry allowance to deputies for doing the business *here.* Let any man consider what an exhausting drain this must be upon us, when ministers are possessed of the power of creating what posts they please, and of affixing to such posts what salaries they please, and he must be convinced how destructive the late act will be. The injured king-

dom lately mentioned, can tell us the mischiefs of ABSENTEES;
and we may perceive already the same disposition taking
place with us. The government of New-York has been exercised by a deputy. That of Virginia is now held so; and we
know of a number of secretary-ships, collector-ships, and other
offices, held in the same manner.

True it is, that if the people of Great-Britain were not too
much blinded by the passions, that have been artfully excited
in their breasts, against their dutiful children the colonists,
these considerations would be nearly as alarming to them as
to us. The influence of the crown was thought by wise men,
many years ago, too great by reason of the multitude of pensions and places bestowed by it. These have been vastly encreased since, and perhaps it would be no difficult matter to
prove that the people have decreased.

Surely therefore, those who wish the welfare of their country,
ought seriously to reflect, what may be the consequence of
such a new creation of offices, in the disposal of the crown. The
army, the *administration of justice,* and the *civil government*
here, with such salaries as the crown shall please to annex, will
extend *ministerial influence* as much beyond its former bounds,
as the late war did the British dominions.

But whatever the people of Great-Britain may think on this
occasion, I hope the people of these colonies will unanimously
join in this sentiment, that the late act of parliament is injurious to their liberty, and that this sentiment will unite them in
a firm opposition to it, in the same manner as the dread of the
Stamp-Act did.

Some persons may imagine the sums to be raised by it, are
but small, and therefore may be inclined to acquiesce under
it. A conduct more dangerous to freedom, as before has been
observed, can never be adopted. Nothing is wanted at home
but a PRECEDENT, the force of which shall be established, by
the tacit submission of the colonies. With what zeal was the
statute erecting the post-office, and another relating to the recovery of debts in America, urged and tortured, as *precedents*

in support of the Stamp-Act, tho' wholly inapplicable. If the parliament succeeds in this attempt, other statutes will impose other duties. Instead of taxing ourselves, as we have been accustomed to do, from the first settlement of these provinces, all our usual taxes will be converted into parliamentary taxes on our importations; and thus the parliament will levy upon us such sums of money as they chuse to take, *without any other* LIMITATION, *than their* PLEASURE.

We know how much labor and care have been bestowed by these colonies, in laying taxes in such a manner, that they should be most *easy* to the people, by being laid on the proper articles; most *equal*, by being proportioned to every man's circumstances; and *cheapest*, by the method directing for collecting them.

But *parliamentary taxes* will be laid on us, without any consideration, whether there is any *easier* mode. The *only point* regarded will be, the *certainty of levying the taxes,* and not the *convenience* of the people on whom they are to be levied; and therefore all statutes on this head will be such as will be most likely, according to the favorite phrase, "*to execute themselves.*"

Taxes in every free state have been, and ought to be, as exactly *proportioned as is possible to the abilities of those who are to pay them.* They cannot otherwise be *just.* Even a Hottentot would comprehend the *unreasonableness* of making a poor man pay as much for "defending" the property of a rich man, as the rich man pays himself.

Let any person look into the late act of parliament, and he will immediately perceive, that the immense estates of Lord Fairfax, Lord Baltimore, and our Proprietaries, which are amongst his Majesty's other "DOMINIONS" to be "defended, protected and secured" by the act, will not pay a *single farthing* for the duties thereby imposed, except Lord Fairfax wants some of his windows glazed; Lord Baltimore and our Proprietaries are quite secure, as they live in England.

I mention these particular cases, as striking instances how

far the late act is a deviation from *that principle of justice,* which has so constantly distinguished our own laws on this continent, and ought to be regarded in all laws.

The third consideration with our continental assemblies in laying taxes, has been the *method* of collecting them. This has been done by a few officers, with moderate allowances, under the inspection of the respective assemblies. *No more was raised from the subject,* than was used for the intended purposes. But by the late act, a minister may appoint *as many officers as he pleases* for collecting the taxes; may assign them *what salaries he thinks* "adequate;" and they are subject to *no inspection but his own.*

In short, if the late act of parliament takes effect, these colonies must dwindle down into "COMMON CORPORATIONS," as their enemies, in the debates concerning the repeal of the Stamp-Act, *strenuously insisted they were;* and it seems not improbable that some future historian may thus record our fall.

"The eighth year of this reign was distinguished by *a very memorable event,* the American colonies then submitting, for the *FIRST* time, to be *taxed* by the British parliament. An attempt of this kind had been made about two years before, but was defeated by the vigorous exertions of the several provinces, in defence of their liberty. Their behavior on that occasion rendered their name very celebrated *for a short time* all over Europe; all states being extremely attentive to a dispute between Great-Britain, and so considerable a part of her dominions. For as she was thought to be grown too powerful, by the successful conclusion of the late war she had been engaged in, it was hoped by many, that as it had happened before to other kingdoms, civil discords would afford opportunities of revenging all the injuries supposed to be received from her. However, the cause of dissention was removed, by a repeal of the statute that had given offence. This affair rendered the SUBMISSIVE CONDUCT of the colonies so soon after, the more extraordinary; there being *no difference* between the mode of taxation which they opposed, and that to which they submitted, but this, that by the first, they were to be continually *reminded* that they *were taxed,* by certain marks *stamped* on every piece of paper or parchment they used. The authors of *that statute* triumphed greatly on this conduct of the colonies, and insisted, that if the people of Great-Britain had persisted in enforcing it, the Americans would have been, in a few months, *so fatigued with the efforts of patriotism,* that they would have yielded obedience.

"Certain it is, that tho' they had before their eyes *so many illustrious examples* in their mother country, of *the constant success* attending *firmness* and *perseverance,* in opposition to dangerous encroachments on liberty, yet they quietly gave up a point of the LAST IMPORTANCE. From thence the decline of their freedom began, and its decay was extremely rapid; for as *money* was always raised upon them by the parliament, their *assemblies* grew immediately *useless,* and in a short time *contemptible:* And in less than one hundred years, the people sunk down into that *tameness* and *supineness* of spirit, by which they still continue to be distinguished."

> *Et majores vestros & posteros cogitate.*
> Remember your ancestors and your posterity.

· 9 ·

The Nature and Extent of Parliamentary
Power Considered (1768)

By William Hicks

The essays printed in this pamphlet appeared in the *Pennsylvania Journal* between January 21 and February 25, 1768, and in whole or in part in the *Boston Gazette* on February 15 and 22, the *Boston Evening Post* between February 15 and March 21, and in Peter Timothy's *South Carolina Gazette* between March 28 and April 11. John Holt in New York and William and Thomas Bradford in Philadelphia published the essays as pamphlets (in somewhat differing form) in 1768.

The full title of the New York edition is *The Nature and Extent Of Parliamentary Power Considered, In some Remarks upon Mr. Pitt's Speech in the House of Commons, previous to the Repeal of the Stamp-Act, With an Introduction. Applicable to the present situation of the Colonies.* It was signed "A Citizen." Omitted here are the portion of the essays in which Hicks argues that the British demand that the colonies obey the Quartering Act is an attempt to

New York, 1768, pp. 2–3, 18–40.

implement the Declaratory Act, his account of the origins of English liberties, and the like.

In reprinting this pamphlet all the italics except those clearly used for emphasis have been omitted, and capitalization has been modernized.

ADVERTISEMENT
TO THE PRINTER.

Any considerations upon the nature of our present political situation, will appear impertinent and ill-timed, while we have a writer so capable and so anxious to support the liberties of his country; but since information cannot be so effectually communicated, as by placing the same object in a variety of lights, the essay which you are now requested to convey to the world, through the channel of your press, may have its use. The patriot Farmer has, with great judgment and precision, applied his observations to those important particulars which have lately occurred. The author of the present performance has endeavoured to support the interests of the colonies, by reasons drawn from general principles; and, if he can but be so happy as to cooperate with his worthy predecessor in correcting the prejudiced, and informing the ignorant, he will have the satisfaction of thinking that he has discharged the duty of
A CITIZEN.

INTRODUCTION

The following piece was written but a short time before the repeal of the Stamp-Act; and as the subject of it was the most general and important nature, the trifling alteration of circumstances which a few months have produced, cannot prevent it's being as applicable to the present state of our affairs, as to those disagreeable controversies, in which we have been heretofore unhappily involved. The conciliating spirit which prevailed upon the first intelligence of the Stamp-Act's being repealed, prevented its publication then; though the author was ever perfectly convinced, the colonies would not long have any reason to flatter themselves, that the repeal of this act was a sacrifice of liberty; or that it proceeded from any thing more than an apprehension of the ill consequences which our brethren of Britain must have felt from the oeconomical resolutions which we had formed. Upon examining the debates, previous to the repeal, if any one could have doubted the sense of the legislature, the act for securing the dependence of the colonies, would have reduced it to a sufficient degree of certainty. Indeed, if this act had been more equivocal, the billeting act was explicit enough to have pointed out clearly to every common understanding, their *generous meaning*—— A meaning evidenced by such measures as could not but excite the most alarming apprehensions. . . .

IV. *"Those laws therefore that I call scripta Leges, or such as are usually called statute laws, which are originally reduced into writing, before they are enacted, or receive any binding power; every such law being formally made, is as it were, an INDENTURE TRIPARTITE, between the King, the Lords, and the Commons; for without the concurrent consent of all these three parts no such law is or can be made."*
                                                    Hale's Hist. of the Common Law.

It seems to me the distinguishing characteristic of the English constitution, that no free man shall be restrained in the exercise of his natural liberty, or, in the use of his acquired property but by those regulations to which he has *really* or *virtually* subscribed. Laws which are the result of such a rational and well-digested compact, may bear hard upon some, but they cannot, with propriety, be complained of by any; since every precaution which the wit of man could devise, was necessarily employed for the benefit of the whole united body, after a due attention to the separate interest of each.

The Lords and Commons with the approbation of the Crown, agree to regulate their trade by well placed restrictions, and settle the establishment of their manufactures in such a manner as shall be most conducive to the public good. In all these disposing and restraining laws, the interest of the whole community is consulted, and spirit of the constitution preserved inviolate.

But when the Lords and Commons of England, by *formal compact* with the Crown, attempt to bind those, who can by no means be considered as parties to their agreement, they discard those noble principles to which they owe the enjoyment of all that is valuable in life, and introduce power in the place of reason to support a system which has its foundation in partial, not in universal good. For, can any thing be more evidently partial, or more inconsistent with the principles of common justice, than that the Lords and Commons of England should *give* and *grant* to his Majesty any sum which they may think proper, to be levied, by any mode which they may be pleased to devise, upon his American subjects— perhaps for the payment of a subsidy to some Prince of the Empire for the defence of his Majesty's electoral dominions? If the absurdity and injustice of such a procedure is to be discovered by every eye, we shall not be long before we clearly perceive, through all the mists of ingenious sophistry, that, upon the indispensible principles of their own constitution, the Lords and Commons of England can no more *covenant* with the Crown for the limitting and restraining our natural liberty, than they can *agree* to *give* and *grant* the most valuable of our property to be disposed of for their own private purposes.

The more I consider this maxim, which I have taken from my Lord C[hief] Justice Hale, the more sensible am I of its weight and importance. To perceive its full force, it will be necessary to look back to the first dawn of freedom, when the good people of England, would no longer submit to have their liberty and property arbitrarily disposed of by the royal fiat. Conscious of their own importance, they, at first, only claimed a privilege of recommending by petition, such measures as they might conceive necessary for the public good. In this humble form did the spirit of liberty first appear, while the power of the Crown continued for ages almost unlimited in its extent, and uncontrouled in its opperation. But, when an attention to the true interests of the nation, established their manufactures and extended their commerce, the common people readily shook off their servile dependence upon their Lords, and gladly embraced an opportunity of acquiring that affluence of riches which was the firmest foundation of their future liberty. Those, whose situation had lately been that of the most abject vassallage, now suddenly found themselves raised, by their own industry, to the possession of wealth and independance. Proud of such valuable and important acquisitions, they only waited for that information, which was the child of time and experience, to direct their steps in the pursuit of measures which were to establish the most solid security for that liberty and property which they had so lately acquired.

Before science extended her happy influence over this rising nation, their progress in the paths of liberty was but slow and irregular—interrupted by events which they were too short sighted to foresee, and obstructed by revolutions which no human prudence could prevent. But, when their acquisition of knowledge, from a careful examination of the past, enabled them not only to regulate the present, but even to penetrate into the remote regions of future contingency, every revolving year furnished them with some opportunity to improve and enlarge their system of liberty. With every assistance which human wisdom could bestow, supported by the experience of ages, they have at last fixed the foundation of their freedom upon such principles as will forever stand the test of the most critical examination. Careful to guard those blessings for which they had so industriously laboured, they established this as a fundamental maxim—that no new regulation could be framed, nor any old law abrogated but by the *general consent* of the nation. Such a consent as must be evidenced by a majority of votes in the different estates of the kingdom—the Lords in their proper persons assenting, while the sense of the common people is known from the voices of their representatives. Can any thing less than infinite wisdom elaborate a system more perfect than that which so effectually secures the happiness of every individual—which admits no law as obligatory but upon those who are *expressly parties,* or have actually subscribed to the obligation?

If these be, as they certainly are, the well digested principles of the English constitution, with what appearance of reason can the warmest zealot for the superiority of Great Britain assert, that the legislative power of parliament is *sovereign and supreme?*

Shall the freemen of New York be reduced to a state of subordination, and deprived of those invaluable privileges enjoyed by the inhabitants of that city, which has given a name to their province, because they are unfortunately placed a thousand leagues further from the presence of their sovereign; and instead of prefering their petitions immediately to the royal ear, can only apply to his deputy for a redress of their grievances, and for the framing such regulations as the infant state of the colony may require? This would be heightening the misfortune of their situation by the most flagrant injustice.

When the emigrants from Great Britain crossed the Atlantic to settle the deserts of America, they brought with them the spirit of the English government. They brought with them the same duties to their sovereign which the freemen of England at that time acknowledged; and they very naturally supposed, that, under his direction, they should be allowed to make such regulations as might answer the purposes of their emigration. Ever mindful of their duty and allegiance to their Prince, they cannot easily conceive that they left their brethren the freemen of England vested with a sovereign, supreme power to restrain their natural liberty, or to dispose of their acquired property. Removed at an immense distance from the seat of government, they could no longer join the national council; but, as the very spirit of the English constitution required it, they naturally applied to their Prince for such protection and assistance as might raise them to an equality with their brethren of England; from whom they only requested their friendly patronage, during the weakness of their infant state.

The formula of their government once settled in some measure to their satisfaction, with the concurrence of those officers appointed by the Crown, the inhabitants of these new settlements, ever faithfully preserving in their memory the principles of that happy government which they had just quitted, totally disclaim all subordination to, and dependence upon, the two inferior estates of their mother country. Without the power, without the inclination to disturb the tranquility of those to whom they stand so nearly related, they wish to promote an amicable intercourse, founded upon reciprocal interest; without allowing or submitting to any laws but those which they themselves have made, by *regular agreement* with the deputy of the Crown, properly authorized for that purpose. To suppose the British parliament to be vested with a sovereign and supreme legislative power over the colonies, is advancing a supposition inconsistent with the principles of their own constitution; and to assert the *necessity* of subordination from the nature of our situation, without attempting to prove that necessity, is really treating an affair of the utmost importance with too little attention. Those who may probably be most seriously affected by this doctrine, very naturally require something stronger than general assertions to support it, although those assertions may be advanced by the best and wisest men of the nation.

Perhaps it may not be such an irreconcileable paradox in policy, to assert, that the freemen settled in America may preserve themselves absolutely independant of their fellow subjects who more immediately surround the throne, and yet discharge, with the strictest fidelity, all their duties to their sovereign. They may not only be loyal and valuable subjects to their Prince, but useful and necessary neighbours to their brethren of Britain.

The colonies may, with no great impropriety, be considered as so many different counties of the same kingdom, the nature of whose situation prevents their joining in the general council, and reduces them to a necessity of applying to their Prince for the establishment of such a partial policy as may be the best adapted to their particular circumstances, and, at the same time, the most conducive to the general good. That this partial policy, settled for every distinct part, may not interfere with the general welfare of the whole, the restraining power lodged in the Crown will always be able to insure; since we cannot suppose that a wise and just Prince would ever consent to sacrifice the interest and happiness of any one part to the selfish views of another.

As a commercial people, while blessed with the same advantages which the inhabitants of Great-Britain enjoy, our interest may sometimes clash with theirs. This is an inconvenience which may, at some future period happen, in the extent of our trade: But shall this *possible inconvenience* be a sufficient authority for stripping us of all the most valuable privileges in society? Shall we be reduced to the most abject state of dependence, because we may possibly become formidable rivals to our jealous brethren, if we are allowed to maintain that equality which we have received from nature, and which we find so firmly supported by the laws of our mother country?

nostri autem magistratus, imperatores que ex hac una re maximam laudem capere stutebant, SI PROVINCIAS, SI SOCIOS EQUITATE ET SIDE DEFENDERENT.
Cic. *de Ofs.*

There is no reasoning against those prejudices which are the support of particular interests, or I would ask why my being born in the island of Great Britain should vest me with a power to tie the hands of my American neighbour, and then justify me in picking his pocket; although this same American should be a loyal subject of the same Prince, and formerly declared to be possessed of all the liberties and privileges of a British subject? How absurd and unmeaning must this specious declaration appear to one who sees and feels the force of the present violent struggles for reducing us to a state of infamous vassallage.

That right honourable and worthy gentleman who exerted his extensive influence to ward off from the devoted colonies that blow which would have effected their immediate ruin, has been pleased to make these declarations in our favour.— *They are the subjects of this* kingdom, *equally entitled with ourselves to all the* natural rights *of mankind, and the peculiar privileges of* Englishmen, *equally bound by the laws, and equally participating of its constitution. The* Americans *are the sons, not the bastards of* England.—And yet, in the same speech he asserts the authority of Great Britain over the colonies to be *sovereign and supreme* in every circumstance of government and legislation whatsoever. If the latter part of this declaration be by any means reconcileable with the former, I must forfeit all pretensions to reason; since, after the most careful disquisition which I am capable of making, I cannot discover how any inhabitant of the colonies can be said to enjoy the *peculiar privileges of Englishmen,* when all that he holds valuable in life must lie at the mercy of that unlimited power, which is so repeatedly said to be *sovereign and supreme,* an authority established upon partial principles, and such as must be supported by the force of arms more than the force of reason, if it is to survive to any distant period.

I have the highest veneration for the character and abilities of Mr. Pitt, and scarcely dare indulge myself in a train of reasoning, which evidently points out to me the most striking inconsistency in the sense of his speech in January, upon American affairs. From the best evidence which I am capable of receiving, I cannot but be clearly convinced that our liberty must be only ideal, and our privileges chimerical, while the omnipotence of parliament can "bind our trade, confine our manufactures, and exercise every power whatever except that of taking money out of our pockets without our consent." If this sovereign power, which they so warmly assert, should be once tamely conceded, to what trifling purpose have we exerted ourselves in our glorious opposition to the Stamp-Act. At best we have but put the evil day afar off.—We have not combated the reality, but the mode of oppression, we have only gained a temporary reprieve, 'till some future minister with as little virtue and more abilities than Mr. G[renville] shall think proper to employ this unbounded legislative power for the horrid purpose of reducing three millions of people to a state of abject slavery.

If our sovereign Lords, the Commons of England, have been led, by their absurd jealousy and envious partiality, under the direction of a rash and impolitic minister, to strike so bold a stroke at both our liberty and property, what danger may we not apprehend from the same selfish principles, when they may be influenced by the deep laid schemes of some able statesman? Under such pernicious influence the chains of America may be forged and rivited on, while her incautious sons are lulled in a state of security. The power of taxation given up to their spirited opposition, the excess of their joy will not suffer them to indulge any gloomy reflections upon that *dangerous reserve* of *legislation*. The present evil averted, the warmth of their sanguine dispositions will not allow them to think that oppression may return at any other time, or in any other form. Their very gratitude and humility prevent their enquiring into a cause of the last importance. In the highest exaltation of heart at a concession scarcely expected, they receive as a matter of *favour* what they demanded as a matter of *right*, and, to avoid an appearance of arrogance in urging any new demands, they neglect the discharge of the most essential duties to themselves and their posterity. Perhaps, they will scarcely thank the man who shall endeavour to convince them, that the simple power of legislation may as effectually ruin the colonies as that of taxation.

Let us borrow and improve upon a thought of our greatest enemy. Mr. G[renville] tells us that *internal and external taxes* are the same in *effect,* and differ but in name. Mr. Pitt has indeed treated this opinion with so little attention, that he has only answered it by a general assertion, *That there is a plain distinction between taxes levied for the purpose of raising a revenue, and duties imposed for the regulation of trade.*

Plain as this distinction is, my most industrious enquiries have not yet led me to it; and I cannot but think with Mr. G[renville] that they are the same *in effect.*—The one is precisely determined, while the other is more uncertain and eventual; but, in proportion to the sum raised, the effect will be exactly the same. It is taken for granted that the collection of a stamp duty would drain us of all the specie which we receive as a balance in our West-India trade. If an exhorbitant duty laid upon sugar and molasses produces the same effect, in what does the difference consist? By either means the treasury of England will be enriched with the whole profit of our labour and we ourselves shall be reduced to that deplorable state of poverty, of which we have, at this very moment, a most affecting instance. General as the calamity is now become, there are few so uninformed as not to know that the power of legislation has done all this mischief, without any assistance from that of taxation. The severe restrictions imposed upon our trade, have made it impracticable for us to answer every foreign demand, and, at the same time reserve a sufficient stock to keep up that circulation of property so necessary to the well being of society.

Involved in heavy debts, without any prospect of discharging them—in want of the necessaries of life, without the means of acquiring them, the very politic Mr. G[renville] has furnished us with the most interesting facts to prove the truth of his doctrine. As great an enemy as he may be to the colonies, he has at least kindly bestowed upon them the most irrefragable proof that internal and external taxes are the same in effect; and that they may be as effectually ruined by the powers of legislation as by those of taxation.

When the parliament of Great Britain arrogate to themselves this sovereign jurisdiction over the colonies, I should be glad to know what principles they found their claim. Do they ground their pretensions on the excellent principles of their own constitution, or is this supremacy a power *virtually inherent* in the name of parliament? A name which should remind them of their original state of humility, when the distinguishing power which they boasted was priviledge of *speaking their mind* and remonstrating their grievances. The Lords indeed may, with some appearance of reason, assert a supreme jurisdiction over the whole body of the nation, as the highest court of judicature: But when an aspiring member of the Commons House confidently declares that he has a power to bind our trade, and restrain our manufactures, I should be glad to know whether he derived this power from the honest freemen his constituents, or whether he acquired it by virtue of his office? From his constituents he could receive no more power than they *naturally possessed;* and, from his office he cannot reasonably be supposed vested with any other authority, than that of deciding upon the formalities, and punctilios annexed to it.

To grasp at a jurisdiction so infinitely extensive, and so little capable of limitation, is expressly declaring, that, from the antiquity of their establishment, they are become sovereigns of the new-discovered world. Upon some such arbitrary principles must they ground their unreasonable pretensions; since no man in his senses will assert that an inhabitant of Birmingham or Manchester has a *natural right,* after having obtained the consent of the Crown, to restrain, and prevent an industrious settler of the colonies from engaging in those particular manufactures which may interfere with the business of his own profession. Absurd as this assertion is, either this must be maintained, or one full as pregnant with absurdity; since one may with as much reason suppose this *natural superiority* in the freemen of Great Britain, as this *acquired sovereignty* in the collective body of their representatives. Whatever reasons they may devise to support this extraordinary claim, the motives to their usurpation are clearly evinced in that part of Mr. Pitt's speech, where he says—"If the legislative power of Great Britain over America ceases to be sovereign and supreme, I would advise every gentleman to sell his lands and embark for that country." A jealous fear, that, from the natural advantages which we possess, we may, in some future age, rival our envious brethren in strength and riches, has urged them to exercise a piece of Ottoman policy, by strangling us in our infancy. When we examine into the nature of those fears which have already proved so fatal to our interest, the slightest examination shews them as contemptible and ill grounded as were ever entertained by the most selfish of mankind.

Had not this refined policy of our *British Machiavel* interfered, and roused us to attention, we should, in all human
probability, have continued for many centuries the faithful
drudges of our indulgent mother; and Great Britain would
have increased in strength and riches in proportion to the
population of her colonies. While our commerce continued unrestrained we should industriously have cultivated every
branch of it, that we might be enabled to pay punctually to
Great Britain, that balance which would every year increase;
since our attention to the settling an immeasureable extent of
country would effectually prevent our establishing such manufactories as would furnish us with the necessaries of life.

Had I sufficient information to enter into a minute detail of
facts, I believe it would be no difficult matter to prove, that,
in the course of our most successful commerce, Great Britain
receives nine-tenths of the profit, whilst we are humbly contented with being well fed and clothed as the wages of our
labour.

If this inferiority be the consequence of a reasonable connection, why would they wish to reduce us to a state of abject
dependence? Or, if with the advantages which they already
possess, a fair unlimited trade would bring into their hands
all the specie which we could draw from the West-Indies,
why would they wantonly use such detestable measures as
they have lately pursued, to effect the same purpose?

If the present severe system of politics be the result of unreasonable jealousy; I will venture to assert that this very
policy will counteract its own intention. Their distresses first
led the colonists into enquiries concerning the nature of their
political situation, and the justice of the treatment which they
had received. That ignorance which had kept them in a state
of peaceable submission, fled before their eager researches
after that information which was so essentially necessary to
the preservation of their liberty. Enraged to find, that, while
they had been amused with the specious title of fellow sub-

jects, and flattered with the rights of British freemen, they
were in reality treated as infants in policy, whose every motion was to be directed by the arbitrary will of their jealous
parent; when every such direction evidently tended to reduce
the one to an abject state of dependence, and to raise the
other to the most *exalted superiority.* That both these purposes could easily have been obtained, by measures artfully
managed, is not to be doubted, since nothing but the most
violent oppression could have roused us from our state of
stupefaction to a proper degree of attention. But when our
sensibility was excited by the most pointed injustice, rage instantly succeeded that tranquility which had been nourished
by our imaginary security. Warmed with a sense of the
injuries which we suffered, neither our gratitude nor our fear
could prevent our asserting those rights, the possession of
which can alone determine us freemen; and, though we could
not but see that superiority of power which could *"crush us
to atoms"* yet could we have found even in the modern history
of Europe so many examples for our encouragement, that we
should not have despaired of assistance sufficient to preserve
us from the *worst of evils.*

> *quam vos facillime agitis, quam estis* maxime potentes,
> *dites, fortunati, nobiles, tam maxime vos aquo*
> *animo aque noscere oportet, si vox*
> *vultis perhiberi* probos.
>   Terent. Adelph

The advocates for the sovereignty of Great Britain enumerate amongst the other obligations by which we are bound, the
favours which she has constantly conferred. If we could reasonably suppose a whole political body actuated by the same
passions which may influence an individual, then, indeed there
would be some foundation for our grateful acknowledgments;
but when we plainly perceive that the bounties which Great

Britain is said so lavishly to have bestowed upon us, are meted out in the common political measure, with an evident intention *finally to promote her own particular benefit,* we can only say that her actions are the result of good policy, not of great generosity. As for the support which they have given us in times of danger, if it did not immediately arise from the same motive which has produced their other favours, I am still amazed that it should even be mentioned by those who have lavished so much blood and treasure, for the maintenance of an *imaginary balance,* or in defending those who never thanked them for their defence.

The most superficial examination must serve to convince us that the battles of Great Britain could no where have been fought with so much advantage as in the woods of America; where her troops could be supplied with all the necessaries of life upon the easiest terms, and, from whence all the money which they expended immediately returned in immense payments for the extraordinary importation of her manufactures which the exigencies of the war required. Thus were the whole expences of the American war very far from lessening the strength or riches of the nation, while her forces, which were not sufficient to make a considerable impression upon the body of her natural enemy, were enabled to lop off one of its most valuable limbs. In effecting this glorious purpose, I will venture to mention the assistance which they received from the provincial troops, as an aid of more importance than is generally allowed. I will even take the liberty to assert, that the colonists, in proportion to their *real ability,* did more for the general cause than could reasonably have been expected, if not more than Great Britain herself. This assertion I fancy will gain more credit now than it would have gained some time ago; since the eyes of the world are at last open, and they must if they are not wilfully blind, plainly discover, that the estimates of our wealth which have been received from ignorant or prejudiced persons, are, in every calculation, grossly erroneous. These misrepresentations, which have been so industriously propagated, are very possibly the offspring of political invention, as they form the best apology for imposing upon us burthens to which we are altogether unequal. The easy faith which every absurd information obtained, and the precipitate measures, which were the consequence of this unreasonable credulity, must sufficiently convince us, that while we are within the reach of parliamentary power, we shall not be suffered to riot in a superfluity of wealth, or to acquire any dangerous degree of strength. Whatever advantages may hereafter present themselves, from an increased population, or a more extended trade, we shall never be able to cultivate them to any valuable purpose; for, how much soever we may possess the ability of acquiring wealth and independence, the partial views of our selfish brethren, supported by the sovereignty of parliament, will most effectually prevent our enjoying such invaluable acquisitions.

If any alteration in our system of agriculture should furnish us with a sufficiency of the necessary articles for the establishment of the most valuable manufactories, and an increase of population should enable us to carry them to the greatest advantage; the manufacturers of Great Britain, jealous of such a formidable encroachment, would easily obtain the interposition of our sovereign directors; who would very naturally ordain, that we should export our unwrought materials to be laboured by our more skilful brethren, and dispatch our superfluous inhabitants in search of another vacant world: And, if the extent of our commerce should draw into our hands the wealth of the Indies, the same unlimited authority would always carefully provide ways and means for conveying the whole into the treasury of England. Perhaps some future G[renvi]lle, refining upon the system of his predecessor, may make the powers of legislation answer the purposes of oppression as effectually as the severest taxation.

The measures which have already been pursued almost give

to conjecture the force of conviction; since no man can have been so inattentive to the most interesting facts as not to know that the power of parliament exerted in the single instance of restraining our trade, has already reduced us to *inconceivable distress*. Denied the means of acquiring specie sufficient for the purposes of a general circulation, and limitted in the emission of our paper currency, men of considerable real estates become unable to answer the most trifling demands; and, when urged by creditors, perhaps as much perplexed as themselves, their lands are sold by execution for less than half their former value. This, as one of the most striking inconveniences, attending the late unseasonable exertion of parliamentary power, I have selected for observation, from a very extensive catalogue of grievances which it has already produced, and of which we are at this moment most severely sensible. I am led to a choice of this particular fact, from a consideration of the fatal consequence by which it may possibly be attended, should the merchants of England immediately demand a rigid payment of the general balance due to them. It is not an easy matter to conceive how much our property may be affected by so unseasonable a demand; since the calamity would by a regular connection, extend from the lowest to the highest member of society. But as it was never my intention to enter into a minute detail of facts, I shall content myself with offering such loose, desultory observations as may serve to direct others in their researches after more particular information upon the most interesting subject. In the further pursuit of this design, I shall just take the liberty to observe upon the resolves of the Commons, of February 1766; that the severe censures which they so liberally bestow upon us, are evidently inconsistent with the principles upon which they are supposed to have voted the repeal of the Stamp-Act.

From these resolves we may very reasonably suppose, that the repeal is more immediately founded upon the *inexpediency* of the act, than upon a conviction that they had exerted an *unconstitutional power.* Had they been willing to allow this act as invasive of an indisputable right, they would not so severely have censured us for our daring opposition, and lavished such praises upon those whose selfish views or slavish principles made them so readily subscribe to the infallibility and omnipotence of parliament.—A peaceable submission to the first attacks of encroaching power, is altogether incompatible with the genius of liberty! nor could it reasonably be expected, that in such a sudden and dangerous invasion of our most estimable rights, the form of opposition could be perfectly model'd by the hand of prudence. Violent and precipitate as our measures were, they wanted nothing but success to sanctify them; since the most superficial observer cannot but have discovered, that in the political world, right and wrong are merely *arbitrary modes* totally dependent upon the rise and fall of contending parties.

The people of England very justly dissatisfied with the tyrannic conduct of a weak prince, made the boldest struggles for the support of their languishing liberty. In their first ill directed efforts under the unfortunate *Monmouth,* the justice of their cause could not save them from the pains and penalties of *open rebellion:* But when a prince of military abilities gave them his powerful assistance, they suddenly effected the preservation of their freedom, and distinguished so important an event by the title of a *glorious revolution:* so much influence has success, in rating the merit of our political conduct.

When the committee of the House resolve in the most general and expressive terms, that the authority of parliament over the colonies is *sovereign and supreme in every respect whatever,* there is no reasoning against so formidable a resolution, supported by the power of the whole kingdom. We can only remark that the same house heretofore resolved to take under their own particular direction, the rights of the people, the privileges of the Lords, and the sovereignty of the Crown; and, for a long time maintained this unnatural usurpation.

If they did not suffer the passions of the man to influence the judgment of the Senator, they would never treat that as a point of honour which should only be considered as a matter of right.

If, upon a cool, dispassionate enquiry, it may appear that the Commons of Great Britain, have no *natural or acquired superiority* over the freemen of America, they will certainly do us the justice to acknowledge this very reasonable independence, and not wickedly endeavour to enslave millions to promote the honour and dignity of a few ambitious individuals.

In supporting this doctrine of independence, I have established as an incontrovertible truth, this very accurate definition of my Lord C. J. Hale,—That every act of parliament is a *tripartite indenture of agreement between the three estates of the kingdom.* If this maxim be not disputable, I very humbly conceive, that every consequence which I have drawn from it, is fairly and logically deduced; for it cannot, but with the most glaring absurdity, be supposed, that the parties to these political agreements may legally bind those who are not in any wise privy to them.

The very spirit of the English constitution requires, that general regulations framed for the government of society, must have the sanction of *general approbation;* and, that no man shall be deprived of life, liberty or property, but by the force of those laws to which he has voluntarily subscribed. These principles once acknowledged as the foundation of English liberty, how can the colonists be said to possess the *natural rights of mankind,* or the *peculiar privileges of Englishmen,* while they are every day liable to receive laws framed by persons ignorant of their abilities—unacquainted with their necessities, and evidently influenced by partial motives? If my zeal for the good of my country has not greatly clouded my judgment, I still dare so far depend upon the principles which I have established, as to assert, that, while the power of the British parliament is acknowledged *sovereign and supreme in every re-*

spect whatsoever, the liberty of America is no more than a flattering dream, and her privileges delusive shadows.

While I relate matters of fact, from the best evidence which I am capable of receiving, if I have misrepresented them, I lie open to contradiction; and, when I recapitulate the principles from which I have drawn my train of reasoning, I am not so obstinately attached to my own opinion as to be proof against conviction. If I am guilty of any errors in the course of this unconnected performance, they must be attributed to my not having received sufficient information, or to my want of ability in using the materials which I had acquired. I have never wilfully misrepresented a fact, nor designedly drawn from it a falacious consequence. I have not laboured to establish any favourite system, and, with the vanity of a projector, supported it at the expence of my veracity.

But however trifling this performance may appear, both my head and my heart have co-operated in its production, and I really sat down "to write what I thought, not to think what I should write."

> *Ardeo, mihi credite—incredibili quodam amore*
> *patria—quod volent denique homines existement;*
> *nemini ego possum esse bene de republica merenti*
> *non amicus.*
> Cicero.
> A Citizen

FINIS.

· 10 ·

Extracts from the Proceedings of the
Court of Vice-Admiralty

By Henry Laurens

After the trial of the *Ann* in the summer of 1768, Laurens sent an
account of the trial and some "General Observations" to one of his
partners in the ownership of the vessel, William Fisher of Philadelphia. Fisher had a portion of the account printed and sent
copies to Laurens, along with opinions of Philadelphia lawyers
questioning Judge Leigh's decision. Meanwhile, Leigh had received orders from England to resign either as judge or as attorney-
general, and he resigned as judge in September, 1768.

    Laurens published the first edition of his pamphlet in February
1769, and at the same time, the Philadelphia publication, which
had circulated privately, was offered for sale. Leigh responded with
a pamphlet, *The Man Unmasked*. Laurens was furious, and in
Timothy's *South Carolina Gazette* on May 23 he announced that

---

Charleston. [February], 1769. pp. iii–iv, 41–42, 1–5, 1–4. The pagination
of the pamphlet is not continuous. For discussion of the background,
with details about the various cases, see David D. Wallace, *The Life of
Henry Laurens* (New York, 1915).

he would answer "that POLE CAT" and his "Billingsgate Rhap-
sody" with a second edition. The new edition appeared in the
summer and included a sixty-four-page appendix in which Laurens
quoted correspondence between himself and Leigh.

The text that follows consists of excerpts from the first Charleston edition of the pamphlet. Omitted are forty-one pages which
consist of copies of documents relating to the proceedings of the
Vice-Admiralty Court. Laurens summarizes these proceedings in
his "Recapitulation," which is included here. Laurens' discussion
of the "oath of calumny" refers to an oath Judge Leigh required
Deputy-Collector George Roupel to take, disclaiming any malice,
before he would try the case of the *Ann*. The case of the French
smuggler refers to a decision of Leigh in 1767, in which no costs
were charged and the wages of the sailors were paid from the
proceeds of the sale of the vessel. For the background of the other
cases, see the general introduction to this volume.

Laurens' use of dashes, colons, italics, and capitalization is so
erratic, and the typographical design of the pamphlet so confusing,
that both have been modernized to a certain extent in an effort to
make the pamphlet comprehensible to the twentieth-century reader.

INTRODUCTION.

Some few interested persons, whose practice it has been of
late to sneer at every complaint of grievances in America, or to
turn from them with disdain, may perhaps object to this publication——that it treats only of private affairs between certain
custom-house officers and a set of merchants, and is therefore
unworthy of publick attention.

This may be the language of a few who call truth "Virulence," and whose mistaken policy and unbounded ambition
lead them to act as if they thought the interest of Great-Britain
would be most effectually promoted by the distress of her
colonies; but it is apprehended, when all the circumstances

relative to the informations and prosecutions, as well as the final sentences passed upon each case, are properly considered and thoroughly understood, the publick in general will not be displeased with this appeal to them. It is also presumed, that an apology is the less necessary in the present times when the powers of Commissioners and other officers in America are increased to an alarming height, and, as if it were to render them still more formidable, the jurisdiction of Vice-Admiralty Courts extended *beyond their antient limits;* when too many men are employed in those offices, whose sole view seems to be amassing fortunes, at the expense of their honour, conscience, and almost ruined country; when such is the unhappy state of America every British merchant is concerned; but in a more particular manner those who reside upon this continent, are interested in the decrees and determinations in the Courts of Admiralty.

The cases before us will afford glaring instances of what pernicious practices may be carried on under colour of law, and shew how the most fair and honest trader may be harrassed and injured in his property, and exposed to vast expence and damages, by intriguing, malicious and temporizing officers. And no one knows how soon he may be ensnared and "tripaned," his ships and cargoes boldly seized and violently prosecuted, and either condemned as forfeited, or *partially* and *incompleatly* restored, without even the *smallest legal* pretence for seizure.

As such the following extracts, &c. are laid before the publick, and it is hoped that the publication will prove of general utility to his Majesty's American Colonies, by putting merchants on their guard against the artifices of wicked officers ——and possibly by drawing the attention of persons in higher stations, from whom such officers pretend to derive authority and to claim protection.

Each case shall be treated of as distinctly and concisely as the several relative circumstances will admit. The remarks,

reasonings and conclusions thereon, are submitted to those
who, from an extensive knowledge of trade and commerce,
free from the *despotism* of *petty office,* or the *bias* of plurality
of *places,* are capable of *truly* judging whereon "the Wealth
and Power of Great-Britain and her Colonies depend;" and
through the whole so strict a regard shall be paid to truth as
will in that respect bear the "most critical Examination," and
make some amends for the imperfection of style.

[*Forty-one pages of documents begin at this point. Laurens
summarizes the essence of these in his "Recapitulation."*]

RECAPITULATION.

1. *The Schooner* WAMBAW.

In this case, said the Judge, "no Fraud was either committed
or intended. . . . The Collector himself, in open Court, dis-
claimed even a suspicion of either." The "Forms and Cere-
monies" required by an act of Parliament, were complied with
as far as the circumstances of the case would admit:

The vessel, &c. were condemned as forfeited, and the claimant ordered to pay all the taxed costs—even those incurred by
the Prosecutor in the promotion of his suit—contrary (it is
presumed) to the true intent and meaning of Statute 4th Geo.
III. Cap. xv [The Revenue Act of 1764].

2. *The Schooner* DORCAS, *a French Smuggler,*

was seized for importing and landing foreign goods by night.
She was condemned; but the costs of prosecution was ordered
to be paid out of the monies arising from the sale of the vessel
and cargo; and, what was more extraordinary, even the men's
wages ordered to be paid likewise out of the same fund to the

great discouragement of the mariners to continue in the smuggling business.

3. *The Schooner* BROTON-ISLAND-PACKET,

was on one day said to have been seized on a most frivolous pretence——and without colour to support such seizure; and upon another day it was said, that in this case "the Letter of the Act had been beyond all Doubt transgressed."

Yet the vessel was acquitted, and the Prosecutor was ordered to pay all the costs that the Judge thought himself justifiable in assigning to him.

"*No Mention was made of probable Cause,*" and the injured owner had his remedy at common law—for damages sustained by the seizure—which the Judge in the person of Mr. Leigh as a barrister, strove to defeat him in, by an attempt to prove that probable cause had been "mentioned."

4. *The Ship* ANN

was seized for lading non-enumerated goods before bond was given.

The tenor of the bond required (filed in the Court of Admiralty) expressly declares that goods are actually loaden *at the time of giving the bond.*

The constant practice of the Custom House had been to take such bond *after the goods were loaden.*

The Collector's agreement with the merchants, that such bond should not be required when a bond for enumerated goods had been previously given, was clearly proved.

A bond for enumerated goods *had been given for the Ann.*

The Judge was convinced that the Master of the said *Ann* had done every thing in his power to comply *with the terms required at the Custom House;* and that he had been artfully hindered from doing so by the Custom-House Officers themselves.

His Honour was also convinced that the said Master's whole conduct had been fair and free even *from suspicion of fraud;* and that he had been trepan'd and surprised by the Custom-House Officers for "private Reasons."

The vessel was acquitted; but the Claimant ordered to pay *all his own Costs,* and the Judge certified a probable cause of seizure, by which the claimant and owners were deprived of *all means of obtaining redress.*

5. *The Schooner ACTIVE.*

The Judge declared that in this case not one of the numerous Acts of Trade had been transgressed, and moreover, that there was not the least shadow or pretence of complaint that the vessel had *at any time* been employed in *any illicit trade whatsoever;* but his Honour nevertheless *thought* that there was a probable cause for the seizure, and the "innocent Owners" were, by that *unlucky thought,* loaded with a vast expense ——without remedy.

6. *The INFORMATION of Manigault and Neufville against Daniel Moore, for taking illegal fees, contrary to Statute Geo. II, Cap. xxx.*

The Statute prohibits the demanding, taking or receiving *any* fee, gratuity or reward, by any officers of the customs, for signing any Indigo-Certificate.

Divers witnesses, men of known veracity and established characters, prove upon oath, that Daniel Moore, Esq., Collector of the Customs at Charlestown, South Carolina, did *demand, take* and *receive,* certain fees, gratuities and rewards, for signing Indigo-Certificates.

But the Judge decreed that he was free and acquitted from the charge; and that he was not guilty of the offence complained of, modo et formd:

That he the Collector had given *some cause* for a prosecution *of this nature* against him; nevertheless his Honour was pleased to abuse the prosecutors, *in particular,* for promoting, and the merchants *in general,* from a mere flimsy out-of-door tale, for a supposed abetting, the prosecution; and finally, to order the informants to pay *all* the costs of suit, except a mere trifle to be paid by Mr. Moore for his two pleas, the first of which had been set aside by exceptions.

"Our Will Is Law—So We Judge It—And So We Will Have It."
TRANSLATION OF A MEMORIAL, &C.

REFLECTIONS ARISING FROM A
RETROSPECT OF A LATE CASE.

First, upon an oath administered under these awful charges, viz. "You shall swear the Truth, the whole Truth, and *nothing but the Truth.*" So Help you God, or God be your Help in your last Hour.

> "An Oath with sacred Awe doth rouse the Soul,
> And thus restrains her from the double Mischief
> Of ang'ring Friends and of offending Heaven."

The very heathen held an oath as a thing of so great force and of such sacred authority, that they believed the sin of perjury was pursued with the severest vengeance; such as extended itself to the posterity of the offender—such as might be incurred by the bare inclination without the act; and that men became partakers of the guilt of perjury by subordination, and also for overlooking and conniving at false swearing, when, from the nature of their office, it was their duty to put the rash or malicious swearer to open shame.

And by some of their laws, persons who had forsworn themselves were adjudged to capital punishment, as being guilty of two of the greatest crimes—in violating that piety which they owed to God, and in destroying faith from amongst men; the strongest pillars of human society.

"From whence dire Plagues and dreadful Slaughters come
On perjured Wretches."

Christians of all denominations and in all ages have held the solemn obligation of an oath in the same sacred light, and in the highest degree of veneration, as being the touchstone of truth, whereupon the properties, characters, and lives of worthy citizens do often depend.

"———Perjury's the Parent of a nameless Issue,
Which without Hands or Feet shall quick Advances make,
And seize and ruin all before him."

When solemn oaths are trifled with in courts of judicature, the false swearer suffered to escape unpunished, and that uncomfortable observation of the wise man confirmed:

"All Things come alike to all—one Event to the Righteous and the Wicked: to him that sweareth and to him that feareth an Oath."

The alarm should be struck—every man is in danger. The judge, "who for the Wages of Unrighteousness," let the wicked go free—should be held in *everlasting*———Remembrance.

Secondly, upon the oath administered *ex officio*, and the dangerous oath of calumny.

An oath of exculpation, offered *ex officio*, should be administered before, or even with the first institution of a suit, lest the party to whom it is to be offered should entangle himself and become unable to retreat.

It is cruel to extort an oath of calumny from an officer, contrary to the repeated desires of the opposite party.

More cruel, when an officer discovers a reluctance to take such an oath, and pleads, that as an officer duly appointed and authorized he had made a seizure, and thought "*that*" a sufficient justification of his conduct.

But still more cruel and unjust must it be in a Judge, after an officer shall openly have declared his motives for making a seizure, peremptorily to demand such an oath under heavy pains and penalties—from no cause of *"suspicion of the officer's character,"* but *"for some some special reasons in his own mind."*

Revenue officers who seize ships and goods for supposed transgressions of the statutes and laws of the realm, may plead their commission and orders from the higher powers, and may of right claim protection from the laws. The laws and not the state of an officer's mind should be given in evidence.

If goods seized by Customs House officers were to be acquitted or forfeited, according to the purity or impurity of the motives of such officers half the produce of France and the Indies might be safely imported duty free.

It is not a mark of wisdom in a Judge of his *own will to drive an officer to such extremities.*

It is a mark of an arbitrary disposition in a Judge, and he may be justly suspected of sinister views when, in opposition to the prayer of both parties, he exacteth, under grievous penalties, such an oath from an officer who hath "other proofs" sufficient to justify the first act of seizure.

If an officer should have such *sufficient proofs* to justify his act, and should therefore magnanimously refuse the oath of calumny, a Judge who had menaced the penalty of quashing the prosecution would be reduced by a foolish declaration to a dangerous dilemma.

Thirdly, upon final sentences and decrees.

A Judge who shall slight or overlook a law founded upon reason and justice, and offered to his consideration as applicable to a case in point in defence of *"innocent persons"* although he may afterwards, from his own pretended discoveries of equity extend partial relief to the defendant, is vain, and cannot escape reprehension.

A Judge who shall refuse or neglect to investigate truth upon a contrariety of oaths laid before him in judgment *is deficient in his duty* and also *injurious to those witnesses who appeal to records and other proofs in support of their testimony.*

A Judge who shall draw conclusions by a strained impli-
cation from the most suspicious side of evidence, and that
only of one person, in opposition to the uniform declarations
of four good and true men, and also contrary to other undeniable proof, doth unrighteousness in judgment.

A Judge betrays either rashness in judgment or want of
integrity if he pronounceth or insinuateth that an assertory
and declaratory clause in an instrument of writing brought
before him as an exhibit of evidence, *"is only a recital."*

If a Judge in one part of a definitive sentence shall pretend
that the reasons for partiality of officers, in oppressing "innocent persons" are "private and inexplicable," and in other parts
of the same sentence, charge such officers as being guilty of
"fraud, artifice, treachery," and *"design to surprise"* the same
"innocent persons," he is inconsistent in judgment. He is a
double-minded man, and unstable in all his ways.

Fourthly, upon the advice and proceedings of crown officers
disengaged in plurality of offices.

I. OF AN ATTORNEY-GENERAL.

An Attorney-General who was to have received no benefits
in another character from multiplied Courts of Admiralty,
and who could acquire neither fame nor profit from weak or
ambiguous counsel, upon hearing the true state of a case,
would have dissuaded an officer from attempting a *fruitless*
and *dishonourable* prosecution, and thereby have prevented
even the institution of a suit and all the pernicious consequences thereof to both parties.

II. OF A JUDGE OF THE ADMIRALTY.

A Judge of the Admiralty who sat independent of the office of Attorney-General if he had discovered, on the part of
the prosecutor, that the principal and only witness had been
guilty, in his depositions to the several interrogatories put to
him, of *"impertinence, impropriety,"* fallacy, equivocation,
prevarication, and of swearing in direct contradiction to an

agreement subscribed by himself, as well as to the constant practice of the office in which he as an officer presided, and also in direct contradiction to the oaths of four impartial men:

That there was reason to believe that measures had been artfully taken by the officers to hinder the claimant from executing a bond, for want of which a pretence for seizure and prosecution was made:

That a trap had been set for the claimant and owner by the officers, who had withdrawn (from them alone) an indulgence which had been universally extended *to all other cases:*

That by cunning and unfair measures the officers had *"trepan'd"* the owner and claimant, and taken base advantages:

That the prosecutor having been many years a constant attendant at the Custom House, it was impossible for him to be ignorant of the constant practice of that office in such cases, or of the tenor and declaration of the bond required:

That on the part of the claimant there had been no transgression either wilful or inadvertent, in as much as his whole conduct had been fair, open, free even from "all suspicion" of guile; and that he had acted in direct conformity to the rules laid down in the Custom House by the supreme officer, and agreeable to the constant practice of that office:

That the goods, on account of which the ship was prosecuted, had been shipped without the knowledge of the owners, and were in quantity but half a ton to one hundred and sixty tons, and in value, as forty pounds to forty-five hundred pounds——and was literally a very *"small thing:"*

That the prosecuting officer had not even insinuated any thing like a suspicion of fraud committed or intended:

That if an act of Parliament, which might truly be said *"to have slept long,"* even from its first existence, had not been *literally complied with,* the blame, *if any,* was not imputable to the owner or claimant of the ship:

That modes not strictly agreeable to the letter of the law, for complying with the revenue acts, and acts for the regulation of trade, are frequently prescribed by principal revenue officers, without prejudice to the King's Revenue or danger to the merchants:

That upon such frivolous pretences for seizure as in a case alluded to, every ship or vessel from one small cause or other might be subjected to the rigour of a prosecution, unless the owners would stoop to some base concessions and pecuniary contributions to rapacious officers:

That from the notoriety of a former illegal seizure, and of what followed in consequence thereof, it was probable the present seizure was made by way of revenge——from hopes of extorting a compensation from the owner for late costs and damages.

Such a Judge sitting independent and with a single eye to his duty, having investigated such facts and circumstances,

Would have pursued every legal measure in his power to expose and to punish each guilty officer according to his demerit:

He would have conducted himself toward an officer whom he had openly charged as being guilty of P[erjury], according to the circumstances of the case in point, carefully avoiding all appearance of *coaxing.*

He would have opposed the oath of calumny to such an officer, if he had "other proofs" sufficient for commencing a prosecution, even if the opposite party had moved for it in the beginning of the suit.

He would have given *some demonstration* of his being "cloathed with Righteousness, and of the equitable jurisdiction of his court," by doing right and complete justice to him that had suffered wrong.

He would have applied a law founded in justice, useful and absolutely necessary for preventing such instances of treachery and violence, to the case in point.

In a word, an honest and upright Judge of Admiralty, to whom *solely* the *whole power* of a bench of judges and of an empanneled jury was delegated, being filled with just indignation from the many discoveries made of fraud, craft, design, treachery, false and evasive swearing on the part of the officers, would, as early as might be consistent with the form, style and dignity of his court, have dismissed the prosecution by a concise definitive sentence, as being groundless and malicious on the part of the prosecutor, discountenancing as much as in him lay such base attempts.

"Contentious Suits (says Lord Bacon) are the surfeit of courts, and ought to be spewed out."

Finally, upon the conduct and proceedings of an officer vested in two offices incongruous and incompatible with each other.

A Judge of the Admiralty embarrassed and entangled in the office of Attorney-General, thereby inhibited or pretendedly inhibited from giving his opinion upon any matter likely to come before him in judgment.

Would, by insnaring silence, half sentences, and "hypothetical answers," and other such *ignes fatui,* mislead a poor officer whose heart was brim full of pride and resentment, and his head not well stored with cases and constructions of law, to commence a prosecution, and to dangle after him at twelve courts of admiralty, pointed at by every man of honesty or understanding; and after extorting an oath of calumny from him, might and probably would take leave of him with this consolatory address.

Sir. This case is so exceedingly fair on the part of the claimant and owner, and the conduct of the officers so villainous, treacherous and unjust, that it is absolutely out of my power to condemn the ship and goods as forfeited. Indeed I begin to wish the suit had never been instituted, and if "giving up my Fees" in this awkward situation, would stop the mouths of these "mercantile Patriots" around me, and obliterate the whole affair, I should think myself happily off by such a surrender.

You know, Sir, the state of your own mind best with respect

to that oath of calumny which you took so reluctantly; however I shall act as if I believed you swore from your heart, and thence fix the *causa movata* of your first act.

The claimant and owner of this ship have undoubtedly been basely "trepan'd" by the Custom House officers; but you appear to have acted in the highest character of any of them. H—— and C—— I perceive were the jackals to decoy; the glory as well as the benefit of *devouring* "seem" to have been reserved for you.

H—— strove hard indeed to secure the prey; but his single testimony being flatly contradicted by the evidence of several honest men, and also by other undeniable proof, could not *be made use of;* however I shall leave his deposition unimpeached, upon record; and although I must *rattle* the officers, and "seem" to be in earnest too, for their horrible misdeeds, yet I shall proceed no further than *the rattle;* faint strictures upon their conduct, and those only from *"presumptions"* and *"suspicions"* shall appear in my final decree.

And now, in order to serve you as far as I can in this *bootless enterprise,* and at the same time to save my faithful colleague the Attorney-General from further attacks by appeals, complaints and *ex parte* oaths, I shall (before you apply for it) declare my resolution to certify a probable cause for seizure. The advice of the Attorney-General, if he had given it never so fully, could not have been more serviceable to you; for he could not have divined that all these notorious equitable circumstances would have come out in the course of the trial; nor is it likely that he would have thought of King Edward's charter granted to his trading subjects, although it is incorporated with the laws of, and made of force in, a province called South Carolina.

I shall take no notice myself of that royal act, but barely acquit the vessel, upon the equity of the case, and make such humble acknowledgments of my own righteousness, delicacy, blindness and infallibility, that I am in hopes the folks in general will think me in earnest.

With respect to the costs of suit——it will be most eligible for me to split the difference, to avoid provoking either side; each party therefore shall pay his own. That may dip you some three or four hundred pounds more it is true, unless you can obtain relief from the American Chest; a fund which may be aptly employed in supporting so good an officer, ever labouring for the "Advantage of the Revenue;" and the certificate for probable cause will probably be a means of procuring you access to it. I am sorry to say there is probable cause too to believe that you will become a subject for publick and private derision, and perhaps you may be reduced to ask a favour from him whom you attempted to plunder; but at the same time remember, that my said certificate, with a handsome prefatory apology, will skreen you from another "Action for damages;" and therefore let me caution you against appealing from my decree. If you aim at such a thing, I know the best security you have to propose, and although it is a matter that does not by any means concern me, if the claimant and owner are content—yet I shall manage the matter so, as to render your offer insufficient and unacceptable; wherefore let us now part good friends, and wait for *a more favourable opportunity* to repair the present disappointment.

What poor searcher of rates and customs, possessed of one spark of expiring honour, could forbear, upon hearing a definitive sentence truly admitting of such a comment and such degrading comparisons, from breaking out into loud complaints against an A[ttorney]-G[eneral]-J[udge], for such selfish double dealing?

What claimant and owner, conscious of their own integrity, acquitted from all suspicion of fraud, "trepan'd" and "surprised" by the Custom House officers, and thus cunningly dismissed with compliments upon their conduct and characters ——partial restitution, exhorbitant fees, and an effectual bar against recovering satisfaction for damages——could refrain from expressing the highest dissatisfaction at the proceedings and final sentence of a _____ officer thus greedily running after the Error of Balaam; or could forbear complaining as we complain against J[udge] and officers all, who, juglers like, trick us and trick one another!

> Friendship and Party with a weak and corrupt Judge
> Is Enmity against God, and Opposition to the publick Good.

A FEW GENERAL OBSERVATIONS ON AMERICAN CUSTOM-HOUSE OFFICERS, AND COURTS OF VICE-ADMIRALTY.[1]

The appointment of officers whose business should be to inspect and superintend the conduct of the trading part of the community was very soon found expedient and necessary in every commercial state. Observation and experience left too little room to doubt, that some men, if at liberty to pursue their inclinations, preferring their own private gain to the public welfare, would prosecute schemes of trade inconsistent with the general good. Policy directs that some articles should be carefully preserved and retained within the country and that others should be entirely excluded, or admitted under peculiar circumstances and with great caution. Such, for instance, as afford materials for useful and advantageous manufactures and such as contribute to the cheap and convenient support of the industrious part of a society should by no means be exported, unless they are produced in superfluous quantities, which seldom can happen, as the plenty of materials and cheapness of living will induce still greater numbers to engage in manufactures. Those articles, on the other hand, which tend to impoverish the community by promoting luxury, idleness, and debauchery, should be wholly prohibited from importation. Some states have, indeed, allowed such articles to be sparingly imported from a neighbouring state or government,

---

1 Published in Philadelphia with the single case of the ship *Ann*.

in order to vend greater quantities of their own commodities; but they have found the increase of idleness, and vice its concomitant, greatly to over-balance their profits.

It was likewise discovered that it would be of very great publick utility to have some articles in greater plenty than they could be produced in the country or procured in the ordinary course of trade; for states and kingdoms are in this respect like the subjects of which they are composed; none is able to live conveniently without being beholden to his neighbour for some of his conveniences. To encourage the importation of such articles, it is necessary in many cases to offer a bounty to the importer.

Further, trade can never flourish in any state whose merchants are not protected and secured from foreign insults. If a government is remiss and negligent in providing and maintaining a proper armament for their defense, foreigners will on many frivolous pretenses, seize and confiscate the merchant's property, which must soon put an end to his trade.

These several purposes, of appointing and supporting officers, of paying bounties and defending and protecting the merchants, cannot be answered without a very great charge and expense to the government. It is therefore but just and reasonable the merchants should contribute a share of their profits for purposes so beneficial to themselves, as well as the rest of the community.

The most fair, just, and impartial method of assessing such contribution is by laying a tax or impost on such articles of commerce as would least affect the industrious manufacturer and afford the greatest profit to the merchant.

From this view it appears consistent with the soundest maxims of policy and the dictates of reason and justice that some duties should be laid on merchandise and rules and regulations established respecting commerce; that officers should be appointed to collect those duties and to enforce a due observance of those rules.

Where the laws relating to trade pursue this plan and keep the original design and intention of their institution in view, and where men can be found to put them in execution who have sufficient resolution and probity to prefer the publick good to their own private emolument, and to act up to the true meaning and spirit of such laws; under such favourable circumstances, commerce must flourish and the community grow rich and happy. But be the laws ever so good and equitable, if bad men are employed as executive officers, who are avaricious, revengeful, and make their private gain the rule and measure of their conduct, under good laws, wrested and perverted by such men, trade must inevitably languish and decay; the spirit of industry and commerce must either submit to them and in the end be entirely extinguished, or by a vigorous exertion of all its faculties such baneful harpies must be expelled.

The mercantile part of the community may be compared to the human body; officers of this stamp may be considered as the cause whereby navigation, the veins and arteries through which the vitals of commerce are conveyed, is clogged and oppressed. A fever naturally ensues. If the strength of the constitution should not be able to expel the morbifick matter and restore the blood to its free and unconstrained circulation, the assistance of some skillful physician should be called, who, by a proper application of medicine, may assist nature and remove the cause of the disorder.

O America! how great would be thy happiness and the happiness of that Empire with which thou art so closely united in interest and affection could a physician be found of sufficient probity and wisdom to undertake a perfect and radical cure of those disorders under which thy trade at present languishes!

The laws relating to the customs in America are become so very numerous and intricate that it is a science which requires a great deal of time and application to comprehend them with any tolerable degree of clearness and perspicuity; and very few merchants have sufficient leisure to acquire a critical knowledge therein, although the conduct of the officers renders such a knowledge absolutely necessary to everyone who would secure his property from seizure: so that while the fair trader is industriously endeavouring to comply with the laws and not to infringe them in the least iota, he finds himself taken in the snare of some intriguing officer. If he can stoop and submit to such a wretch, an handsome bribe may gain his clearance; if not, he is put to the trouble and expense of prosecution in the Court of Vice-Admiralty, where his property is at the disposal of a single judge, whom *it is possible to suppose* equally weak and corrupt; for recent instances shew that such have been entrusted in offices of great importance to the publick weal.

It is by no means intended to arraign the wisdom or good intentions of the compilers of the laws relating to navigation; but this must be said, there are some particulars therein which appear to an American hard and peculiarly grievous.

An American thinks it hard he should be obliged to purchase almost all the articles he makes use of from Great Britain at an high price, and at the same time be prohibited from carrying his own produce to the most advantageous market; whereby the British merchant is enabled to set his own price, not only on British goods, but also on the produce of America. By this means the American pays a much greater tax than any person of equal fortune on the other side of the Atlantic, exclusive of the sums he is bound to contribute towards the support of the provincial government under which he resides.

He esteems it an additional hardship that, super-added to the high price he is obliged to pay for British goods, he should be saddled with an heavy duty payable on many of them; particularly at a time when, from the reason above-mentioned, of not being suffered to carry his own produce to the best market, he is not able to pay the first cost of them in Britain. And it is no small mortification to him, that the great sums thus exacted from him should be employed to enrich and aggrandize a numerous tribe of greedy rapacious officers, many of whom he apprehends are useless; and many others of them he knows are become contemptible, by their dirty, tricking, disingenuous behaviour.

But he thinks it most peculiarly hard and grievous that the little share of property left him, after so many and so great deductions, should be rendered a precarious and uncertain possession.

Were he sure that an honest, upright deportment, and peaceable, inoffensive behaviour would render him secure, he might perhaps sit down quietly and enjoy the pittance left him; but when he reflects, he trembles even for that pittance! When he reflects on the amazing accession of jurisdiction given to courts of admiralty and the numerous cases in which trials by jury are abolished, he is almost led to suspect he places too great a value upon this boasted privilege, otherwise it would not be so lightly taken from him. He recurs to the history of his ancestors to know what were their sentiments of this flower of English liberty? He finds they esteemed it the Palladium of their constitution. He finds in every period of their history that they asserted it with great firmness, as their unalienable birthright; and, from his searches into history, he is led to conclude, with a late sensible judicious author (Blackstone),

That it is the most transcendant privilege which any subject can enjoy or wish for, that he cannot be affected either in his property, his liberty or his person, but by the unanimous consent of twelve of his neighbors and equals. A constitution that, I may venture to affirm, has, under Providence, secured the just liberties of this nation for a long succession of ages. And therefore a celebrated French writer, who concludes that because Rome, Sparta and Carthage, have lost their liberties, therefore those of England in time must perish, should have recollected that Rome, Sparta and Carthage were strangers to the trial by jury. It is therefore upon the whole (adds the same elegant writer in another place) a duty which every man owes to his country, his friends, his posterity and himself to maintain to the utmost of his power this valuable constitution in all its rights, and to guard with the most jealous circumspection against the introduction of new and arbitrary methods of trial, which, under a variety of plausible pretenses, may in time imperceptibly undermine this best preservative of English liberty.

Upon examination, he finds, on the other hand, that his ancestors were very cautious of admitting the jurisdiction of admiralty courts. The ancient law of England, both common and statute, confined it to things arising on the sea only, as is learnedly proved by the judges, in answer to the articles of complaint exhibited by the Lord Admiral to King James the First (*Vide* 4. Inst. 134) "And in case part of the cause of action arose at land and part at sea, the whole was determined in the courts of common law."

He asks how causes relating to the revenue are decided in Great Britain? Whether they are given to the Admiral? He is answered, No. In Ireland? No. America is the only place where cognizance of such causes is given to the admiralty. And what has America done to be thus particularized, to be disfranchised and stript of so invaluable a privilege as the trial by jury? Are the liberties of an American less dear to him or of smaller consequence than those of any other subject of the British Empire? He would presume they are not. Have the Americans abused this privilege, or are they less capable of judging and determining with propriety in cases of property than the other inhabitants of the British Empire? It must be allowed even by their enemies that they are in general intelligent, honest men. What, therefore, can be the reason for dealing thus harshly with the inhabitants of America?

However difficult the solution of this question may seem to be, he can easily foretell, and the prospect affords him the utmost concern, what will be the consequence of this deviation from what our ancestors looked upon as the bulwark of their liberties, and a fundamental principle of the British constitution. Merchants will consider their property as precarious; being liable to be called into the Admiralty to claim it, where the whole decision of the cause, of however great importance, rests on the arbitrary will of one man: And from this consideration they will be induced to draw their effects out of trade as much as possible, and secure what they can. Those who have not already engaged in foreign commerce will consider this method of decision as an additional, if not the most considerable risque attending trade, and many of them will no doubt be discouraged from the attempt, who might otherwise have become eminent merchants. The lands must of consequence be better settled. Necessity will oblige the colonists to pursue and extend agriculture and manufactures, and in time they will be able to live wholly independent of the mother country; which will undoubtedly prove a fatal wound to her trade and influence.

These are the sentiments of an American who glories in the British constitution and in being a member of the British Empire—whose heart bleeds to think that the interests of Great Britain and America should be separated in idea when they are in reality so closely united; and who would wish to preserve and perpetuate that Empire and that Constitution great and inviolate to latest times.

· 11 ·

A Short Narrative of the
Horrid Massacre in Boston

*By James Bowdoin, Dr. Joseph Warren
and Samuel Pemberton*

The day after the Boston Massacre the town meeting was in almost continuous session. It demanded the removal of the troops, and put so much pressure on Lieutenant-Governor Thomas Hutchinson and Colonel Dalrymple that they agreed to move the troops to Castle William on an island in the harbor. By March 16 the last of them had left. Meanwhile, the preparation of an account of the Massacre was under way. On March 6 the town meeting ordered that depositions be taken, describing the events of the previous

A Short Narrative Of The horrid Massacre in Boston, Perpetrated In the Evening of the Fifth Day of March, 1770, By Soldiers of the XXIXth Regiment; Which With the XIVth Regiment Were then Quartered there & With Some Observations On The State Of Things Prior To That Catastrophe, Boston, 1770. For a quite different version of the Boston Massacre, see Captain Thomas Preston's account in Merrill Jensen, ed., *American Colonial Documents to 1776,* pp. 752–755.

night. On March 13 the meeting appointed James Bowdoin, Dr. Joseph Warren, and Samuel Pemberton as a committee to find out who had committed the "murders and massacres," and to do everything in their power to see that the murderers were tried and punished.

The committee presented a written account of the "late horrid Massacre" to the town meeting on March 19. The meeting approved of the account, suggested some revisions, and ordered it printed. At the same time the town ordered the hiring of a fishing boat to carry copies of dispatches and of the printed pamphlet to England.

On March 26, the town voted that all printed copies of the pamphlet, except those sent to England, should be retained by the committee that had written it. The reason given was that sale of the pamphlet might be regarded by "the unhappy persons now in custody for trial as tending to give an undue Byass to the minds of the jury who are to try the same. . . ." The town meeting, of course, had already declared the soldiers guilty, and was demanding an immediate trial before the Superior Court. But with considerable courage, the government put off the trial until fall.

On July 10, a motion was made in town meeting to permit the printers to sell the pamphlet, but according to the *Boston Town Records* the motion passed "in the Narrative." Presumably this is a misprint for "passed in the negative." If so, Bostonians were not long denied copies. The next week, on July 16, the *Boston Evening Post* announced that it would publish the pamphlet "[from the London edition]," and on July 23, the *Post* reported that it had been published. Whether this was a trick to get around the vote of the town meeting, or was an actual copy of a London edition, is unknown: the pamphlet was available publicly, as it doubtless had been privately ever since it was printed.

During 1770 there were two different editions of the pamphlet in Boston, three in London, and one in Dublin. In reprinting the pamphlet here, the ninety-four depositions appended to it have been omitted. It should be noted that the committee had collected some twenty depositions defending the soldiers, but that it did not include them in the pamphlet.

The text of the pamphlet printed here is based on the reprint in Frederic Kidder, *History of the Boston Massacre. . . .* (Albany, 1870), pp. 25–46. Kidder modernized punctuation, capitalization, and spelling. Most of his changes have been accepted. However, the text has been proofread and corrected against the microcard copy of the first edition.

It may be a proper introduction to this narrative, briefly to represent the state of things for some time previous to the said massacre; and this seems necessary in order to the forming a just idea of the causes of it.

At the end of the late war, in which this province bore so distinguished a part, a happy union subsisted between Great Britain and the colonies. This was unfortunately interrupted by the Stamp Act; but it was in some measure restored by the repeal of it. It was again interrupted by other acts of parliament for taxing America; and by the appointment of a board of commissioners, in pursuance of an act, which by the face of it was made for the relief and encouragement of commerce, but which in its operation, it was apprehended, would have, and it has in fact had, a contrary effect. By the said act the said commissioners were "to be resident in some convenient part of his majesty's dominions in America." This must be understood to be in some part convenient for the whole. But it does not appear that, in fixing the place of their residence, the convenience of the whole was at all consulted, for Boston, being very far from the centre of the colonies, could not be the place most convenient for the whole. Judging by the act, it may seem this town was intended to be favored, by the commissioners being appointed to reside here; and that the consequence of that residence would be the relief and encouragement of commerce; but the reverse has been the constant and uniform effect of it; so that the commerce of the town, from the embarrassments in which it has been lately involved, is greatly reduced. For the particulars on this head, see the state of the trade not long since drawn up and transmitted to England by a committee of the merchants of Boston.

The residence of the commissioners here has been detrimental, not only to the commerce, but to the political interests of the town and province; and not only so, but we can trace from it the causes of the late horrid massacre. Soon after their arrival here in November, 1767, instead of confining themselves to the proper business of their office, they became partisans of Governor Bernard in his political schemes; and had the weakness and temerity to infringe upon one of the most essential rights of the house of commons of this province—that of giving their votes with freedom, and not being accountable therefor but to their constituents. One of the members of that house, Capt. Timothy Folger, having voted in some affair contrary to the mind of the said commissioners, was for so doing dismissed from the office he held under them.

These proceedings of theirs, the difficulty of access to them on office business, and a supercilious behavior, rendered them disgustful to people in general, who in consequence thereof treated them with neglect. This probably stimulated them to resent it; and to make their resentment felt, they and their coadjutor, Governor Bernard, made such representations to his majesty's ministers as they thought best calculated to bring the displeasure of the nation upon the town and province; and in order that those representations might have the more weight, they are said to have contrived and executed plans for exciting disturbances and tumults, which otherwise would probably never have existed; and, when excited, to have transmitted to the ministry the most exaggerated accounts of them.

These particulars of their conduct his majesty's council of this province have fully laid open in their proceeding in council, and in their address to General Gage, in July and October,

1768; and in their letter to Lord Hillsborough of the 15th of April, 1769. Unfortunately for us, they have been too successful in their said representations, which, in conjunction with Governor Bernard's, have occasioned his majesty's faithful subjects of this town and province to be treated as enemies and rebels, by an invasion of the town by sea and land; to which the approaches were made with all the circumspection usual where a vigorous opposition is expected. While the town was surrounded by a considerable number of his majesty's ships of war, two regiments landed and took possession of it; and to support these, two other regiments arrived some time after from Ireland; one of which landed at Castle Island, and the other in the town.

Thus were we, in aggravation of our other embarrassments, embarrassed with troops, forced upon us contrary to our inclination—contrary to the spirit of Magna Charta—contrary to the very letter of the Bill of Rights, in which it is declared, that the raising or keeping a standing army within the kingdom in time of peace, unless it be with the consent of parliament, is against law, and without the desire of the civil magistrates, to aid whom was the pretence for sending the troops hither; who were quartered in the town in direct violation of an act of parliament for quartering troops in America; and all this in consequence of the representations of the said commissioners and the said governor, as appears by their memorials and letters lately published.

As they were the procuring cause of troops being sent hither, they must therefore be the remote and a blameable cause of all the disturbances and bloodshed that have taken place in consequence of that measure.

But we shall leave them to their own reflections, after observing, that as they had some months before the arrival of the troops, under pretence of safety to their persons, retired from the town to the Castle, so after the arrival of the troops, and their being quartered in the town, they thought proper to return; having answered as they doubtless thought, the purpose of their voluntary flight.

We shall next attend to the conduct of the troops, and to some circumstances relative to them. Governor Bernard without consulting the council, having given up the State-house to the troops at their landing, they took possession of the chambers, where the representatives of the province and the courts of law held their meetings; and (except the council-chamber) of all other parts of that house; in which they continued a considerable time, to the great annoyance of those courts while they sat, and of the merchants and gentlemen of the town, who had always made the lower floor of it their exchange. They had a right so to do, as the property of it was in the town; but they were deprived of that right by mere power. The said governor soon after, by every stratagem and by every method but a forcible entry, endeavored to get possession of the Manufactory house, to make a barrack of it for the troops; and for that purpose caused it to be besieged by the troops, and the people in it to be used very cruelly; which extraordinary proceedings created universal uneasiness, arising from the apprehension that the troops under the influence of such a man would be employed to effect the most dangerous purposes; but failing of that, other houses were procured, in which, contrary to act of parliament, he caused the troops to be quartered. After their quarters were settled, the main guard was posted at one of the said houses, directly opposite to, and not twelve yards from, the State-house (where the general court, and all the law courts for the county were held), with two field pieces pointed to the State-house. This situation of the main guard and field pieces seemed to indicate an attack upon the constitution, and a defiance of law; and to be intended to affront the legislative and executive authority of the province.

The general court, at the first session after the arrival of the troops, viewed it in this light, and applied to Governor Bernard to cause such a nuisance to be removed; but to no purpose. Disgusted at such an indignity, and at the appearance of being under duress, they refused to do business in such circumstances; and in consequence thereof were adjourned to Cambridge, to the great inconvenience of the members.

Besides this, the challenging the inhabitants by sentinels posted in all parts of the town before the lodgings of officers, which (for about six months, while it lasted), occasioned many quarrels and uneasiness.

Capt. Wilson, of the 59th, exciting the negroes of the town to take away their masters' lives and property, and repair to the army for protection, which was fully proved against him—the attack of a party of soldiers on some of the magistrates of the town—the repeated rescues of soldiers from peace officers—the firing of a loaded musket in a public street, to the endangering a great number of peaceable inhabitants—the frequent wounding of persons by their bayonets and cutlasses, and the numerous instances of bad behavior in the soldiery, made us early sensible that the troops were not sent here for any benefit to the town or province, and that we had no good to expect from such conservators of the peace.[1]

It was not expected, however, that such an outrage and massacre, as happened here on the evening of the fifth instant, would have been perpetrated. There were then killed and wounded, by a discharge of musketry, eleven of his majesty's subjects, viz:

Mr. Samuel Gray, killed on the spot by a ball entering his head.

Crispus Attucks, a mulatto, killed on the spot, two balls entering his breast.

---

[1] The inhabitants, instead of making application to the military officers on these occasions, chose rather to oppose the civil authority and the laws of the land to such offenders; and had not the soldiery found means to evade legal punishments, it is more than probable their insolence would have received a check and some of the most melancholy effects of it been prevented.

Mr. James Caldwell, killed on the spot, by two balls entering his back.

Mr. Samuel Maverick, a youth of seventeen years of age, mortally wounded; he died the next morning.

Mr. Patrick Carr mortally wounded; he died the 14th instant.

Christopher Monk and John Clark, youths about seventeen years of age, dangerously wounded. It is apprehended they will die.

Mr. Edward Payne, merchant, standing at his door; wounded.

Messrs. John Green, Robert Patterson, and David Parker; all dangerously wounded.

The actors in this dreadful tragedy were a party of soldiers commanded by Capt. Preston of the 29th regiment. This party, including the captain, consisted of eight, who are all committed to jail.

There are depositions in this affair which mention, that several guns were fired at the same time from the Custom-house; before which this shocking scene was exhibited. Into this matter inquisition is now making. In the meantime it may be proper to insert here the substance of some of those depositions.

Benjamin Frizell, on the evening of the 5th of March, having taken his station near the west corner of the Custom-house in King street, before and at the time of the soldiers firing their guns, declares (among other things) that the first discharge was only of one gun, the next of two guns, upon which he the deponent thinks he saw a man stumble; the third discharge was of three guns, upon which he thinks he saw two men fall; and immediately after were discharged five guns, two of which were by soldiers on his right hand; the other three, as appeared to the deponent, were discharged from the balcony, or the chamber window of the Custom-house, the flashes appearing on the left hand, and higher than the right hand flashes appeared to be, and of which the deponent was very sensible, although his eyes were much turned to the soldiers, who were all on his right hand.

Gillam Bass, being in King street at the same time, declares that they (the party of soldiers from the main guard) posted themselves between the Custom-house door and the west corner of it; and in a few minutes began to fire upon the people: two or three of the flashes so high above the rest, that he the deponent verily believes they must have come from the Custom-house windows.

Jeremiah Allen declares, that in the evening of the 5th day of March current, being at about nine o'clock in the front chamber in the house occupied by Col. Ingersoll in King street, he heard some guns fired, which occasioned his going into the balcony of the said house. That when he was in the said balcony in company with Mr. William Molineux, jun., and John Simpson, he heard the discharge of four or five guns, the flashes of which appeared to be to the westward of the sentry-box, and immediately after, he the deponent heard two or three more guns and saw the flashes thereof from out of the house, now called the Custom-house, as they evidently appeared to him, and which he the said deponent at the same time declared to the aforesaid Molineux and Simpson, being then near him, saying to them (at the same time pointing his hand towards the Custom-house), "there they are out of the Custom-house."

George Coster, being in King street at the time above mentioned, declares that in five or six minutes after he stopped, he heard the word of command given to the soldiers *fire;* upon which one gun was fired, which did no execution, as the deponent observed; about half a minute after two guns, one of which killed one Samuel Gray a rope-maker, the other a mulatto man, between which two men the deponent stood; after this the deponent heard the discharge of four or five guns more, by the soldiers; immediately after which the deponent heard the discharge of two guns or pistols, from an open window of the middle story of the Custom-house, near to the place where the sentry-box is placed, and being but a small distance from the window, he heard the people from within speak and laugh, and soon after saw the casement lowered down; after which the deponent assisted others in carrying off one of the corpses.

Cato, a negro man, servant to Tuthill Hubbart, Esq., declares that on Monday evening the 5th of March current, on hearing the cry of fire, he ran into King street, where he saw a number of people assembled before the Custom-house; that he stood near the sentry-box and saw the soldiers fire on the people, who stood in the middle of said street; directly after which he saw two flashes of guns, one quick upon the other, from the chamber window of the Custom-house; and that after the firing was all over, while the people were carrying away the dead and wounded, he saw the Custom-house door opened, and several soldiers (one of whom had a cutlass), go into the Custom-house and shut the door after them.

Benjamin Andrews declares, that being desired by the committee of inquiry to take the ranges of the holes made by musket balls, in two houses nearly opposite to the Custom-house, he finds the bullet hole in the entry-door post of Mr. Payne's house (and which grazed the edge of the door, before it entered the post, where it lodged, two and a half inches deep), ranges just under the stool of the westernmost lower chamber window of the Custom-house.

Samuel Drowne, towards the end of his deposition (which contains a pretty full account of the proceedings of the soldiers on the evening of the 5th instant), declares, that he saw the flashes of two guns fired from the Custom-house, one of which was out of a window of the chamber westward of the balcony, and the other from the balcony; the gun (which he clearly discerned), being pointed through the ballisters, and the person who held the gun, in a stooping posture withdrew himself into the house, having a handkerchief or some kind of cloth over his face.

These depositions show clearly that a number of guns were fired from the Custom-house. As this affair is now inquiring into, all the notice we shall take of it is, that it distinguishes the actors in it into street-actors and house-actors; which is necessary to be observed.

What gave occasion to the melancholy event of that evening seems to have been this. A difference having happened near Mr. Gray's ropewalk, between a soldier and a man belonging to it, the soldier challenged the ropemakers to a boxing match. The challenge was accepted by one of them, and the soldier worsted. He ran to the barrack in the neighborhood, and returned with several of his companions. The fray was renewed, and the soldiers were driven off. They soon returned with recruits, and were again worsted. This happened several times, till at length a considerable body of soldiers was collected, and they also were driven off, the ropemakers having been joined by their brethren of the contiguous ropewalks. By this time Mr. Gray being alarmed interposed, and with the assistance of some gentlemen prevented any further disturbance. To satisfy the soldiers and punish the man who had been the occasion of the first difference, and as an example to the rest, he turned him out of his service; and waited on Col. Dalrymple, the commanding officer of the troops, and with him concerted measures for preventing further mischief. Though this affair ended thus, it made a strong impression on the minds of the soldiers in general, who thought the honor of the regiment concerned to revenge those repeated repulses. For this purpose they seemed to have formed a combination to commit some outrage upon the inhabitants of the town indiscriminately; and this was to be done on the evening of the 5th instant or soon after; as appears by the depositions of the following persons, viz:

William Newhall declares, that on Thursday night the 1st of March instant, he met four soldiers of the 29th regiment, and that he heard them say, "there were a great many that would eat their dinners on Monday next, that should not eat any on Tuesday."

Daniel Calfe declares, that on Saturday evening the 3d of March, a camp-woman, wife to James McDeed, a grenadier of the 29th, came into his father's shop, and the people talking about the affrays at the ropewalks, and blaming the soldiers for the part they had acted in it, the woman said, "the soldiers were in the right;" adding, "that before Tuesday or Wednesday night they would wet their swords or bayonets in New England people's blood."

Mary Brailsford declares, that on sabbath evening the 4th of March instant, a soldier came to the house of Mr. Amos Thayer, where she then was. He desiring to speak with Mr. Thayer, was told by Mrs. Mary Thayer, that her brother was engaged and could not be spoke with. He said, "your brother as you call him, is a man I have a great regard for, and I came on purpose to tell him to keep in his house, for *before Tuesday night next at twelve o'clock, there will be a great deal of bloodshed, and a great many lives lost;*" and added, "that he came out of a particular regard to her brother to advise him to keep in his house, for then he would be out of harm's way." He said, "your brother knows me very well; my name is Charles Malone." He then went away. Of the same import, and in confirmation of this declaration, are the depositions of Mary Thayer and Asa Copeland, who both live with the said Mr. Thayer, and heard what the soldier said as above mentioned. It is also confirmed by the deposition of Nicholas Ferriter.

Jane Usher declares, that about 9 o'clock on Monday morning the 5th of March current, from a window she saw two persons in the habit of soldiers, one of whom being on horseback appeared to be an officer's servant. The person on the horse first spoke to the other, but what he said, she is not able to say, though the window was open, and she not more than twenty feet distant; the other replied, "he hoped he should see blood enough spilt before morning."

Matthew Adams declares, that on Monday evening the 5th of March instant, between the hours of 7 and 8 o'clock, he went to the house of Corporal Pershall of the 29th regiment, near Quaker lane, where he saw the corporal and his wife, with one of the fifers of said regiment. When he had got what he went for, and was coming away, the corporal called him back, and desired him with great earnestness to go home to his master's house as soon as business was over, and not to be abroad on any account that night in particular, for "the soldiers were determined to be revenged on the ropewalk people; and that much mischief would be done." Upon which the fifer (about eighteen or nineteen years of age), said "he hoped in God they would burn the town down." On this he left the house, and the said corporal called after him again, and begged he would mind what he said to him.

Caleb Swan declares, that on Monday night, the 5th of March instant, at the time of the bells ringing for fire, he heard a woman's voice, whom he knew to be the supposed wife of one Montgomery, a grenadier of the 29th regiment, standing at her door, and heard her say, *"it was not fire; the town was too haughty and too proud; and that many of their arses would be laid low before the morning."*

Margaret Swansborough declares, that a free woman named Black Peg, who has kept much with the soldiers, on hearing the disturbance on Monday evening the 5th instant, said, "the soldiers were not to be trod upon by the inhabitants, but would know before morning, whether they or the inhabitants were to be masters."

Joseph Hooton, jun., declares, that coming from the Southend of Boston on Monday evening the 5th of March instant, against Dr. Sewall's meeting he heard a great noise and tumult, with the cry of murder often repeated. Proceeding towards the

Town-house he was passed by several soldiers running that way, with naked cutlasses and bayonets in their hands. He asked one of them what was the matter, and was answered by him, "by God you shall all know what is the matter soon." Between 9 and 10 o'clock he went into King street, and was present at the tragical scene exhibited near the Custom-house; as particularly set forth in his deposition.

Mrs. Mary Russell declares, that John Brailsford a private soldier of the 14th regiment, who had frequently been employed by her (when he was ordered with his company to the castle, in consequence of the murders committed by the soldiers on the evening of the 5th of March), coming to the deponent's house declared, that *their* regiment were *ordered* to hold themselves in readiness, and accordingly was ready *that evening*, upon the inhabitants firing on the soldiery, to come to the assistance of the soldiery. On which she asked him, if he would have fired upon any of the inhabitants of this town. To which he replied, " yes, if he had orders; but that if he saw Mr. Russell, he would have fired wide of him." He also said, "It's well there was no gun fired by the inhabitants, for had there been, *we* should have come to the soldiers' assistance."

By the foregoing depositions it appears very clearly, there was a general combination among the soldiers of the 29th regiment at least, to commit some extraordinary act of violence upon the town; that if the inhabitants attempted to repel it by firing even one gun upon those soldiers, the 14th regiment were ordered to be in readiness to assist them; and that on the late butchery in King street they actually were ready for that purpose, had a single gun been fired on the perpetrators of it.

It appears by a variety of depositions, that on the same evening between the hours of six and half after nine (at which time the firing began), many persons, without the least provocation, were in various parts of the town insulted and abused by parties of armed soldiers patrolling the streets; particularly:

Mr. Robert Pierpont declares, that between the hours of 7

and 8 in the same evening, three armed soldiers passing him, one of them who had a bayonet gave him a back-handed stroke with it. On complaint of this treatment, he said the deponent should soon hear more of it, and threatened him very hard.

Mr. Henry Bass declares, that at 9 o'clock, a party of soldiers came out of Draper's alley, leading to and from Murray's barracks, and they being armed with large naked cutlasses, made at every body coming in their way, cutting and slashing, and that he himself very narrowly escaped receiving a cut from the foremost of them, who pursued him.

Samuel Atwood declares, that ten or twelve soldiers armed with drawn cutlasses bolted out of the alley leading from Murray's barracks into Dock square, and met the deponent, who asked them if they intended to murder people? They answered, "Yes, by God, root and branch;" saying, "here is one of them;" with that one of them struck the deponent with a club, which was repeated by another. The deponent being unarmed turned to go off, and he received a wound on the left shoulder, which reached the bone, disabled him and gave him much pain. Having gone a few steps the deponent met two officers, and asked them, "Gentlemen, what is the matter?" they answered "you will see by and by;" and as he passed by Col. Jackson's he heard the cry, turn out the guards.

Capt. James Kirkwood declares, that about 9 of the clock in the evening of the 5th day of March current, he was going by Murray's barracks: hearing a noise he stopped at Mr. Rhoads's door, opposite the said barracks, where said Rhoads was standing, and stood some time, and saw the soldiers coming out of the yard from the barracks, armed with cutlasses and bayonets, and rushing through Boylston's alley into Cornhill, two officers, namely, Lieuts. Minchin and Dickson, came out of the mess-house, and said to the soldiers, "My lads, come into the barracks and don't hurt the inhabitants," and then retired into the mess-house. Soon after they came to the door

again, and found the soldiers in the yard; and directly upon
it, Ensign Mall came to the gate of the barrack-yard and said
to the soldiers, "*Turn out, and I will stand by you;*" this he repeated frequently, adding, "*Kill them! stick them! knock them
down; run your bayonets through them;*" with a great deal of
language of like import. Upon which a great number of soldiers came out of the barracks with naked cutlasses, headed by
said Mall, and went through the aforesaid alley; that some officers came and got the soldiers into their barracks, and that
Mall, with his sword or cutlass drawn in his hand, as often
had them out again, but were at last drove into their barracks
by the aforesaid Minchin and Dickson.

Mr. Henry Rhoads's declaration agrees with Captain Kirkwood's.

Mr. Matthias King, of Halifax, in Nova Scotia, declares that
in the evening of the fifth day of March instant, about nine
o'clock, he was at his lodgings at Mrs. Torrey's, near the town
pump, and heard the bells ring and the cry of "fire;" upon
which he went to the door and saw several soldiers come
round the south side of the Town-house, armed with bayonets,
and something which he took to be broadswords; that one of
those people came up almost to him and Mr. Bartholomew
Kneeland; and that they had but just time to shut the door
upon him; otherwise he is well assured they must have fell
victims to their boundless cruelty. He afterwards went into
the upper chamber of the said house, and was looking out of
the window when the drum and the guard went into the barrack, and he saw one of the guards kneel and present his piece,
with a bayonet fixed, and heard him swear he would fire upon
a parcel of boys who were then in the street, but he did not.
He further declares that when the body of troops was drawn
up before the guard house (which was presently after the
massacre), he heard an officer say to another, that this was
fine work, and just what he wanted; but in the hurry he could
not see him, so as to know him again.

Robert Polley declares, that on Monday evening, the 5th instant, as he was going home, he observed about ten persons standing near Mr. Taylor's door; after standing there a small space of time, he went with them towards Boylston's alley, opposite to Murray's barracks; we met in the alley about eight or nine armed soldiers; they assaulted us, and gave us a great deal of abusive language; we then drove them back to the barracks with sticks only; we looked for stones or bricks, but could find none, the ground being covered with snow. Some of the lads dispersed, and he, the said Polley, with a few others, were returning peaceably home, when we met about nine or ten other soldiers armed: one of them said, "Where are the sons of bitches?" They struck at several persons in the street, and went towards the head of the alley. Two officers came and endeavored to get them into their barracks; one of the lads proposed to ring the bell; the soldiers went through the alley, and the boys huzzaed, and said they were gone through Royal Exchange lane into King street.

Samuel Drowne declares that, about nine o'clock of the evening of the fifth of March current, standing at his own door in Cornhill, he saw about fourteen or fifteen soldiers of the 29th regiment, who came from Murray's barracks, armed with naked cutlasses, swords, &c., and came upon the inhabitants of the town, then standing or walking in Cornhill, and abused some, and violently assaulted others as they met them; most of whom were without so much as a stick in their hand to defend themselves, as he very clearly could discern, it being moonlight, and himself being one of the assaulted persons. All or most of the said soldiers he saw go into King street (some of them through Royal Exchange lane), and there followed them, and soon discovered them to be quarrelling and fighting with the people whom they saw there, which he thinks were not more than a dozen, when the soldiers came there first, armed as aforesaid. Of those dozen people, the most of them were gentlemen, standing together a little below the

Town-house, upon the Exchange. At the appearance of those soldiers so armed, the most of the twelve persons went off, some of them being first assaulted.

The violent proceedings of this party, and their going into King street, "quarrelling and fighting with the people whom they saw there" (mentioned in Mr. Drowne's deposition), was immediately introductory to the grand catastrophe.

These assailants, who issued from Murray's barracks (so called), after attacking and wounding divers persons in Corn-hill, as above mentioned, being armed, proceeded (most of them) up the Royal Exchange lane into King street; where, making a short stop, and after assaulting and driving away the few they met there, they brandished their arms and cried out, "Where are the boogers! where are the cowards!" At this time there were very few persons in the street beside themselves. This party in proceeding from Exchange lane into King street, must pass the sentry posted at the westerly corner of the Custom-house, which butts on that lane and fronts on that street. This is needful to be mentioned, as near that spot and in that street the bloody tragedy was acted, and the street actors in it were stationed: their station being but a few feet from the front side of the said Custom-house. The outrageous behavior and the threats of the said party occasioned the ringing of the meeting-house bell near the head of King street, which bell ringing quick, as for fire, it presently brought out a number of the inhabitants, who being soon sensible of the occasion of it, were naturally led to King street, where the said party had made a stop but a little while before, and where their stopping had drawn together a number of boys, round the sentry at the Custom-house. Whether the boys mistook the sentry for one of the said party, and thence took occasion to differ with him, or whether he first affronted them, which is affirmed in several depositions; however that may be, there was much foul language between them, and some of them, in consequence of his pushing at them with his bayonet, threw snowballs at him,[2] which occasioned him to knock hastily at the door of the Custom-house. From hence two persons thereupon proceeded immediately to the mainguard, which was posted (opposite to the State-house) at a small distance, near the head of the said street. The officer on guard was Capt. Preston, who with seven or eight soldiers, with fire-arms and charged bayonets, issued from the guard house, and in great haste posted himself and his soldiers in the front of the Custom-house, near the corner aforesaid. In passing to this station the soldiers pushed several persons with their bayonets, driving through the people in so rough a manner that it appeared they intended to create a disturbance. This occasioned some snowballs to be thrown at them, which seems to have been the only provocation that was given. Mr. Knox (between whom and Capt. Preston there was some conversation on the spot) declares, that while he was talking with Capt. Preston, the soldiers of his detachment had attacked the people with their bayonets; and that there was not the least provocation given to Capt. Preston or his party; the backs of the people being toward them when the people were attacked. He also declares that Capt. Preston seemed to be in great haste and much agi-

---

[2] Since writing this narrative, several depositions have appeared, which make it clear that the sentry was first in fault. He overheard a barber's boy saying, that a captain of the 14th (who had just passed by) was so mean a fellow as not to pay his barber for shaving him. Upon this the sentry left his post and followed the boy into the middle of the street, where he told him to show his face. The boy pertly replied, "I am not ashamed to show my face to any man." Upon this the sentry gave him sweeping stroke on the head with his musket, which made him reel and stagger, and cry much. A fellow-apprentice asked the sentry, what he meant by this abuse? He replied, "Damn your blood, if you do not get out of the way, I will give you something;" and then fixed his bayonet and pushed at the lads, who both ran out of his way. This dispute collected a few persons about the boy, near the Custom-house. Presently after this, the party above-mentioned came into King street, which was a further occasion of drawing people thither, as above related. (See deposition of Benjamin Broaders and others).

tated, and that, according to his opinion, there were not then present in King street above seventy or eighty persons at the extent.

The said party was formed into a half circle; and within a short time after they had been posted at the Custom-house, began to fire upon the people.

Captain Preston is said to have ordered them to fire, and to have repeated that order. One gun was fired first; then others in succession, and with deliberation, till ten or a dozen guns were fired; or till that number of discharges were made from the guns that were fired. By which means eleven persons were killed and wounded, as above represented.

These facts, with divers circumstances attending them, are supported by the depositions of a considerable number of persons, and among others of the following, viz: Messrs. Henry Bass, Samuel Atwood, Samuel Drowne, James Kirkwood, Robert Polley, Samuel Condon, Daniel Usher, Josiah Simpson, Henry Knox, Gillam Bass, John Hickling, Richard Palmes, Benjamin Frizzel, and others, whose depositions are in the appendix.

Soon after the firing, a drum with a party from the main guard went to Murray's and the other barracks, beating an alarm as they went, which, with the firing, had the effect of a signal for action. Whereupon all the soldiers of the 29th regiment, or the main body of them, appeared in King street under arms, and seemed bent on a further massacre of the inhabitants, which was with great difficulty prevented. They were drawn up between the State-house and main guard, their lines extending across the street and facing down King street, where the town-people were assembled. The first line kneeled, and the whole of the first platoon presented their guns ready to fire, as soon as the word should be given. They continued in that posture a considerable time; but by the good providence of God they were restrained from firing. That they then went into King street with such a disposition will appear probable by the two following depositions.

Mrs. Mary Gardner, living in Atkinson street, declares, that on Monday evening the 5th of March current, and before the guns fired in King street, there were a number of soldiers assembled from Green's barracks towards the street, and opposite to her gate; that they stood very still until the guns were fired in King street; then they clapped their hands and gave a cheer, saying, "This is all that we want." They ran to their barrack, and came out again in a few minutes, all with their arms, and ran towards King street.

William Fallass declares, that (after the murder in King street) on the evening of the 5th instant, upon his return home, he had occasion to stop opposite to the lane leading to Green's barracks, and while he stood there, the soldiers rushed by him with their arms, towards King street, saying: "This is our time or chance;" and that he never saw men or dogs so greedy for their prey as those soldiers seemed to be, and the sergeants could hardly keep them in their ranks.

These circumstances, with those already mentioned, amount to a clear proof of a combination among them to commit some outrage upon the town on that evening; and that after the enormous one committed in King street, they intended to add to the horrors of that night by making a further slaughter.

At the time Capt. Preston's party issued from the main guard, there were in King street about two hundred persons, and those were collected there by the ringing of the bell in consequence of the violences of another party, that had been there a very little while before. When Captain Preston had got to the Custom-house, so great a part of the people dispersed at sight of the soldiers, that not more than twenty or thirty then remained in King street, as Mr. Drowne declares, and at the time of the firing not seventy, as Mr. Palmes thinks.

But after the firing, and when the slaughter was known, which occasioned the ringing of all the bells of the town, a large body of the inhabitants soon assembled in King street, and continued there the whole time the 29th regiment was there under arms, and would not retire till that regiment, and all the soldiers that appeared, were ordered, and actually went, to their barracks: after which, having been assured by the Lieutenant-Governor, and a number of the civil magistrates present, that every legal step should be taken to bring the criminals to justice, they gradually dispersed. For some time the appearance of things was dismal. The soldiers outrageous on the one hand, and the inhabitants justly incensed against them on the other; both parties seeming disposed to come to action. In this case the consequences would have been terrible. But by the interposition of his honor, some of his majesty's council, a number of civil magistrates, and other gentlemen of weight and influence, who all endeavored to calm and pacify the people, and by the two principal officers interposing their authority with regard to the soldiers, there was happily no further bloodshed ensued; and by two o'clock the town was restored to a tolerable state of quiet. About that time, Capt Preston, and a few hours after, the party that had fired, were committed to safe custody.

One happy effect has arisen from this melancholy affair, and it is the general voice of the town and province it may be a lasting one—all the troops are removed from the town. They are quartered for the present in the barracks at Castle island; from whence it is hoped they will have a speedy order to remove entirely out of the province, together with those persons who were the occasion of their coming hither.

In what manner this was effected, it is not foreign from the subject of this narrative to relate.

The morning after the massacre, a town meeting was held; at which attended a very great number of the freeholders and other inhabitants of the town. They were deeply impressed and affected by the tragedy of the preceding night, and were unanimously of opinion, it was incompatible with their safety that the troops should remain any longer in the town. In consequence thereof they chose a committee of fifteen gentlemen to wait upon his honor the Lieutenant-Governor in Council to request of him to issue his orders for the immediate removal of the troops.

The message was in these words:

"That it is the unanimous opinion of this meeting that the inhabitants and soldiery can no longer live together in safety; that nothing can rationally be expected to restore the peace of the town and prevent further blood and carnage, but the immediate removal of the troops; and that we therefore most fervently pray his honor, that his power and influence may be exerted for their instant removal."

His honor's reply, which was laid before the town then adjourned to the old south meeting-house, was as follows:

"Gentlemen,

"I am extremely sorry for the unhappy differences between the inhabitants and troops, and especially for the action of the last evening, and I have exerted myself upon that occasion, that a due inquiry may be made, and that the law may have its course. I have in council consulted with the commanding officers of the two regiments who are now in the town. They have their orders from the general at New York. It is not in my power to countermand those orders. The Council have desired that the two regiments may be removed to the Castle. From the particular concern which the 29th regiment has had in your differences, Col. Dalrymple, who is the commanding officer of the troops, has signified that that regiment shall without delay be placed in the barracks at the Castle, until he can send to the general and receive his further orders concerning both the regiments, and that the main-guard shall be removed, and the 14th regiment so disposed, and laid under such restraint, that all occasion of future disturbances may be prevented."

The foregoing reply having been read and fully considered —the question was put, Whether the report be satisfactory? Passed in the negative (only one dissentient) out of upwards of 4,000 voters.

A respectable committee was then appointed to wait on his honor the Lieutenant-Governor, and inform him, *that it is the unanimous opinion of this meeting, that the reply made to a vote of the inhabitants presented his honor in the morning, is by no means satisfactory; and that nothing less will satisfy than a total and immediate removal of all the troops.*

The committee having waited upon the Lieutenant-Governor, agreeable to the foregoing vote, laid before the inhabitants the following vote of Council received from his honor.

His honor the Lieutenant-Governor laid before the board a vote of the town of Boston, passed this afternoon, and then addressed the board as follows:

"Gentlemen of the Council,

"I lay before you a vote of the town of Boston, which I have just now received from them, and I now ask your advice what you judge necessary to be done upon it."

The Council thereupon expressed themselves to be unanimously of opinion, "that it was absolutely necessary for his majesty's service, the good order of the town, and the peace of the province, that the troops should be immediately removed out of the town of Boston, and thereupon advised his honor to communicate this advice of the council to Col. Dalrymple, and to pray that he would order the troops down to Castle William." The committee also informed the town, that Col. Dalrymple after having seen the vote of Council, said to the committee,

"That he now gave his word of honor that he would begin his preparations in the morning, and that there should be no unnecessary delay until the whole of the two regiments were removed to the Castle."

Upon the above report being read, the inhabitants could not avoid expressing the high satisfaction it afforded them.

After measures were taken for the security of the town in the night by a strong military watch, the meeting was dissolved.

In the concluding paragraph of the foregoing narrative it is said, that the town meeting was dissolved after the measures were taken for the security of the town in the night, by a strong military watch.

Our implacable enemies, in pursuance of their plan of misrepresentation, have taken pains to misrepresent this most necessary measure, by declaring it to have been contrary to the mind of the commander-in-chief, and against law.

This matter will be judged of, by stating the fact, and producing the law.

When the committee, who had waited on the Lieutenant-Governor, had reported to the town that the troops would be removed to Castle island (at which time it was near night), it was thought necessary for the safety of the town, and for preventing a rescue of the persons committed to jail for firing upon and killing a number of his majesty's subjects, that there should be a military watch; and divers gentlemen were desired to take the needful steps for that purpose. It being then night, it was impossible a regular notification should issue from the officers of the militia; a considerable number of respectable persons therefore offered themselves volunteers, and did the duty of a military watch under the direction of the lieutenant-colonel, who attended that service with the approbation of the chief colonel of the Boston regiment. The next day, with two of the select men of the town, the chief colonel went to the Lieutenant-Governor, and they informed him it was apprehended absolutely necessary for the safety of the town there should be a military watch kept; and that the colonel then waited upon him to receive his orders. The Lieutenant-Governor declined giving any orders concerning it, but said the law was clear, that the colonel, as chief officer of the regiment, might order a military watch; and that he might do about it as he thought fit. In consequence of this, and knowing the law gave him such a power, the colonel issued his orders for that purpose, and a regular watch was kept the following night. The next day the Lieutenant-Governor sent for the colonel, and let him know, that he was in doubt about the legality of the appointment of the military watch; and recommended to the colonel to take good advice whether he had a right by law to order such a watch.

This being quite unexpected, occasioned the colonel to express himself with some fervor. He also said, he had already taken advice, and had no doubt of his own power; but had the preceding day waited upon his honor as commander-in-chief to receive his orders; which, as his honor had declined giving, and left the matter with himself, he had appointed a military watch; and judged it a necessary measure to quiet the fears and apprehensions of the town. The interview ended with the Lieut.-Governor's recommending again, that the colonel would take care to proceed according to law; and without his forbidding a military watch.

This military watch was continued every night, till Col. Dalrymple had caused the two regiments under his command to be removed to the barracks at Castle Island. During the continuance of the watch, the justices of the peace in their turns attended every night; and the utmost order and regularity took place through the whole of it.

This is the state of the fact, upon which every one is left to make his own observations.

Now for the law; with respect to which nothing more is necessary than just to recite it. It runs thus, "That there be military watches appointed and kept in every town, at such times, in such places, and in such numbers, and under such regulation, as the chief military officers of each town shall appoint, or as they may receive orders from the chief officer of the regiment."[3] This needs no comment. It clearly authorizes the chief officer of the regiment to appoint military watches. The late military watch in Boston being founded on such an appointment was therefore according to law.

---

[3] See a Law of the Province for regulating the Militia, made in the 5th year of William and Mary, Chap. 7, Sec. 10.

· 12 ·

A State of the Rights

of the Colonists (1772)

[*By Samuel Adams?*]

Samuel Adams' political fortunes reached a low ebb in the spring of 1772, when an effort was made to defeat his re-election to the legislature. He was re-elected, but received only 505 votes, as compared with 699 for Thomas Cushing, 690 for John Hancock, and 668 for William Phillips. Then in July, the ministry in England decided to pay the salaries of the Superior Court judges from British customs revenues. That decision, soon known in Boston, gave Adams an opportunity and he began the attack in the *Boston Gazette*. He denounced Governor Thomas Hutchinson as a pensioned "tool" of the Crown and then turned to the issue of the judges' salaries, beseeching God to save the country from ruin and to not let "the iron hand of tyranny ravish our laws and seize the

A Report of the Record Commissioners of the City of Boston, Containing the Boston Town Records, 1770 Through 1777 (Boston, 1887), pp. 95–108.

badge of freedom, nor avowed corruption and murderous rage of lawless power be ever seen on the sacred seat of justice."

His remedy was the formation of associations to recover the just rights of Americans. Petitions were prepared, and on October 28 the Boston Town Meeting considered them. The town petitioned Governor Hutchinson for information and he refused to give any. Two days later the Town Meeting asked him to allow the legislature to meet at the appointed time. Hutchinson put off the session and replied it was none of the town's business when the legislature met. At that point Samuel Adams moved the appointment of a Committee of Correspondence of twenty-one men to state the rights of the colonists and the violations of those rights. The meeting agreed without dissent. The committee appointed was controlled by men who supported Adams.

"A State of the Rights of the Colonists" was probably the work of Samuel Adams, for a draft still exists in his handwriting. It was carefully prepared with an eye to arousing popular opinion. Thus the correspondence between Adams and Elbridge Gerry of Marblehead shows that Adams planned deliberately to appeal to religious prejudice. The result was presented to the town meeting on November 20. It suggested some additions to the list of violations of American rights, and then ordered the report printed as a pamphlet and directed that 600 copies be sent to the selectmen of the Massachusetts towns and to "such other gentlemen as the committee shall think fit."

The pamphlet consists of four parts: the theoretical basis of American rights, the list of violations of those rights, a circular letter to the towns of Massachusetts, and an appendix containing correspondence between Governor Hutchinson and the town of Boston. The first three are reprinted here.

In addition to the pamphlet published in Boston by Edes and Gill, editions were printed in London and Dublin. The official title of the pamphlet is *The Votes and Proceedings of the Freeholders and other Inhabitants of The Town of Boston, In Town Meeting assembled, According To Law.* The copy printed here is as it appears in the *Boston Town Records*, with certain punctuation revised for clarity. Although the original pamphlet is extremely rare, a copy of it can be found in Clifford K. Shipton's *Early American Imprints*.

First, a State of the *Rights* of the Colonists and of this Province in particular.

Secondly, A List of the *Infringements*, and Violations of those Rights.

Thirdly, A Letter of Correspondence with the other Towns.

1st. Natural Rights of the Colonists as Men.

Among the natural Rights of the Colonists are these: First, a Right to *Life*; Secondly to *Liberty*; thirdly to *Property*; together with the Right to support and defend them in the best manner they can. Those are evident Branches of, rather than deductions from the Duty of Self Preservation, commonly called the first Law of Nature.

All Men have a Right to remain in a State of Nature as long as they please; And in case of intollerable Oppression, Civil or Religious, to leave the Society they belong to, and enter into another.

When Men enter into Society, it is by voluntary consent; and they have a right to demand and insist upon the performance of such conditions, And previous limitations as form an equitable *original compact*.

Every natural Right not expressly given up or from the nature of a Social Compact necessarily ceded remains.

All positive and civil laws, should conform as far as possible, to the Law of natural reason and equity.

As neither reason requires, nor religion permits the contrary, every Man living in or out of a state of civil society, has a right peaceably and quietly to worship God according to the dictates of his conscience.

"Just and true liberty, equal and impartial liberty" in matters spiritual and temporal, is a thing that all Men are clearly entitled to, by the eternal and immutable laws Of God and nature, as well as by the law of Nations, & all well grounded municipal laws, which must have their foundation in the former.

In regard to Religeon, mutual tolleration in the different professions thereof, is what all good and candid minds in all ages have ever practiced; and both by precept and example inculcated on mankind. And it is now generally agreed among christians that this spirit of toleration in the fullest extent consistent with the being of civil society "is the chief characteristical mark of the true church" & In so much that M^r. Lock has asserted, and proved beyond the possibility of contradiction on any solid ground, that such toleration ought to be extended to all whose doctrines are not subversive of society. The only Sects which he thinks ought to be, and which by all wise laws are excluded from such toleration, are those who teach Doctrines subversive of the Civil Government under which they live. The Roman Catholicks or Papists are excluded by reason of such Doctrines as these "that Princes excommunicated may be deposed, and those they call *Hereticks* may be destroyed without mercy; besides their recognizing the Pope in so absolute a manner, in subversion of Government, by introducing as far as possible into the states, under whose protection they enjoy life, liberty and property, that solecism in politicks, Imperium in imperio leading directly to the worst anarchy and confusion, civil discord, war and blood shed.

The natural liberty of Men by entring into society is abridg'd or restrained so far only as is necessary for the Great end of Society the best good of the whole.

In the state of nature, every man is under God, Judge and sole Judge, of his own rights and the injuries done him. By entering into society, he agrees to an Arbiter or indifferent Judge between him and his neighbours; but he no more renounces his original right, than by taking a cause out of the ordinary course of law, and leaving the decision to Referees or indifferent Arbitrations. In the last case he must pay the Referees for time and trouble; he should be also willing to pay his Just quota for the support of government, the law and constitution; the end of which is to furnish indifferent and impartial Judges in all cases that may happen, whether civil ecclesiastical, marine or military.

"The natural liberty of man is to be free from any superior power on earth, and not to be under the will or legislative authority of man; but only to have the law of nature for his rule."

In the state of nature men may as the *Patriarchs* did, employ hired servants for the defence of their lives, liberty and property; and they should pay them reasonable wages. Government was instituted for the purposes of common defence; and those who hold the reins of government have an equitable natural right to an honourable support from the same principle "that the labourer is worthy of his hire" but then the same community which they serve, ought to be assessors of their pay: Governors have no right to seek what they please; by this, instead of being content with the station assigned them, that of honourable servants of the society, they would soon become Absolute masters, Despots, and Tyrants. Hence as a private man has a right to say, what wages he will give in his private affairs, so has a Community to determine what they will give and grant of their Substance, for the Administration of publick affairs. And in both cases more are ready generally to offer their Service at the proposed and stipulated price, than are able and willing to perform their duty.

In short it is the greatest absurdity to suppose it in the power of one or any number of men at the entering into society, to renounce their essential natural rights, or the means of preserving those rights when the great end of civil government from the very nature of its institution is for the support, protection and defence of those very rights: the principal of which as is before observed, are life, liberty and property. If men through fear, fraud or mistake, should *in terms* renounce & give up any essential natural right, the eternal law of reason and the great end of society, would absolutely vacate such renunciation; the right to freedom being *the gift* of God Almighty, it is not in the power of Man to alienate this gift, and voluntarily become a slave.

2ᵈ. *The Rights of the Colonists as Christians.*

These may be best understood by reading and carefully studying the institutes of the great Lawgiver and head of the Christian Church: which are to be found closely written and promulgated in the *New Testament.*

By the Act of the British Parliament commonly called the Toleration Act, every Subject in England Except Papists etc. was restored to, and re-established in, his natural right to worship God according to the dictates of his own conscience. And by the Charter of this Province it is granted ordained and established (that it is declared as an original right) that there shall be liberty of conscience allowed in the worship of God, to all christians except Papists, inhabiting or which shall inhabit or be resident within said Province or Teritory. Magna Charta itself is in substance but a constrained Declaration, or proclamation, and promulgation in the name of King, Lord, and Commons of the sense the latter had of their original inherent, indefeazible natural Rights, as also those of free Citizens equally perdurable with the other. That great author, that great jurist, and even that Court writer Mʳ. Justice Blackstone holds that this recognition was justly obtained of King John sword in hand, and peradventure it must be one day sword in hand again rescued and preserved from total destruction and oblivion.

3ᵈ. *The Rights of the Colonists as Subjects*

A Common Wealth or state is a body politick or civil society of men, united together to promote their mutual safety and prosperity, by means of their union.

The *absolute Rights* of Englishmen, and all freemen in or out of Civil society, are principally, *personal security, personal liberty* and *private property.*

All Persons born in the British American Colonies are by the laws of God and nature, and by the Common law of England, *exclusive of all charters from the Crown,* well Entitled, and by Acts of the British Parliament are declared to be entitled to all the natural essential, inherent & inseperable Rights Liberties and Privileges of Subjects born in Great Britain, or within the Realm. Among those Rights are the following; which no men or body of men, consistently with their own rights as men and citizens or members of society, can for themselves give up, or take away from others.

First, "The first fundamental positive law of all Commonwealths or States, is the establishing the legislative power; as the first fundamental *natural* law also, which is to govern even the legislative power itself, is the preservation of the Society."

Secondly, The Legislative has no right to absolute arbitrary power over the lives and fortunes of the people. Nor can mortals assume a prerogative, not only too high for men, but for Angels; and therefore reserved for the exercise of the *Deity* alone.

"The Legislative cannot Justly *assume* to itself a power to rule by extempore arbitrary decrees; but it is bound to see that Justice is dispensed, and that the rights of the subjects be decided, by promulgated, standing and known laws, and authorized *independent Judges;*" that is independent as far as possible of Prince or People. *"There shall be one rule of Justice for rich and poor; for the favorite in Court, and the Countryman at the Plough."*

Thirdly, The supreme power cannot Justly take from any man, any part of his property without his consent, in person or by his Representative.

These are some of the first principles of natural law & Justice, and the great Barriers of all free states, and of the British Constitution in particular. It is utterly irreconcileable to these principles, and to many other fundamental maxims of the common law, common sense and reason, that a British house of commons, should have a right, at pleasure, to give and grant the property of the Colonists. That these Colonists are well entitled to all the essential rights, liberties and privileges of men and freemen, born in Britain, is manifest, not only from the Colony charter, in general, but acts of the British Parliament. The statute of the 13th of George 2. c. 7. naturalizes even foreigners after seven years residence. The words of the Massachusetts Charter are these, "And further our will and pleasure is, and we do hereby for us, our heirs and successors, grant establish and ordain, that all and every of the subjects of us, our heirs and successors, which shall go to and inhabit within our said province or territory and every of their children which shall happen to be born there, or on the seas in going thither, or returning from thence shall have and enjoy, all liberties and immunities of free and natural subjects within any of the dominions of us, our heirs and successors, to all intents constructions & purposes whatsover as if they every of them were born within this our Realm of England." Now what liberty can there be, where property is taken away without consent? Can it be said with any colour of truth and Justice, that this Continent of three thousand miles in length, and of a breadth as yet unexplored, in which however, its supposed, there are five millions of people, has the least voice, vote or influence in the decisions of the British Parliament? Have they, all together, any more right or power to return a single number to that house of commons, who have not inadvertently, but deliberately assumed a power to dispose of their lives, Liberties and properties, then to choose an Emperor of China! Had the Colonists a right to return members to the british parliament, it would only be hurtfull; as from their local situation and circumstances it is impossible they should be ever truly and properly represented there. The inhabitants of this country in all probability in a few years will be more numerous, than those of Great Britain and Ireland together; yet it is absurdly expected by the promoters of the present measures, that these, with their posterity to all generations, should be easy while their property, shall be disposed of by a house of commons at three thousand miles distant from them; and who cannot be supposed to have the least care or concern for their real interest: Who have not only no natural care for their interest, but must be *in effect* bribed against it; as every burden they lay on the colonists is so much saved or gained to themselves. Hitherto many of the Colonists have been free from Quit Rents; but if the breath of a british house of commons can originate an act for taking away all our money, our lands will go next or be subject to rack rents from haughty and relentless landlords who will ride at ease, while we are trodden in the dirt. The Colonists have been branded with the odious names of traitors and rebels, only for complaining of their grievances; How long such treatment will, or ought to born is submitted.

A List of Infringements & Violations of Rights.

We cannot help thinking, that an enumeration of some of the most open infringments of our rights, will by every candid Person be Judged sufficient to Justify whatever measures have been already taken, or may be thought proper to be taken, in order to obtain a redress of the Grievances under which we labour. Among many others we Humbly conceive, that the following will not fail to excite the attention of all who consider themselves interested in the happiness and freedom of mankind in general, and of this continent and province in particular.

1st. The British Parliament have assumed the power of legislation for the Colonists in all cases whatsoever, without obtaining the consent of the Inhabitants, which is ever essentially necessary to the right establishment of such a legislative.

2^d. They have exerted that assumed power, in raising a Revenue in the Colonies without their consent; thereby depriving them of that right which every man has to keep his own earnings in his own hands untill he shall in person, or by his Representative, think fit to part with the whole or any portion of it. This infringement is the more extraordinary, when we consider the laudable care which the British House of Commons have taken to reserve intirely and absolutely to themselves the powers of giving and granting moneys. They not only insist on originating every money bill in their own house, but will not even allow the House of Lords to make an amendment in these bills. So tenacious are they of this privilege, so jealous of any infringement of the sole & absolute right the people have to dispose of their own money. And what renders this infringement the more grievous is, that what of our earnings still remains in our own hands is in a great measure deprived of its value, so long as the British Parliament continue to claim and exercise this power of taxing us; for we cannot Justly call that *our* property which *others* may, when they please take away from us against our will.

In this respect we are treated with less decency and regard than the Romans shewed even to the Provinces which They had conquered. *They* only determined upon the sum which each should furnish, and left every Province to raise it in the manner most easy and convenient to themselves.

3ᵈ. A number of new Officers, unknown in the Charter of this Province, have been appointed to superintend this Revenue, whereas by our Charter the Great & General Court or Assembly of this Province has the sole right of appointing all civil officers, excepting only such officers, the election and constitution of whom is in said charter expressly excepted; among whom these Officers are not included.

4ᵗʰ. These Officers are by their Commission invested with powers altogether unconstitutional, and entirely destructive to that security which we have a right to enjoy; and to the last degree dangerous, not only to our property; but to our lives: For the Commissioners of his Majestys customs in America, or any three of them, are by their Commission impowered, "by writing under their hands and seals to constitute and appoint inferior Officers in all and singular the Port within the limits of their commissions. Each of these petty officers so made is intrusted with power more absolute and arbitrary than ought to be lodged in the hands of any man or body of men whatsoever; for in the commission aforementioned, his Majesty gives & grants unto his said Commissioners, or any three of them, and to all and every the Collectors Deputy Collectors, Ministers, Servants, and all other Officers serving and attending in all and every the Ports and other places within the limits of their Commission, full power and authority from time to time, at their and any of their wills and pleasures, as well By Night as by day to enter and go on board any Ship, Boat, or other Vessel, riding lying or being within, or coming into any Port, Harbour, Creek or Haven, within the limits of their commission; and also in the day time to go into any house, shop, cellar, or any other place, where any goods wares or merchandizes lie concealed, or are *suspected* to lie concealed, whereof the customs & other duties, have not been, or shall not be, duly paid and truly satisfied, answered or paid unto the Collectors, Deputy Collectors, Ministers, Servants, and other Officers respectively, or otherwise agreed for; and the said house, shop, warehouse, cellar, and other place to search and survey, and all and every the boxes, trunks, chests and packs then and there found to break open.

Thus our homes and even our bed chambers, are exposed to be ransacked, our boxes chests & trunks broke open ravaged and plundered by wretches, whom no prudent man would venture to employ even as menial servants; whenever they are pleased to say they *suspect* there are in the house wares etc. for which the dutys have not been paid. Flagrant instances of the wanton exercise of this power, have frequently happened in this and other sea port Towns. By this we are cut off from that domestick security which renders the lives of the most unhappy in some measure agreable. Those Officers may under colour of law and the cloak of a general warrant, break thro' the sacred rights of the *Domicil,* ransack mens houses, destroy their securities, carry off their property, and with little danger to themselves commit the most horred murders.

And we complain of it as a further grievance, that notwithstanding by the Charter of this Province, the Governor and the Great and General Court or Assembly of this Province or Territory, for the time being shall have full power and authority, from time to time, to make, ordain and establish all manner of wholesome and reasonable laws, orders, statutes, and ordinances, directions and instructions, and that if the same shall not within the term of three years after presenting the same to his Majesty in privy council be disallowed, they shall be and continue in full force and effect, untill the same shall be repealed by the Great and General Assembly of this Province. Yet the Parliament of Great Britain have rendered or attempted to render, null and void a law of this Province made and passed in the Reign of his late Majesty George the first, intitled "An Act stating the Fees of the Custom-house Officers within this Province" and by meer dint of power, in violation of the Charter aforesaid, established other and exorbitant fees, for the same Officers; any law of the Province to the contrary notwithstanding.

5th. Fleets and Armies have been introduced to support these unconstitutional Officers in collecting and managing this unconstitutional Revenue; and troops have been quarter'd in this Metropolis for that purpose. Introducing and quartering standing Armies in a free Country in times of peace without the consent of the people either by themselves or by their Representatives, is, and always has been deemed a violation of their rights as freemen; and of the Charter or Compact made between the King of Great Britain, and the People of this Province, whereby all the rights of British Subjects are confirmed to us.

6th. The Revenue arising from this tax unconstitutionally laid, and committed to the management of persons arbitrarily appointed and supported by an armed force quartered in a free City, has been in part applyed to the most destructive purposes. It is absolutely necessary in a mixt government like that of this Province, that a due proportion or balance of power should be established among the several branches of legislative. Our Ancestors received from King William & Queen Mary a Charter by which it was understood by both parties in the contract, that such a proportion or balance was fixed; and therefore every thing which renders any one branch of the Legislative more independent of the other two than it was originally designed, is an alteration of the constitution as settled by the Charter; and as it has been untill the establishment of this Revenue, the constant practise of the General Assembly to provide for the support of Government, so it is an essential part of our constitution, as it is a necessary means of preserving an *equilibrium,* without which we cannot continue a free state.

In particular it has always been held, that the dependence of the Governor of this Province upon the General Assembly for his support, was necessary for the preservation of this *equilibrium;* nevertheless his Majesty has been pleased to apply fifteen hundred pounds sterling annually out of the American revenue, for the support of the Governor of this Providence independent of the Assembly, whereby the ancient connection between him and this people is weakened, the confidence in the Governor lessened and the equilibrium destroyed, and the constitution essentially altered.

And we look upon it highly probable from the best intelligence we have been able to obtain, that not only our Governor and Lieuvetenant Governor, but the Judges of the Superior Court of Judicature, as also the Kings Attorney and Solicitor General are to receive their support from this Grievous tribute. This will if accomplished compleat our slavery. For if taxes are raised from us by the Parliament of Great Britain without our consent, and the men on whose opinions and decisions our properties liberties and lives, in a great measure depend, receive their support from the Revenues arising from these taxes, we cannot, when we think on the depravity of mankind, avoid looking with horror on the danger to which we are exposed? The British Parliament have shewn their wisdom in making the Judges there as independent as possible both on the Prince and People, both for place and support: But our Judges hold their Commissions only during pleasure; the granting them salaries out of this Revenue is rendering them dependent on the Crown for their support. The King upon his first accession to the Throne, for giving the last hand to the independency of the Judges in England, not only upon himself but his Successors by recommending and consenting to an act of Parliament, by which the Judges are continued in office, notwithstanding the demise of a King, which vacates all other Commissions, was applauded by the whole Nation. How alarming must it then be to the Inhabitants of this Province, to find so wide a difference made between the Subjects in Britain and America, as the rendering the Judges here altogether dependent on the Crown for their support.

7th. We find ourselves greatly oppressed by Instructions sent to our Governor from the Court of Great Britain, whereby the first branch of our legislature is made merely a ministerial engine. And the Province has already felt such effects from these Instructions, as We think Justly intitle us to say that they threaten an entire destruction of our liberties, and must soon, if not checked, render every branch of our Government a useless burthen upon the people. We shall point out some of the alarming effects of these Instructions which have already taken place.

In consequence of Instructions, the Governor has called and adjourned our General Assemblies to a place highly inconvenient to the Members and grately disadvantageous to the interest of the Province, even against his own declared intention.

In consequence of Instructions, the Assembly has been prorogued from time to time, when the important concerns of the Province required their Meeting.

In obedience to Instructions, the General Assembly was Anno 1768 dissolved by Governor Bernard, because they would not consent to *rescind* the resolution of a *former* house, and thereby sacrifise the rights of their constituents.

By an Instruction, the honourable his Majesty Council are forbid to meet and transact matters of publick concern as a Council of advice to the Governor, unless called by the Governor; and if they should from a zealous regard to the interest of the Province so meet at any time, the Governor is ordered to negative them at the next Election of Councellors. And although by the Charter of this Province the Great & General Court have full power and authority to impose taxes upon the estates and persons of all and every the proprietors and inhabitants of this Province, yet the Governor has been forbidden to give his consent to act imposing a tax for the necessary support of government, unless such persons as were pointed out In the said instruction, were exempted from paying their Just proportion of said tax.

His Excellency has also pleaded Instructions for giving up the provincial fortress, Castle William into the hands of troops, over whom he had declared he had no controul (and that at a time when they were menaceing the Slaughter of the Inhabitants of the Town, and our Streets were stained with the blood which they had barbariously shed). Thus our Governor, appointed and paid from Great Britain with money forced from us, is made an instrument of totally preventing or at least of rendering, every attempt of the other two branches of the Legislative in favor of a distressed and wronged people; And least the complaints naturally occasioned by such oppression should excite compassion in the Royal breast, and induce his Majesty seriously to set about relieving us from the cruel bondage and insults which we his loyal Subjects have so long suffered, the Governor is forbidden to consent to the payment of an Agent to represent our grievances at the Court of Great Britain, unless he the Governor consent to his election, and we very well knew what *the man must be* to whose appointment a Governor in such circumstances will consent.

While we are mentioning the infringement of the rights of this Colony in particular by means of Instructions, we cannot help calling to remembrance the late unexampled suspension of the legislative of a Sister Colony, *New York* by force of an Instruction, untill they should comply with an Arbitrary Act of the British Parliament for quartering troops, designed by military execution, to enforce the raising of a tribute.

8th. The extending the power of the Courts of Vice Admiral/ity to so enormous a degree as deprives the people in the Colonies in a great measure of their inestimable right to tryals by *Juries:* which has ever been Justly considered as the grand Bulwark and security of English property.

This alone is sufficient to rouse our jealousy. And we are again obliged to take notice of the remarkable contrast, which the British Parliament have been pleased to exhibit between the Subjects in Great Britain & the Colonies. In the same Statute, by which they give up to the decision of one dependent interested Judge of Admirality the estates and properties of the Colonists, they expressly guard the estates & properties of the people of Great Britain; for all forfeitures & penalties inflicted by the Statute of George the Third, or any other Act of Parliament relative to the trade of the Colonies, may be sued for in any Court of Admiralty in the Colonies; but all penalties and forfeitures which shall be incurred in great Britain, may be sued for in any of his Majestys Courts of Record in Westminster or in the Court of Exchequer in Scotland, respectively. Thus our Birth Rights are taken from us; and that too with every mark of indignity, insult and contempt. We may be harrassed and dragged from one part of the Continent to the other (which some of our Brethren here and in the Country Towns already have been) and finally be deprived of our whole property, by the arbitrary determination of one biassed, capricious Judge of the Admirality.

9th. The restraining us from erecting Stilling Mills for manufacturing our Iron the natural produce of this Country, Is an infringement of that right with which God and nature have invested us, to make use of our skill and industry in procuring the necessaries and conveniences of life. And we look upon the restraint laid upon the manufacture and transportation of Hatts to be altogether unreasonable and grievous. Although by the Charter all Havens, Rivers, Ports, Waters &c. are expressly granted the Inhabitants of the Province and their Successors, to their only proper use and behoof forever, yet the British Parliament passed an Act, whereby they restrain us from carrying our Wool, the produce of our own farms, even over a ferry; whereby the Inhabitants have often been put to the expence of carrying a Bag of Wool near an hundred miles by land, when passing over a River or Water of one quarter of a mile, of which the Province are the absolute Proprietors, would have prevented all that trouble.

10th. The Act passed in the last Session of the British Parliament, intitled, *An Act for the better preserving his Majestys Dock Yards, Magizines, Ships, Ammunition and Stores,* is, as we apprehend a violent infringement of our Rights. By this Act any one of us may be taken from his Family, and carried to any part of Great Britain, there to be tried whenever it shall be pretended that he has been concerned in burning or otherwise destroying any Boat or Vessel, or any Materials for building etc. any Naval or Victualling Store etc. belonging to his Majesty. For by this Act all Persons in the Realm, or in any of the places thereto belonging (under which denomination we know the Colonies are meant to be included) may be indicted and tryed either in any County or Shire within this Realm, in like manner and form as if the offence had been committed in said County, as his Majesty and his Successors may deem Most expedient. Thus we are not only deprived of our grand right to *tryal by our Peers in the Vicinity,* but any Person suspected, or pretended to be suspected, may be hurried to Great Britain, to take his tryal in any County the King or his Successors shall please to direct; where, innocent or guilty he is in great danger of being condemned; and whether condemned or acquitted he will probably be ruined by the expense attending the tryal, and his long absence from his Family and business; and we have the strongest reason to apprehend that we shall soon experience the fatal effects of this Act, as about the year 1769 the British Parliament passed Resolves for taking up a number of Persons in the Colonies and carrying them to Great Britain for tryal, pretending that they were authorised so to do, by a Statute passed in the Reign of Henry the Eighth, in which they say the Colonies were included, although the Act was passed long before any Colonies were settled, or even in contemplation.

11th. As our Ancestors came over to this Country that they might not only enjoy their civil but their religeous rights, and particularly desired to be free from the Prelates, who in those times cruilly persecuted all who differed in sentiment from the established Church; we cannot see without concern the various attempts, which have been made and are now making, to establish an American Episcopate. Our Episcopal Brethren of the Colonies do enjoy, and rightfully ought ever to enjoy, the free exercise of their religeon, we cannot help fearing that they who are so warmly contending for such an establishment, have views altogether inconsistent with the universal and peaceful enjoyment of our christian privileges. And doing or attempting to do any thing which has even the remotest tendency to endanger this enjoyment, is Justly looked upon a great grievance, and also an infringement of our Rights, which is not barely to exercise, but peaceably & securely to enjoy, that liberty wherewith CHRIST has made us free.

And we are further of Opinion, that no power on Earth can justly give either temporal or spiritual Jurisdiction within this Province, except the Great & General Court. We think therefore that every design for establishing the Jurisdiction of a Bishop in this Province, is a design both against our Civil and Religeous rights. And we are well informed, that the more candid and Judicious of our Brethren of the Church of England in this and the other Colonies, both Clergy and Laity, conceive of the establishing an American Episcopate both unnecessary and unreasonable.

12th. Another Grievance under which we labour is the frequent alteration of the bounds of the Colonies by decisions before the King and Council, explanatory of former grants and Charters. This not only subjects Men to live under a constitution to which they have not consented, which in itself is a great Grievance; but moreover under color, that the *right of Soil* is affected by such declarations, some Governors, or Ministers, or both in conjunction, have pretended to Grant in consequence of a Mandamus many thousands of Acres of Lands appropriated near a Century past; and rendered valuable by the labours of the present Cultivators and their Ancestors. There are very notable instances of Setlers, who having first purchased the Soil of the Natives, have at considerable expence obtained confermation of title from this Province; and on being transferred to the Jurisdiction of the Province of *New Hampshire* have been put to the trouble and cost of a new Grant or confermation from thence; and after all this there has been a third declaration of Royal Will, that they should thence forth be considered as pertaining To the Province of *New York*. The troubles, expences and dangers which hundreds have been put to on such occasions, cannot here be recited; but so much may be said, that they have been most cruelly harrassed, and even threatned with a military force, to dragoon them into a compliance, with the most unreasonable demands.

A *Letter* of Correspondence to the other Towns.

Boston November 20: 1772

Gentlemen   We the Freeholders and other Inhabitants of *Boston* in Town Meeting duly Assembled, according to Law, apprehending there is abundant to be alarmed at the plan of

Despotism, which the enemies of our invaluable rights have concerted, is rapidly hastening to a completion, can no longer conceal our impatience under a constant, unremitted, uniform aim to enslave us, or confide in an Administration which threatens us with certain and inevitable destruction. But, when in addition to the repeated inroads made upon the Rights and Liberties of the Colonists, and of those in this Province in particular, we reflect on the late extraordinary measure in affixing stipends or Salaries from the Crown to the Offices of the Judges of the Superior Court of Judicature, making them not only intirely independent of the people, whose lives and properties are so much in their power, but absolutely dependent on the Crown (which may hereafter, be worn by a *Tyrant*) both for their appointment and support, we cannot but be extremely alarmed at the mischievous tendency of this innovation; which in our opinion is directly contrary to the spirit of the British Constitution, pregnant with innumerable evils, and hath a direct tendency To deprive us of every thing valuable as Men, as Christians and as Subjects, entitled, by the Royal Charter, to all the Rights, liberties and privileges of native Britons. Such being the critical state of this Province, we think it our duty on this truly distressing occasion, to ask you, What can withstand the Attacks of mere power? What can preserve the liberties of the Subject, when the Barriers of the Constitution are taken away? The Town of Boston consulting on the matter above mentioned, thought proper to make application to the Governor by a Committee; requesting his Excellency to communicate such intelligence as he might have received relative to the report of the Judges having their support independent of the grants of this Province a Copy of which you have herewith in Paper N. 1. To which we received as answer the Paper N. 2. The Town on further deliberation, thought it advisable to refer the matter to the Great and General Assembly; and accordingly in a second address as N. 3 they requested his Excellency that the General Court might Convene at the time to which they then stood prorogued; to which the Town received the reply as in N. 4. in which we are acquainted with his intentions further to prorogue the General Assembly, which has since taken place. Thus Gentlemen it is evident his Excellency declines giving the least satisfaction as to the matter in request. The affair being of publick concernment, the Town of Boston thought it necessary to consult with their Brethren throughout the Province; and for this purpose, appointed a Committee, to communicate with our fellow Sufferers, respecting this recent instance of oppression, as well as the many other violations of our Rights under which we have groaned for several Years past. This Committee have briefly Recapitulated the sense we have of our invaluable Rights as Men, as Christians, and as Subjects; and wherein we conceive those Rights to have been violated, which we are desirous may be laid before your Town, that the subject may be weighed as its importance requires, and the collected wisdom of the whole People, as far as possible, be obtained, on a deliberation of such great and lasting moment as to involve in it the fate of all our Posterity. Great pains has been taken to perswade the British Administration to think that the good People of this Province in general are quiet and undisturbed at the late measures; and that any uneasiness that appears, arises from a few factious designing and disaffected men. This renders it the more necessary, that the sense of the People should be explicitly declared. A free communication of your sentiments to this Town, of our common danger, is earnestly solicited and will be gratefully received. If you concur with us in opinion, that our Rights are properly stated, and that the several Acts of Parliament, and Measures of Administration, pointed out by us are subversive of these Rights, you will doubtless think it of the utmost importance that we stand firm as one man, to recover and support them; and to take such measures by directing our Representatives, or otherwise, as your wisdom and fortitude shall dictate, to rescue from impending ruin our happy and glorious constitution. But if it should be the general voice of this Province, that the Rights as we have stated them, do not belong to us; or that the several measures of Administration in the British Court, are no violations of these Rights, or that if they are thus violated or infringed, they are not worth contending for, or resolutely maintaining; should this be the general voice of the Province, we must be resigned to our wretched fate; but shall forever lament the extinction of that generous ardor for Civil and Religeous liberty, which in the face of every danger, and even death itself, induced our fathers to forsake the bosom of their Native Country, and begin a settlement on bare Creation. But we trust this cannot be the case: We are sure your wisdom, your regard to yourselves and the rising Generation, cannot suffer you to dose, or set supinely indifferent on the brink of destruction, while the Iron hand of oppression is dayly tearing the choisest Fruit from the fair Tree of Liberty, planted by our worthy Predecessors, at the expence of their treasure, & abundantly water'd with their blood. It is an observation of an eminent Patriot, that a People long inured to hardships, loose by degrees the very notions of liberty; they look upon themselves as Creatures *at mercy,* and that all impositions laid on by superior hands, are legal and obligatory. But thank Heaven this is not yet verified in *America!* We have yet some share of publick virtue remaining: we are not afraid of poverty, but disdain slavery. The fate of Nations is so Precarious and resolutions in States so often take place at an unexpected moment, when the hand of power by fraud or flattery, has secured every Avenue of retreat, and the minds of the Subject debased to its purpose, that it becomes every will wisher to his Country, while it has any remains of freedom, to keep an Eagle Eye upon every inovation and stretch of power, in those that have the rule over us. A recent instance of this we have in the late Revolutions in *Sweden,* by which the Prince once subject to the laws of the State, has been able of a sudden to declare himself absolute Monarch. The Sweeds were once a free, martial and valient people. Their minds are now so debaced, that they rejoice at being subject to the caprice and arbitrary power of a Tyrant & kiss their Chains. It makes us shudder to think, the late measures of Administration may be productive of the like Catastrophe; which Heaven forbid! Let us consider Brethren, we are struggling for our best Birth Rights & Inheritance; which being infringed, renders all our blessings precarious in their enjoyments, and consequently triffling in their value. Let us disappoint the Men who are raising themselves on the ruin of this Country. Let us convince every Invader of our freedom, that we will be as free as the Constitution our Fathers recognized, will Justify.

· 13 ·

A Summary View of the Rights

of British America (1774)

By Thomas Jefferson

News of the Boston Port Bill reached Virginia while the House of Burgesses was in session. On May 24 the House proclaimed a day of fasting and the governor, Lord Dunmore, dissolved it for usurping his prerogative. On May 29 Boston's appeal for the complete stoppage of trade with Britain reached Williamsburg. The members of the former House of Burgesses who were still in town called a convention to meet on August 1. Before it met it was generally known that a continental congress would meet in Philadelphia in September.

Jefferson was elected to the convention, but became ill and could not attend. He therefore sent the convention two copies of resolutions he had prepared to serve as a basis for instructions to the Virginia delegates to the continental congress. The convention read the resolutions, but adopted more mild instructions. Jefferson's friends, without consulting him, gave his resolutions the title they

Williamsburg [August], 1774.

bear and had them printed as a pamphlet in Williamsburg in August. The pamphlet was reprinted in Philadelphia and London before the end of the year.[1]

The full title of the pamphlet is *A Summary View of the Rights of British America. Set Forth in Some Resolutions Intended for the Inspection of the Present Delegates of the People of Virginia Now in Convention.*

The footnotes have been omitted from the following text.

THE PREFACE OF THE EDITORS.

THE *following piece was intended to convey to the late meeting of* DELEGATES *the sentiments of one of their body, whose personal attendance was prevented by an accidental illness. In it the sources of our present unhappy differences are traced with such faithful accuracy, and the opinions entertained by every free American expressed with such a manly firmness, that it must be pleasing to the present, and may be useful to future ages. It will evince to the world the moderation of our late convention, who have only touched with tenderness many of the claims insisted on in this pamphlet, though every heart acknowledged their justice. Without the knowledge of the author, we have ventured to communicate his sentiments to the public; who have certainly a right to know what the best and wisest of their members have thought on a subject in which they are so deeply interested.*

Resolved, that it be an instruction to the said deputies, when assembled in general congress with the deputies from the other states of British America, to propose to the said congress that

---

[1] See Julian Boyd, ed., *The Papers of Thomas Jefferson,* I (1950), Appendix I, "Historical and Bibliographical Notes on *A Summary View of the Rights of British America.*"

an humble and dutiful address be presented to his majesty, begging leave to lay before him, as chief magistrate of the British empire, the united complaints of his majesty's subjects in America; complaints which are excited by many unwarrantable encroachments and usurpations, attempted to be made by the legislature of one part of the empire, upon those rights which God and the laws have given equally and independently to all. To represent to his majesty that these his states have often individually made humble application to his imperial throne to obtain, through its intervention, some redress of their injured rights, to none of which was ever even an answer condescended; humbly to hope that this their joint address, penned in the language of truth, and divested of those expressions of servility which would persuade his majesty that we are asking favours, and not rights, shall obtain from his majesty a more respectful acceptance. And this his majesty will think we have reason to expect when he reflects that he is no more than the chief officer of the people, appointed by the laws, and circumscribed with definite powers, to assist in working the great machine of government, erected for their use, and consequently subject to their superintendance. And in order that these our rights, as well as the invasions of them, may be laid more fully before his majesty, to take a view of them from the origin and first settlement of these countries.

To remind him that our ancestors, before their emigration to America, were the free inhabitants of the British dominions in Europe, and possessed a right which nature has given to all men, of departing from the country in which chance, not choice, has placed them, of going in quest of new habitations, and of there establishing new societies, under such laws and regulations as to them shall seem most likely to promote public happiness. That their Saxon ancestors had, under this universal law, in like manner left their native wilds and woods in the north of Europe, had possessed themselves of the island of Britain, then less charged with inhabitants, and had established there that system of laws which has so long been the glory and protection of that country. Nor was ever any claim of superiority or dependence asserted over them by that mother country from which they had migrated; and were such a claim made, it is believed that his majesty's subjects in Great Britain have too firm a feeling of the rights derived to them from their ancestors, to bow down the sovereignty of their state before such visionary pretensions. And it is thought that no circumstance has occurred to distinguish materially the British from the Saxon emigration. America was conquered, and her settlements made, and firmly established, at the expence of individuals, and not of the British public. Their own blood was spilt in acquiring lands for their settlement, their own fortunes expended in making that settlement effectual; for themselves they fought, for themselves they conquered, and for themselves alone they have right to hold. Not a shilling was ever issued from the public treasures of his majesty, or his ancestors, for their assistance, till of very late times, after the colonies had become established on a firm and permanent footing. That then, indeed, having become valuable to Great Britain for her commercial purposes, his parliament was pleased to lend them assistance against an enemy, who would fain have drawn to herself the benefits of their commerce, to the great aggrandizement of herself, and danger of Great Britain. Such assistance, and in such circumstances, they had often before given to Portugal, and other allied states, with whom they carry on a commercial intercourse; yet these states never supposed, that by calling in her aid, they thereby submitted themselves to her sovereignty. Had such terms been proposed, they would have rejected them with disdain, and trusted for better to the moderation of their enemies, or to a vigorous exertion of their own force. We do not, however, mean to under-rate those aids, which to us were doubtless valuable, on whatever principles granted; but we would shew that they cannot give a title to that authority which the British parliament would arrogate over us, and that they may amply be repaid by our giving to the inhabitants of Great Britain such exclusive privileges in trade as may be advantageous to them, and at the same time not too restrictive to ourselves. That settlements having been thus effected in the wilds of America, the emigrants thought proper to adopt that system of laws under which they had hitherto lived in the mother country, and to continue their union with her by submitting themselves to the same common sovereign, who was thereby made the central link connecting the several parts of the empire thus newly multiplied.

But that not long were they permitted, however far they thought themselves removed from the hand of oppression, to hold undisturbed the rights thus acquired, at the hazard of their lives, and loss of their fortunes. A family of princes was then on the British throne, whose treasonable crimes against their people brought on them afterwards the exertion of those sacred and sovereign rights of punishment reserved in the hands of the people for cases of extreme necessity, and judged by the constitution unsafe to be delegated to any other judicature. While every day brought forth some new and unjustifiable exertion of power over their subjects on that side the water, it was not to be expected that those here, much less able at that time to oppose the designs of despotism, should be exempted from injury.

Accordingly that country, which had been acquired by the lives, the labours, and the fortunes, of individual adventurers, was by these princes, at several times, parted out and distributed among the favourites and followers of their fortunes, and, by an assumed right of the crown alone, were erected into distinct and independent governments; a measure which it is believed his majesty's prudence and understanding would prevent him from imitating at this day, as no exercise of such a power, of dividing and dismembering a country, has ever occurred in his majesty's realm of England, though now of very antient standing; nor could it be justified or acquiesced under there, or in any other part of his majesty's empire.

That the exercise of a free trade with all parts of the world, possessed by the American colonists, as of natural right, and which no law of their own had taken away or abridged, was next the object of unjust encroachment. Some of the colonies having thought proper to continue the administration of their government in the name and under the authority of his majesty king Charles the first, whom, notwithstanding his late deposition by the commonwealth of England, they continued in the sovereignty of their state; the parliament for the commonwealth took the same in high offence, and assumed upon themselves the power of prohibiting their trade with all other parts of the world, except the island of Great Britain. This arbitrary act, however, they soon recalled, and by solemn treaty, entered into on the 12th day of March, 1651, between the said commonwealth by their commissioners, and the colony of Virginia by their house of burgesses, it was expressly stipulated, by the 8th article of the said treaty, that they should have "free trade as the people of England do enjoy to all places and with all nations, according to the laws of that commonwealth." But that, upon the restoration of his majesty king Charles the second, their rights of free commerce fell once more a victim to arbitrary power; and by several acts of his reign, as well as of some of his successors, the trade of the colonies was laid under such restrictions, as shew what hopes they might form from the justice of a British parliament, were its uncontrouled power admitted over the states. History has informed us that bodies of men, as well as individuals, are susceptible of the spirit of tyranny. A view of these acts of parliament for regulation, as it has been affectedly called, of the American trade, if all other evidence were removed out of the case, would undeniably evince the truth of this observation. Besides the duties they impose on our articles of export and import, they prohibit our going to any markets northward of Cape Finesterre, in the kingdom of Spain, for the sale of commodities which Great Britain will not take from us, and for the purchase of others, with which she cannot supply us, and that for no other than the arbitrary purposes of purchasing for themselves, by a sacrifice of our rights and interests, certain privileges in their commerce with an allied state, who in confidence that their exclusive trade with America will be continued, while the principles and power of the British parliament be the same, have indulged themselves in every exorbitance which their avarice could dictate, or our necessities extort; have raised their commodities, called for in America, to the double and treble of what they sold for before such exclusive privileges were given them, and of what better commodities of the same kind would cost us elsewhere, and at the same time give us much less for what we carry thither than might be had at more convenient ports. That these acts prohibit us from carrying in quest of other purchasers the surplus of our tobaccoes remaining after the consumption of Great Britain is supplied; so that we must leave them with the British merchant for whatever he will please to allow us, to be by him reshipped to foreign markets, where he will reap the benefits of making sale of them for full value. That to heighten still the idea of parliamentary justice, and to shew with what moderation they are like to exercise power, where themselves are to feel no part of its weight, we take leave to mention to his majesty certain other acts of British parliament, by which they would prohibit us from manufacturing for our own use the articles we raise on our own lands with our own labour. By an act passed in the 5th Year of the reign of his late majesty king George the second, an American subject is forbidden to make a hat for himself of the fur which he has taken perhaps on his own soil; an instance of despotism to which no parrallel can be produced in the most arbitrary ages of British history. By one other act, passed in the 23d year of the same reign, the iron which we make we are forbidden to manufacture, and heavy as that article is, and necessary in every branch of husbandry, besides commission and insurance, we are to pay freight for it to Great Britain, and freight for it back again, for the purpose of supporting not men, but machines, in the island of Great Britain. In the same spirit of equal and impartial legislation is to be viewed the act of parliament, passed in the 5th year of the same reign, by which American lands are made subject to the demands of British creditors, while their own lands were still continued unanswerable for their debts; from which one of these conclusions must necessarily follow, either that justice is not the same in America as in Britain, or else that the British parliament pay less regard to it here than there. But that we do not point out to his majesty the injustice of these acts, with intent to rest on that principle the cause of their nullity; but to shew that experience confirms the propriety of those political principles which exempt us from the jurisdiction of the British parliament. The true ground on which we declare these acts void is, that the British parliament has no right to exercise authority over us.

That these exercises of usurped power have not been confined to instances alone, in which themselves were interested, but they have also intermeddled with the regulation of the internal affairs of the colonies. The act of the 9th of Anne for establishing a post office in America seems to have had little connection with British convenience, except that of accommodating his majesty's ministers and favourites with the sale of a lucrative and easy office.

That thus have we hastened through the reigns which preceded his majesty's, during which the violations of our right were less alarming, because repeated at more distant intervals than that rapid and bold succession of injuries which is likely to distinguish the present from all other periods of American story. Scarcely have our minds been able to emerge from the astonishment into which one stroke of parliamentary thunder has involved us, before another more heavy, and more alarming, is fallen on us. Single acts of tyranny may be ascribed to the accidental opinion of a day; but a series of oppressions, begun at a distinguished period, and pursued unalterably through every change of ministers, too plainly prove a deliberate and systematical plan of reducing us to slavery.

That the act passed in the 4th year of his majesty's reign, intitled "An act for granting certain duties in the British colonies and plantations in America, &c."

One other act, passed in the 5th year of his reign, intitled "An act for granting and applying certain stamp duties and other duties in the British colonies and plantations in America, &c."

One other act, passed in the 6th year of his reign, intituled "An act for the better securing the dependency of his majesty's dominions in America upon the crown and parliament of Great Britain;" and one other act, passed in the 7th year of his reign, intituled "An act for granting duties on paper, tea, &c." form that connected chain of parliamentary usurpation, which has already been the subject of frequent applications to his majesty, and the houses of lords and commons of Great Britain; and no answers having yet been condescended to any of these, we shall not trouble his majesty with a repetition of the matters they contained.

But that one other act, passed in the same 7th year of the reign, having been a peculiar attempt, must ever require peculiar mention; it is intituled "An act for suspending the legislature of New York." One free and independent legislature hereby takes upon itself to suspend the powers of another, free and independent as itself; thus exhibiting a phœnomenon unknown in nature, the creator and creature of its own power. Not only the principles of common sense, but the common feelings of human nature, must be surrendered up before his majesty's subjects here can be persuaded to believe that they hold their political existence at the will of a British parliament. Shall these governments be dissolved, their property annihilated, and their people reduced to a state of nature, at the imperious breath of a body of men, whom they never saw, in whom they never confided, and over whom they have no powers of punishment or removal, let their crimes against the American public be ever so great? Can any one reason be assigned why 160,000 electors in the island of Great Britain should give law to four millions in the states of America, every individual of whom is equal to every individual of them, in virtue, in understanding, and in bodily strength? Were this to be admitted, instead of being a free people, as we have hitherto supposed, and mean to continue ourselves, we should suddenly be found the slaves, not of one, but of 160,000 tyrants, distinguished too from all others by this singular circumstance, that they are removed from the reach of fear, the only restraining motive which may hold the hand of a tyrant.

That by "an act to discontinue in such manner and for such time as are therein mentioned the landing and discharging, lading or shipping, of goods, wares, and merchandize, at the town and within the harbour of Boston, in the province of Massachusetts Bay, in North America," which was passed at the last session of British parliament; a large and populous town, whose trade was their sole subsistence, was deprived of that trade, and involved in utter ruin. Let us for a while suppose the question of right suspended, in order to examine this act on principles of justice: An act of parliament had been passed imposing duties on teas, to be paid in America, against which act the Americans had protested as inauthoritative. The East India company, who till that time had never sent a pound of tea to America on their own account, step forth on that occasion the assertors of parliamentary right, and send hither many ship loads of that obnoxious commodity. The masters of their several vessels, however, on their arrival in America, wisely attended to admonition, and returned with their cargoes. In the province of New England alone the remonstrances of the people were disregarded, and a compliance, after being many days waited for, was flatly refused. Whether in this the master of the vessel was governed by his obstinacy, or his instructions, let those who know, say. There are extraordinary situations which require extraordinary interposition. An exasperated people, who feel that they possess power, are not easily restrained within limits strictly regular. A number of them assembled in the town of Boston, threw the tea into the ocean, and dispersed without doing any other act of violence. If in this they did wrong, they were known and were amenable to the laws of the land, against which it could not be objected that they had ever, in any instance, been obstructed or diverted from their regular course in favour of popular offenders. They should therefore not have been distrusted on this occasion. But that ill fated colony had formerly been bold in their enmities against the house of Stuart, and were now devoted to ruin by that unseen hand which governs the momentous affairs of this great empire. On the partial representations of a few worthless ministerial dependents, whose constant office it has been to keep that government embroiled, and who, by their treacheries, hope to obtain the dignity of the British knighthood, without calling for a party accused, without asking a proof, without attempting a distinction between the guilty and the innocent, the whole of that antient and wealthy town is in a moment reduced from opulence to beggary. Men who had spent their lives in extending the British commerce, who had invested in that place the wealth their honest endeavours had merited, found themselves and their families thrown at once on the world for subsistence by its charities. Not the hundredth part of the inhabitants of that town had been concerned in the act complained of; many of them were in Great Britain and in other parts beyond sea; yet all were involved in one indiscriminate ruin, by a new executive power, unheard of till then, that of a British parliament. A property, of the value of many millions of money, was sacrificed to revenge, not repay, the loss of a few thousands. This is administering justice with a heavy hand indeed! and when is this tempest to be arrested in its course? Two wharfs are to be opened again when his majesty shall think proper. The residue which lined the extensive shores of the bay of Boston are forever interdicted the exercise of commerce. This little exception seems to have been thrown in for no other purpose than that of setting a precedent for investing his majesty with legislative powers. If the pulse of his people shall beat calmly under this experiment, another and another will be tried, till the measure of despotism be filled up. It would be an insult on common sense to pretend that this exception was made in order to restore its commerce to that great town. The trade which cannot be received at two wharfs alone must of necessity be transferred to some other place; to which it will soon be followed by that of the two wharfs. Considered in this light, it would be an insolent and cruel mockery at the annihilation of the town of Boston.

By the act for the suppression of riots and tumults in the town of Boston, passed also in the last session of parliament, a murder committed there is, if the governor pleases, to be tried in the court of King's Bench, in the island of Great Britain, by a jury of Middlesex. The witnesses, too, on receipt of such a sum as the governor shall think it reasonable for them to expend, are to enter into recognizance to appear at the trial. This is, in other words, taxing them to the amount of their recognizance, and that amount may be whatever a governor pleases; for who does his majesty think can be prevailed on to cross the Atlantic for the sole purpose of bearing evidence to a fact? His expences are to be borne, indeed, as they shall be estimated by a governor; but who are to feed the wife and children whom he leaves behind, and who have had no other subsistence but his daily labour? Those epidemical disorders, too, so terrible in a foreign climate, is the cure of them to be estimated among the articles of expence, and their danger to be warded off by the almighty power of parliament? And the wretched criminal, if he happen to have offended on the American side, stripped of his privilege of trial by peers of his vicinage, removed from the place where alone full evidence could be obtained, without money, without counsel, without

friends, without exculpatory proof, is tried before judges pre-
determined to condemn. The cowards who would suffer a
countryman to be torn from the bowels of their society, in
order to be thus offered a sacrifice to parliamentary tyranny,
would merit that everlasting infamy now fixed on the authors
of the act! A clause for a similar purpose had been introduced
into an act, passed in the 12th year of his majesty's reign, intitled "An act for the better securing and preserving his majesty's dockyards, magazines, ships, ammunition, and stores;"
against which, as meriting the same censures, the several colonies have already protested.

That these are the acts of power, assumed by a body of men,
foreign to our constitutions, and unacknowledged by our laws,
against which we do, on behalf of the inhabitants of British
America, enter this our solemn and determined protest; and we
do earnestly entreat his majesty, as yet the only mediatory
power between the several states of the British empire, to recommend to his parliament of Great Britain the total revocation
of these acts, which, however nugatory they be, may yet prove
the cause of further discontents and jealousies among us.

That we next proceed to consider the conduct of his majesty,
as holding the executive powers of the laws of these states,
and mark out his deviations from the line of duty: By the
constitution of Great Britain, as well as of the several American
states, his majesty possesses the power of refusing to pass into
a law any bill which has already passed the other two branches
of legislature. His majesty, however, and his ancestors, conscious of the impropriety of opposing their single opinion to
the united wisdom of two houses of parliament, while their
proceedings were unbiassed by interested principles, for several ages past have modestly declined the exercise of this
power in that part of his empire called Great Britain. But by
change of circumstances, other principles than those of justice
simply have obtained an influence on their determinations; the
addition of new states to the British empire has produced an

addition of new, and sometimes opposite interests. It is now, therefore, the great office of his majesty, to resume the exercise of his negative power, and to prevent the passage of laws by any one legislature of the empire, which might bear injuriously on the rights and interests of another. Yet this will not excuse the wanton exercise of this power which we have seen his majesty practise on the laws of the American legislatures. For the most trifling reasons, and sometimes for no conceivable reason at all, his majesty has rejected laws of the most salutary tendency. The abolition of domestic slavery is the great object of desire in those colonies, where it was unhappily introduced in their infant state. But previous to the enfranchisement of the slaves we have, it is necessary to exclude all further importations from Africa; yet our repeated attempts to effect this by prohibitions, and by imposing duties which might amount to a prohibition, have been hitherto defeated by his majesty's negative: Thus preferring the immediate advantages of a few African corsairs to the lasting interests of the American states, and to the rights of human nature, deeply wounded by this infamous practice. Nay, the single interposition of an interested individual against a law was scarcely ever known to fail of success, though in the opposite scale were placed the interests of a whole country. That this is so shameful an abuse of a power trusted with his majesty for other purposes, as if not reformed, would call for some legal restrictions.

With equal inattention to the necessities of his people here has his majesty permitted our laws to lie neglected in England for years, neither confirming them by his assent, nor annulling them by his negative; so that such of them as have no suspending clause we hold on the most precarious of all tenures, his majesty's will, and such of them as suspend themselves till his majesty's assent be obtained, we have feared, might be called into existence at some future and distant period, when time, and change of circumstances, shall have rendered them destructive to his people here. And to render this grievance still more oppressive, his majesty by his instructions has laid his governors under such restrictions that they can pass no law of any moment unless it have such suspending clause; so that, however immediate may be the call for legislative interposition, the law cannot be executed till it has twice crossed the atlantic, by which time the evil may have spent its whole force.

But in what terms, reconcileable to majesty, and at the same time to truth, shall we speak of a late instruction to his majesty's governor of the colony of Virginia, by which he is forbidden to assent to any law for the division of a county, unless the new county will consent to have no representative in assembly? That colony has as yet fixed no boundary to the westward. Their western counties, therefore, are of indefinite extent; some of them are actually seated many hundred miles from their eastern limits. Is it possible, then, that his majesty can have bestowed a single thought on the situation of those people, who, in order to obtain justice for injuries, however great or small, must, by the laws of that colony, attend their county court, at such a distance, with all their witnesses, monthly, till their litigation be determined? Or does his majesty seriously wish, and publish it to the world, that his subjects should give up the glorious right of representation, with all the benefits derived from that, and submit themselves the absolute slaves of his sovereign will? Or is it rather meant to confine the legislative body to their present numbers, that they may be the cheaper bargain whenever they shall become worth a purchase.

One of the articles of impeachment against Tresilian, and the other judges of Westminster Hall, in the reign of Richard the second, for which they suffered death, as traitors to their country, was, that they had advised the king that he might dissolve his parliament at any time; and succeeding kings have adopted the opinion of the unjust judges. Since the establishment, however, of the British constitution, at the glorious revolution, on its free and antient principles, neither his maj-

esty, nor his ancestors, have exercised such a power of dissolution in the island of Great Britain; and when his majesty was
petitioned, by the united voice of his people there, to dissolve
the present parliament, who had become obnoxious to them,
his ministers were heard to declare, in open parliament, that
his majesty possessed no such power by the constitution. But
how different their language and his practice here! To declare,
as their duty required, the known rights of their country, to
oppose the usurpations of every foreign judicature, to disregard
the imperious mandates of a minister or governor, have been
the avowed causes of dissolving houses of representatives in
America. But if such powers be really vested in his majesty,
can he suppose they are there placed to awe the members from
such purposes as these? When the representative body have
lost the confidence of their constituents, when they have no-
toriously made sale of their most valuable rights, when they
have assumed to themselves powers which the people never
put into their hands, then indeed their continuing in office becomes dangerous to the state, and calls for an exercise of the
power of dissolution. Such being the causes for which the representative body should, and should not, be dissolved, will it
not appear strange to an unbiassed observer, that that of Great
Britain was not dissolved, while those of the colonies have repeatedly incurred that sentence?

But your majesty, or your governors, have carried this power
beyond every limit known, or provided for, by the laws: After
dissolving one house of representatives, they have refused to
call another, so that, for a great length of time, the legislature
provided by the laws has been out of existence. From the nature of things, every society must at all times possess within
itself the sovereign powers of legislation. The feelings of human
nature revolt against the supposition of a state so situated as
that it may not in any emergency provide against dangers
which perhaps threaten immediate ruin. While those bodies
are in existence to whom the people have delegated the powers

of legislation, they alone possess and may exercise those powers; but when they are dissolved by the lopping off one or more of their branches, the power reverts to the people, who may exercise it to unlimited extent, either assembling together in person, sending deputies, or in any other way they may think proper. We forbear to trace consequences further; the dangers are conspicuous with which this practice is replete.

That we shall at this time also take notice of an error in the nature of our land holdings, which crept in at a very early period of our settlement. The introduction of the feudal tenures into the kingdom of England, though antient, is well enough understood to set this matter in a proper light. In the earlier ages of the Saxon settlement feudal holdings were certainly altogether unknown; and very few, if any, had been introduced at the time of the Norman conquest. Our Saxon ancestors held their lands, as they did their personal property, in absolute dominion, disencumbered with any superior, answering nearly to the nature of those possessions which the feudalists term allodial. William, the Norman, first introduced that system generally. The lands which had belonged to those who fell in the battle of Hastings, and in the subsequent insurrections of his reign, formed a considerable proportion of the lands of the whole kingdom. These he granted out, subject to feudal duties, as did he also those of a great number of his new subjects, who, by persuasions or threats, were induced to surrender them for that purpose. But still much was left in the hands of his Saxon subjects; held of no superior, and not subject to feudal conditions. These, therefore, by express laws, enacted to render uniform the system of military defence, were made liable to the same military duties as if they had been feuds; and the Norman lawyers soon found means to saddle them also with all the other feudal burthens. But still they had not been surrendered to the king, they were not derived from his grant, and therefore they were not holden of him. A general principle, indeed, was introduced, that "all lands in England were held either mediately or immediately of the crown," but this was borrowed from those holdings, which were truly feudal, and only applied to others for the purposes of illustration. Feudal holdings were therefore but exceptions out of the Saxon laws of possession, under which all lands were held in absolute right. These, therefore, still form the basis, or groundwork, of the common law, to prevail wheresoever the exceptions have not taken place. America was not conquered by William the Norman, nor its lands surrendered to him, or any of his successors. Possessions there are undoubtedly of the allodial nature. Our ancestors, however, who migrated hither, were farmers, not lawyers. The fictitious principle that all lands belong originally to the king, they were early persuaded to believe real; and accordingly took grants of their own lands from the crown. And while the crown continued to grant for small sums, and on reasonable rents; there was no inducement to arrest the error, and lay it open to public view. But his majesty has lately taken on him to advance the terms of purchase, and of holding to the double of what they were; by which means the acquisition of lands being rendered difficult, the population of our country is likely to be checked. It is time, therefore, for us to lay this matter before his majesty, and to declare that he has no right to grant lands of himself. From the nature and purpose of civil institutions, all the lands within the limits which any particular society has circumscribed around itself are assumed by that society, and subject to their allotment only. This may be done by themselves, assembled collectively, or by their legislature, to whom they may have delegated sovereign authority; and if they are allotted in neither of these ways, each individual of the society may appropriate to himself such lands as he finds vacant, and occupancy will give him title.

That in order to enforce the arbitrary measures before complained of, his majesty has from time to time sent among us large bodies of armed forces, not made up of the people here, nor raised by the authority of our laws: Did his majesty possess such a right as this, it might swallow up all our other rights whenever he should think proper. But his majesty has no right to land a single armed man on our shores, and those whom he sends here are liable to our laws made for the suppression and punishment of riots, routs, and unlawful assemblies; or are hostile bodies, invading us in defiance of law. When in the course of the late war it became expedient that a body of Hanoverian troops should be brought over for the defence of Great Britain, his majesty's grandfather, our late sovereign, did not pretend to introduce them under any authority he possessed. Such a measure would have given just alarm to his subjects in Great Britain, whose liberties would not be safe if armed men of another country, and of another spirit, might be brought into the realm at any time without the consent of their legislature. He therefore applied to parliament, who passed an act for that purpose, limiting the number to be brought in and the time they were to continue. In like manner is his majesty restrained in every part of the empire. He possesses, indeed, the executive power of the laws in every state; but they are the laws of the particular state which he is to administer within that state, and not those of any one within the limits of another. Every state must judge for itself the number of armed men which they may safely trust among them, of whom they are to consist, and under what restrictions they shall be laid.

To render these proceedings still more criminal against our laws, instead of subjecting the military to the civil powers, his majesty has expressly made the civil subordinate to the military. But can his majesty thus put down all law under his feet? Can he erect a power superior to that which erected himself? He has done it indeed by force; but let him remember that force cannot give right.

That these are our grievances which we have thus laid before his majesty, with that freedom of language and sentiment which becomes a free people claiming their rights, as derived from the laws of nature, and not as the gift of their chief magistrate: Let those flatter who fear; it is not an American art. To give praise which is not due might be well from the venal, but would ill beseem those who are asserting the rights of human nature. They know, and will therefore say, that kings are the servants, not the proprietors of the people. Open your breast, sire, to liberal and expanded thought. Let not the name of George the third be a blot in the page of history. You are surrounded by British counsellors, but remember that they are parties. You have no ministers for American affairs, because you have none taken from among us, nor amenable to the laws on which they are to give you advice. It behoves you, therefore, to think and to act for yourself and your people. The great principles of right and wrong are legible to every reader; to pursue them requires not the aid of many counsellors. The whole art of government consists in the art of being honest. Only aim to do your duty, and mankind will give you credit where you fail. No longer persevere in sacrificing the rights of one part of the empire to the inordinate desires of another; but deal out to all equal and impartial right. Let no act be passed by any one legislature which may infringe on the rights and liberties of another. This is the important post in which fortune has placed you, holding the balance of a great, if a well poised empire. This, sire, is the advice of your great American council, on the observance of which may perhaps depend your felicity and future fame, and the preservation of that harmony which alone can continue both to Great Britain and America the reciprocal advantages of their connection. It is neither our wish, nor our interest, to separate from her. We are willing, on our part, to sacrifice every thing which reason can ask to the restoration of that tranquility for which all must wish. On their part, let them be ready to establish union and a generous plan. Let them name their terms, but let them be just. Accept of every commercial preference it is in our power to give for such things as we can raise for their use, or they make for ours. But let them not think to exclude us from going to other markets to dispose of those commodities which they cannot use, or to supply those wants which they cannot supply. Still less let it be proposed that our properties within our own territories shall be taxed or regulated by any power on earth but our own. The God who gave us life gave us liberty at the same time; the hand of force may destroy, but cannot disjoin them. This, sire, is our last, our determined resolution; and that you will be pleased to interpose with that efficacy which your earnest endeavours may ensure to procure redress of these our great grievances, to quiet the minds of your subjects in British America, against any apprehensions of future encroachment, to establish fraternal love and harmony through the whole empire, and that these may continue to the latest ages of time, is the fervent prayer of all British America!

· 14 ·

Massachusettensis and Novanglus

By Daniel Leonard and John Adams

The first of seventeen essays signed *Massachusettensis* appeared in the *Massachusetts Gazette and Boston Post-Boy* on December 12, 1774, and the last on April 3, 1775. The first of twelve essays signed *Novanglus*, in reply to *Massachusettensis*, appeared in the *Boston Gazette* on January 23, 1775, and the last on April 17, 1775. The participants in this newspaper debate were Daniel Leonard and John Adams.

The first eight of Leonard's essays were published by James Rivington in New York early in 1775, and later on in the year, all of them were published as a pamphlet in Boston. During 1776 four editions were published in London and one in Dublin. John Adams' *Novanglus* essays were never published as a pamphlet in America, but John Almon, the London publisher, printed them in abridged form in his *Remembrancer* for 1775. In 1782 when John Adams was in Holland seeking a loan for the United States, they were published in a Dutch translation, and in 1784 they were pub-

Novanglus and Massachusettensis; or Political Essays Published in the years 1774 and 1775. . . . (Boston, 1819), pp. 146–158, 203–209, 15–23, 34–35, 49–59.

lished in English in London, with John Adams named as the author.

In 1819 the two sets of essays were published in Boston as a single volume with a preface by John Adams. At that time he still believed that Jonathan Sewall was the author of *Massachusettensis*. He did not find out until two years later that Daniel Leonard had been his opponent.

Charles Francis Adams republished *Novanglus* in the fourth volume of his edition of *The Works of John Adams* in 1856. The information concerning the previous publication of both sets of essays is from Adams' preface to *Novanglus* in 1856.

The text of the essays reprinted here is that of the Boston edition of 1819. Included here are *Massachusettensis* for December 19 and 26, 1774 and March 6, 1775; and *Novanglus* for January 30, February 13, and a portion of the essay of February 20, 1775.

MASSACHUSETTENSIS, December 19, 1774

I endeavoured last week to convince you of our real danger, not to render you desperate, but to induce you to seek immediately some effectual remedy. Our case is not yet remediless, as we have to deal with a nation not less generous and humane, than powerful and brave; just indeed, but not vindictive.

I shall, in this and successive papers, trace this yet growing distemper through its several stages, from the first rise to the present hour, point out the causes, mark the effects, shew the madness of persevering in our present line of conduct, and recommend what, I have been long convinced, is our only remedy. I confess myself to be one of those, that think our present calamity is in a great measure to be attributed to the bad policy of a popular party in this province; and that their measures for several years past, whatever may have been their intention, have been diametrically opposite to their profession,—the public good; and cannot, at present, but compare their leaders to a false guide, that having led a benighted traveller through many mazes and windings in a thick wood, finds himself at length on the brink of a horrid precipice, and, to save himself, seizes fast hold of his follower, to the utmost hazard of plunging both headlong down the steep, and being dashed in pieces together against the rocks below.

In ordinary cases we may talk in the measured language of a courtier; but when such a weight of vengeance is suspended over our heads, by a single thread, as threatens every moment to crush us to atoms, delicacy itself would be ill-timed. I will declare the plain truth wherever I find it, and claim it as a right to canvass popular measures and expose their errors and pernicious tendency, as freely as governmental measures are canvassed, so long as I confine myself within the limits of the law.

At the conclusion of the late war, Great Britain found that though she had humbled her enemies, and greatly enlarged her own empire, that the national debt amounted to almost one hundred and fifty millions, and that the annual expence of keeping her extended dominions in a state of defence, which good policy dictates no less in a time of peace than war, was increased in proportion to the new acquisitions. Heavy taxes and duties were already laid, not only upon the luxuries and conveniences, but even the necessaries of life in Great Britain and Ireland. She knew that the colonies were as much bene-fitted by the conquests in the late war, as any part of the empire, and indeed more so, as their continental foes were subdued, and they might now extend their settlements not only to Canada, but even to the western ocean.—The greatest opening was given to agriculture, the natural livelihood of the country, that ever was known in the history of the world, and their trade was protected by the British navy. The revenue to the crown, from America, amounted to but little more than the charges of collecting it. She thought it as reasonable that the colonies should bear a part of the national burden, as that they should share in the national benefit. For this purpose the stamp-act was passed. The colonies soon found that the duties imposed by the stamp-act would be grievous, as they were laid upon custom-house papers, law proceedings, conveyancing, and indeed extended to almost all their internal trade and dealings. It was generally believed through the colonies, that this was a tax not only exceeding our proportion, but beyond our utmost ability to pay. This idea, united the colonies generally in opposing it. At first we did not dream of denying the *authority* of parliament to tax us, much less to legislate for us. We had always considered ourselves, as a part of the British empire, and the parliament, as the supreme legislature of the whole. Acts of parliament for regulating our internal polity were familiar. We had paid postage agreeable to act of parliament, for establishing a post-office, duties imposed for regulating trade, and even for raising a revenue to the crown without questioning the right, though we closely adverted to the rate or quantum. We knew that in all those acts of government, the good of the whole had been consulted, and whenever through want of information any thing grievous had been ordained, we were sure of obtaining redress by a proper representation of it. We were happy in our subordination; but in an evil hour, under the influence of some malignant planet, the design was formed of opposing the stamp-act, by a denial of the right of parliament to make it. The love of empire is so predominant in the human breast, that we rarely find an individual content with relinquishing a power that he is able to retain; never a body of men. Some few months after it was known that the stamp-act was passed, some resolves of the house of burgesses in Virginia, denying the right of parliament to tax the colonies, made their appearance. We read them with wonder; they savoured of independence; they flattered the human passions; the reasoning was specious; we wished it conclusive. The transition, to believing it so, was easy; and we, and almost all America, followed their example, in resolving that the parliament had no such right. It now became unpopular to suggest the contrary; his life would be in danger that asserted it. The newspapers were open to but one side of the question, and the inflammatory pieces that issued weekly from the press, worked up the populace to a fit temper to commit the outrages that ensued. A non-importation was agreed upon, which alarmed the merchants and manufacturers in England. It was novel, and the people in England then supposed, that the love of liberty was so powerful in an American merchant, as to stifle his love of gain, and that the agreement would be religiously adhered to. It has been said, that several thousands were expended in England, to foment the disturbances there. However that may be, opposition to the ministry was then gaining ground, from circumstances, foreign to this. The ministry was changed, and the stamp-act repealed. The repealing statute passed, with difficulty however, through the house of peers, near forty noble lords protested against giving way to such an opposition, and foretold what has since literally come to pass in consequence of it. When the statute was made, imposing duties upon glass, paper, India teas, &c. imported into the colonies, it was said, that this was another instance of taxation, for some of the dutied commodities were necessaries, we had them not within ourselves, were prohibited from importing them from any place except Great Britain, were therefore obliged to import them from Great Britain, and consequently, were obliged to pay the duties. Accordingly newspaper publications, pamphlets, resolves, non-importation agreements, and the whole system of American opposition was again put in motion. We obtained a partial repeal of this statute, which took off the duties from all the articles except teas. This was the lucky moment when to have closed the dispute. We might have made a safe and honorable retreat. We had gained much, perhaps more than we expected. If the parliament had passed an act declaratory of their right to tax us, our assemblies had resolved, ten times, that they had no such right. We could not complain of the three-penny duty on tea as burdensome, for a shilling which had been laid upon it, for the purpose of regulating trade, and therefore was allowed to be constitutional, was taken off; so that we were in fact gainers nine-pence in a pound by the new regulation. If the appropriation of the revenue, arising from this statute was disrelished, it was only our striking off one article of luxury from our manner of living, an article too, which if we may believe the resolves of most of the towns in this province, or rely on its collected wisdom in a resolve of the house of representatives, was to the last degree ruinous to health. It was futile to urge its being a precedent, as a reason for keeping up the ball of contention; for, allowing the supreme legislature ever to want a precedent, they had many for laying duties on commodities imported into the colonies. And beside we had great reason to believe that the remaining part of the statute would be repealed, as soon as the parliament should suppose it could be done with honor to themselves, as the incidental revenue arising from the former regulation, was four fold to the revenue arising from the latter. A claim of the right, could work no injury, so long as there was no grievous exercise of it, especially as we had protested against it, through the whole, and could not be said to have departed from our claims in the least. We might now upon good terms have dropped the dispute, and been happy in the affections of our mother country; but that is yet to come. Party is inseperable from a free state. The several distributions of power, as they are limited by, so they create perpetual dissentions between each other, about their respective boundaries; but the greatest source is the competition of individuals for preferment in the state. Popularity is the ladder by which the partizans usually climb. Accordingly, the struggle is, who shall have the greatest share of it. Each party professes disinterested patriotism, though some cynical writers have ventured to assert, that self-love is the ruling passion of the whole. There were two parties in this province of pretty long standing, known by the name of whig and tory, which at this time were not a little imbittered against each other. Men of abilities and acknowledged probity were on both sides. If the tories were suspected of pursuing their private interest through the medium of court favor, there was equal reason to suspect the whigs of pursuing their private interest by the means of popularity. Indeed some of them owed all their importance to it, and must in a little time have sunk into obscurity, had these turbulent commotions then subsided.

The tories and whigs took different routs, as usual. The tories were for closing the controversy with Great Britain, the whigs for continuing it; the tories were for restoring government in the province, which had become greatly relaxed by these convulsions, to its former tone; the whigs were averse to it; they even refused to revive a temporary riot act, which expired about this time. Perhaps they thought that mobs were a necessary ingredient in their system of opposition. However, the whigs had great advantages in the unequal combat; their scheme flattered the people with the idea of independence; the tories' plan supposed a degree of subordination, which is rather an humiliating idea; besides there is a propensity in men to believe themselves injured and oppressed whenever they are told so. The ferment, raised in their minds in the time of the stamp-act, was not yet allayed, and the leaders of the whigs had gained the confidence of the people by their successes in their former struggles, so that they had nothing to do but to keep up the spirit among the people, and they were sure of commanding in this province. It required some pains to prevent their minds settling into that calm, which is ordinarily the effect of a mild government; the whigs were sensible that there was no oppression that could be either seen or felt; if any thing was in reality amiss in government, it was its being too lax. So far was it from the innocent being in danger of suffering, that the most atrocious offenders escaped with impunity. They accordingly applied themselves to work upon the imagination, and to inflame the passions; for this work they possessed great talents; I will do justice to their ingenuity; they were intimately acquainted with the feelings of man, and knew all the avenues to the human heart. Effigies, paintings, and other imagery were exhibited; the fourteenth of August was celebrated annually as a festival in commemoration of a mob's destroying a building, owned by the late Lieutenant Governor, which was supposed to have been erected for a stamp-office; and compelling him to resign his office of stamp-master under liberty tree; annual orations were delivered in the old south meeting house, on the fifth of March, the day when some persons were unfortunately killed by a party of the twenty-ninth regiment; lists of imaginary grievances were continually published; the people were told weekly that the ministry had formed a plan to enslave them; that the duty upon tea was only a prelude to a window tax, hearth tax, land tax, and poll tax; and these were only paving the way for reducing the country to lordships. This last bait was the more easily swallowed, as there seems to be an apprehension of that kind hereditary to the people of New-England; and were conjured by the duty they owed themselves, their country, and their God, by the reverence due to the sacred memory of their ancestors, and all their toils and sufferings in this once inhospitable wilderness, and by their affections for unborn millions, to rouse and exert themselves in the common cause. This perpetual incantation kept the people in continual alarm. We were further stimulated by being told, that the people of England were depraved, the parliament venal, and the ministry corrupt; nor were attempts wanting to traduce Majesty itself. The kingdom of Great Britain was depicted as an ancient structure, once the admiration of the world, now sliding from its base, and rushing to its fall. At the same time we were called upon to mark our own rapid growth, and behold the certain evidence that America was upon the eve of independent empire.

When we consider what effect a well written tragedy or

novel has on the human passions, though we know it to be all fictitious, what effect must all this be supposed to have had upon those, that believed these high wrought images to be realities?

The tories have been censured for remissness in not having exerted themselves sufficiently at this period. The truth of the case is this; they saw and shuddered at the gathering storm, but durst not attempt to dispel it, lest it should burst on their own heads. Printers were threatened with the loss of their bread, for publishing freely on the tory side. One Mr. Mein was forced to fly the country for persisting in it.

All our dissenting ministers were not inactive on this occasion. When the clergy engage in a political warfare, religion becomes a most powerful engine, either to support or overthrow the state. What effect must it have had upon the audience to hear the same sentiments and principles, which they had before read in a newspaper, delivered on Sundays from the sacred desk, with religious awe, and the most solemn appeals to heaven, from lips which they had been taught, from their cradles, to believe could utter nothing but eternal truths? What was it natural to expect from a people bred under a free constitution, jealous of their liberty, credulous, even to a proverb, when told their privileges were in danger, thus wrought upon in the extreme? I answer, outrages disgraceful to humanity itself. What mischief was not an artful man, who had obtained the confidence and guidance of such an enraged multitude, capable of doing? He had only to point out this or the other man, as an enemy of his country; and no character, station, age, or merit could protect the proscribed from their fury. Happy was it for him, if he could secrete his person, and subject his property only to their lawless ravages. By such means, many people naturally brave and humane, have been wrought upon to commit such acts of private mischief and public violence, as will blacken many a page in the history of our country.

I shall next trace the effects of this spirit, which the whigs had thus infused into the body of the people, through the courts of common law, and the general assembly, and mark the ways and means, whereby they availed themselves of it, to the subversion of our charter constitution, antecedent to the late acts of parliament.

MASSACHUSETTENSIS

MASSACHUSETTENSIS, December 26, 1775

To undertake to convince a person of his error, is the indispensible duty, the certain, though dangerous test of friendship. He that could see his friend persevering in a fatal error, without reminding him of it, and striving to reclaim him, through fear that he might thereby incur his displeasure, would little deserve the sacred name himself. Such delicacy is not only false, but criminal. Were I not fully convinced upon the most mature deliberation, that I am capable of, that the temporal salvation of this province depends upon an entire and speedy change of measures, which must depend upon a change of sentiment, respecting our own conduct, and the justice of the British nation, I never should have obtruded myself on the public. I repeat my promise, to avoid personal reflection, as much as the nature of the task will admit of; but will continue faithfully to expose the wretched policy of the whigs, though I may be obliged to penetrate the arcana, and discover such things as, were there not a necessity for it, I should be infinitely happier in drawing a veil over, or covering with a mantle. Should I be so unfortunate as to incur your displeasure, I shall nevertheless think myself happy, if I can but snatch one of my fellow-subjects as a brand out of the burning.

Perhaps some may imagine that I have represented too many of my countrymen, as well as the leading whigs, in an unjust point of light, by supposing these so wicked as to mislead, or those so little circumspect as to be misled, in matters of the last importance. Whoever has been conversant with the history of man, must know that it abounds with such instances. The same game, and with the same success, has been played in all ages, and all countries.

The bulk of the people are generally but little versed in matters of state. Want of inclination or opportunity to figure in public life, makes them content to rest the affairs of government in the hands, where accident or merit has placed them. Their views and employments are confined to the humbler walks of business or retirement. There is a latent spark however, in their breasts, capable of being kindled into a flame; to do this has always been the employment of the disaffected. They begin by reminding the people of the elevated rank they hold in the universe, as men; that all men by nature are equal; that kings are but the ministers of the people; that their authority is delegated to them by the people for their good, and they have a right to resume it, and place it in other hands, or keep it themselves, whenever it is made use of to oppress them. Doubtless there have been instances where these principles have been inculcated to obtain a redress of real grievances, but they have been much oftener perverted to the worst of purposes. No government, however perfect in theory, is administered in perfection; the frailty of man does not admit of it. A small mistake, in point of policy, often furnishes a pretence to libel government, and persuade the people that their rulers are tyrants, and the whole government a system of oppression. Thus the seeds of sedition are usually sown, and the people are led to sacrifice real liberty to licentiousness, which gradually ripens into rebellion and civil war. And what is still more to be lamented, the generality of the people, who are thus made the dupes of artifice, and the mere stilts of ambition, are sure to be losers in the end. The best they can expect, is to be thrown neglected by, when they are no longer wanted;

but they are seldom so happy; if they are subdued, confiscation of estate and ignominious death are their portion; if they conquer, their own army is often turned upon them, to subjugate them to a more tyranical government than that they rebelled against. History is replete with instances of this kind; we can trace them in remote antiquity, we find them in modern times, and have a remarkable one in the very country from which we are derived. It is an universal truth, that he that would excite a rebellion, whatever professions of philanthropy he may make, when he is insinuating and worming himself into the good graces of the people, is at heart as great a tyrant as ever wielded the iron rod of oppression. I shall have occasion hereafter to consider this matter more fully, when I shall endeavour to convince you how little we can gain, and how much we may lose, by this unequal, unnatural, and desperate contest. My present business is, to trace the spirit of opposition to Great Britain through the general court, and the courts of common law. In moderate times, a representative that votes for an unpopular measure, or opposes a popular one, is in danger of losing his election the next year; when party runs high, he is sure to do it. It was the policy of the whigs to have their questions, upon high matters, determined by yea and nay votes, which were published with the representatives' names in the next gazette. This was commonly followed by severe strictures and the most illiberal invectives upon the dissentients; sometimes they were held up as objects of resentment, of contempt at others; the abuse was in proportion to the extravagance of the measure they opposed. This may seem not worth notice, but its consequences were important. The scurrility made its way into the dissentient's town, it furnished his competitor with means to supplant him, and he took care to shun the rock his predecessor had split upon. In this temper of the times, it was enough to know who voted with Cassius and who with Lucius, to determine who was a friend and who an enemy to the country, without once adverting to the question before the house. The loss of a seat in the house was not of so much consequence; but when once he became stigmatized as an enemy to his country, he was exposed to insult; and if his profession or business was such, that his livelihood depended much on the good graces of his fellow citizens, he was in danger of losing his bread, and involving his whole family in ruin.

One particular set of members, in committee, always prepared the resolves and other spirited measures. At first they were canvassed freely, at length would slide through the house without meeting an obstacle. The lips of the dissentients were sealed up; they sat in silence, and beheld with infinite regret the measures they durst not oppose. Many were borne down against their wills, by the violence of the current; upon no other principle can we reconcile their ostensible conduct in the house to their declarations in private circles. The apparent unanimity in the house encouraged the opposition out of doors, and that in its turn strengthened the party in the house. Thus they went on mutually supporting and up-lifting each other. Assemblies and towns resolved alternately; some of them only omitted resolving to snatch the sceptre out of the hands of our sovereign, and to strike the imperial crown from his sacred head.

A master stroke in politics respecting the agent, ought not to be neglected. Each colony has usually an agent residing at the court of Great Britain. These agents are appointed by the three branches of their several assemblies; and indeed there cannot be a provincial agent without such appointment. The whigs soon found that they could not have such services rendered them from a provincial agent, as would answer their purposes. The house therefore refused to join with the other two branches of the general court in the appointment. The house chose an agent for themselves, and the council appointed another. Thus we had two agents for private purposes, and the expence of agency doubled; and with equal reason a third might have been added, as agent for the Governor, and the charges been trebled.

The additional expence was of little consideration, compared with another inconvenience that attended this new mode of agency. The person appointed by the house was the ostensible agent of the province, though in fact he was only the agent of a few individuals that had got the art of managing the house at their pleasure. He knew his continuing in office depended upon them. An office, that yielded several hundred pounds sterling annually, the business of which consisted in little more than attending the levees of the great, and writing letters to America, was worth preserving. Thus he was under a strong temptation to sacrifice the province to a party; and ecchoed back the sentiments of his patrons.

The advices continually received from one of the persons, that was thus appointed agent, had great influence upon the members of the house of more moderate principles. He had pushed his researches deep into nature, and made important discoveries; they thought he had done the same in politics, and did not admire him less as a politician, than as a philosopher. His intelligence as to the disposition of his majesty, the ministry, the parliament and the nation in general, was deemed the most authentic. He advised us to keep up our opposition, to resolve, and re-resolve, to cherish a military spirit, uniformly holding up this idea, that if we continued firm, we had nothing to fear from the government in England. He even proposed some modes of opposition himself. The spirited measures were always ushered into the house with a letter from him. I have been sometimes almost ready to suspect him of being the *primum mobile,* and, that like the man behind the curtain at a puppet-shew, he was playing off the figures here with his own secret wires. If he advised to these measures contrary to his better knowledge, from sinister views, and to serve a private purpose, he has *wilfully* done the province irreparable injury. However, I will do him justice; he enjoined it upon us to refrain from violence, as that would unite the nation against us; and I am rather inclined to think that he was deceived himself, with respect to the measures he recommended, as he has already felt the resentment of that very government, which he told us there was nothing to fear from. This disposition of the house could not have produced such fatal effects, had the other two branches of the legislature retained their constitutional freedom and influence. They might have been a sufficient check.

The councellors depended upon the general assembly for their political existence; the whigs reminded the council of their mortality. If a councellor opposed the violent measures of the whigs with any spirit, he lost his election the next May. The council consisted of twenty-eight. From this principle, near half that number, mostly men of the first families, note and abilities, with every possible attachment to their native country, and as far from temptation as wealth and independence could remove them, were tumbled from their seats in disgrace. Thus the board, which was intended to moderate between the two extremes of prerogative and privilege, lost its weight in the scale, and the political balance of the province was destroyed.

Had the chair been able to retain its own constitutional influence, the loss of the board would have been less felt; but no longer supported by the board, that fell likewise. The Governor by the charter could do little or nothing without the council. If he called upon a military officer to raise the militia, he was answered, they were there already. If he called upon his council for their assistance, they must first enquire into the cause. If he wrote to government at home to strengthen his hands, some officious person procured and sent back his letters.

It was not the person of a Bernard or Hutchinson that made them obnoxious; any other governors would have met with the same fate, had they discharged their duty with equal fidelity; that is, had they strenuously opposed the principles and practices of the whigs; and when they found that the government here could not support itself, wrote home for aid sufficient to do it. And let me tell you, had the intimations in those letters, which you are taught to execrate, been timely attended to, we had now been as happy a people as good government could make us. Gov. Bernard came here recommended by the affections of the province over which he had presided. His abilities are acknowledged. True British honesty and punctuality are traits in his character, too strongly marked to escape the eye of prejudice itself. We know Governor Hutchinson to be amiable and exemplary in private life. His great abilities, integrity and humanity were conspicuous, in the several important departments that he filled, before his appointment to the chair, and reflect honour on his native country. But his abilities and integrity, added to his thorough knowledge of the province, in all its interests and connexions, were insufficient in this case. The constitution itself was gone, though the ancient form remained; the spirit was truly republican. He endeavoured to reclaim us by gentle means. He strove to convince us by arguments, drawn from the first principles of government; our several charters, and the express acknowledgments of our ancestors, that our claims were inconsistent with the subordination due to Great Britain; and if persisted in, might work the destruction of those that we were entitled to. For this he was called an enemy to his country, and set up as a mark for the envenomed arrows of malice and party rage. Had I entertained a doubt about its being the governor, and not the man that was aimed at, the admirable facility with which the newspaper abuse was transferred from Gov. Hutchinson to his humane and benevolent successor, Gen. Gage, almost as soon as he set foot on our shore, would have removed it.

Thus, disaffection to Great Britain being infused into the body of the people, the subtle poison stole through all the veins and arteries, contaminated the blood, and destroyed the very stamina of the constitution. Had not the courts of justice been tainted in the early stages, our government might have expelled the virus, purged off the peccant humors, and recovered its former vigour by its own strength. The judges of the superior court were dependant upon the annual grants of the general court for their support. Their salaries were small, in proportion to the salaries of other officers in the government, of less importance.

They had often petitioned the assembly to enlarge them, without success. They were at this time reminded of their dependance. However, it is but justice to say, that the judges remained unshaken, amid the raging tempests, which is to be attributed rather to their firmness than situation. But the spirit of the times was very apparent in the juries. The grand jurors were elective; and in such places where libels, riots, and insurrections were the most frequent, the high whigs took care to get themselves chosen. The judges pointed out to them the seditious libels on governors, magistrates, and the whole government to no effect. They were enjoined to present riots and insurrections, of which there was ample evidence, with as little success.

It is difficult to account for so many of the first rate whigs being returned to serve on the petit jury at the term next after extraordinary insurrections, without supposing some legerdemain in drawing their names out of the box. It is certain that notwithstanding swarms of the most virulent libels infested the province, and there were so many riots and insurrections, scarce one offender was indicted, and I think not one convicted and punished. Causes of *meum et tuum* were not always exempt from party influence. The mere circumstance of the whigs gaining the ascendency over the tories, is trifling. Had the whigs divided the province between them, as they once flattered themselves they should be able to do, it would have been of little consequence to the community, had they not cut asunder the very sinews of government, and broke in pieces the ligaments of social life in the attempt. I will mention two instances, which I have selected out of many, of the weakness of our government, as they are recent and unconnected with acts of parliament. One Malcolm, a loyal subject, and as such entitled to protection, the evening before the last winter sessions of the general court, was dragged out of his house, stript, tarred and feathered, and carted several hours in the severest frost of that winter, to the utmost hazard of his life. He was carried to the gallows with an halter about his neck, and in his passage to and from the gallows, was beaten with as cruel stripes as ever were administered by the hands of a savage. The whipping, however, kept up the circulation of his blood, and saved the poor man's life. When they had satiated their malice, they dispersed in good order. This was transacted in the presence of thousands of spectators; some of whom were members of the general court. Malcolm's life was despaired of several days, but he survived and presented a memorial to the general assembly, praying their interposition. The petition was read, and all he obtained was leave to withdraw it. So that he was destitute of protection every hour, until he left the country, as were thousands beside, until the arrival of the king's troops. This originated from a small fracas in the street, wherein Malcolm struck, or threatened to strike a person that insulted him, with a cutlass, and had no connection with the quarrel of the times, unless his sustaining a small post in the customs made it.

The other instance is much stronger than this, as it was totally detached from politics. It had been suspected that infection had been communicated from an hospital, lately erected at Marblehead, for the purpose of innoculating the small-pox, to the town's people. This caused a great insurrection; the insurgents burnt the hospital; not content with that, threatened the proprietors, and many others, some of the first fortunes and characters in the town, with burning their houses over their heads, and continued parading the streets, to the utmost terror of the inhabitants several days. A massacre and general devastation was apprehended. The persons threatened, armed themselves, and petitioned the general assembly, which was then sitting, for assistance, as there was little or no civil authority in the place. A committee was ordered to repair to Marblehead, report the facts, and enquire into the cause. The committee reported the facts nearly as stated in the petition. The report was accepted, and nothing farther done by the assembly. Such demonstrations of the weakness of government induced many persons to join the whigs, to seek from them that protection, which the constitutional authority of the province was unable to afford.

Government at home, early in the day, made an effort to check us in our career, and to enable us to recover from anarchy without her being driven to the necessity of altering our provincial constitution, knowing the predilection that people always have for an ancient form of government. The judges of the superior court had not been staggered, though their feet stood in slippery places, they depended upon the leading whigs for their support. To keep them steady, they were made independent of the grants of the general assembly: but it was not a remedy any way adequate to the disease. The whigs now turned their artillery against them, and it played briskly. The chief justice, for accepting the crown grant, was accused of receiving a royal bribe.

Thus, my friends, those very persons that had made you believe that every attempt to strengthen government and save our charter was an infringement of your privileges, by little and little destroyed your real liberty, subverted your charter constitution, abridged the freedom of the house, annihilated the freedom of the board, and rendered the governor a mere doge of Venice. They engrossed all the power of the province into their own hands. A democracy or republic it has been called, but it does not deserve the name of either; it was, however, a despotism cruelly carried into execution by mobs and riots, and more incompatible with the rights of mankind, than the enormous monarchies of the East. The absolute necessity of the interposition of parliament is apparent. The good policy of the act for regulating the government in this province, will be the subject of some future paper. A particular enquiry into the despotism of the whigs will be deferred for a chapter on congresses. I shall next ask your attention to a transaction, as important in its consequences, and perhaps more so, than any I have yet mentioned; I mean the destruction of the tea, belonging to the East-India company. I am sensible of the difficulty of the task, in combating generally received opinions. It is hard work to eradicate deep-rooted prejudice. But I will persevere. There are hundreds, if not thousands, in the province, that will feel the truth of what I have written, line by line as they read it, and as to those who obstinately shut their eyes against it now, haply the fever of the times may intermit, there may be some lucid interval, when their minds shall be open to truth, before it is too late to serve them; otherwise it will be revealed to them in bitter moments, attended with keen remorse and unutterable anguish. *Magna est veritas et prevalebit.*

MASSACHUSETTENSIS

NOVANGLUS, January 23, 1775

A writer, under the signature of Massachusettensis, has addressed you, in a series of papers, on the great national subject of the present quarrel between the British administration and the Colonies. As I have not in my possession, more than one of his Essays, and that is in the Gazette of December 26, I will take the liberty, in the spirit of candor, and decency, to bespeak your attention, upon the same subject.

There may be occasion, to say very severe things, before I shall have finished what I propose, in opposition to this writer but there ought to be no reviling. *Rem ipsam dic, mitte male loqui,* which may be justly translated, speak out the whole truth boldly, but use no bad language.

It is not very material to enquire, as others have done, who is the author of the speculations in question. If he is a disinterested writer, and has nothing to gain or to lose, to hope or to fear, for himself more than other individuals of your community; but engages in this controversy from the purest principles, the noblest motives of benevolence to men, and of love to his country, he ought to have no influence with you, further than truth and justice will support his argument. On the other hand, if he hopes to acquire or preserve a lucrative employment, to screen himself from the just detestation of his countrymen, or whatever other sinister inducement he may have, as far as the truth of facts and the weight of argument, are in his favor, he ought to be duly regarded.

He tells you "that the temporal salvation of this province depends upon an entire and speedy change of measures, which must depend upon a change of sentiments respecting our own conduct and the justice of the British nation."

The task, of effecting these great changes, this courageous writer, has undertaken in a course of publications in a newspaper. *Nil desperandum* is a good motto, and *Nil admirari,* is another. He is welcome to the first, and I hope will be willing that I should assume the last. The public, if they are not mistaken in their conjecture, have been so long acquainted with this gentleman, and have seen him so often disappointed, that if they were not habituated to strange things, they would wonder at his hopes, at this time to accomplish, the most unpromising project of his whole life. In the character of Philanthrop, he attempted to reconcile you to Mr. Bernard. But the only fruit of his labor was, to expose his client to more general examination, and consequently to more general resentment and aversion. In the character of Philalethes, he essayed to prove Mr. Hutchinson a patriot, and his letters not only innocent, but meritorious. But the more you read and considered, the more you were convinced of the ambition and avarice, the simulation and dissimulation, the hypocricy and perfidy of that destroying angel.

This illfated and unsuccessful, though persevering writer, still hopes to change your sentiments and conduct—by which it is supposed that he means to convince you that the system of Colony administration, which has been pursued for these ten or twelve years past, is a wise, righteous and humane plan; that sir Francis Bernard and Mr. Hutchinson, with their connections, who have been the principal instruments of it, are your best friends;—and that those gentle in this province, and in all the other Colonies, who have been in opposition to it, are from ignorance, error, or from worse and baser causes, your worst enemies.

This is certainly an inquiry that is worthy of you; and I promise to accompany this writer, in his ingenious labours to assist you in it. And I earnestly intreat you, as the result of all shall be, to change your sentiments or persevere in them, as the evidence shall appear to you, upon the most dispassionate and impartial consideration, without regard to his opinion or mine.

He promises to avoid personal reflections, but to penetrate the arcana, and expose the wretched policy of the whigs. The cause of the whigs is not conducted by intrigues at a distant court, but by constant appeals to a sensible and virtuous people; it depends intirely on their good will, and cannot be pursued a single step without their concurrence, to obtain which of all designs, measures, and means, are constantly published to the collective body. The whigs therefore can have no arcana; but if they had, I dare say they were never so left, as to communicate them to this writer; you will therefore be disappointed if you expect from him any thing which is true, but what has been as public as records and newspapers could make it.

I, on my part, may perhaps in a course of papers, penetrate

arcana too. Shew the wicked policy of the tories—trace their plan from its first rude sketches to its present complete draught. Shew that it has been much longer in contemplation, than is generally known,—who were the first in it—their views, motives and secret springs of action—and the means they have employed. This will necessarily bring before your eyes many characters, living and dead. From such a research and detail of facts, it will clearly appear, who were the aggressors—and who have acted on the defensive from first to last—who are still struggling, at the expense of their ease, health, peace, wealth and preferment, against the encroachments of the tories on their country—and who are determined to continue struggling, at much greater hazards still, and like the Prince of Orange, resolve never to see its entire subjection to arbitrary power, but rather to die fighting against it, in the last ditch.

It is true, as this writer observes, "that the bulk of the people are generally, but little versed in the affairs of State; that they left the affairs of government where accident has placed them." If this had not been true, the designs of the tories had been many years ago, entirely defeated. It was clearly seen, by a few, more than ten years since, that they were planning and pursuing the very measures, we now see executing. The people were informed of it, and warned of their danger: But they had been accustomed to confide in certain persons, and could never be persuaded to believe, until prophecy, became history. Now they see and feel, that the horrible calamities are come upon them, which were foretold so many years ago, and they now sufficiently execrate the men who have brought these things upon them. Now alas! when perhaps it is too late. If they had withdrawn their confidence from them in season, they would have wholly disarmed them.

The same game, with the same success, has been played in all ages and countries as Massachusettensis observes. When a favourable conjuncture has presented, some of the most intrigueing and powerful citizens have conceived the design of enslaving their country, and building their own greatness on its ruins. Philip and Alexander, are examples of this in Greece —Cæsar in Rome—Charles the fifth in Spain—Lewis the eleventh in France—and ten thousand others.

"There is a latent spark in the breasts of the people capable of being kindled into a flame, and to do this has always been the employment of the disaffected." What is this latent spark? The love of Liberty? *a Deo hominis est indita naturæ.* Human nature itself is evermore an advocate for liberty. There is also in human nature, a resentment of injury, and indignation against wrong. A love of truth and a veneration for virtue.

These amiable passions, are the "latent spark" to which those whom this writer calls the "disaffected" apply. If the people are capable of understanding, seeing and feeling the difference between true and false, right and wrong, virtue and vice, to what better principle can the friends of mankind apply, than to the sense of this difference.

Is it better to apply as this writer and his friends do, to the basest passions in the human breast to their fear, their vanity, their avarice, ambition, and every kind of corruption? I appeal to all experience, and to universal history, if it has ever been in the power of popular leaders, uninvested with other authority than what is conferred by the popular suffrage, to persuade a large people, for any length of time together, to think themselves wronged, injured, and oppressed, unless they really were, and saw and felt it to be so.

"They," the popular leaders, "begin by reminding the people of the elevated rank they hold in the universe as men; that all men by nature are equal; that kings are but the ministers of the people; that their authority is delegated to them by the people, for their good, and they have a right to resume it, and place it in other hands, or keep it themselves, whenever it is made use of to oppress them. Doubtless there have been instances, when these principles have been inculcated to obtain a redress of real grievances, but they have been much oftener perverted to the worst of purposes."

These are what are called revolution principles. They are the principles of Aristotle and Plato, of Livy and Cicero, and Sydney, Harrington and Locke. The principles of nature and eternal reason. The principles on which the whole government over us, now stands. It is therefore astonishing, if any thing can be so, that writers, who call themselves friends of government, should in this age and country, be so inconsistent with themselves, so indiscreet, so immodest, as to insinuate a doubt concerning them.

Yet we find that these principles stand in the way of Massachusettensis, and all the writers of his class. The veteran, in his letter to the officers of the army, allows them to be noble, and true, but says the application of them to particular cases is wild and utopian. How they can be in general true, and not applicable to particular cases, I cannot comprehend. I thought their being true in general, was because they were applicable in most particular cases.

Gravity is a principle in nature. Why? because all particular bodies are found to gravitate. How would it sound to say, that bodies in general are heavy; yet to apply this to particular bodies and say, that a guinea, or a ball is heavy, is wild, &c.—

"Adopted in private life," says the honest amiable veteran, "they would introduce perpetual discord." This I deny, and I think it plain, that there never was an happy private family where they were not adopted. "In the State perpetual discord." This I deny, and affirm that order, concord and stability in this State, never was or can be preserved without them. "The least failure in the reciprocal duties of worship and obedience in the matrimonial contract would justify a divorce." This is no consequence from those principles,—a total departure from the ends and designs of the contract it is true, as elopement and adultery, would by these principles justify a divorce, but not the least failure, or many smaller failures in the reciprocal duties, &c. "In the political compact, the smallest defect in the Prince a revolution"—By no means. But a manifest design in the Prince, to annul the contract on his part, will annul it on the part of the people. A settled plan to deprive the people of all the benefits, blessings and ends of the contract, to subvert the fundamentals of the constitution, to deprive them of all share in making and executing laws, will justify a revolution.

The author of a "Friendly Address to all reasonable Americans," discovers his rancour against these principles, in a more explicit manner, and makes no scruples to advance the principles of Hobbs and Filmer, boldly, and to pronounce damnation, *ore rotundo,* on all who do not practice implicit passive obedience, to an established government, of whatever character it may be. It is not reviling, it is not bad language, it is strictly decent to say, that this angry bigot, this ignorant dogmatist, this foul mouthed scold, deserves no other answer than silent contempt. Massachusettensis and the veteran, I admire, the first for his art, the last for his honesty.

Massachusettensis, is more discreet than either of the others; sensible that these principles would be very troublesome to him, yet conscious of their truth, he has neither admitted nor denied them. But we have a right to his opinion of them, before we dispute with him. He finds fault with the application of them. They have been invariably applied in support of the revolution and the present establishment—against the Stuart's, the Charles' and the James',—in support of the reformation and the Protestant religion, against the worst tyranny, that the genius of toryism, has ever yet invented, I mean the Roman superstition. Does this writer rank the revolution and present establishment, the reformation and Protestant religion among his worst of purposes? What "worse purpose" is there than established tyranny? Were these principles ever inculcated in favor of such tyranny? Have they not always been used against such tyrannies, when the people have had knowledge enough to be apprized of them, and courage to assert them? Do not those who aim at depriving the people of their liberties, always inculcate opposite principles, or discredit these?

"A small mistake in point of policy," says he, "often furnishes a pretence to libel government and persuade the people that their rulers are tyrants, and the whole government, a system of oppression." This is not only untrue, but inconsistent with what he said before. The people are in their nature so gentle, that there never was a government yet, in which thousands of mistakes were not overlooked. The most sensible and jealous people are so little attentive to government, that there are no instances of resistance, until repeated, multiplied oppressions have placed it beyond a doubt, that their rulers had formed settled plans to deprive them of their liberties; not to oppress an individual or a few, but to break down the fences of a free constitution, and deprive the people at large of all share in the government and all the checks by which it is limited. Even Machiavel himself allows, that not ingratitude to their rulers, but much love is the constant fault of the people.

This writer is equally mistaken, when he says, the people are sure to be loosers in the end. They can hardly be loosers, if unsuccessful; because if they live, they can but be slaves, after an unfortunate effort, and slaves they would have been, if they had not resisted. So that nothing is lost. If they die, they cannot be said to lose, for death is better than slavery. If they succeed, their gains are immense. They preserve their liberties. The instances in antiquity, which this writer alludes to, are not mentioned, and therefore cannot be answered, but that in the country from whence we are derived, is the most unfortunate for his purpose, that could have been chosen. The resistance to Charles the First and the case of Cromwell, no doubt he means. But the people of England, and the cause of liberty, truth, virtue and humanity, gained infinite advantages by that resistance. In all human probability, liberty civil and religious, not only in England but in all Europe, would have been lost. Charles would undoubtedly have established the Romish religion and a despotism as wild as any in the world. And as England has been a principal bulwark from that period to this, of civil liberty and the Protestant religion in all Europe, if

Charles' schemes had succeeded, there is great reason to apprehend that the right of science would have been extinguished,
and mankind, drawn back to a state of darkness and misery,
like that which prevailed from the fourth to the fourteenth
century. It is true and to be lamented that Cromwell did not
establish a government as free, as he might and ought; but his
government was infinately more glorious and happy to the
people than Charles'. Did not the people gain by the resistance
to James the second? Did not the Romans gain by the resistance
to Tarquin? Throughout that resistance and the liberty that
was restored by it, would the great Roman orators, poets and
historians, the great teachers of humanity and politeness, the
pride of human nature, and the delight and glory of mankind,
for seventeen hundred years, ever have existed? Did not the
Romans gain by resistance to the Decemvirs? Did not the English gain by resistance to John, when Magna Charta was
obtained? Did not the seven united provinces gain by resistance
to Philip, Alva, and Granvell? Did not the Swiss Cantons, the
Genevans and Grissons, gain by resistance to Albert and
Grisler?

NOVANGLUS

NOVANGLUS, January 30, 1775

I have heretofore intimated my intention, of pursuing the
tories, through all their dark intrigues, and wicked machina-
tions; and to shew the rise, and progress of their schemes for
enslaving this country. The honor of inventing and contriving
these measures, is not their due. They have been but servile
copiers of the designs of Andross, Randolph, Dudley, and other
champions of their cause towards the close of the last century.
These latter worthies accomplished but little; and their plans
had been buried with them, for a long course of years, until in

the administration of the late Governor Shirley, they were re-vived, by the persons who are now principally concerned in carrying them into execution. Shirley, was a crafty, busy, ambi-tious, intrigueing, enterprising man; and having mounted, no matter by what means, to the chair of this province, he saw, in a young growing country, vast prospects of ambition opening before his eyes, and he conceived great designs of aggrandizing himself, his family and his friends. Mr. Hutchinson and Mr. Oliver, the two famous letter writers, were his principal minis-ters of State. Russell, Paxton, Ruggles, and a few others, were *subordinate* instruments. Among other schemes of this Junto, one was to have a Revenue in America by authority of Parlia-ment.

In order to effect their purpose it was necessary to concert measures with the other Colonies. Dr. Franklin, who was known to be an active, and very able man, and to have great influence, in the province of Pennsylvania, was in Boston, in the year 1754, and Mr. Shirley communicated to him the profound secret, the great design of taxing the Colonies by act of Parlia-ment. This sagacious gentleman, this eminent philosopher, and distinguished patriot, to his lasting honor, sent the Governor an answer in writing with the following remarks upon his scheme. Remarks which would have discouraged any honest man from the pursuit. The remarks are these:—

"That the people always bear the burden best, when they have, or think they have, some *share* in the direction.

"That when public measures are generally distasteful to the people, the wheels of government must move more heavily.

"That excluding the people of America from all share in the choice of a grand council for their own defence, and taxing them in Parliament, where they have no representative, would probably give extreme dissatisfaction.

"That there was no reason to doubt the willingness of the Colonists to contribute for their own defence. That the people themselves, whose all was at stake, could better judge of the force necessary for their defence, and of the means for raising money for the purpose, than a British Parliament at so great distance.

"That natives of America, would be as likely to consult wisely and faithfully for the safety of their native country, as the Governors sent from Britain, whose object is generally to make fortunes, and then return home, and who might therefore be expected to carry on the war against France, rather in a way, by which themselves were likely to be gainers, than for the greatest advantage of the cause.

"That compelling the Colonies to pay money for their own defence, without their consent, would shew a suspicion of their loyalty, or of their regard for their country, or of their common sense, and would be treating them as conquered enemies, and not as free Britains, who hold it for their undoubted right not to be taxed but by their own consent, given through their representatives.

"That parliamentary taxes, once laid on, are often continued, after the necessity for laying them on, ceases; but that if the Colonists were trusted to tax themselves, they would remove the burden from the people, as soon as it should become un-necessary for them to bear it any longer.

"That if Parliament is to tax the Colonies, their assemblies of representatives may be dismissed as useless.

"That taxing the Colonies in Parliament for their own defence against the French, is not more just, than it would be to oblige the cinque ports, and other parts of Britain, to maintain a force against France, and to tax them for this purpose, without allow-ing them representatives in Parliament.

"That the Colonists have always been indirectly taxed by the mother country (besides paying the taxes necessarily laid on by their own assemblies) inasmuch as they are obliged to pur-chase the manufactures of Britain, charged with innumerable heavy taxes; some of which manufactures they could make, and others could purchase cheaper at other markets.

"That the Colonists are besides taxed by the mother country, by being obliged to carry great part of their produce to Britain, and accept a lower price, than they might have at other markets. The difference is a tax paid to Britain.

"That the whole wealth of the Colonists centres at last in the mother country, which enables her to pay her taxes.

"That the Colonies have, at the hazard of their lives and fortunes, extended the dominions, and increased the commerce and riches of the mother country, that therefore the Colonists do not deserve to be deprived of the native right of Britons, the right of being taxed only by representatives chosen by themselves.

"That an adequate representation in parliament would probably be acceptable to the Colonists, and would best raise the views and interests of the whole empire."

The last of these propositions seems not to have been well considered, because an adequate representation in parliament, is totally impracticable; but the others have exhausted the subject. If any one should ask what authority or evidence I have of this anecdote, I refer to the second volume of the Political Disquisitions,[1] page 276, 7, 8, 9. A book which ought to be in the hands of every American who has learned to read.

Whether the ministry at home or the junto here, were discouraged by these masterly remarks, or by any other cause, the project of taxing the Colonies was laid aside. Mr. Shirley was removed from this government, and Mr. Pownal was placed in his stead.

Mr. Pownal seems to have been a friend to liberty and to our Constitution, and to have had an aversion to all plots against either, and consequently to have given his confidence to other persons than Hutchinson and Oliver, who, stung with envy against Mr. Pratt and others, who had the lead in affairs, set

---

[1] James Burgh, *Political Disquisitions,* 3 vols. (London, 1774–1775). [—ED.]

themselves, by propagating slanders against the Governor, among the people, and especially among the clergy, to raise discontents, and make him uneasy in his seat. Pownal averse to wrangling, and fond of the delights of England, solicited to be recalled, and after some time Mr. Bernard was removed from New Jersey to the chair of this Province.

Bernard was the man for the purpose of the junto; educated in the highest principles of monarchy, naturally daring and courageous, skilled enough in law and policy to do mischief, and avaricious to a most infamous degree; needy at the same time, and having a numerous family to provide for,—he was an instrument, suitable in every respect, excepting one, for this junto, to employ. The exception I mean, was blunt frankness, very opposite to that cautious cunning, that deep dissimulation, to which they had by long practice disciplined themselves. However, they did not despair of teaching him this necessary artful quality by degrees, and the event shewed they were not wholly unsuccessful, in their endeavors to do it.

While the war lasted, these simple Provinces were of too much importance in the conduct of it, to be disgusted, by any open attempt against their liberties. The junto therefore, contented themselves with preparing their ground by extending their connection and correspondencies in England, and by conciliating the friendship of the crown officers occasionally here, and insinuating their designs as necessary to be undertaken in some future favorable opportunity, for the good of the empire, as well of the Colonies.

The designs of Providence are inscrutable. It affords to bad men conjunctures favourable for their designs, as well as to good. The conclusion of the peace, was the most critical opportunity for our junto, that could have presented. A peace founded on the destruction of that system of policy, the most glorious for the nation, that ever was formed, and which was never equalled in the conduct of the English government, except in the interregnum, and perhaps in the reign of Elizabeth; which system however, by its being abruptly broken off and its chief conductor discarded before it was completed, proved unfortunate to the nation by leaving it sinking in a bottomless gulf of debt, oppressed and borne down with taxes.

At this lucky time, when the British financier, was driven out of his wits for ways and means, to supply the demands upon him, Bernard is employed by the junto, to suggest to him the project of taxing the Colonies by act of Parliament.

I do not advance this without evidence. I appeal to a publication made by Sir Francis Bernard himself, the last year of his own select letters on the trade and government of America, and the principles of law and polity applied to the American Colonies. I shall make much use of this pamphlet before I have done.

In the year 1764, Mr. Bernard transmitted home to different noblemen, and gentlemen, four copies of his principles of law and polity, with a preface, which proves incontestibly, that the project of new regulating the American Colonies were not first suggested to him by the ministry, but by him to them. The words of this preface are these:—"The present expectation, that a new regulation of the American governments will soon take place, probably arises more from the opinion the public has of the abilities of the present ministry, than from any thing that has transpired from the cabinet; it cannot be supposed that their penetration can overlook the necessity of such a regulation, nor their public spirit fail to carry it into execution. But it may be a question, whether the present is a proper time for this work; more urgent business may stand before it, some preparatory steps may be required to precede it; but these will only serve to postpone. As we may expect that this reformation, like all others, will be opposed by powerful prejudices, it may not be amiss to reason with them at leisure, and endeavor to take off their force before they become opposed to government."

These are the words of that arch enemy of North America, written in 1764, and then transmitted to four persons, with a desire that they might be communicated to others.

Upon these words, it is impossible not to observe, first, That the ministry had never signified to him, any intention of new regulating the Colonies; and therefore, that it was he who most officiously and impertinently put them upon the pursuit of this *will with a whisp*, which has led him and them into so much mire. 2. The artful flattery with which he insinuates these projects into the minds of the ministry, as matters of absolute necessity, which their great penetration could not fail to discover, nor their great regard to the public, omit. 3. The importunity with which he urges a speedy accomplishment of his pretended reformation of the governments, and 4. His consciousness that these schemes would be opposed, although he affects to expect from powerful prejudices only, that opposition, which all Americans say, has been dictated by sound reason, true policy, and eternal justice. The last thing I shall take notice of is, the artful, yet most false and wicked insinuation, that such new regulations were then generally expected. This is so absolutely false, that excepting Bernard himself, and his junto, scarcely any body on this side the water had any suspicion of it,—insomuch that if Bernard had made public, at that time, his preface and principles, as he sent them to the ministry, it is much to be doubted whether he could have lived in this country—certain it is, he would have had no friends in this province out of the junto.

The intention of the junto, was, to procure a revenue to be raised in America by act of parliament. Nothing was further from their designs and wishes, than the drawing or sending this revenue into the exchequer in England to be spent there in discharging the national debt, and lessening the burdens of the poor people there. They were more selfish. They chose to have the fingering of the money themselves. Their design was, that the money should be applied, first in a large salary to the governor. This would gratify Bernard's avarice, and then it would render him and all other governors, not only independent of the people, but still more absolutely a slave to the will of the minister. They intended likewise a salary for the lieutenant governor. This would appease in some degree the gnawings of Hutchinson's avidity, in which he was not a whit behind Bernard himself. In the next place, they intended a salary to the judges of the common law, as well as admiralty. And thus the whole government, executive and judicial, was to be rendered wholly independent of the people, (and their representatives rendered useless, insignificant and even burthensome) and absolutely dependant upon, and under the direction of the will of the minister of State. They intended further to new model the whole continent of North America, make an entire new division of it, into distinct, though more extensive and less numerous Colonies, to sweep away all the charters upon the continent, with the destroying besom of an act of parliament, and reduce all the governments to the plan of the royal governments, with a nobility in each Colony, not hereditary indeed, at first, but for life. They did indeed flatter the ministry and people in England, with distant hopes of a revenue from America, at some future period, to be appropriated to national uses there. But this was not to happen in their minds for some time. The governments must be new modelled, new regulated, reformed first and then the governments here would be able and willing to carry into execution any acts of Parliament or measures of the ministry, for fleecing the people here, to pay debts, or support pensioners, on the American establishment, or bribe electors, or members of parliament, or any other purpose that a virtuous ministry could desire.

But as ill luck would have it, the British financier, was as selfish as themselves, and instead of raising money for them, chose to raise it for himself. He put the cart before the horse. He chose to get the revenue into the exchequer, because he had hungry cormorants enough about him in England whose *coo-*

ings were more troublesome to his ears, than the croaking of the ravens in America. And he thought if America could afford any revenue at all, and he could get it by authority of parliament, he might have it himself, to give to his friends, as well as raise it for the junto here, to spend themselves, or give to theirs. This unfortunate preposterous improvement of Mr. Grenville, upon the plan of the junto, had well nigh ruined the whole.

I will proceed no further without producing my evidence. Indeed to a man who was acquainted with this junto, and had any opportunity to watch their motions, observe their language, and remark their countenances, for these last twelve years, no other evidence is necessary; it was plain to such persons, what this junto was about. But we have evidence enough now under their own hands of the whole of what was said of them by their opposers, through this whole period.

Governor Bernard, in his letter July 11, 1764, says, "that a general reformation of the American governments would become not only a desirable but a necessary measure." What his idea was, of a general reformation of the American governments, is to be learnt from his principles of law and polity, which he sent to the ministry in 1764. I shall select a few of them in his own words; but I wish the whole of them could be printed in the newspapers, that America might know more generally the principles and designs and exertions of our junto.

His 29th proposition is, "The rule that a British subject shall not be bound by laws, or liable to taxes, but what he has consented to, by his representatives, must be confined to the inihabitants of Great Britain only; and is not strictly true even there. 30. The parliament of Great Britain, as well from its rights of sovereignty, as from occasional exigences, has a right to make laws for and impose taxes upon its subjects in its external dominions, although they are not represented in such parliament. But 31. Taxes imposed upon the external dominions, ought to be applied to the use of the people, from whom they are raised. 32. The parliament of Great Britain has a right and duty to take care to provide for the defence of the American Colonies; especially as such Colonies are unable to defend themselves. 33. The parliament of Great Britain has a right and a duty to take care that provision be made for a sufficient support of the American governments. Because 34. The support of the government is one of the principal conditions upon which a Colony is allowed the power of legislation. Also because 35. Some of the American Colonies have shewn themselves deficient in the support of their several governments, both as to sufficiency and independency."

His 75th proposition is, "Every American government is capable of having its constitution altered for the better. 76. The grants of the powers of governments to the American Colonies by charters cannot be understood to be intended for other than their infant or growing States. 77. They cannot be intended for their mature state, that is for perpetuity; because they are in many things unconstitutional and contrary to the very nature of a British government; therefore 78. They must be considered as designed only as temporary means, for settling and bringing forward the peopling the Colonies; which being effected, the cause of the peculiarity of their constitution ceases. 79. If the charters can be pleaded against the authority of Parliament they amount to an alienation of the dominions of Great Britain, and are in effect acts' of dismembering the British empire, and will operate as such, if care is not taken to prevent it. 83. The notion which has heretofore prevailed, that the dividing America into many governments, and different modes of government will be the means to prevent their uniting to revolt, is ill founded; since, if the governments were ever so much consolidated, it will be necessary to have so many distinct States, as to make a union to revolt, impracticable. Whereas 84. The splitting America into many small governments, weakens the governing power, and strengthens that of the people; and thereby makes revolting more probable and more practicable. 85. To prevent revolts in future times (for there is no room to fear them in the present) the most effectual means would be, to make the governments large and respectable, and balance the powers of them. 86. There is no government in America at present, whose powers are properly balanced; there not being in any of them, a real and distinct third legislative power mediating between the king and the people, which is the peculiar excellence of the British constitution. 87. The want of such a third legislative power, adds weight to the popular, and lightens the royal scale; so as to destroy the balance between the royal and popular powers. 88. Although America is not now (and probably will not be for many years to come) ripe enough for an hereditary nobility; yet it is now capable of a nobility for life. 89. A nobility appointed by the king for life, and made independent, would probably give strength and stability to the American governments, as effectually as an hereditary nobility does to that of Great Britain. 90. The reformation of American governments should not be controuled by the present boundaries of the Colonies; as they were mostly settled upon partial, occasional, and accidental considerations, without any regard to a whole. 91. To settle the American governments to the greatest possible advantage, it will be necessary to reduce the number of them; in some places to unite and consolidate, in others to separate and transfer; and in general to divide by natural boundaries, instead of imaginary lines. 92. If there should be but one form of government established for all the North American provinces, it would greatly facilitate the reformation of them; since, if the mode of government was every where the same, people would be more indifferent under what division they were ranged. 93. No objections ought to arise to the alteration of the boundaries of provinces from proprietors, on account of their property only; since there is no occasion that it should in the least affect the boundaries of properties. 94. The present distinction of one government being more free or more popular than another, tends to embarrass and to weaken the whole; and should not be allowed to subsist among people, subject to one king and one law, and all equally fit for one form of government. 95. The American Colonies, in general, are, at this time, arrived at that state, which qualifies them to receive the most perfect form of government, which their situation and relation to Great Britain, make them capable of. 96. The people of North America at this time, expect a revisal and reformation of the American governments, and are better disposed to submit to it, than ever they were, or perhaps ever will be again. 97. This is therefore the proper, and critical time to reform the American governments, upon a general, constitutional, firm, and durable plan; and if it is not done now, it will probably every day grow more difficult, till at last it becomes impracticable."

My friends, these are the words, the plans, principles, and endeavours of governor Bernard in the year 1764. That Hutchinson and Oliver, notwithstanding all their disguises which you well remember, were in unison with him in the whole of his measures, can be doubted by no man. It appeared sufficiently in the part they all along acted, notwithstanding their professions. And it appears incontestibly from their detected letters, of which more hereafter.

Now let me ask you, if the parliament of Great Britain, had all the natural foundations of authority, wisdom, goodness, justice, power, in as great perfection as they ever existed in any body of men since Adam's fall; and if the English nation was the most virtuous, pure and free, that ever was; would not such an unlimited subjection of three millions of people to that parliament, at three thousand miles distance be real slavery? There are but two sorts of men in the world, freemen and slaves. The very definition of a freeman, is one who is bound by no law to which he has not consented. Americans would have no way of giving or withholding their consent to the acts of this parliament, therefore they would not be freemen. But, when luxury, effeminacy and venality are arrived at such a shocking pitch in England, when both electors and elected, are become one mass of corruption, when the nation is oppressed to death with debts and taxes, owing to their own extravagance, and want of wisdom, what would be your condition under such an absolute subjection to parliament? You would not only be slaves. But the most abject sort of slaves to the worst sort of masters! at least this is my opinion. Judge you for yourselves between Massachusettensis and

NOVANGLUS.

NOVANGLUS, February 13, 1775

Massachusettensis, whose pen can wheedle with the tongue of king Richard the third, in his first paper, threatens you with the vengeance of Great Britain, and assures you that if she had no authority over you, yet she would support her claims by her fleets and armies, Canadians and Indians. In his next he alters his tone, and soothes you with the generosity, justice and humanity of the nation.

I shall leave him to show how a nation can claim an authority which they have not by right, and support it by fire and sword, and yet be generous and just. The nation I believe is not vindictive, but the minister has discovered himself to be so, in a degree that would disgrace a warrior of a savage tribe.

The wily Massachusettensis thinks our present calamity is to be attributed to the bad policy of a popular party, whose measures, whatever their intentions were, have been opposite to their profession, the public good. The present calamity seems to be nothing more nor less, than reviving the plans of Mr. Bernard and the junto, and Mr. Grenville and his friends in 1764. Surely this party, are and have been rather unpopular. The popular party did not write Bernard's letters, who so long ago pressed for the demolition of all the charters upon the continent, and a parliamentary taxation to support government, and the administration of justice in America.

The popular party did not write Oliver's letters, who enforces Bernard's plans, nor Hutchinson's, who pleads with all his eloquence and pathos for parliamentary penalties, ministerial vengeance and an abridgement of English liberties.

There is not in human nature a more wonderful phenomenon; nor in the whole theory of it, a more intricate speculation; than the *shiftings, turnings, windings* and *evasions* of a guilty conscience. Such is our unalterable moral constitution, that an internal inclination to do wrong, is criminal; and a wicked thought, stains the mind with guilt, and makes it tingle with pain. Hence it comes to pass that the guilty mind, can never bear to think that its guilt is known to God or man, no, nor to itself.

> ————*Cur tamen hos tu*
> *Evasisse putes, quos diri conscia facti*
> *Mens habet attonitos, et surdo verbere cædit*
> *Occultum quatiente animo tortore flagellum?*
> *Pæna autem vehemens ac multo sævior illis,*
> *Quos et cæditius gravis invenit aut Rhadamanthus,*
> *Nocte dieque suum gestare in pectore testem.*
>
> Juv. Sat. 13. 192.

Massachusettensis and his friends the tories, are startled at the calamities they have brought upon their country, and their conscious guilt, their smarting, wounded mind, will not suffer them to confess, even to themselves, what they have done. Their silly denials of their own share in it before a people, who they know have abundant evidence against them, never fail to remind me of an ancient *fugitive,* whose conscience could not bear the recollection of what he had done. "I know not, am I my brother's keeper?" He replies, with all the apparent simplicity of truth and innocence, to one from whom he was very sensible his guilt could not be hid. The still more absurd and ridiculous attempts of the tories, to throw off the blame of these calamities from themselves to the whigs, remind me of another story, which I have read in the Old Testament. When Joseph's brethren had sold him to the Ishmaelites for twenty pieces of silver, in order to conceal their own avarice, malice and envy, they dip the coat of many colours in the blood of a kid, and say that an evil beast had rent him in pieces and devoured him.

However, what the sons of Israel intended for ruin to Joseph, proved the salvation of the family; and I hope and believe that the whigs, will have the magnanimity, like him, to suppress their resentment, and the felicity of saving their ungrateful brothers.

This writer has a faculty of insinuating errors into the mind, almost imperceptibly, he dresses them so in the guise of truth. He says "that the revenue to the crown, from America amounted to but little more than the charges of collecting it," at the close of the last war. I believe it did not to so much. The truth is, there was never any pretence of raising a revenue in America before that time, and when the claim was first set up, it gave an alarm, like a warlike expedition against us. True it is that some duties had been laid before by parliament, under pretence of regulating our trade, and by a collusion and combination between the West India planters, and the North American governors, some years before, duties had been laid upon molasses, &c. under the same pretence, but in reality merely to advance the value of the estates of the planters in the West India Islands, and to put some plunder, under the name of thirds of seisures into the pockets of the governors. But these duties, though more had been collected in this province, than in any other in proportion, were never regularly collected in any of the Colonies. So that the idea of an American revenue for one purpose or another had never, at this time, been formed in American minds.

Our writer goes on, "She, (Great Britain,) thought it as reasonable that the Colonies should bear a part of the national burdens, as that they should share in the national benefit."

Upon this subject Americans have a great deal to say. The national debt before the last war, was near an hundred millions.

Surely America had no share in running into that debt. What is the reason then that she should pay it? But a small part of the sixty millions spent in the last war, was for her benefit. Did she not bear her full share of the burden of the last war in America? Did not the province pay twelve shillings in the pound in taxes for the support of it; and send a sixth or seventh part of her sons into actual service? And at the conclusion of the war, was she not left half a million sterling in debt? Did not all the rest of New England exert itself in proportion? What is the reason that the Massachusetts has paid its debt, and the British minister in thirteen years of peace has paid none of his? Much of it might have been paid in this time, had not such extravagance and speculation prevailed, as ought to be an eternal warning to America, never to trust such a minister with her money. What is the reason that the great and necessary virtues of simplicity, frugality and economy cannot live in England, Scotland and Ireland, as well as America?

We have much more to say still. Great Britain has confined all our trade to herself. We are willing she should, as far as it can be for the good of the empire. But we say that we ought to be allowed as credit, in the account of public burdens and expenses, so much paid in taxes, as we are obliged to sell our commodities to her cheaper than we could get for them at foreign markets. The difference is really a tax upon us, for the good of the empire. We are obliged to take from Great Britain commodities, that we could purchase cheaper elsewhere. This difference is a tax upon us for the good of the empire. We submit to this cheerfully, but insist that we ought to have credit for it, in the account of the expenses of the empire, because it is really a tax upon us. Another thing. I will venture a bold assertion. Let Massachusettensis, or any other friend of the minister, confute me. The three million Americans, by the tax aforesaid, upon what they are obliged to export to Great Britain only, what they are obliged to import from Great Britain only, and the quantities of British manufactures which in these climates they are obliged to consume, more than the like number of people in any part of the three kingdoms, ultimately pay more of the taxes and duties that are apparently paid in Great Britain, than any three million subjects in the three kingdoms. All this may be computed and reduced to stubborn figures, by the minister, if he pleases. We cannot do it. We have not the accounts, records, &c. Now let this account be fairly stated, and I will engage for America, upon any penalty, that she will pay the overplus, if any, in her own constitutional way, provided it is to be applied for national purposes, as paying off the national debt, maintaining the fleet, &c. not to the support of a standing army in time of peace, placemen, pensioners, &c.

Besides, every farthing of expense which has been incurred on pretence of protecting, defending and securing America, since the last war, has been worse than thrown away; it has been applied to do mischief. Keeping an army in America has been nothing but a public nuisance.

Furthermore, we see that all the public money that is raised here, and have reason to believe all that will or can be raised, will be applied not for public purposes, national or provincial, but merely to corrupt the sons of America, and create a faction to destroy its interest and happiness.

There are scarcely three sentences together, in all the voluminous productions of this plausible writer, which do not convey some error in fact or principle, tinged with a colouring to make it pass for truth. He says, "the idea, that the stamps were a tax, not only exceeding our proportion, but beyond our utmost ability to pay, united the Colonies generally in opposing it." That we thought it beyond our proportion and ability is true, but it was not this thought which united the Colonies in opposing it. When he says that at first, we did not dream of denying the authority of parliament to tax us, much less to legislate for us, he discovers plainly either a total inattention to the sentiments of America at that time, or a disregard of what he affirms.

The truth is, the authority of parliament was never generally acknowledged in America. More than a century since, Massachusetts and Virginia, both protested against even the act of navigation and refused obedience, for this very reason, because they were not represented in parliament and were therefore not bound; and afterwards confirmed it by their own provincial authority. And from that time to this, the general sense of the Colonies has been, that the authority of parliament was confined to the regulation of trade, and did not extend to taxation or internal legislation.

In the year 1764, your house of representatives sent home a petition to the king, against the plan of taxing them. Mr. Hutchinson, Oliver and their relations and connections were then in the legislature, and had great influence there. It was by their influence that the two houses were induced to wave the word rights, and an express denial of the right of parliament to tax us, to the great grief and distress of the friends of liberty in both houses. Mr. Otis and Mr. Thatcher laboured in the committee to obtain an express denial. Mr. Hutchinson expressly said he agreed with them in opinion, that parliament had no right, but thought it ill policy to express this opinion in the petition. In truth, I will be bold to say, there was not any member of either house, who thought that parliament had such a right at that time. The house of representatives, at that time, gave their approbation to Mr. Otis's rights of the Colonies, in which it was shewn to be inconsistent with the right of British subjects to be taxed, but by their own representatives.

In 1765, our house expressly resolved against the right of parliament to tax us. The congress at New York resolved 3. "That it is inseparably essential to the freedom of a people, and the undoubted right of Englishmen, that no tax be imposed on them, but with their own consent given personally, or by their representatives. 4. That the people of the Colonies are not, and from their local circumstances cannot be represented in the house of commons of Great Britain. 5. That the only representatives of the people of the Colonies, are the persons chosen therein by themselves; and that no taxes ever have been or can be constitutionally imposed on them, but by their respective legislatures." Is it not a striking disregard to truth in the artful Massachusettensis to say, that at first we did not dream of denying the right of parliament to tax us? It was the principle that united the Colonies to oppose it, not the quantum of the tax. Did not Dr. Franklin deny the right in 1754, in his remarks upon governor Shirley's scheme, and supposed that all America would deny it? We had considered ourselves as connected with Great Britain, but we never thought parliament the supreme legislature over us. We never generally supposed it to have any authority over us, but from necessity, and that necessity we thought confined to the regulation of trade, and to such matters as concerned all the colonies together. We never allowed them any authority in our internal concerns.

This writer says, acts of parliament for regulating our internal polity were familiar. This I deny. So far otherwise, that the hatter's act was never regarded; the act to destroy the Land Bank Scheme raised a greater ferment in this province, than the stamp-act did, which was appeased only by passing province laws directly in opposition to it. The act against slitting mills, and tilt hammers, never was executed here. As to the postage, it was so useful a regulation, so few persons paid it, and they found such a benefit by it, that little opposition was made to it. Yet every man who thought about it called it an usurpation. Duties for regulating trade we paid, because we thought it just and necessary that they should regulate the trade which their power protected. As for duties for a revenue, none were ever laid by parliament for that purpose until 1764, when, and ever since, its authority to do it has been constantly denied. Nor is this complaisant writer near the truth, when he says, "We know that in all those acts of government, the good of the whole had been consulted." On the contrary, we know that the private interest of provincial governors and West India planters, had been consulted in the duties on foreign molasses,

&c. and the private interest of a few Portugal merchants, in obliging us to touch at Falmouth with fruit, &c. in opposition to the good of the whole, and in many other instances.

The resolves of the house of Burgesses of Virginia, upon the stamp act, did great honor to that province, and to the eminent patriot Patrick Henry, Esq. who composed them. But these resolves made no alteration in the opinion of the Colonies, concerning the right of parliament to make that act. They expressed the universal opinion of the continent at that time, and the alacrity with which every other Colony, and the congress at New York, adopted the same sentiment in similar resolves, proves the entire union of the Colonies in it, and their universal determination to avow and support it.

What follows here, that it became so popular that his life was in danger, who suggested the contrary, and that the press was open to one side only, are direct misrepresentations and wicked calumnies.

Then we are told, by this sincere writer, that when we obtained a partial repeal of the statute imposing duties on glass, paper, and teas, this was the lucky moment, when to have closed the dispute. What? With a Board of commissioners remaining the sole end of whose creation was to form and conduct a revenue—with an act of parliament remaining, the professed design of which expressed in the preamble, was to raise a revenue, and appropriate it to the payment of governors' and judges' salaries, the duty remaining too upon an article, which must raise a large sum, the consumption of which would constantly increase? Was this a time to retreat? Let me ask this sincere writer a simple question. Does he seriously believe that the designs of imposing other taxes, and of new modelling our governments, would have been laid aside, by the ministry or by the servants of the crown here? Does he think that Mr. Bernard, Mr. Hutchinson, the commissioners and others, would have been content then to have desisted? If he really thinks so, he knows little of the human heart, and still less of those gentlemen's hearts. It was at this very time that the salary was given to the governor, and an order soliciting for that to the judges.

Then we are entertained with a great deal of ingenious talk about whigs and tories, and at last are told that some of the whigs owed all their importance to popularity. And what then? Did not as many of the tories owe their importance to popularity?—And did not many more owe all their importance to unpopularity? If it had not been for their taking an active part on the side of the ministry, would not some of the most conspicuous and eminent of them have been unimportant enough? Indeed, through the two last administrations to despise and hate the people, and to be despised and hated by them were the principal recommendations to the favours of government, and all the qualification that was required.

The tories, says he, were for closing the controversy. That is, they were for contending no more, and it was equally true that they never were for contending at all, but lying at mercy. It was the very end they had aimed at from the beginning. They had now got the governor's salary out of the revenue—a number of pensions and places, and they knew they could at any time get the judges' salaries from the same fountain, and they wanted to get the people reconciled and familiarised to this, before they went upon any new projects.

The whigs were averse to restoring government, they even refused to revive a temporary riot act, which expired about this time. Government had as much vigour then as ever, excepting only in those cases which affected this dispute. The riot act expired in 1770, immediately after the massacre in King Street. It was not revived and never will be in this Colony, nor will any one ever be made in any other, while a standing army is illegally posted here, to butcher the people, whenever a governor, or a magistrate, who may be a tool, shall order it. "Perhaps the whigs thought that mobs were a necessary ingredient in their system of opposition." Whether they did or no, it is certain that mobs have been thought a necessary ingredient by the tories in their system of administration, mobs of the worst sort with red coats, fuzees and bayonets, and the lives and limbs of the whigs have been in greater danger from these, than ever the tories were from others.

"The scheme of the whigs flattered the people with the idea of independence; the tories' plan supposed a degree of subordination." This is artful enough, as usual, not to say jesuitical. The word independence is one of those, which this writer uses, as he does treason and rebellion, to impose upon the undistinguishing on both sides of the Atlantic. But let us take him to pieces. What does he mean by independence? Does he mean independent of the crown of Great Britain, and an independent republic in America, or a confederation of independent republics? No doubt he intended the undistinguishing should understand him so. If he did; nothing can be more wicked, or a greater slander on the whigs; because he knows there is not a man in the province, among the whigs, nor ever was, who harbours a wish of that sort. Does he mean that the people were flattered with the idea of total independence on parliament? If he does, this is equally malicious and injurious; because he knows that the equity and necessity of parliament's regulating trade has always been acknowledged, our determination to consent and submit to such regulations constantly expressed, and all the acts of trade in fact, to this very day, much more submitted to and strictly executed in this province, than any other in America.

There is equal ambiguity in the words "degree of subordination." The whigs acknowledge a subordination to the king, in as strict and strong a sense as the tories. The whigs acknowledge a voluntary subordination to parliament, as far as the regulation of trade. What degree of subordination then do the tories acknowledge? An absolute dependance upon parliament as their supreme legislative, in all cases whatever, in their internal polity as well as taxation? This would be too gross and would lose him all his readers; for there is nobody here who will expose his understanding so much, as explicitly to adopt such a sentiment. Yet it is such an absolute dependance and submission, that these writers would persuade us to, or else there is no need of changing our sentiments and conduct. Why will not these gentlemen speak out, shew us plainly their opinion that the new government, they have fabricated for this province, is better than the old, and that all the other measures, we complain of, are for our and the public good, and exhort us directly to submit to them? The reason is, because they know they should lose their readers.

"The whigs were sensible that there was no oppression that could be seen or felt." The tories have so often said and wrote this to one another, that I sometimes suspect they believe it to be true. But it is quite otherwise. The castle of the province was taken out of their hand and garrisoned by regular soldiers: this they could see, and they thought it indicated an hostile intention and disposition towards them. They continually paid their money to collectors of duties: this they could both see and feel. An host of placemen, whose whole business it was to collect a revenue, were continually rolling before them in their chariots. These they saw. Their governor was no longer paid by themselves, according to their charter, but out of the new revenue, in order to render their assemblies useless and indeed contemptible. The judges' salaries were threatened every day to be paid in the same unconstitutional manner. The dullest eye-sight could not but see to what all this tended, viz.; to prepare the way for greater innovations and oppressions. They knew a minister would never spend his money in this way, if he had not some end to answer by it. Another thing they both saw and felt. Every man, of every character, who by voting, writing, speaking, or otherwise, had favoured the stamp act, the tea act, and every other measure of a minister or governor, who they knew was aiming at the destruction of their form of government, and introducing parliamentary taxation, was uniformly, in some department or other, promoted to some place of honour or profit for ten years together: and, on the other hand, every man who favoured the people in their opposition to those innovations, was depressed, degraded and persecuted, as far as it was in the power of the government to do it.

This they considered as a systematical means of encouraging every man of abilities to espouse the cause of parliamentary taxation, and the plan of destroying their charter privilege, and to discourage all from exerting themselves, in opposition to them. This they thought a plan to enslave them, for they uniformly think that the destruction of their charter, making the council and judges wholly dependant on the crown, and the people subject to the unlimited power of parliament, as their supreme legislative, is slavery. They were certainly rightly told, then, that the ministry and their governors together had formed a design to enslave them; and that when once this was done, they had the highest reason to expect window taxes, hearth taxes, land taxes and all others: and that these were only paving the way for reducing the country to lordships. Were the people mistaken in these suspicions? Is it not now certain that governor Bernard in 1764, had formed a design of this sort? Read his principles of polity—And that lieutenant governor Oliver as late as 1768 or 9, inforced the same plan? Read his letters.

Now if Massachusettensis will be ingenuous, avow this design, shew the people its utility, and that it ought to be done by parliament, he will act the part of an honest man. But to insinuate that there was no such plan, when he knows there was, is acting the part of one of the junto.

It is true that the people of this country in general, and of this province in special, have an hereditary apprehension of and aversion to lordships, temporal and spiritual. Their ancestors fled to this wilderness to avoid them—they suffered sufficiently under them in England. And there are few of the present generation, who have not been warned of the danger of them by their fathers or grandfathers, and injoined to oppose them. And neither Bernard nor Oliver ever dared to avow, before them, the designs which they had certainly formed to introduce them. Nor does Massachusettensis dare to avow his opinion in their favour. I do not mean that such avowal would expose their persons to danger, but their characters and writings to universal contempt.

When you were told that the people of England were depraved, the parliament venal, and the ministry corrupt, were you not told most melancholy truths? Will Massachusettensis deny any of them? Does not every man, who comes from England, whig or tory, tell you the same thing? Do they make any secret of it, or use any delicacy about it? Do they not most of them avow that corruption is so established there, as to be incurable, and a necessary instrument of government? Is not the British constitution arrived nearly to that point, where the Roman republic was, when Jugurtha left it, and pronounced it a venal city ripe for destruction, if it can only find a purchaser? If Massachusettensis can prove that it is not, he will remove from my mind, one of the heaviest loads which lies upon it.

Who has censured the tories for remissness, I know not. Whoever it was, he did them great injustice. Every one that I know of that character has been through the whole tempestuous period, as indefatigable as human nature will admit, going about seeking whom he might devour, making use of art, flattery, terror, temptation and allurements in every shape, in which human wit could dress it up, in public and private. But all to no purpose. The people have grown more and more weary of them every day, until now the land mourns under them.

Massachusettensis is then seized with a violent fit of anger at the clergy. It is curious to observe the conduct of the tories towards this sacred body. If a clergyman preaches against the principles of the revolution, and tells the people that upon pain of damnation, they must submit to an established government, of whatever character the tories cry him up, as an excellent man, and a wonderful preacher, invite him to their tables, procure him missions from the society, and chaplainships to the navy, and flatter him with the hopes of lawn sleeves. But if a clergyman preaches christianity, and tells the magistrates that they were not distinguished from their brethren, for their private emolument, but for the good of the people; that the people are bound in conscience to obey a good government, but are not bound to submit to one, that aims at destroying all the ends of government—Oh Sedition! Treason!

The clergy in all ages and countries, and in this in particular, are disposed enough to be on the side of government, as long as it is tolerable. If they have not been generally, in the late administrations, on that side, it is a demonstration that the late administration has been universally odious.

The clergy of this province are a virtuous, sensible and learned set of men; and they do not take their sermons from newspapers, but the bible; unless it be a few, who preach passive obedience. These are not generally curious enough to read Hobbs.

It is the duty of the clergy to accommodate their discourses to the times, to preach against such sins, as are most prevalent, and recommend such virtues, as are most wanted. For example; if exorbitant ambition, and venality are predominant, ought they not to warn their hearers against their vices? If public spirit is much wanted, should they not inculcate this great virtue? If the rights and duties of christian magistrates and subjects are disputed, should they not explain them, shew their nature, ends, limitations and restrictions, how much soever it may move the gall of Massachusettensis?

Let me put a supposition:—Justice is a great christian, as well as moral duty and virtue, which the clergy ought to inculcate and explain. Suppose a great man of a parish should for seven years together receive 600 sterling a year, for discharging the duties of an important office; but during the whole time, should never do one act or take one step about it. Would not this be great injustice to the public? And ought not the parson of that parish to cry aloud and spare not, and shew such a bold transgressor his sin? shew that justice was due to the public as well as to an individual? and that cheating the public of four thousand two hundred pounds sterling, is at least as great a sin, as taking a chicken from a private hen roost, or perhaps a watch from a fob?

Then we are told that newspapers and preachers have excited outrages disgraceful to humanity. Upon this subject I will venture to say, that there have been outrages in this province, which I neither justify, excuse or extenuate; but these were not excited, that I know of, by newspapers or sermons: that however, if we run through the last ten years, and consider all the tumults and outrages that have happened, and at the same time recollect the insults, provocations and oppressions which this people have endured; we shall find the two characteristics of this people, religion and humanity, strongly marked on all their proceedings. Not a life, nor, that I have ever heard, a single limb has been lost through the whole. I will take upon me to say, there is not another province on this continent, nor in his majesty's dominions, where the people, under the same indignities, would not have gone greater lengths. Consider the tumults in the three kingdoms, consider the tumults in ancient Rome, in the most virtuous of her periods, and compare them with ours. It is a saying of Machiavel, which no wise man ever contradicted, which has been literally verified in this province; that "while the mass of the people is not corrupted, tumults do no hurt." By which he means, that they leave no lasting ill effects behind.

But let us consider the outrages committed by the tories. Half a dozen men shot dead in an instant, in King Street, frequent resistance and affronts to civil officers and magistrates, officers, watchmen, citizens, cut and mangle in a most inhuman manner. Not to mention the shootings for desertion, and the frequent cruel whippings for other faults, cutting and mangling men's bodies before the eyes of citizens; spectacles which ought never to be introduced into populous places. The worst sort of tumults and outrages, ever committed in this province, were excited by the tories. But more of this hereafter.

We are then told that the whigs erected a provincial democracy, or republic, in the province. I wish Massachusettensis knew what a democracy, or republic is. But this subject must be considered another time.

NOVANGLUS.

Messieurs Printers. Instead of *Cawings* of Cormorants, in a former paper, you have printed *Cooings,* too dove-like a word for the birds intended.

NOVANGLUS, February 20, 1775

· · · · · · · · ·

From the date of our charter, to the time of the stamp act, and indeed since that time (notwithstanding the misrepresentations of our charter constitution, as too popular and republican) the council of this province have been generally on the side of the governor and the prerogative. For the truth of this, I appeal to our whole history and experience. The art and power of governors, and especially the negative, have been a stronger motive on the one hand, than the annual election of the two houses on the other. In disputes between the governor and the house, the council have generally adhered to the former, and in many cases have complied with his humour, when scarcely any council by mandamus, upon this continent, would have done it.

But in the time of the stamp act, it was found productive of many mischiefs and dangers, to have officers of the crown, who were dependant on the ministry, and judges of the superior court, whose offices were thought incompatible with a voice in the legislature, members of council.

In May 1765, Lt. Gov. Hutchinson, Sec. Oliver, and Mr.

Belcher were officers of the crown, the judges of the superior court, and some other gentlemen, who held commissions under the governor, were members of council. Mr. Hutchinson was chief justice and a judge of probate for the first county, as well as lieutenant governor, and a counsellor; too many offices for the greatest and best man in the world to hold, too much business for any man to do; besides, that these offices were frequently clashing and interfering with each other. Two other justices of the superior court were counsellors, and nearly and closely connected with him by family alliances. One other justice was judge of admiralty during pleasure. Such a jumble of offices never got together before in any English government. It was found in short, that the famous triumvirate, Bernard, Hutchinson and Oliver, the ever memorable, secret, confidential letter writers, whom I call the junto, had by degrees, and before the people were aware of it, erected a tyranny in the province. Bernard had all the executive, and a negative on the legislative; Hutchinson and Oliver, by their popular arts and secret intrigues, had elevated to the board, such a collection of crown officers, and their own relations, as to have too much influence there; and they had three of a family on the superior bench, which is the supreme tribunal in all causes civil and criminal, vested with all the powers of the king's bench, common pleas and exchequer, which gave them power over every act of this court. This junto therefore had the legislative and executive in their controul, and more natural influence over the judicial, than is ever to be trusted to any set of men in the world. The public accordingly found all these springs and wheels in the constitution set in motion to promote submission to the stamp act, and to discountenance resistance to it; and they thought they had a violent presumption, that they would forever be employed to encourage a compliance with all ministerial measures and parliamentary claims, of whatever character they might be.

The designs of the junto, however, were concealed as carefully as possible. Most persons were jealous; few were certain. When the assembly met in May, 1766, after the stamp act was repealed, the whigs flattered themselves with hopes of peace and liberty for the future. Mr. Otis, whose abilities and integrity, whose great exertions, and most exemplary sacrifices of his private interest to the public service, had entitled him to all the promotion, which the people could bestow, was chosen speaker of the house. Bernard negatived the choice. It can scarcely be conceived by a stranger, what an alarm this manœuvre gave to the public. It was thought equivalent to a declaration, that although the people had been so successful as to obtain a repeal of the stamp act, yet they must not hope to be quiet long, for parliament, by the declaratory act, had asserted its supreme authority, and new taxations and regulations should be made, if the junto could obtain them: and every man who should dare to oppose such projects, let his powers, or virtues, his family or fortune be what they would, should be surely cut off from all hopes of advancement. The electors thought it high time to be upon their guard. All the foregoing reasons and motives prevailed with the electors; and the crown officers and justices of the supreme court, were left out of council in the new choice. Those who were elected in their places were all negatived by Bernard, which was considered as a fresh proof, that the junto still persevered in their designs of obtaining a revenue, to divide among themselves.

The gentlemen elected anew, were of equal fortune and integrity, at least, and not much inferior in abilities to those left out, and indeed, in point of fortune, family, note or abilities, the councils which have been chosen from that time to this, taken on an average, have been very little inferior, if any, to those chosen before. Let Massachusettensis descend if he will, to every particular gentleman by name through the whole period, and I will make out my assertion.

Every impartial person will not only think these reasons a full vindication of the conduct of the two houses, but that it was their indispensable duty to their country, to act the part they did; and the course of time, which has developed the dark intrigues of the junto, before and since, has confirmed the rectitude and necessity of the measure. Had Bernard's principles of polity been published and known at that time, no member of the house, who should have voted for any of the persons then left out, if it was known to his constituents, would ever have obtained another election.

By the next step we rise to the chair. "With the board, the chair fell likewise," he says. But what a slander is this? Neither fell; both remained in as much vigour as ever. The junto it is true, and some other gentlemen who were not in their secret, but however had been misled to concur in their measures, were left out of council. But the board had as much authority as ever. The board of 1766 could not have influenced the people to acknowledge the supreme uncontroulable authority of parliament, nor could that of 1765, have done it. So that by the chair, and the board's falling, he means no more, if his meaning has any truth in it, than that the junto fell; the designs of taxing the Colonies fell, and the schemes for destroying all the charters on the continent and for erecting lordships fell. These, it must be acknowledged, fell very low indeed, in the esteem of the people, and the two houses.

"The governor," says our wily writer, "could do little or nothing without the council, by the charter." "If he called upon a military officer to raise the militia, he was answered they were there already," &c. The council, by the charter, had nothing to do with the militia. The governor alone had all authority over them. The council therefore are not to blame for their conduct. If the militia refused obedience to the captain general, or his subordinate officer, when commanded to assist in carrying into execution the stamp act, or in dispersing those who were opposing it, does not this prove the universal sense and resolution of the people not to submit to it? Did not a regular army do more to James the second? If those, over whom the governor had the most absolute authority and decisive influence, refused obedience, does not this show how deeply rooted in all men's minds was the abhorrence of that unconstitutional power which was usurping over them? "If he called upon the council for their assistance, they must first inquire into the cause." An unpardonable crime, no doubt! But is it the duty of a middle branch of legislature, to do as the first shall command them, implicitly, or to judge for themselves? Is it the duty of a privy council, to understand the subject before they give advice, or only to lend their names to any edict, in order to make it less unpopular? It would be a shame to answer such observations as these, if it was not for their wickedness. Our council, all along however did as much as any council could have done. Was the mandamus council at New York able to do more, to influence the people to a submission to the stamp act? Was the chair, the board, the septennial house, with the assistance of general Gage and his troops, able to do more, in that city, than our branches did in this province? Not one iota. Nor could Bernard, his council, and house, if they had been unanimous, have induced submission. The people would have spurned them all, for they are not to be wheedled out of their liberties by their own representatives, any more than by strangers. "If he wrote to government at home to strengthen his hands, some officious person procured and sent back his letters." At last it seems to be acknowledged, that the governor did write for a military force, to strengthen government. For what? to enable it to enforce stamp acts, tea acts, and other internal regulations, the authority of which the people were determined never to acknowledge.

But what a pity it was, that these worthy gentlemen could not be allowed, from the dearest affection to their native country, to which they had every possible attachment, to go on in profound confidential secrecy, procuring troops to cut our throats, acts of parliament to drain our purses, destroy our charters and assemblies, getting estates and dignities for themselves and their own families, and all the while most devoutly professing to be friends to our charter, enemies to parliamentary taxation, and to all pensions, without being detected? How happy! if they could have annihilated all our charters, and yet have been beloved, nay deified by the people, as friends and advocates for their charters? What masterly politicians! to have made themselves nobles for life, and yet have been thought very sorry, that the two houses were denied the privilege of choosing the council? How sagacious, to get large pensions for themselves, and yet be thought to mourn, that pensions and venality were introduced into the country? How sweet and pleasant! to have been the most popular men in the community, for being staunch and zealous dissenters, true blue Calvinists, and able advocates for public virtue and popular government, after they had introduced an American Episcopate, universal corruption among the leading men, and deprived the people of all share in their supreme legislative council? I mention an Episcopate, for although I do not know that governors Hutchinson and Oliver ever directly solicited for bishops, yet they must have seen, that these would have been one effect, very soon, of establishing the unlimited authority of parliament!

I agree with this writer, that it was not the persons of Bernard, Hutchinson or Oliver, that made them obnoxious; but their principles and practices. And I will agree, that if Chatham, Campden and St. Asaph, (I beg pardon for introducing these reverend names into such company, and for making a supposition which is absurd) had been here, and prosecuted such schemes, they would have met with contempt and execration from this people. But when he says, "that had the intimations in those letters been attended to, we had now been as happy a people as good government could make us," it is too gross to make us angry. We can do nothing but smile. Have not these intimations been attended to? Have not fleets and armies been sent here, whenever they requested? Have not governors', lieutenant governors', secretaries', judges', attorney generals', and solicitor generals' salaries been paid out of the revenue as they solicited? Have not taxes been laid, and continued? Have not English liberties been abridged as Hutchinson desired? Have not "penalties of another kind" been inflicted, as he desired? Has not our charter been destroyed, and the council put into the king's hands, as Bernard requested? In short, almost all the wild mock pranks of this desperate triumvirate have been attended to and adopted, and we are now as miserable as tyranny can well make us. That Bernard came here with the affections of New Jersey, I never heard nor read, but in this writer. His abilities were considerable, or he could not have done such extensive mischief. His true British honesty and punctuality will be acknowledged by none, but such as owe all their importance to flattering him.

That Hutchinson was amiable and exemplary, in some respects, and very unamiable and unexemplary, in others, is a certain truth; otherwise he never would have retained so much popularity on one hand, nor made so pernicious a use of it on the other. His behavior, in several important departments, was with ability and integrity, in cases which did not effect his political system, but he bent all his offices to that. Had he continued stedfast to those principles in religion and government, which in his former life he professed, and which alone had procured him the confidence of the people and all his importance, he would have lived and died, respected and beloved, and have done honor to his native country. But by renouncing these principles and that conduct, which had made him and all his ancestors respectable, his character is now considered by all America, and the best part of the three kingdoms, notwithstanding the countenance he receives from the ministry, as a reproach to the province that gave him birth, as a man who by all his actions aimed at making himself great, at the expense of the liberties of his native country. This gentleman was open to flattery, in so remarkable a degree, that any man who would flatter him was sure of his friendship, and every one who would not, was sure of his enmity. He was credulous, in a rediculous degree, of every thing that favoured his own plans, and equally incredulous of every thing which made against them. His natural abilities which have been greatly exaggerated by persons whom he had advanced to power, were far from being of the first rate. His industry was prodigious. His knowledge lay chiefly in the laws of politics and history of this province, in which he had a long experience. Yet with all his advantages, he never was master of the true character of his native country, not even of New England and the Massachusetts Bay. Through the whole troublesome period since the last war, he manifestly mistook the temper, principles, and opinions of this people. He had resolved upon a system, and never could or would see the impracticability of it.

It is very true that all his abilities, virtues, interests and connections, were insufficient; but for what? To prevail on the people to acquiesce in the mighty claim of parliamentary authority. The constitution was not gone. The suggestion, that it was, is a vile slander. It had as much vigour as ever, and even the governor had as much power as ever, excepting in cases which affected that claim. "The spirit" says this writer "was truly republican." It was not so in any one case whatever; any further than the spirit of the British constitution is republican. Even in the grand fundamental dispute, the people arranged themselves under their house of representatives and council, with as much order as ever, and conducted their opposition as much by the constitution as ever. It is true their constitution was employed against the measures of the junto, which created their enmity to it. However I have not such an horror of republican spirit, which is a spirit of true virtue, and honest independence; I do not mean on the king, but on men in power. This spirit is so far from being incompatible with the British constitution, that it is the greatest glory of it, and the nation has always been most prosperous, when it has most prevailed and been most encouraged by the crown. I wish it increased in every part of the world, especially in America; and I think the measures, the tories are now pursuing, will increase it to a degree that will ensure us, in the end, redress of grievances and an happy reconciliation with Great Britain.

"Governor Hutchinson strove to convince us, by the principles of government, our charters and acknowledgments, that our claims were inconsistent with the subordination due to Great Britain," &c. says this writer.

Suffer me to introduce here, a little history. In 1764, when the system of taxing and new modelling the Colonies was first apprehended, lieutenant governor Hutchinson's friends struggled in several successive sessions of the general court, to get him chosen agent for the province at the court of Great Britain. At this time he declared freely, *that he was of the same sentiment with the people, that parliament had no right to tax them; but differed from the country party, only in his opinion of the policy of denying that right, in their petitions,* &c. I would not injure him; I was told this by three gentlemen who were of the committee of both houses, to prepare that petition, that he made this declaration explicitly before that committee. I have been told by other gentlemen that he made the same declaration to them. It is possible that he might make use of expressions studied for the purpose, which would not strictly bear this construction. But it is certain that they understood him so, and that this was the general opinion of his sentiments until he came to the chair.

The country party saw, that this aspiring genius aimed at keeping fair with the ministry, by supporting their measures, and with the people, by pretending to be of our principles, and between both to trim himself up to the chair. The only reason why he did not obtain an election at one time, and was excused from the service at another, after he had been chosen by a small majority, was because the members knew he would not openly deny the right, and assure his majesty, the parliament, and ministry, that the people never would submit to it. For the same reason he was left out of council. But he continued to cultivate his popularity, and to maintain a general opinion among the people, that he denied the right in his private judgment, and this idea preserved most of those who continued their esteem for him.

But upon Bernard's removal, and his taking the chair as lieutenant governor, he had no farther expectations from the people nor complaisance for their opinions. In one of his first speeches he took care to advance the supreme authority of parliament. This astonished many of his friends. They were heard to say, we have been deceived. We thought he had been abused, but we now find what has been said of him is true. He is determined to join in the designs against this country. After his promotion to the government, finding that the people had little confidence in him, and shewing that he had no interest at home to support him, but what he had acquired by joining with Bernard in kicking up a dust, he determined to strike a bold stroke, and in a formal speech to both houses, became a champion for the unbounded authority of parliament, over the Colonies. This he thought would lay the ministry under obligation to support him in the government, or else to provide for him out of it, not considering that starting that question before that assembly, and calling upon them, as he did, to dispute with him upon it, was scattering firebrands, arrows and death in sport. The arguments he then advanced were inconclusive indeed; but they shall be considered, when I come to the feeble attempt of Massachusettensis to give a colour to the same position.

The house, thus called upon, either to acknowledge the unlimited authority of parliament, or confute his arguments, were bound by their duty to God, their country and posterity, to give him a full and explicit answer. They proved incontestibly, that he was out in his facts, inconsistent with himself, and in every principle of his law, he had committed a blunder. Thus the fowler was caught in his own snare; and although this country has suffered severe temporary calamities, in consequence of this speech, yet I hope they will not be durable; but his ruin was certainly in part owing to it. Nothing ever opened the eyes of the people so much, as his designs, excepting his letters. Thus it is the fate of Massachusettensis to praise this gentleman, for these things which the wise part of mankind condemn in him, as the most insidious and mischievous of actions. If it was out of his power to do us any more injuries, I should wish to forget the past; but as there is reason to fear he is still to continue his malevolent labours against this country, although he is out of our sight, he ought not to be out of our minds. This country has every thing to fear, in the present state of the British court, while the lords Bute, Mansfield and North have the principal conduct of affairs, from the deep intrigues of that artful man.

. . . .

NOVANGLUS

MASSACHUSETTENSIS, March 13, 1775

Novanglus, and all others, have an indisputable right to publish their sentiments and opinions to the world, provided they conform to truth, decency, and the municipal laws, of the society of which they are members. He has wrote with a professed design of exposing the errors and sophistry which he supposes are frequent in my publications. His design is so far laudable, and I intend to correct them wherever he convinces me there is an instance of either. I have no objection to the minutest disquisition; contradiction and disputation, like the collision of flint and steel, often strike out new light; the bare opinions of either of us, unaccompanied by the grounds and reasons upon which they were formed, must be considered only as propositions made to the reader, for him to adopt, or reject as his own reason may judge, or feelings dictate. A large proportion of the labours of Novanglus consists in denials of my allegations in matters of such public notoriety, as that no reply is necessary. He has alleged many things destitute of foundation; those that affect the main object of our pursuit, but remotely, if at all, I shall pass by without particular remark; others, of a more interesting nature, I shall review minutely. After some general observations upon Massachusettensis, he slides into a most virulent attack upon particular persons, by names, with such incomparable ease, that shews him to be a great proficient in the modern art of detraction and calumny. He accuses the late governor Shirley, governor Hutchinson, the late lieutenant governor Oliver, the late judge Russell, Mr. Paxton, and brigadier Ruggles, of a conspiracy to enslave their country. The charge is high coloured; if it be just, they merit the epithets dealt about so indiscriminately, of enemies to their country. If it be groundless, Novanglus has acted the part of an assassin, in thus attempting to destroy the reputation of the living; and of something worse than an assassin, in entering those hallowed mansions, where the wicked commonly cease from troubling, and the weary are at rest, to disturb the repose of the dead. That the charge is groundless respecting governor Bernard, governor Hutchinson, and the late lieutenant governor, I dare assert, because they have been acquitted of it in such a manner, as every good citizen must acquiesce in. Our house of representatives, acting as the grand inquest of the province, presented them before the king in council, and after a full hearing, they were acquitted with honour, and the several impeachments dismissed, as groundless, vexatious, and scandalous. The accusation of the house was similar to this of Novanglus; the court they chose to institute their suit in, was of competent and high jurisdiction, and its decision final. This is a sufficient answer to the state charges made by this writer, so far as they respect the governors Bernard, Hutchinson and Oliver, whom he accuses as principals; and it is a general rule, that if the principal be innocent, the accessary cannot be guilty. A determination of a constitutional arbiter ought to seal up the lips of even prejudice itself, in silence; otherwise litigation must be endless. This calumniator, nevertheless, has the effrontery to renew the charge in a public news paper, although thereby he arraigns our most gracious Sovereign, and the lords of the privy council, as well as the gentlemen he has named. Not content with wounding the honour of judges, counsellors and governors, with missile weapons, darted from an obscure corner, he now aims a blow at majesty itself. Any one may accuse; but accusation, unsupported by proof, recoils upon the head of the accuser. It is entertaining enough to consider the crimes and misdemeanors alleged, and then examine the evidence he adduces, stript of the false glare he has thrown upon it.

The crimes are these; the persons named by him conspired together to *enslave* their country, in consequence of a plan, the outlines of which have been drawn by sir Edmund Andross and others, and handed down by tradition to the present times. He tells us that governor Shirley, in 1754, communicated the profound secret, the great design of taxing the colonies by act of parliament, to the sagacious gentleman, eminent philosopher, and distinguished patriot, Dr. Franklin. The profound secret is this; after the commencement of hostilities between the English and French colonies in the last war, a convention of committees from several provinces were called by the king, to agree upon some general plan of defence. The principal difficulty they met with was in devising means whereby each colony might be obliged to contribute its proportionable part. General Shirley proposed *that application should be made to parliament to impower the committees of the several colonies to tax the whole according to their several proportions.* This plan was adopted by the convention, and approved of by the assembly in New York, who passed a resolve in these words: "That the scheme proposed by governor Shirley for the defence of the British colonies in North America, is well concerted, and that this colony joins therein." This however did not succeed, and he proposed another, viz. for the parliament to assess each one's proportion, and in case of failure to raise it on their part, that it should be done by parliament. This is the profound secret. His assiduity in endeavouring to have some effectual plan of general defence established, is, by the false colouring of this writer, represented as an attempt to aggrandise himself, family and friends; and that gentleman, under whose administration the several parties in the province were as much united, and the whole province rendered as happy as it ever was, for so long a time together, is called a "crafty, busy, ambitious, intriguing, enterprizing man." This attempt of Governor Shirley for a parliamentary taxation, is however a circumstance strongly militating with this writer's hypothesis, for the approbation shewn to the Governor's proposal by the convention, which consisted of persons from the several colonies, not inferior in point of discernment, integrity, knowledge or patriotism to the members of our late *grand congress,* and the vote of the New York assembly furnishes pretty strong evidence that the authority of parliament, even in point of taxation, was not doubted in that day. Even Dr. Franklin, in the letter alluded to, does not deny the right. His objections go to the inexpediency of the measure. He supposes it would create uneasiness in the minds of the colonists should they be thus taxed, unless they were previously allowed to send representatives to parliament. If Dr. Franklin really supposes that the parliament has no constitutional right to raise a revenue in America, I must confess myself at a loss to reconcile his conduct in accepting the office of post-master, and his assiduity in increasing the revenue in that department, to the patriotism predicated of him by Novanglus, especially as this unfortunately happens to be an internal tax. This writer then tells us, that the plan was interrupted by the war, and afterwards by Governor Pownal's administration. That Messieurs Hutchinson and Oliver, stung with envy at Governor Pownal's favourites, propagated slanders respecting him to render him uneasy in his seat. My answer is this, that he that publishes such falsehoods as these in a public newspaper, with an air of seriousness, insults the understanding of the public, more than he injures the individuals he defames. In the next place we are told, that Governor Bernard was the proper man for this purpose, and he was employed by the junto to suggest to the ministry the project of taxing the colonies by act of parliament. Sometimes Governor Bernard is the arch enemy of America, the source of all our troubles, now only a tool in the hands of others. I wish Novanglus's memory had served him better, his tale might have been consistent with itself, however variant from truth. After making these assertions with equal gravity and assurance, he tells us, he does not advance this without evidence. I had been looking out for evidence a long time, and was all attention when it was promised, but my disappointment was equal to the expectation he had raised, when I found the evidence amounted to nothing more than Governor Bernard's letters and principles of law and polity, wherein he asserts the supremacy of parliament over the colonies both as to legislation and taxation. Where this writer got his logic, I do not know. Reduced to a syllogism, his argument stands thus; Governor Bernard, in 1764, wrote and transmitted to England certain letters and principles of law and polity, wherein he asserts the right of parliament to tax the colonies; Messieurs Hutchinson and Oliver were in unison with him in all his measures; therefore Messieurs Hutchinson and Oliver employed Governor Bernard to suggest to the ministry the project of taxing the colonies by act of parliament. The letters and principles are the whole of the evidence, and this is all the appearance of argument contained in his publication. Let us examine the premises. That Governor Bernard asserted the right of parliament to tax the colonies in 1764, is true. So did Mr. Otis, in a pamphlet he published the self-same year,[2] from which I have already taken an extract. In a pamphlet published in 1765,

---

[2] Pamphlet 2. [—ED.]

Mr. Otis tells us, "it is certain that the parliament of Great Britain hath a just, clear, equitable and constitutional right, power and authority to bind the colonies by all acts wherein they are named. Every lawyer, nay every Tyro, knows this; no less certain is it that the parliament of Great Britain has a just and *equitable* right, power and authority to impose taxes on the colonies *internal and external, on lands as well as on trade.*" But does it follow from Governor Bernard's transmitting his principles of polity to four persons in England, or from Mr. Otis's publishing to the whole world similar principles, that either the one or the other suggested to the ministry the project of taxing the colonies by act of parliament? Hardly, supposing the transmission and publication had been prior to the resolution of parliament to that purpose; but very unfortunately for our reasoner, they were both subsequent to it, and were the effect and not the cause.

The history of the stamp act is this. At the close of the last war, which was a native of America, and increased the national debt upwards of sixty millions, it was thought by parliament to be but equitable, that an additional revenue should be raised in America, towards defraying the necessary charges of keeping it in a state of defence. A resolve of this nature was passed, and the colonies made acquainted with it through their agents, in 1764, that their assemblies might make the necessary provision if they would. The assemblies neglected doing any thing, and the parliament passed the stamp act. There is not so much as a colourable pretence that any American had a hand in the matter. Had governor Bernard, governor Hutchinson, or the late lieutenant governor been any way instrumental in obtaining the stamp act, it is very strange that not a glimpse of evidence should ever have appeared, especially when we consider that their private correspondence has been published, letters which were written in the full confidence of unsuspecting friendship. The evidence, as Novanglus calls it, is wretchedly deficient as to fixing the charge upon governor

Bernard; but, even admitting that governor Bernard suggested to the ministry the design of taxing, there is no kind of evidence to prove that the junto, as this elegant writer calls the others, approved of it, much less that they employed him to do it. But, says he, no one can doubt but that Messieurs Hutchinson and Oliver were in unison with governor Bernard, in all his measures. This is not a fact, Mr. Hutchinson dissented from him respecting the alteration of our charter, and wrote to his friends in England to prevent it. Whether governor Bernard wrote in favour of the stamp act being replaced or not I cannot say, but I know that governor Hutchinson did, and have reason to think his letters had great weight in turning the scale, which hung doubtful a long time, in favour of the repeal. These facts are known to many in the province, whigs as well as tories, yet such was the infatuation that prevailed, that the mob destroyed his house upon supposition that he was the patron of the stamp act. Even in the letters wrote to the late Mr. Whately, we find him advising to a total repeal of the tea act. It cannot be fairly inferred from persons' intimacy or mutual confidence, that they always approve of each others plans. Messieurs Otis, Cushing, Hancock and Adams were as confidential friends, and made common cause equally with the other gentlemen. May we thence infer, that the three latter hold that the parliament has a just and *equitable right* to impose taxes on the colonies? Or, that "the time may come, when the real interest of the whole may require an act of parliament to annihilate all our charters?" For these also are Mr. Otis's words. Or may we lay it down as a principle to reason from, that these gentlemen never disagree respecting measures? We know they do often, very materially. This writer is unlucky both in his principles and inferences. But where is the evidence respecting brigadier Ruggles, Mr. Paxton, and the late judge Russel? He does not produce even the shadow of a shade. He does not even pretend that they were in unison with governor Bernard in all his measures. In matters of small moment a man may be allowed to amuse with ingenious fiction, but in personal accusation, in matters so interesting both to the individual and to the public, reason and candour require something more than assertion, without proof, declamation without argument, and censure without dignity or moderation: this however, is characteristic of Novanglus. It is the stale trick of the whig writer feloniously to stab the reputation, when their antagonists are invulnerable in their public conduct.

These gentlemen were all of them, and the survivers still continue to be, friends of the English constitution, equally tenacious of the privileges of the people, and of the prerogative of the crown, zealous advocates for the colonies continuing their constitutional dependance upon Great Britain, as they think it no less the interest than the duty of the colonists; averse to tyranny and oppression in all their forms, and always ready to exert themselves for the relief of the oppressed, though they differ materially from the whigs in the mode of obtaining it; they discharged the duties of the several important departments they were called to fill, with equal faithfulness and ability; their public services gained them the confidence of the people, real merit drew after it popularity; their principles, firmness and popularity rendered them obnoxious to certain persons amongst us, who have long been indulging themselves, in hopes of rearing up an American commonwealth, upon the ruin of the British constitution. This republican party is of long standing; they lay however, in a great measure, dormant for several years. The distrust, jealousy and ferment raised by the stamp act, afforded scope for action. At first they wore the garb of hypocrisy, they professed to be friends to the British constitution in general, but claimed some exemptions from their local circumstances; at length threw off their disguise, and now stand confessed to the world in their true characters, American republicans. These republicans knew, that it would be impossible for them to succeed in their darling projects, without first destroying the influence of these adherents to the constitution. Their only method to accomplish it, was by publications charged with falshood and scurrility. Notwithstanding the favorable opportunity the stamp act gave of imposing upon the ignorant and credulous, I have sometimes been amazed, to see with how little hesitation, some slovenly baits were swallowed. Sometimes the adherents to the constitution were called ministerial tools, at others, kings, lords and commons, were the tools of them; for almost every act of parliament that has been made respecting America, in the present reign, we were told was drafted in Boston, or its environs, and only sent to England to run through the forms of parliament. Such stories, however improbable, gained credit; even the fictitious bill for restraining marriages and murdering bastard children, met with some simple enough to think it real. He that readily imbibes such absurdities, may claim affinity with the person mentioned by Mr. Addison, that made it his practice to swallow a chimera every morning for breakfast. To be more serious, I pity the weakness of those that are capable of being thus duped, almost as much as I despise the wretch that would avail himself of it, to destroy private characters and the public tranquility. By such infamous methods, many of the ancient, trusty and skilful pilots, who had steered the community safely in the most perilous times, were driven from the helm, and their places occupied by different persons, some of whom, bankrupts in fortune, business and fame, are now striving to run the ship on the rocks, that they may have an opportunity of plundering the wreck. The gentlemen named by Novanglus, have nevertheless persevered with unshaken constancy and firmness, in their patriotic principles and conduct, through a variety of fortune; and have at present, the mournful consolation of reflecting, that had their admonitions and councils been timely attended to, their country would never have been involved in its present calamity.

MASSACHUSETTENSIS.

· 15 ·

A Candid Examination of the Mutual

Claims of Great Britain and the Colonies

By Joseph Galloway

After the adjournment of the First Continental Congress, Joseph Galloway went to New York, where he talked with men who believed as he did. When he returned to Philadelphia in December 1774, he found that the Pennsylvania Assembly had approved the proceedings of the first Congress and elected him a delegate to the second Congress. He told the Assembly flatly that he did not approve of the first Congress and that he would not serve as a delegate to the second Congress.

During this period he was writing the pamphlet which was published in New York by James Rivington in February 1775. The pamphlet appealed to men who thought like Galloway, but it was bitterly denounced by those who opposed any closer connection with Britain. Among others who attacked Galloway was his old political enemy John Dickinson, in *An Address to the Author of the Pamphlet.* It is one of the many ironies of the history of the

---

New York, February, 1775.

times that the course of events soon placed Dickinson in Galloway's role as a leading opponent of independence and as a supporter of a strong central government in America.

By the end of 1775, Galloway said later, his life was in danger. The next year he fled to the protection of the British army. During the British occupation of Philadelphia in 1777–1778, Galloway served as the civil administrator of the city; when the British evacuated it, he went to England. There, during the remainder of the war, and even afterwards, he continued his efforts to bring about a reconciliation between Britain and America.

The full title of the New York edition of the pamphlet is: *A Candid Examination of the Mutual Claims of Great Britain, And the Colonies: With A Plan of Accommodation on Constitutional Principles.* Galloway republished the pamphlet in London in 1780; it has not been reprinted since then.

In the following text some of the punctuation has been modified to clarify the meaning.

When we see the country we live in, where agriculture, elegant and beneficial improvements, philosophy, and all the liberal arts and sciences have been nourished and ripened to a degree of perfection, astonishing to mankind; where wisdom and sound policy have even sustained their due authority, kept the licentious in awe, and rendered them subservient to their own, and the public welfare; and where freedom, peace and order, have always triumphed over those enemies to human happiness, oppression and licentiousness; now governed by the barbarian rule of frantic folly, and lawless ambition; When we see freedom of speech suppressed, the liberty and secrecy of the press destroyed, the voice of truth silenced; A lawless power established throughout the colonies, forming laws for the government of their conduct, depriving men of their natural rights, and inflicting penalties more severe than death itself, upon a disobedience to their edicts, to which the constitutional magistracy, in some places by force, and in others willingly, submit; The property of the subject arbitrarily, and without law, taken from him, in pursuance of those edicts; When, under their influence, America is arming in the east and west, against the parent state: I say, when we see the colonies, needlessly, and while the path to their safety and happiness is plain, and open before them; thus pushing on with precipitation and madness, in the high road of sedition and rebellion, which must ultimately terminate in their misery and ruin, it is the duty of every man of the least abilities, to try to reclaim them from their folly, and save them from destruction, before it be too late. With this design I am resolved to review the most important controversy, that ever was agitated between a state and its members; in hope, that my countrymen, too long seduced from their true interest, by false tho' specious arguments, will, at length, listen to reason and truth, and pursue those measures only, which lead to their safety and happiness.

In a controversy of so great moment, it is of the first importance to ascertain the standard by which it ought to be decided. This being unsettled, the merits can never be determined, nor any just decision formed. Hence it is, that we have seen all the American writers on the subject, adopting untenable principles, and thence rearing the most wild and chimerical superstructures. Some of them have fixed on, as a source from whence to draw American Right, "the laws of God and nature," the common rights of mankind, "and American charters." Others finding that the claims of the colonies could not be supported upon those pillars, have racked their inventions to find out distinctions, which never existed, nor can exist, in reason or common sense: A distinction between a right in parliament to legislate for the colonies, and a right to tax them— between internal and external taxation—and between taxes laid for the regulation of trade, and for the purpose of revenue. And after all of them have been fully considered, even the authors themselves, finding that they have conveyed no satisfactory idea to the intelligent mind, either of the extent of parliamentary authority, or of the rights of America, have exploded them, and taken new ground, which will be found equally indefensible. I shall not attempt to account for a conduct which must appear so strange, when it is considered, that the subject itself naturally, and familiarly, led to the only just and proper means of deciding it. It is a dispute between the supreme authority of the state, and a number of its members, respecting its supremacy, and their constitutional rights. What other source to draw them from, or standard to decide them by, can reason point out, but the principles of government in general, and of that constitution in particular, where both are to be found, defined and established? Whoever searches for them elsewhere, will search for them in vain, and ever confound the subject, perplex himself, and bewilder the reader.

In order then to ascertain the constitutional extent of parliamentary authority; to determine whether the colonies are members of the British state; and if they are, to mark out their just rights, and to propose a remedy to reconcile them, upon principles of government and liberty; it is necessary, first, to delineate those principles, which are essential in the constitution of all societies, and particularly in that of the British government.

There is no position more firmly established, in the conduct of mankind, Than that there must be in every state a supreme legislative authority, universal in its extent, over every member. This truth, the principles upon which all governments from the earliest ages have been established, uniformly demonstrate. This truth, the authority of all authors of credit will ever support. This truth, the nature and reason of civil societies will for ever evince. Tully gives us this definition of government, "Multitudo juris consensu et utilitatis communione fociata. A multitude of people united together by a communion of interests, and *common laws* to which *they all submit with one accord.*" Mr. Locke tells us, that "the first *fundamental positive law* of all commonwealths is, the establishing *the legislative power*. This legislative is not only the *supreme power of the common-wealth;* but is sacred and unalterable in the hands where the community have placed it." And in another place, he says, "there can be but one *supreme power,* which is the *legislative,* to which *all the rest* are, and must be, *subordinate.*" The judicious Burlamaqui, in treating of the essential constitution of states, and of the manner in which they are formed, declares that in forming a society, "it is necessary to *unite forever* the *wills of all the members* in such a manner, that from that time forward they should never desire *but one and the same thing,* in whatever relates to the end and purpose of society. It is afterwards necessary, to establish a *supreme power,* supported by the strength of the whole body. That it is from this *union of wills and strength,* that the *body politic, or state, results;* and *without* it we could never conceive a *civil society.* That the state is considered as a body, or moral person, of which the *Sovereign* is the chief head, and the *subjects are the members.*" And afterwards, in another part he says, "The state is a body, or society, animated by *one soul,* which directs *all its motions,* and makes *all its members* act after a *constant and uniform manner,* with a view to one and the *same end,* namely the *public utility.*" And in another chapter, speaking of the characters of sovereignty, its modifications and extent, he avers, "that in every government there should be such a *supreme power,* is a point absolutely *necessary;* the very nature of the thing requires it; otherwise *it is impossible for it to subsist.* That this power is that *from which all others flow,* it being a supreme and independent power; that is, a power that judges finally of whatever is *susceptible of human direction,* and relates to the welfare and advantage of society." And *Acherley,* in his treatise on the Britannic constitution, proves with great strength of argument, "That the *supreme power* in every government and nation, is the *legislative power of making and altering those laws* of it, by which *every man is to be bound,* and to which he is to *yield obedience.*"

The evidence of all other authors of credit, even of those the most attached to republican forms of government, might be adduced, to demonstrate the same truths; but this must be unnecessary, when we refer to the forms of all civilized societies, whether monarchical, aristocratical, democratical, or mixed; and there find a sovereign legislature established, to which it is the duty of *every member uniformly to yield obedience.* A due attention to this universal principle, which seems too firmly settled to be shaken by any sophistical distinctions, would have saved the American writers from all their numerous absurdities. It would have shewn them, that the legislative authority in every government must of necessity be *equally supreme over all its members.* That to divide this supremacy, by allowing it to exist in some cases, and not in all, over a part of the members, and not the whole, is to weaken and confound the operations of the system, and to subvert the very end and purpose for which it was formed; in as much as the vigour and strength of every machine, whether mechanical or political, must depend upon the consistency of its parts, and their corresponding obedience to the supreme *acting power:* And it would have shewn that there can be no alternative; either the colonies must be considered as complete members of the state, or so many distinct communities, in a state of nature, as independant of it, as Hanover, France, or Spain.

That there is such a supreme power established in the British society, which has from the time of its origin, exercised this universal authority over all its members, will not be denied. But where it is lodged; what are its modifications; and what are the powers subordinate to it, is a necessary enquiry. It will lead us to those principles which must decide many important questions in this great controversy; and in particular point out the absurdity, in the colonists, when they acknowledge allegiance to the King, and deny obedience to the laws of parliament.

The government of Great-Britain is of a particular kind. There is none now in the world like it. It is of a mixed form, composed partly of the principles of a monarchy, aristocracy, and democracy; and yet cannot with propriety be described, by the name of either of them. Its supreme legislative head is *lodged* in the King, Lords and Commons. To their authority every other power of the state is subordinate, and every member must yield full and perfect obedience. These three branches constituting but one supreme politic head, their power is equal and concurrent; their joint assent being necessary to the validity of every act of legislation. So that even in this department of the state, which is the highest and first in order, the King is not supreme; being only one of three equal in power. It cannot therefore be to the King, as legislator, that the colonists owe obedience and allegiance; because he has no such complete, independent capacity; he is not, by the constitution, a legislator, but only a part of one; and to submit to the power of a *part*, and not to the *whole*, is too great an absurdity for men of sense to adopt.

But as the legislature does not always exist, it could avail little, without some power to superintend the execution of its regulations. The appointment of a representative of the whole state, to see that its laws are duly carried into execution, was absolutely necessary. The King is that representative; and as such is vested with the executive power of the British government. But this power is a subordinate one, and perpetually liable to the alterations and controul of the supreme legislative authority; whose will, enacted into laws, is the sole guide and rule of its actions. Mr. Locke tells us, that the King "is to be considered as the image, phantom, or *representative of the common wealth, and by the will of the society declared in its laws,* and thus *has no will, no power,* but *that of the law.*"

To him, in this representative capacity, and as supreme executor of the laws, made by *a joint power of him and others,* the oaths of allegiance are taken; and by him, that obedience in the subjects to the laws, which intitle them to protection in their persons and properties, is received. Is it then to him, as representative of the state, and executor of its laws, that the Americans profess their allegiance? This cannot be; because it would be owning an obedience to the laws of the state which he represents, and is bound to execute, and of which they uniformly deny the force and obligation. Hence these professions are not made to him either in his legislative, or executive capacities; but yet it seems they are made to the King. And into this distinction, which is no where to be found, either in the constitution of the government, in reason or common sense, the ignorant and thoughtless have been deluded ever since the passing of the stamp-act, and they have rested satisfied with it without the least examination; for we find it in all the resolves and petitions of the American assemblies, town meetings, provincial committees, and even in the proceedings of the continental congress. And such have been the unhappy effects, that we have seen the officers of justice in America, who have taken the oaths to the British government, resolutely opposing the execution of those very laws, which they have sworn to obey and execute; and thus unwittingly sliding into the most palpable perjuries. I do not mean to offend the inventors of this refined distinction, when I ask them—Is this acknowledgment made to the King, in his politic capacity, as King of Great-Britain, or of America? If to him in the first, it includes a promise of obedience to the British laws, as I shall more fully prove hereafter. If in the second, as King of America, when did he assume that title, and by whom was it conferred? When was he crowned? On the contrary has he not invariably denied the existence of any such capacity in him, by an uniform conduct, in exerting his authority, to execute the British statutes in America?

In his representative capacity, the King also holds the great seal, or the seal of the state, and has right to affix it to all acts of the legislature, and such as he is impowered to do by his prerogative, and *no other*. He has also certain prerogatives, which are defined and known. By one of them he has right, under the great seal, to form any circle of territory, within the realm, and the subjects on it, into inferior bodies politic, and to vest them with the power to make municipal laws, for the regulation of its internal police, so far as it relates to the welfare of that circle only: But by no means to discharge them from their obedience to the supreme legislative authority. Because this would be to weaken, dismember, and in the end destroy the state, contrary to the intent for which the prerogative was vested in him, namely, the public good and safety.

Having thus established the necessity of a supreme legislative authority in every government, and shewn that it is an essential principle in the English state, and explained such other parts of the constitution as are necessary to my purpose; let us next enquire whether the colonies of right are members of that state, or so many independent communities, in a state of nature, with respect to it. For seeing a legislative authority competent, in all cases whatsoever, over every member, is necessary in every government; the colonies must stand in one or other of these predicaments.

The lands upon which the colonies are established must be considered, as they truly are, either discovered, or conquered territories. In either case the right of property is in the state, under the license or authority of which they were discovered or conquered. This property being vested in the state, no subject can lawfully enter upon, and appropriate any part of it to his own use, without a commission or grant from the immediate representative for that purpose. Hence we find in the histories of all civilized states, from the earliest ages to this day, the heads, or representatives of all governments, distributing such lands, by special grants, among their people, who in every instance which history affords, still retain the duties of subjects. And there is no position better established by the practice and usage of all societies, than that where a subject removes from one part of the territory of a government, to another part of the same, his political rights and duties remain as before; but where the subject of one state removes to the territory of another, and settles there, his political rights and duties are changed from those of the state from whence he removed, to those of the state under which he settles, and from which he receives protection. No person acquainted with politic law, or the practice of societies, in these respects, will assert the contrary. What then are the circumstances of America? Under what authority was it discovered? What was the intent of the discovery? By whom, and under what authority, has it been settled? A decision of these questions will lead us to a very important truth, viz. That the colonies are of Right members of the British government.

America was discovered in the latter end of the 15th century, by Sebastian Cabot, authorised for that special purpose, under the great seal of the state, affixed to his commission, by *Henry 7.* Representative of the British government. The *signature* of the great seal fully proves that the King did not in the granting this commission, consider himself as acting in his private, but in his politic capacity. In the first he had no right to affix it, in the second he had. The design in view was to encrease the territories, extend the commerce, and add to the wealth and power of the state. And therefore the discovery was made to the use of the state, and the territories became immediately subject to its supreme authority. No man in his sober senses will, I imagine, affirm that *Henry 7.* had in view the discovery of a country, into which his successors might give license to the members of the state to emigrate, with intent to become independent of its authority. Such a design is too absurd to be supposed ever to have been admitted into any system of policy; much less that of a Prince so justly famed for his wisdom.

Every colony in America, as well those under charters, as

others, has been settled under the licence and authority of the great seal, affixed by the representative of the body politic of the British state. The property of the territory of America being in the state, and its members removing under its authority from one part of it to another, equally subject to its supreme jurisdiction; they of consequence, brought over with them all their political rights and *duties,* and amongst the rest, that of perfect obedience to its laws; nor could they be lost or changed by an alteration of their local circumstances. Indeed nothing can be more explicitly confessed than this truth, in all the American declarations of their rights. I shall cite only those of the congresses which met at New-York in 1765, and at Philadelphia in 1774. By the first we are told, "that his *Majesty's* subjects in these colonies *are entitled to* all the *inherent rights and liberties* of his *natural* born subjects within the kingdom of Great-Britain." And in the second, "That our ancestors, who first settled these colonies, were, at the time of their emigration from the mother-country, *entitled to all the rights, liberties* and immunities of free and natural born subjects within the realm of England." And that by such emigration they by no means forfeited, surrendered, or lost any of those rights;" Thus evidently deducing their title to their right, from the relation they bore, as members of the mother state. Conscious that they could not deduce them from any other source but the English government, as they no where else exist, they claim them under its title and authority. But can the wisest among them inform us, by what law, or upon what principle, they claim rights under the British government, and yet deny the obligation of those duties which subjects of that government owe to it? The rights and duties of the members of all societies are reciprocal. The one is the continuing consideration for the other. Either of them being destroyed, without the consent of the subjects to which both of them adhere, the other ceases. Therefore, should a state arbitrarily deprive its members of their just rights, and refuse to restore them, after it has been repeatedly, and respectfully required so to do, then their duties and obedience to the state cease, but not before, It being the design of every society, when formed, that its existence should be permanent, not of a temporary duration.

Here we may perceive some of those many inconsistencies and absurdities in which the advocates of America have weakly involved her cause. We see them calling the subjects in America, "subjects of his *Majesty*," in his political capacity, and as representative of the British state, bound in duty to execute its laws, in *every part* of its dominions; and in the same breath denying obedience to those laws. We see them claiming "all the inherent rights and liberties of natural born subjects" of the state, and denying the force of those duties, which are so inseparably united with those "rights and liberties." We hear them declare that they have not "forfeited, surrendered, or lost" the rights they enjoyed at the time of their emigration;" and yet they will not comply with the duties upon the performance of which those rights depend. Thus it seems the American subjects have neither "forfeited, surrendered, nor lost," but still retain the rights they derive from the government of Great-Britain; but the government has either forfeited, surrendered, or lost its rights over Them. Indeed they have not told us how, or by what means, this forfeiture, surrender, or loss of rights in the British state, has happened. This, I believe, was a task impossible; and therefore carefully avoided. But what shall we think of the sagacity and foresight of these able politicians, when we find that the right claimed by parliament, and which they deny, may be established with equal reason and solidity, upon the same principles and deductions, on which they have rested the claims of America? May not the advocates for the parliamentary authority assert, "That at the time of the emigration of our ancestors," the legislative power had a constitutional authority over them, and every other member of the state; that by such emigration, which was an act of their own, as well as of the state, it neither "forfeited, surrendered, nor lost" that authority? And would not such a declaration be in reason, truth, and on the principles of the English constitution, as well founded, as that upon which the defenders of American rights have endeavoured to establish them?

But it may be said that America is settled by others, besides British subjects. Are They also members of the state, and subject to its authority? They most certainly are. They have by their own act become subjects; and owe obedience to its laws, as fully as any other members, as I have before shewn. But to confirm what I have already advanced upon this head, I shall add the opinion of Mr. *Locke,* because it has been often heretofore relied on by the American advocates, as worthy of credit. His words are, "Whoever by *inheritance, purchase, permission, or otherwise,* enjoys *any part of the land* annexed to, and under the government of a common wealth, must take it with the condition it is under, that is of *submitting* to the government of the common wealth, under whose jurisdiction it is, as *far as any subject of it.*" If the preceding principles and arguments be well founded, as they appear to be, from the usage, practice and policy of all societies; it follows, that whatever British subject, or foreigner, has, either under the sanction of the American charters, or otherwise, become an occupant of the English territories in the colonies, he is truly a member of the British state, and subject to the laws of its supreme authority.

I have thus far drawn my arguments chiefly from the policy of government in general, and of the English constitution in particular; and, I hope, with sufficient evidence, to prove the justness and truth of them. But as I mean fully to investigate, with the strictest candour, the rights of both the parties, and place them in their true light; it is of importance to consider whether their conduct, for upwards of a century, affords evidence of a denial, or confirmation of the principles I have maintained. And here we shall find, that the prerogatives of this supreme representative of the state, ever since the first settlement of the colonies, have been uniformly exercised, and submitted to, in all the colonies. All their political Executive powers have been derived from, and all their governments established by, it. It is in this representative capacity that the King has granted all the charters, appointed the governors, custom-house officers, &c. and granted authority to the governors to commissionate the inferior officers of justice, as well judicial as ministerial. From this source only all his legal powers, in respect to the colonies, can be drawn; there being no other capacity vested in him, from whence he could derive them. So that every officer in America, appointed by him, or under his authority, is truly the inferior and subordinate delegate of the King, Lords and Commons; receiving his authority from the supreme executive representative of the British state; all their powers being originally derived from, and limited by, its constitution and laws.

Upon the same principle, the supreme legislature has, upon many occasions, and at a variety of times, held forth and exercised its authority over the colonies; and they have yielded obedience to all the British statutes, in which they have been named; as well those imposing taxes on them, as those for regulating their internal police. The learned judges in England, and the judges and other officers concerned in the administration of justice in America, in conformity to this idea, of their being the inferior delegates of the British state, and of its authority over the colonies, have ever made those laws of parliament, where by words they have been extended to them, the test of their decisions, in all American disputes, without doubt or hesitation, until the year 1765, when our unhappy controversy commenced.

All the officers of government, every member of assembly, every foreigner before his naturalization, had always taken the oaths of allegiance, under the directions of the statutes, that have been made for that purpose. The words of the oath are the same with that administered to the subject in Britain, on the like occasions; and consequently must be of the same import, and carry with them the same obligations in every respect. Both in Britain and America the oaths are taken to the King, not in his private, but politic capacity; they are taken to him as representative of the whole state, whose duty it is to superintend the administration of justice, and to see that a faithful obedience is paid to the laws. These oaths are no more than renewals of the original covenant, upon which all governments are formed: For in the constitution of all societies two covenants are essential; one on the part of the state, that it will ever consult and promote the public good and safety; and the other on the part of the subject, that he will bear fidelity and true allegiance to the *sovereign, or supreme authority.* "This last covenant," says the judicious Burlamaqui, "includes a submission of the *strength* and *will* of each *individual* to the *will* and *head* of the society, as far as the public good requires; and thus it is that a *regular state,* and *perfect government* is formed." And the words of Mr. Locke are equally apposite,

The oaths of allegiance are taken to the King, it is not to him as supreme legislator, but as *supreme executor of the law,* made by a joint power of *him and others; allegiance* being nothing but *obedience according to law,* which, when he *violates,* he has no right to *obedience,* nor can *claim it* otherwise than in his *public person,* vested with the *power of the law.*

And in another place he says,

That all obedience which by the most solemn ties any one can be obliged to pay, *ultimately terminates in the supreme power of the legislature,* and is directed by those laws which it enacts.

This being the nature of the oath of allegiance, and of the obligations it enforces, no man of any understanding will call for further proof, That all the officers of government in America, who have taken these oaths, and those who have submitted to their administration, while they were executing the British statutes, considered themselves as subjects of the state, owing obedience to its legislative authority.

In every government, protection and allegiance, or obedience, are reciprocal duties. They are so inseparably united that one cannot exist without the other. Protection from the state demands, and entitles it to receive, obedience and submission to its laws from the subject; And obedience to the will of the state, communicated in its laws, entitles the subject to its protection. A just sense of this truth has governed the conduct of the state towards the colonies, and that of the colonies towards the state, ever since their settlement. The colonists have not only settled upon the lands of the state, under its licence and authority, granted by its representative; but they have been fostered, nourished and sheltered under its wings, and protected by its wealth and power. And as they have ever yielded obedience to its laws, they have, whenever in danger, called for its protection; and in the last war were saved from all the misery and slavery, which popish superstition and tyranny could inflict, when their inability to save themselves was universally known and acknowledged.

Seeing then that the colonies have, ever since their existence, considered themselves, and acted as perfect members of the British state, obedient to its laws, untill the year 1765: There must, one would imagine, be something lately discovered, which has convinced them of their mistake, and that they have a right to cast off their allegiance to the British government. We can look for this in no place so properly, as in the late declaration of American rights. Here we find it drawn from "the immutable laws of nature, the principles of the English constitution, and their several charters, or compacts." Should we fail in discovering it here, we may safely determine it is not any where to be found. We shall not find it in "the laws of nature;" the principles upon which those laws are founded, are reason and immutable justice, which require a rigid performance of every lawful contract; to suppose therefore, that a right can thence be derived to violate the most solemn and sacred of all covenants; those upon which the existence of societies, and the welfare of millions depend; is, in the highest degree, absurd. And, I believe, we shall be equally unsuccessful in searching for it in the principles of the English constitution; because that constitution is formed to bind all the members of the state together, and to compel an obedience to its laws. We must therefore find it in the American charters or compacts, or no where. And after we have looked there, we can discover no exemption, or discharge from the authority of parliament in any of them, save one, and there it is only partial; while other parts of the same charter declare the contrary, and expressly retain the submission of the subject to the British laws. But suppose there had been such an exemption in all of them, as clear as words could express it, it is a question which demands a solution, whether the King had a right, by the constitution, to grant it.

The original intent of the prerogative, under which the inhabitants of particular districts of territory have been incorporated into bodies politic, was to enable the representative of the state, to form inferior communities, with municipal rights and privileges. This was necessary to enable the executive power to carry into execution the operations of government with regularity and order. And in some instances it has been beneficial in promoting the trade, arts, and particular pursuits in business of such districts. This prerogative is very antient, and well defined by usage and prescription. London held peculiar privileges long before the conquest. William the conqueror granted to that city two charters soon after. A great number of inferior societies have been since incorporated, by succeeding Kings, upon these principles; all of them under the great seal, and by the same authority under which the American charters were granted. Having so many precedents before us, we cannot be at a loss to ascertain the extent of this prerogative. The exercise of it for so many centuries will give satisfaction to every candid enquirer. Making this the test of decision, we shall find that no King has ever presumed to grant more than merely municipal powers and privileges, always leaving the subjects and the territory incorporated, under the supreme legislative authority. There being no *traces* of a farther extent of this prerogative, in the conduct of all the British Kings; the conclusion is, that no such power does, or ever did exist. Besides, this prerogative, like all others, is vested in the King, in trust, to promote, not to injure, the public good. And therefore, to assert that he may, under it, discharge these incorporated societies from their obedience to the supreme power, is to contend that, by virtue of the power which he holds in trust to strengthen, he may weaken, and instead of maintaining and defending, he may destroy, the common wealth; which involves the most palpable contradiction.

Sufficient has been said to convince us, that the Kings of England can have no authority to discharge inferior bodies politic, from parliamentary authority. But as upon a satisfactory decision of the question, the claim of independency must stand or fall, I shall farther corroborate what I have said, with the most respectable authorities. The learned Pufendorf tells us,

With regard to all *lawful bodies*, it is to be observed, that whatever right they possess, or whatever power they hold over their members, is all under *the determination of the supreme authority*, which it ought on *no account to oppose or over ballance*. For otherways, if there could be a body of men, not *subject to the regulation of the civil government*, there would be *a state within a state*.—If we look on these bodies, or systems, in a state already settled, we are then to consider what was the *intent of the supreme Governor*, in founding, or confirming, such a company. For if he hath given, or ascertained to them, in express words, *an absolute and independent* right, with regard to *some particular affairs* which concern the *pub-lick administration;* then he hath *plainly* ABDICATED *part of his au-thority,* and by admitting *two heads* in the constitution, hath ren-dered it *irregular and monstrous.*

Mr. Locke says, "That the legislative authority *must needs be supreme;* and *all other powers,* in any members, or parts of society, *derived from, and subordinate* to it." And speaking of the King's exceeding his public trust, he affirms, "That when he quits his *representative capacity,* his *public will,* and acts by his own *private will, he degrades* himself, and is but *a single, private person, without power, without will, that has any right to obedience."* And the same author would not scruple to declare, upon the principles he establishes in the latter part of his treatise that a King who should have granted, in the American charters, a licence to the subjects of the state to emigrate, with a discharge from their obedience to the legislative authority, and should open such a door to a deser-tion of the principal territory, and dissolution of its government, would thereby forfeit his crown; and to prevent the mischief of such grant, the people might resume their original authority, if the mischief could not otherwise be prevented.

I have said before, whenever a state refuses to give protec-tion to its subjects, and maintain their rights, their duty ceases. It may with equal truth be affirmed, that whenever subjects shall refuse to perform those duties, and yield that obedience which they are bound to perform and yield by the constitution, or original compact of society, they forfeit not only their right to the protection of the state, but every other right or claim under it; and the government may either punish them agree-ably to its laws, or cease its protection over them, and annul the rights and privileges they derive from it. There is no truth more evident than that where a mutual covenant subsists, in-cluding a consideration perpetually to be performed on both sides, upon which the validity of the covenant rests, if either party refuse the performance on his part, the other is discharged of course, and the party refusing loses his right and claim to the performance of the other. If this assertion be just, and that it is we shall find, whether we apply to the laws of nature, or civil societies, into what a dangerous predicament are the Americans thrown by a denial of obedience to the authority of parliament, which is one of the most essential duties! That they have not, as the congress affirms, forfeited, surrendered, or lost their rights, by their emigration, is true. But that this wise body of men have used their best endeavours, and pursued the most effectual measures to forfeit them, is equally true. Let us suppose that the late congress had been a regular and legal representative of all America, vested with authority, by the consent of the colonists, to deny and withdraw their obedience to the laws of the British state, as they have endeavoured to do; would not Great-Britain be justifiable in declaring, by an act of state, that all the rights and privileges which the colonists derive under her, are forfeited? Shall the Americans have a right to withdraw from the state the performance of their duties, and the state be bound to continue *them* in the enjoyment of all their rights? Every principle of government and common sense denies it.

Thus, in whatever light we view the subject; whether we reason from the principles and policy upon which all governments are established, or those of the English constitution in particular; the right of property in the territory, the authority under which the colonists have been settled, the persons by whom settled, their rights under the several charters and compacts, their conduct ever since their settlement, down to the year 1765, or from the conduct of the state down to this day; we find that they are members of the British state, and owe obedience to its legislative authority.

That America has been wandering in a wrong path, bewildered among the erroneous principles upon which her advocates have attempted in vain to support her rights, is apparent from all her conduct; she began by denying the authority of parliament, to lay internal taxes: But finding that ground not tenable, she next denied its power to lay either internal or external taxes: And at length has declared, that it can neither lay internal nor external taxes, nor regulate the internal police of the colonies. And yet such has been the implicit confidence, such the infatuation of the unthinking and deluded people, that they have believed at the time, that all those principles were so many solid pillars—and supports of their rights, and *truths as sacred as those in holy writ.*

It would not be unreasonable to think, that the arguments before offered, to expose the present unhappy measures of the colonies, would be sufficient for that purpose. But however that may be, as I am convinced they lead to the ruin of my country, I think it my duty to take a more particular view of them. The claims made by the last congress, and upon which, it seems, all America now rests, are, "That the colonies are entitled to *a free and exclusive right, or power of legislation,* in their several provincial legislatures, where their right of representation can alone be preserved, *in all cases of taxation and internal polity, subject only to the negative of their Sovereign, in such manner as has been heretofore used and accustomed.*" No words can convey a more perfect claim of independency, on the British legislature, than those I have just transcribed. Because there is no act within the power of any legislature to pass, binding on any member of the state, but what must, in either the regulation or execution of it affect the internal police. States may make laws for the government of their subjects, while in foreign countries, or upon the sea; but as those laws can only be executed within the society, there being no jurisdiction, no officer of justice without; its internal police must be affected by them, according to the nature of the penalties, and the mode of recovering, or inflicting them, and in the most sacred things, life, liberty and property; these being the objects upon which penalties are laid. If this be true, and the colonies have a "free and exclusive legislation, in all cases of internal polity," the legislature of Great-Britain can have no more authority over them, than the parliament of Paris; and the colonies are as independent of the one as the other. But it seems under this claim of right, though the legislature of Great-Britain, which is supreme in power, having no superior, as I have shewn, shall have no right to make laws for us, nor even to repeal an act of assembly, of the colonies, however inconsistent with the laws of England, or destructive to the rights and interests of the nation; yet the legislation of the colonies is to be subject to the *repeal of the King*. Does not this ill-founded claim involve the cause of America in an inextricable absurdity? Is not this acknowledging a power in an inferior, and denying it in the superior, from whom that inferior draws all its authority, and by whom all its prerogatives, rights, and powers are governed, and controuled? The King, by the constitution, has no capacity in which he does not represent the supreme legislature, or head of the state, as I have proved before. Nor can he assume any other inconsistent with its rights. The power of repeal, being a compleat legislative act, he can draw it from no other fountain, but from his representation of the *whole legislative body.* Because as legislator, he holds only a third part of the right, and upon no ground of reason, or propriety, can an entire superior power be derived, from any part of the same power.

Here we have a full view of the plan of the delegates of North-America, which, when examined, appears to be that of absolute independence on the mother state. But conscious that a scheme, which has so great a tendency to a forfeiture of her rights, and so destructive to her safety and happiness, could not meet with the approbation and support of the colonists in general, unless in some measure disguised; they have endeavoured to throw a veil over it, by graciously conceding to the mother-state, a whimsical authority, useless and impracticable, in its nature. This is a stale device, common to wrong-headed politicians, who have not reason and truth to support their pretensions. But the veil is too thin. The herbage is not sufficiently thick to conceal the covered snake, from the eye of the candid and sensible enquirer. But let us hear them. "But from the necessity of the case, and a regard to the mutual interest of both countries," not from any *constitutional right,* for this they have denied in the preceeding part of the resolve, in all cases whatsoever, "we consent;" but to what do they consent? "to the operations of," not to the right of making, "such acts of the British Parliament as are," not such as shall be hereafter, for they are, no doubt, to receive the sanction of this wise and learned body, before they are valid, "bona fide restrained, to the regulation of our external commerce, for the purpose of *securing* the commercial advantages of the *whole,* (i.e. of our commerce) to the *mother country,* and the commercial benefits of its *respective members."* Here is more art and finesse, than an honest mind would wish to find in the conduct of any men, much less in those of character. It is easy to perceive from the import of these words, that should the British parliament be obliged to accept of their *concessions,* they concede nothing. They have taken especial care, that what they have consented to in one breath, should be blasted by the next. For there is no law of trade, that I know of, nor can such a law be formed, as shall *secure the* commercial advantages *of all the external American commerce* to the mother country, which is a part of the realm distinct from the colonies, and yet "secure to the colonies," as members, their commercial benefit. It would not have been any great deviation from the public duty of these gentlemen, had they dealt less in mysteries, and explained what laws they were, which answered those excellent purposes. Surely they could not mean those statutes, which enumerate American commodities, and compel us to land them in Britain, before they can be exported to foreign markets; nor those which oblige us to purchase their manufactures, and forbid us to get them from other countries. These are so far from "securing," that they greatly diminish the commercial benefits of the colonies; and I know of no other that "secure" the advantages of our commerce "to the mother country." But suppose there are such laws, who are to point them out in the volumes of the statutes? Who is to say whether a law answers this description? Is the legislature of Great-Britain to do this? No. Who then?—Why, the assemblies.— But the assemblies are disunited, and may differ as they have done, even in matters which concerned their essential safety, and there is no constitutional union, declaring the voices of a majority, binding on all. Why then, since it can be no otherways, the point must be determined by an illegal, motley congress; some few of them to be appointed by the assemblies, if they can be so lost to their own, and the true interest of their constituents, as ever to appoint another; and the rest by a twentieth part of the people, the most ignorant and violent to be found among them. A blessed American constitution!

But should there by any such laws as the congress have described, it seems, they are to be still further limited, and to "exclude every idea of internal and external taxation, for raising a revenue in America." All the laws of trade, from whence the least aid arises to the crown for the protection of its dominions, are invalid, for want of this "consent," and to be abolished: But those which amount to an absolute prohibition, are agreed to. The statute imposing a small duty on foreign sugars and molasses, on their importation, and thereby enabling the colonists to establish new manufactures, and open new sources of foreign trade, shall not be obeyed; but had the parliament instead thereof passed an act totally prohibiting this part of our foreign commerce, under forfeiture of vessel and cargo, it would have met with the approbation and consent of these great and wise men, at least as to its "operations." Is it not strange, that when they were about to bring forth this ruinous principle, they could not perceive, that every greater power includes every inferior, relative power; and that the power to prohibit a particular trade includes *from necessity,* that of permitting it, *on condition of paying an advantageous duty?*

To conclude my remarks upon this famous American bill of rights, this pillar of American liberties. It seems implicitly agreed, that with the "consent of America," both internal and external taxes may be laid by Parliament; But they have not informed us in what constitutional, or legal mode, this consent is to be obtained, or given. They must have known, if they knew any thing, that there was none; and yet so far were they from meaning to propose any, that they ordered, in direct violation of their own rules, the only constitutional plan which was offered for that purpose, to be *rescinded* from their minutes, after it had been debated, and referred to further consideration; lest the good people of America should see and approve of it, depriving the member who proposed it, of that security, against misrepresentation, which he was in justice entitled to, and contrary to their duty to the colonies. Such are the proceedings of the men, intrusted with the sacred rights and liberties of America! Such the disappointment of their constituents. They thought that all wisdom, justice and policy were concentred in that learned body. And therefore they expected that some permanent system of union, between Great-Britain and the colonies, upon principles of government and liberty, would have been proposed to the mother state, and a path opened to a lasting and happy reconciliation. But alas! How mistaken! Nothing has been the production of their two months labour, but the ill-shapen, diminutive brat, INDEPENDENCY. And conscious of its inability to defend itself, they have exerted every nerve, to prevail on the people to adopt the spurious infant of a day, and take up arms in its defence; to rush into the blackest rebellion, and all the horrors of an unnatural civil war. To effect this wicked and horrid design, they, in all their *sham* majesty of illegal power, resolve that "if the late acts of parliament shall be attempted to be carried into execution *by force,* that in such case, *All America* ought to support the inhabitants of the Massachusets Bay, *in their opposition.*" Who is to superintend the execution of the laws, against which this opposition is advised? This is the duty of his Majesty, as representative of the state, who is authorised to do it, by first calling on the aid of the civil power, and if that is not sufficient, the military? The essential principles of government justify it. Search for yourselves, my dear countrymen, look into all the treatises on the crown law, and they will tell you, that this opposition is clear, palpable treason and rebellion, which will incur the forfeiture of your estates, and your lives. But this is not all the mischief they have done, or attempted to do—as if nothing would satisfy them, but your inevitable ruin. They have surrounded you with misery on all sides—have used their utmost endeavours, to raise the hostile resentment of one of the most powerful states upon earth against you, when nothing but her affection, lenity and mercy towards you, can prevent her from reducing you, in a short time, to the deplorable condition of a conquered people. But if she should be so blind to your and her own interest, as to give you independency, which is the great aim of their conduct, they have prepared the rods and scourges of their own tyranny to subdue your spirits, and triumph over your invaluable rights and liberties. Under this tyranny, edicts have been made and published; and so sacred are they to be held, that none is to presume to *meddle* with, or determine any dispute arising on them, but the creatures of this illegal power. The severest of all penalties are ordained for a disobedience to them. Taxes have been imposed on your property, and that property arbitrarily taken from you; the liberty of the press, and even the liberty of speech is destroyed. The unthinking, ignorant multitude, in the east and west, are arming against the mother state, and the authority of government, is silenced by the din of war. What think you, O my countrymen, what think you will be your condition, when you shall see the designs of these men carried a little farther into execution? Companies of armed, but undisciplined men, headed by men un-principled, travelling over your estates, entering your houses—your castles—and sacred repositories of safety for all you hold dear and valuable—seizing your property, and carrying havock and devastation wherever they head—ravishing your wives and daughters, and afterwards plunging the dagger into their tender bosoms, while you are obliged to stand the speech-less, the helpless spectators. Tell me, oh! tell me—whether your hearts are so obdurate as to be prepared for such shocking scenes of confusion and death. And yet, believe me, this is a real and not an exaggerated picture of that distress, into which the schemes of those men, who have assumed the characters of your guardians, and dare to stile themselves his *Majesty's most loyal subjects,* will inevitably plunge you, unless you oppose them with all the fortitude which reason and virtue can inspire.

I have thus thought it my duty, in a case of such infinite importance to my country, to give the full weight to the argu-ments in favour of the right of parliament, and against those rash and violent measures which are hastening the ruin of America. I do not know, that I have exaggerated any. I mean, with the most benevolent attachment to her true interest, to lay the truth, the whole truth, and nothing but the truth, be-fore my country, that she may impartially consider it, and give it that weight which reason and her own preservation shall dictate; but hitherto I have only performed a part of my engagement. The rights of America remain to be considered and established. A task which the undertaker must perform with ineffable pleasure, as he is pleading a cause founded on the immutable principles of reason and justice—the cause of his country, and the latest posterity. He is endeavouring to restore an union between two great countries whose interest and welfare are inseparable; and to recover those rights upon the enjoyment whereof the happiness of millions depends.

That America has rights, and most important rights, which

she does not at present enjoy, I know; and that they are as firmly established, as those of the parliament, may be easily proved; but what those rights are—whence derived—how the exercise of them has been lost—and what is the only possible and safe mode of recovering them, are questions, a candid solution of which will throw full light upon this unhappy controversy.

After what has been said respecting the rights of parliament, and the duties of the British state, it cannot be difficult to determine from whence the rights of America are derived. They can be traced to no other fountain, but that wherein they were originally established. This was in the constitution of the British state. Protection from all manner of unjust violence, is the great object which men have in view, when they surrender up their natural rights, and enter into society. I have said before, that the right to this protection, and the duties of allegiance were reciprocal. By protection I do not mean protection from foreign powers only; but also against the private injustice of individuals, the arbitrary and lawless power of the state, and of every subordinate authority. Such being the right, unless the government be so formed, as to afford the subject a security in the enjoyment of it, the right itself would be of little estimation. The tenure would be precarious, and its existence of a short duration. In proportion to the stability of this security, all governments are more or less free, and the subject happy under them. Much therefore depends on the particular form, or constitution of the society. In a monarchy, where the supreme power is lodged in a single person, without any check or controul, the tenure is precarious; because it depends on the discretion and integrity of the Monarch. But in a free government of the mixt form, where the people have a right to a share, and compose a part of the supreme authority, its foundation will be solid, and its continuance permanent; because the people themselves, who are interested in its preservation, partake of the power which is necessary to defend it.

There is no society in the world where this right of protection is settled with so much wisdom and policy, as in the English constitution. The experience of ages affords numerous instances of its being invaded and impaired, but in a short time restored by its own energetic power. It is this part of the English government upon which authors dwell with rapture; as it constitutes its whole excellence, and forms its freedom.

Power naturally arising from property, it is evident from a view of the British constitution, in all its different stages, that the English government derives its power from the landed interest; that being the most permanent and unchangeable in its nature, of all kinds of property, and therefore most worthy of protection. And although we cannot trace this truth up to its origin, the necessary antient records being buried in the ruins of the monasteries, either before or after the conquest, yet the fact is sufficiently evident from very ancient histories and documents, as well as from the plan of government, used in England from time immemorial. All historians agree that the present form of government was settled in Britain, by our ancestors, the Anglo-saxons; and so far as we have any knowledge of their government in their own country, we know that the *proprietors of the land,* gave their personal attendance in *the legislative council,* and *shared the power of making their laws.* After their conquest of Britain, *all those to whom the land* was apportioned, held a right to assist in the Saxon parliaments. And by the feudal law *every landholde*r, met in the feudal courts, and gave his assent, or dissent, to the laws there proposed.

Such continued to be the form of the British government, until the dissolution of the heptarchy, and union of the seven kingdoms, when, we should not have thought it strange, had this principle been destroyed, or greatly impaired, in the convulsions which effected so great a revolution. But, on the contrary, although the numbers of people, and their remoteness from the place of convention, were greatly encreased by the union which rendered a personal exercise of the legislative power impracticable; yet in order to preserve in the government, this important principle, upon which all their rights and freedom depended, they adopted the policy of vesting the landed interest in each tything and borough, with a right to send representatives to their Wittena-Gemot, or Parliament.

Nor could the rage of conquest, and all the power of arms, abolish this first principle of English liberty and safety. William the first, at the time he conquered Britain, found it consistent with his interest and security, to preserve it inviolate. And when he thought it necessary to lessen the exorbitant power of the Saxon Earls, which endangered his safety, by dismembering the baronies from the counties, the Barons were vested with a right to represent their baronies, in the great national council. This was all the change which that great man ventured to make in the constitution; a change which made no essential difference, as to its freedom. For as every spot of land was before the conquest within some tything, so under this alteration every part of it was included, in some barony or borough, and all of them were represented in the legislative power, by the Barons, or Burgesses.

Upon this solid foundation continued the freedom of the English government, during the reigns of William Rufus, and Henry the first. In the civil war between Stephen and Maud and Henry the second, each party finding the power and influence of the Barons over their vassals too great, divided the conquered baronies into smaller *tenancies in chief*, and rewarded their friends with them. By this measure, and the like policy, which was afterwards pursued by King John, tenants in capite, or the lesser Barons, were so multiplied, that a very unequal representation of the landed interest arose. They held an equal share in the legislature, with the greater Barons; and being more numerous, and their interest in many respects different, they over-ruled, and often deprived the greater nobility of their rights. This grievance grew intolerable; and therefore, when

King John found himself obliged to do justice to the nation, and restore the antient principle of the constitution, two several clauses were inserted in Magna Charta. By the first "the Archbishops, Abbots, Earls and *great Barons* of the realm," were to be "summoned *singly*" by the King's writs; and by the second, "all others who held in chief," viz. the lesser Barons, or tenants in capite, were to be "summoned in general." By this clause the lesser barons were separated from the greater, and lost their hereditary right of representing their lands *singly*, or in person; but being summoned to parliament "in general," they held the right of electing some of their body to represent them in the house of commons; and of participating the supreme legislative authority, by their delegates, who were thence forward stiled Knights of the shire.

Thus this right to protection from the state, stood secured in every alteration of the constitution, by preserving to the landholders a share in the authority of the supreme head, who were to regulate that protection, and every other matter susceptible of human direction, until the reign of Henry VI. when our ancestors, conceiving that it could not be rendered too secure, nor founded on a base too broad, they obtained, by act of parliament, a right in every freeholder of forty shillings per annum, to vote for knights of the shire.

In confirmation of this right, I shall only add that King John, in the great charter I have before mentioned, granted for the restoration of the rights of the subject, engages "not to impose any taxes without summoning the archbishops, the bishops, the abbots, the earls, the greater barons, and the *tenants in capite*." And by the 17th of Edward III. another charter, granted on the like occasion, it is expressly declared, that "*whatever concerns the estate of the realm, and the people,* shall be treated of in parliament by the King, with the consent of the prelates, earls, barons, and commonality of the realm."

It would be endless to trace this truth through all the pages of the history of the English government. I have offered proofs sufficient to demonstrate that the Lords and Commons, who hold so large a share of the legislative authority, derive their *right from, and represent the lands* within the realm. I shall therefore only add, before I leave this point, That this power of legislation in the people, derived from the share they held in the lands, was originally, and yet is, of the essence of the English government; and ever was, and still continues to be, the only check upon the encroachments of power, the great security against oppression, and the main support of the freedom and liberty of the English subjects. And its excellence consists in affording, to every part of the realm, an opportunity of representing, by their delegates, at all times, their true circumstances, their wants, their necessities, and their danger, to the supreme authority of the nation, without a knowledge of which it is impossible to form just or adequate laws; and when represented, to consult, advise and decide upon such provisions, as are proposed for their relief, or safety; giving their negative to such as are mischievous or improper, and their assent to those which remove the mischief, or afford a remedy. Here we have a perfect idea of civil liberty, and free government, such as is enjoyed by the subject in Great-Britain.

But what are the circumstancees of the American British subjects? Is there a *part or spot of the lands in America,* or are the owners or proprietors thereof *in right of such lands,* represented in the British parliament; or do they in any other manner partake of the supreme power of the state? In this situation of the colonies, is not the British government as absolute and despotic over them, as any Monarch whatever, who singly holds the legislative authority? Are not the persons, lives and estates of the subjects in America at the disposal of an absolute power, without the least security for the enjoyment of their rights? Most certain it is, that this is a situation which people accustomed to liberty cannot sit easy under.

From the preceeding remarks it partly appears in what manner the American subjects have lost the enjoyment of this inestimable right, though not the right itself, viz. by their emigration to a part of the territory of the state, for which the constitution had not provided a representation. America not being known or thought of when the constitution was formed, no such provision was then made. But the right to a share in the supreme authority was confined to the territory at that time, intended to be governed by it. And at the time our ancestors left the mother country, it seems none was established. How this happened is not material to my subject—they came over, perhaps, without thinking of the importance of the right or their poverty, which rendered the obtaining of it in any form impracticable, prevented their claim of it. However, it is certain that it was passed over in silence, as well by the state, as the people who emigrated; but has been neither forfeited, surrendered, nor lost. And therefore it ought to be restored to them, in such manner as their circumstances will admit of, whenever it shall be decently and respectfully asked for. Justice to the Americans, and sound policy, in respect to both countries, manifestly require it.

The emigrants enjoyed in Britain the perfect rights of English subjects. They left their native country with the consent of the state, to encrease her commerce, to add to her wealth, and extend her dominions. All this they have effected with infinite labour and expence, and through innumerable difficulties and dangers. In the infant state of their societies, they were incapable of exercising this right of participating the legislative authority in any mode. The power of parliament was justifiable from necessity at that time over them; they stood in as much need of its protection, as children in an infant-state require the aid and protection of a parent, to save them from a foreign enemy, as well as from those injuries which might arise from their own indiscretions. But now they are arrived at a degree of opulence, and circumstances so respectable, as not only to be capable of enjoying this right, but from necessity, and for the security of both countries to require it.

The subjects of a free state, in every part of its dominions ought, in good policy, to enjoy the same fundamental rights and privileges. Every distinction between them must be offensive and odious, and cannot fail to create uneasiness and jealousies, which will ever weaken the government, and frequently terminate in insurrections; which, in every society, ought to be particularly guarded against. If the British state therefore means to retain the colonies in a due obedience on her government, it will be wisdom in her to restore to her American subjects, the enjoyment of the right of assenting to, and dissenting from, such bills as shall be proposed to regulate their conduct. Laws thus made will ever be obeyed; because by their assent, they become their own acts. It will place them in the same condition with their brethren in Britain, and remove all cause of complaint; or, if they should conceive any regulations inconvenient, or unjust, they will petition, not rebel. Without this it is easy to perceive that the union and harmony, which is peculiarly essential to a free society, whose members are resident in regions so very remote from each other, cannot long subsist.

The genius, temper, and circumstances of the Americans should be also duly attended to. No people in the world have higher notions of liberty. It would be impossible ever to eradicate them; should an attempt so unjust be ever made, Their late spirit and conduct fully prove this assertion, and will serve as a clue to that policy by which they ought to be governed. The distance of America from Britain, her vast extent of territory, her numerous ports and conveniencies of commerce, her various productions, her increasing numbers, and consequently her growing strength and power, when duly considered—all point out the policy of uniting the two countries together, upon principles of English liberty. Should this be omitted the colonies will infallibly throw off their connexion with the mother country. Their distance will encourage the attempt, their discontent will give them spirit, and their numbers wealth and power, at some future day, will enable them to effect it.

If it be the interest of the mother country, to be united with the colonies, it is still more Their interest that the union should take place. Their future safety and happiness depends on it. A little attention to their circumstances will prove it. Each colony, in the present constitution, is capable, by its own internal legislature, to regulate its own internal police, within its particular circle of territory. But here it is confined; thus far, and no farther, can its authority extend, one cannot travel into the bounds of the other, and there make, or execute, its regulations. They are, therefore, in respect to each other, so many perfect and independent societies; destitute of any political connection, or supreme authority, to compel them to act in concert for common safety. They are different in their forms of government, productions of soil, and views of commerce. They have different religions, tempers, and private interests. They, of course, entertain high prejudices against, and jealousies of, each other; all which must from the nature and reason of things always conspire to create such a diversity of interests, inclinations, judgements, and conduct, that it will ever be impossible for them to unite in any general measure whatever, either to avoid any general mischief, or to promote any general good. A retrospect to the conduct of the colonies, during the last war, will shew that this assertion is founded in fatal experience. It was owing to this disunited state of the colonies, and their conducting their policy upon these principles, that a small number of French subjects in Canada, acting on the reverse, were enabled to concert their plans with such superior wisdom, and to exert such a superior degree of strength, as to endanger the safety of all North America, which contained upwards of two millions of people, and obliged them to implore the assistance of the British government. In the application to the mother country for protection, this is fully acknowledged. "It now evidently appears," say the council and assembly of the Massachusets Bay, "That the French are advanced in the execution of a *plan, projected more than fifty years since,* for extending their possessions from the mouth of the Mississippi on the south, to Hudson's Bay on the north, for securing the vast body of Indians in that inland country, and for subjecting *this whole continent to the crown of France.*"[1] And from what cause did it happen that the English colonies, possessed of an hundred fold more wealth, and twenty times the number of people, could not oppose, with success, the force and schemes of a few? The same gentlemen tell us, The French have but one interest, and keep but one point in view: The English governments have different interests, are disunited: some of them have their frontiers covered by their neighbours; and not being immediately affected, seem unconcerned. The commissioners from the several colonies at Albany, assign the same cause. "The colonies," they inform the crown, being "in a divided, disunited state, there has never been any joint exertion of their force, or councils, to repel or defeat the measures of the French;" and "particular colonies are unable and unwilling to maintain the cause of the whole." "That it seems absolutely necessary, that speedy and effectual measures be taken to secure the colonies from the slavery they are threatened with." The prediction contained in these declarations turned out strictly true. As it was most just that the colonies should contribute towards their own protection, while the mother country was lavishing millions in their defence; requisitions were annually made of them. But what was the conduct of the colonies in this scene, so very interesting to them? It is enough for me here to assert, what was known to all at the time, and what there still remains abundant documents to prove——That altho' some of the colonies, which were in immediate danger, complied chearfully and in time; yet others, from various causes, complied too late to be of real service; and some gave nothing towards the general defence, even at times when the enemy was within their borders, and a considerable part of the colony was evacuated. What must have been the direful consequences of those omissions of duty in

[1] Message from the Council and House of Representatives of the Massachusets Bay, in 1754.

the colonies towards each other, had not the mother-country exerted her military abilities to save them? The danger, and all the horrors of French slavery, and popish superstition, which then threw us, at times, into the greatest despondency, are past, and we have forgot them! But let us not deceive ourselves; the same causes will ever produce the same effects. The ambition of France is still alive and active, her power indeed is asleep, but only to wake at some future day. America is daily growing a more alluring object of her ambition. Her fleets, and those of her natural ally, the King of Spain, are encreasing. The practice of conquering and dividing territories and kingdoms, is become fashionable in Europe. Under this prospect of things, what can America expect, while she denies the authority of the mother-state; and by that denial incurs a forfeiture of her protection, and refuses to be united with her upon such principles as will entitle her to it. She must in all probability soon become the slave of arbitrary power, of Popish bigotry and superstition.

But the miseries of a foreign yoke are not all the mischiefs which may attend her scheme of independency. Disputes will ever arise among the colonies. The seeds of controversy, respecting their several interests and boundaries, are already sown, and in full vegetation. Ambition and avarice are ever ready to exert their influence, whenever opportunity offers. America has many men of abilities and intrigue, who will at all times be ready to rise on the misfortunes and calamities of others. Disputes between Pennsylvania and Maryland began, and would have ended in a civil war, had not the authority of the state interposed. Similar disputes have subsisted between New-York and Connecticut; New-York and New-Jersey, and still subsist between New-York and New-Hampshire, Connecticut and Pennsylvania, and Pennsylvania and Virginia; all arising from the uncertainty of their boundaries, and right to the soil. In 1606 King James granted two charters, one to the Plymouth company, and the other to Sir Thomas Gates, and others; *including all the colonies.* The resumption of the first of these charters has been publickly avowed and attempted; and we have great reason to believe, that of the other is in contemplation. These, with many other causes, will afford plentiful sources of dispute between the several colonies; which can only be decided by the sword, there being no other power to appeal to. The northern colonies, inured to military discipline and hardships, will, in all probability, be the first to enter the list of military controversy; and, like the northern Saxons and Danes, carry devastation and havock over the southern; who, weak for want of discipline, and having a dangerous enemy within their own bowels, must, after suffering all the horrors of a civil war, yield to the superior force, and submit to the will of the conquerors.

We have now before us, all that we are to gain by this frantic attempt, to separate the colonies from Great-Britain. Should America fail in her military opposition, which she must infallibly do, they immediately become a conquered people, subject to such laws as the conquerors shall think proper to impose—All our rights and privileges forfeited, our loyalty justly distrusted, our ports secured by men of war, our capital cities burthened with British troops, and our wealth exhausted for their support. On the contrary, should we by any miraculous event succeed in this mad design, we must soon either become a prey to a foreign power; our laws, our manners and customs, our rights both civil and religious, and our inestimable religion itself, will be changed for the arbitrary customs, the slavery and bloody superstition of Rome: Or should we by any unforeseen accident, escape this deplorable situation, another awaits us, almost as shocking and distressing. Ambition and avarice will soon furnish the fewel, and blow up the flame of civil discord among ourselves. Some of these calamities must inevitably be the blessed consequences of this unnatural scheme.

It will now be asked, what then is to be done? Must we submit to parliamentary regulations, when we are not represented in that body? My answer is—That I am a friend to true liberty. I esteem it above all other temporal blessings, and *because* I esteem it, I disapprove of the independent measures of the congress; which, instead of tending to secure, or obtain it, lead to the destruction of *all liberty,* and the *most dangerous tyranny.* I do not differ from them in opinion, that America has grievances to complain of; but I differ from them in the mode of *obtaining redress.* I ever was convinced that Great-Britain was not so despicable in her power as to be hectored out of her rights by her subjects; or that she was so ignorant of the condition of the colonies, as to believe our pretensions to independency could be maintained. I foresaw what has now come to pass, that we must either submit to parliamentary authority, or to be a conquered people, or seek for redress in an *union* with the mother state. And my duty as a subject, my own interest, and the safety and happiness of my country, ever prevailed on me to prefer the last. Had this measure been adopted in the year 1766, in all probability, the rights of America would have been restored, and the most perfect harmony would have this day subsisted between the two countries. But unfortunately for America, such ground was at that time taken, as rendered it inconsistent with the honour and dignity of parliament to meet us.

Great pains have been taken by the American demagogues, to delude the unhappy people, whom they have doomed to be the dupes of their ambition, into a belief that no justice was to be obtained of his Majesty, and his houses of parliament; and that they had refused to hear our most reasonable petitions. Hence we have seen the best of Sovereigns treated with the grossest abuse and insult, the affections of his people alienated, and many of his faithful subjects, desponding of relief, taking up arms against his authority. It is high time that this fatal delusion should be exposed, and the good people of America disabused. It is true, that his Majesty and the two houses of parliament have treated petitions from the colonies with neglect; but what were those petitions? Did they rest on a denial of the essential rights of Parliament, or did they ask for the rights of the subject in America? A retrospect of all the petitions, ever presented to the throne on this subject, will shew that they conveyed to the royal ear, nothing but the language of independence. They disowned the power of the supreme legislature, to which, as subjects, they owe obedience, and denied a capacity in the colonies to be represented—and upon this ground they insisted on a repeal of the laws. Here they ended. *No prayer, nor the least intimation of a desire to be united with Britain upon a just restoration of their rights!* Such were the petitions of the colonies, which were treated with neglect by the supreme power of the nation. And the reasonable and sensible man will now, on reflection, determine, whether it becomes us to resent a conduct of this kind, in our superiors, or rather to look back with astonishment at our folly, in permitting ourselves to be led by designing men, into such acts of disrespect and insult. Let us bring the case home to ourselves. The relation between the sovereign authority and its members, bears a true resemblance to that between parent and child. Their rights and duties are similar. Should a child take umbrage at the conduct of a parent, tell him that he was not his father, nor would he consider himself, or act, as his child *on any terms;* ought the parent to listen to such undutiful language, or could he be justly censured for treating it with neglect, or even with contempt?

In order to prevail on the congress to desert their scheme of independence, and to pursue those measures for restoring the rights of America, which carried with them a prospect of success; a member of the congress, as I mentioned before, proposed a plan of union between the two countries, which would have restored to the colonies the full enjoyment of their rights. I have often conversed with him on the subject, and well understand his principles, and what passed on the occasion. He waited with patience to see whether any rational scheme of union would be adopted by the congress, determined to unite with them in any measure which might tend to a reconciliation between the two countries; but he waited in vain. And when he found them bewildered, perpetually changing their ground, taking up principles one day, and shifting them the next, he thought it his duty, however little the prospect of success, to speak his sentiments with firmness, and to endeavour to show them the true line of their duty. After proving the necessity of a supreme authority over every member of the state, tracing the rights of the colonies to their origin, and fixing them on the most solid principles; and thence shewing the necessity of an union with the mother state, for the recovery of them; he introduced the plan with the resolve which precedes it. But before he delivered it to be read, he declared, that he was sensible it was not perfect; that knowing the fundamental principles of every system must be first settled, he had, to avoid perplexity, contented himself with only laying down the great out-lines of the union; and should they be approved of, that he had several propositions of lesser consequence to make, in order to render the system more complete. The plan read, and warmly seconded by several gentlemen of the first abilities, after a long debate, was so far approved as to be thought worthy of further consideration, and referred under a rule for that purpose, by a majority of the colonies. Under this promising aspect of things, and an expectation that the rule would have been regarded, or at least that something rational would take place to reconcile our unhappy differences, the member proposing it was weakly led to sign the non-importation agreement, although he had uniformly opposed it; but in this he was disappointed. The measures of *independence and sedition,* were soon after preferred to those of *harmony and liberty;* and no arguments, however reasonable and just, could prevail on a majority of the colonies to desert them. The resolve, plan, and rule referring them to further consideration, so inconsistent with the measures now resolved on, were expunged from the minutes; with what view let America determine. And while the enemies to the gentleman who proposed them, are abusing him for offering and publishing to the world the most infamous falshood, in representing it as ministerial, and sent over to him by Lord N[ort]h; they have copies of it in their pockets, industriously concealing it from the world. With what view can this be, but that their malevolent aspersions may take the greater effect? In justice therefore to the character of this gentleman, and that America may see and judge for itself, they are here offered to its consideration.

Resolved,

That the Congress will apply to his Majesty for a redress of grievances under which his faithful subjects in America labour; and assure him, that the Colonies hold in abhorrence the idea of being considered independent communities on the British government, and most ardently desire the establishment of a Political Union, not only among themselves, but with the Mother State, upon those principles of safety and freedom which are essential in the constitution of all free governments, and particularly that of the British Legislature; and as the Colonies from their local circumstances, cannot be represented in the Parliament of Great Britain, they will humbly propose to his Majesty and his two Houses of Parliament, the following plan, under which the strength of the whole Empire may be drawn together on any emergency, the interest of both countries advanced, and the rights and liberties of America secured.

A PLAN OF A PROPOSED UNION BETWEEN GREAT-BRITAIN AND THE COLONIES.

That a British and American legislature, for regulating the Administration of the general affairs of America, be proposed and established in America, including all the said colonies;

within, and under which government, each colony shall retain its present constitution, and powers of regulating and governing its own internal police, in all cases whatever.

That the said government be administered by a President General, to be appointed by the King and a grand Council, to be chosen by the Representatives of the people of the several colonies, in their respective Assemblies, once in every three years.

That the several assemblies shall choose members for the grand Council in the following proportions, viz.

New-Hampshire,	Delaware Counties,
Massachusetts-Bay,	Maryland,
Rhode-Island,	Virginia,
Connecticut,	North-Carolina,
New-York,	South-Carolina,
New-Jersey,	and
Pennsylvania,	Georgia.

Who shall meet at the city of ——— for the first time, being called by the President-General, as soon as conveniently may be after his appointment.

That there shall be a new election of members for the Grand Council every three years; and on the death, removal or resignation of any member, his place shall be supplied by a new choice, at the next sitting of Assembly of the Colony he represented.

That the Grand Council shall meet once in every year, if they shall think it necessary, and oftner, if occasions shall require, at such time and place as they shall adjourn to, at the last preceding meeting, or as they shall be called to meet at, by the President-General, on any emergency.

That the grand Council shall have power to choose their Speaker, and shall hold and exercise all the like rights, liberties and privileges, as are held and exercised by and in the House of Commons of Great-Britain.

That the President-General shall hold his Office during the

pleasure of the King, and his assent shall be requisite to all acts of the Grand Council, and it shall be his office and duty to cause them to be carried into execution.

That the President-General, by and with the advice and consent of the Grand-Council, hold and exercise all the legislative rights, powers, and authorities, necessary for regulating and administering all the general police and affairs of the colonies, in which Great-Britain and the colonies, or any of them, the colonies in general, or more than one colony, are in any manner concerned, as well civil and criminal as commercial.

That the said President-General and Grand Council, be an inferior and distinct branch of the British legislature, united and incorporated with it, for the aforesaid general purposes; and that any of the said general regulations may originate and be formed and digested, either in the Parliament of Great-Britain, or in the said Grand Council, and being prepared, transmitted to the other for their approbation or dissent; and that the assent of both shall be requisite to the validity of all such general acts or statutes.

That in time of war, all bills for granting aids to the crown, prepared by the Grand Council, and approved by the President-General, shall be valid and passed into a law, without the assent of the British Parliament.

I shall not affirm that this plan is formed upon the most perfect principles of policy and government; but as it is an universally prevailing opinion, that the colonies cannot be represented in parliament, I know of none other which comes so near to them; and it is most evident, upon a due consideration of it, that the rights of America would have been fully restored, and her freedom effectually secured by it. For under it, no law can be binding on America, to which the people, by their representatives, have not previously given their consent: This is the essence of liberty, and what more would her people desire?

The author of this plan seems to have formed it on a comprehensive view, of the regulations necessary to the interest and safety of the colonies. These he has divided into two classes: the first contain all such as the colony legislatures have a right to make, under the several constitutions, and to which they are adequate; these to remain under their decisions; it being declared in the plan, that "each colony shall retain its present constitution and powers of regulating and governing its own internal police in all cases whatever." The others, which are to be the objects of the deliberations and decisions of the grand council, relate to the general interests and security of the colonies, and are absolutely necessary for those purposes; such laws for granting aids to the crown, and levying taxes in just and reasonable proportions in the colonies—for regulating a general paper currency, and the value of foreign coins, which ought in all good policy, to be established on funds equally solid, and ascertained at the same value: Laws for regulating and quartering troops, which may be necessary for their general protection; for settling disputes between the colonies, respecting their boundaries—with a variety of other matters that must naturally arise from the jarring interests of the colonies, which will continually encrease with the encrease of their wealth and commerce. And as to those, it must be owned, that the colony legislatures are not adequate; but that they must be made either by the parliament, or by some new establishment for those purposes. The authority of the first was objected to; and as to the second, or any other system of union, it being incompatible with the scheme of independence, it was not thought worthy of attention.

Objections were indeed made to this plan, which it may not be improper here to mention. It was said, "that the delegates did not come with authority to consent to a political union between the two countries." To which many arguments were opposed, to show that they had such authority or none;

and concluded with desiring, that if that was, in the opinion
of the members, the case, yet that the congress ought in justice to their country to digest and form one, and recommend
it to their respective assemblies; by whom it would be presented with more constitutional propriety than by any other
body of men. It was further said, "that the members of the
grand council would be corrupted, and betray the interest of
the colonies." To this it was answered—That if American virtue was not firm enough to maintain American liberty, it could
be supported by no wisdom or policy whatever; but suppose
the people to be in so corrupt a state; yet as the election of
the members was to be triennial, they might change them every
3 years, and the sums of money, necessary to bribe the new
members, would be too great to be supplied; That the most
sensible writers on the side of liberty agreed, if the parliament
of England was triennial, it would destroy the system of corruption. Besides, to avoid all risque of the contrary, they
might, by altering one word in the plan, make the election
duennial, or annual, which must certainly remove the objection. A third objection was, That it deprived the colony legislatures of a part of their rights. To which it was replied, that
a colony legislature is capable of passing laws to regulate its
internal police; but not adequate to any general regulation,
not even in the necessary one of taxation. That there is no
proposition more just, than that every colony, as a member
of the state, ought to be obliged to contribute towards the
defence of the whole, in proportion to the property and wealth
which each colony possesses. That this is a primary consideration in every society; and that no one colony had a constitutional power to obtain the amount and value of the property
of the others, by which to ascertain its proportion. Nor was
there any authority whatever, save the British Parliament, to
compel refractory colonies to do their reasonable duty, in this
or any other general measure: and that this plan was so far
from diminishing the rights of any colony legislature, that it

extended them; by giving to each a new jurisdiction, to decide upon regulations which relate to the general police of all the colonies.

Such was the plan laid before the congress, the objections against, and the arguments in favour of it. They are here laid before the public, to enable them to judge for themselves, whether, as a representation in parliament, is generally supposed to be impracticable, any thing more consistent with their safety could have been adopted.

Had this unhappy controversy been of the first impression in the English government, I should not be surprised to find the advocates of America so much at a loss for principles upon which to ask for, and obtain her rights. I confess I know not whether to attribute their strange conduct to a total ignorance of the merits, or to a design from the beginning to throw off all political connections with the British government. However this may be, precedents are not wanting upon which to reason, and to form a remedy. The principality of Wales, the Bishoprick of Durham, and the Palatinate of Chester, laboured under the like grievances; being bound by the laws of parliament for many years, without holding a share in the supreme authority. Great discontent arose from the slavish distinction between the subjects of the same state. The oppressed thought it their duty, as members of the state, to petition the parliament for a share in their authority. And such was the equity and justice of their claims, that they became thereupon vested with this important privilege. When Henry III conquered Calais, and settled it with English merchants, with intent to extend his dominions, and encrease the commerce of the nation; and it was held so incompatible with English liberty, that the authority of parliament should extend to members who did not partake of it, that they were incorporated with the English government, and shared in its legislature.

What then is to be done? Is it too late to recover from our madness, and to pursue the dictates of reason and duty? By no means. But it is high time we had changed our measures, and retreated from the dangers with which we are threatened. Let us, like men who love order and government, boldly oppose the illegal edicts of the congress, before it is too late, pull down the licentious tyranny they have established, dissolve their inferior committees, their instruments to trample on the sacred laws of your country, and your invaluable rights. This done, and peace and order restored within your several provinces; apply to your assemblies, who are your constitutional guardians, and can alone procure a redress of your grievances. Intreat them in a respectful and dutiful manner, to petition his Majesty and his two houses of parliament—and in their petitions to assure them,

That you are sensible of the necessity of a supreme legislature over every member of the state; that you acknowledge yourselves subjects of the British government; that you have, through innumerable difficulties and perils, settled and improved a wilderness, extended the territories, and greatly encreased the wealth and power of the nation; That by such settlement you have lost the enjoyment of, though not the right to, some of the first and most excellent of the privileges of Englishmen; That the English government is founded on freedom; That this freedom depends on its particular constitution, in which it is and ever was essential, that the landed interest, or the freeholders of every part of its territory, should participate in the supreme legislative authority, having a right to regulate their conduct, and a power over their lives, liberties and properties. That this privilege alone distinguishes British subjects from the slaves of the most despotic governments: That no *part of the lands in America,* nor the *proportion thereof in right of such lands,* enjoy their antient right of participating in the authority of parliament. And yet that laws have been made, by that authority, for levying taxes upon your property, for restraining and prohibiting your trade and commerce, for suppressing your manufactures, for regulating your internal police, and depriving you of many other rights, to which you are entitled as English subjects. That by such regulations you have been aggrieved and oppressed, and great discontent has arisen in the breasts of his Majesty's faithful American subjects, to the destruction of that harmony which ought to subsist between members of the same community, and great prejudice of the common wealth. That it is not for want of inclination, but capacity, arising from the disunited state of the colonies, that you have not discharged, with justice among yourselves, those duties which appertain to members of the state. And therefore pray, That you may not only be restored to this capacity, but to all the rights of Englishmen, upon such principles of liberty and policy, as shall best suit your local circumstances.

A petition of this kind, so reasonable and just, and so well founded and established on the principles of their own government, attended with such a plan of union as may be wisely digested by your several assemblies, there is no room to doubt, will be graciously received, and duly attended to by his Majesty and his two houses of parliament, and finally terminate in a full redress of your grievances, and a permanent system of union and harmony, upon principles of liberty and safety. But let me entreat you, not to trust these petitions to your agents alone; but follow the wise examples of the Grecian and Roman colonists, send over with them one or more delegates, to remove the present prejudices, to create friends, and to solicit your cause. The expence will be trifling, their utility may be great, the importance of your rights is infinite.

Thus I have, my dear countrymen, with the utmost candour and freedom, and the most benevolent regard for your true interest and happiness, laid before you the constitutional extent of parliamentary jurisdiction, and *deduced* your rights from the most solid foundation, and explained your duties. I have pointed out the mode which I am convinced, you ought to pursue for a restoration of those rights. I have showed you the folly of the scheme now in agitation for that purpose. My most sincere wish is, that you may avail yourselves of the information, and retreat from the danger and distress which threatens you, before it is too late. Permit me, before I conclude, to ask you a few serious questions. Do you mean to forfeit, by your rash and imprudent conduct, your right to the protection of the British state, and cut yourselves and your posterity off for ever from all the privileges of Englishmen? To relinquish your trade up the Mediterranean, in the British seas, and all the British ports? And suffer the produce of your soil, and the effects of your labour and industry to perish on your hands, for want of a market to dispose of them? Do you mean to desert all your present blessings, & retreat from superior force into a wilderness inhabited by wild beasts and savages, destitute of the necessaries of life, and incapable of obtaining them? Or do you mean to submit to the deplorable condition of a conquered people, subject to the oppression and tyranny of a military government, with British fleets directing that pittance of trade, which the conqueror may allow you to enjoy; and with British forces in all your capital cities, commanding your allegiance to the British state?

Do you wish to exchange the mild and equal rule of English customs and manners, and your inestimable religion, for the tyranny of a foreign yoke, and the bloody superstitions of popery? Or if you design to give up your present enjoyment of all the blessings of life, for the horrors and distress of a civil war, and the fatal consequences which must infallibly attend yourselves, and your latest posterity? Are you *still* resolved to surrender up your reason to the miserable sophistry and gargon of designing men, and to hazard all these direful misfortunes, rather than be united with your brethren and fellow subjects in Britain? If such be your dreadful resolutions, I, who have all that I hold dear and valuable among you, must content myself with sharing along with you the calamitous consequences of your frenzy, and the miserable fate of an American; with this only consolation, that I have honestly discharged my duty in warning you of your dangers; and endeavoured to pilot you into the haven of security and happiness.

F   I   N   I   S   .

· 16 ·

Common Sense

By Thomas Paine

The full title of the first edition, published on January 9, 1776, is: COMMON SENSE, *Addressed to the Inhabitants of America, On the following Interesting Subjects. I. Of the Origin and Design of Government in general, with concise Remarks on the English Constitution. II. Of Monarchy and Hereditary Succession. III. Thoughts on the present State of American Affairs. IV. Of the present Ability of America, with some miscellaneous Reflections.*

The pamphlet sold so fast that a new edition was run off on January 20, and a rival Philadelphia printer brought out an edition of his own a few days later. The pamphlet was soon translated into German, and within a short time printers all the way from Boston to Charleston were publishing the pamphlet and selling it in numbers undreamed of by even the most ambitious printers before 1776. The pamphlet soon arrived in Europe, and it was reprinted in England, Scotland, Holland, and France.

Men have been writing biographies of Paine ever since the

Third edition, Philadelphia, February 14, 1776. There are no essential variations in the first three editions published by Robert Bell between January 9 and February 14, 1776.

1790's. With the exception of that by Moncure D. Conway in 1892, they vary from bad to worthless. The most understanding and sensitive short account is Crane Brinton's sketch in the *Dictionary of American Biography*, XIV, 159–166. The best discussion of Paine's writings and a detailed bibliography may be found in Harry Hayden Clark, *Thomas Paine: Representative Selections, With Introduction, Bibliography, and Notes* (New York: American Book Company, 1944). A detailed bibliographical account of the publication of *Common Sense* can be found in Richard Gimbel, *Thomas Paine: A Bibliographical Check List of Common Sense With an Account of its Publication* (New Haven: Yale University Press, 1956).

In reprinting this pamphlet, I have altered the punctuation slightly for the sake of clarity.

INTRODUCTION.

Perhaps the Sentiments contained in the following pages, are not *yet* sufficiently fashionable to procure them general Favor; a long Habit of not thinking a Thing *wrong*, gives it a superficial appearance of being *right*, and raises at first a formidable outcry in defence of Custom. But the Tumult soon subsides. Time makes more Converts than Reason.

As a long and violent abuse of power is generally the means of calling the right of it in question (and in matters too which might never have been thought of, had not the sufferers been aggravated into the inquiry) and as the King of England hath undertaken in his *own Right* to suport the Parliament in what he calls *Theirs*, and as the good People of this Country are grievously oppressed by the Combination, they have an undoubted privilege to enquire into the Pretensions of both, and equally to reject the Usurpation of *either*.

In the following Sheets, the Author hath studiously avoided every thing which is personal among ourselves. Compliments as well as censure to individuals make no part thereof. The wise, and the worthy, need not the triumph of a Pamphlet; and those whose sentiments are injudicious, or unfriendly, will cease of themselves unless too much pains are bestowed upon their conversion.

The cause of America is in a great measure the cause of all mankind. Many circumstances have, and will arise, which are not local, but universal, and through which the principles of all lovers of mankind are affected, and in the event of which, their affections are interested. The laying a country desolate with fire and sword, declaring war against the natural rights of all mankind, and extirpating the defenders thereof from the face of the earth, is the concern of every man to whom nature hath given the power of feeling; of which class, regardless of party censure, is the   AUTHOR.

P. S. The Publication of this new Edition hath been delayed, with a view of taking notice (had it been necessary) of any attempt to refute the Doctrine of Independance. As no answer hath yet appeared, it is now presumed that none will, the time needful for getting such a Performance ready for the Public being considerably past.

Who the Author of this Production is, is wholly unnecessary to the Public, as the Object for Attention is the *Doctrine itself,* not the *Man.* Yet it may not be unnecessary to say, That he is unconnected with any party, and under no sort of Influence public or private, but the influence of reason and principle.

Philadelphia, February 14, 1776.

COMMON SENSE.

Of the Origin and Design of GOVERNMENT *in general, with concise Remarks on the* ENGLISH CONSTITUTION.

Some writers have so confounded society with government, as to leave little or no distinction between them; whereas, they are not only different, but have different origins. Society is produced by our wants, and government by our wickedness; the former promotes our happiness *possitively* by uniting our affections, the latter *negatively* by restraining our vices. The one encourages intercourse, the other creates distinctions. The first is a patron, the last a punisher.

Society in every state is a blessing, but Government even in its best state is but a necessary evil; in its worst state an intolerable one: for when we suffer, or are exposed to the same miseries *by a Government*, which we might expect in a country *without Government*, our calamity is heightened by reflecting that we furnish the means by which we suffer. Government like dress is the badge of lost innocence; the palaces of kings are built on the ruins of the bowers of paradise. For were the impulses of conscience clear, uniform, and irresistibly obeyed, man would need no other lawgiver; but that not being the case, he finds it necessary to surrender up a part of his property to furnish means for the protection of the rest; and this he is induced to do, by the same prudence which in every other case advises him, out of two evils to chuse the least. Wherefore, security being the true design and end of government, it unanswerably follows, that whatever form thereof appears most likely to ensure it to us, with the least expence and greatest benefit, is preferable to all others.

In order to gain a clear and just idea of the design and end of government, let us suppose a small number of persons settled in some sequestered part of the earth, unconnected with the rest; they will then represent the first peopling of any country; or of the world. In this state of natural liberty, society will be their first thought. A thousand motives will excite them thereto, the strength of one man is so unequal to his wants, and his mind so unfitted for perpetual solitude, that he is soon obliged to seek assistance and relief of another, who in his turn requires the same. Four or five united would be able to raise a tolerable dwelling in the midst of a wilderness, but one man might labour out the common period of life without accomplishing any thing; when he had felled his timber he could not remove it, nor erect it after it was removed; hunger in the mean time would urge him to quit his work, and every different want call him a different way. Disease, nay even misfortune would be death; for though neither might be mortal, yet either would disable him from living, and reduce him to a state in which he might rather be said to perish, than to die.

Thus necessity like a gravitating power would soon form our newly arrived emigrants into society, the reciprocal blessings of which, would supersede, and render the obligations of law and government unnecessary while they remained perfectly just to each other: but as nothing but Heaven is impregnable to vice, it will unavoidably happen that in proportion as they surmount the first difficulties of emigration, which bound them together in a common cause, they will begin to relax in their duty and attachment to each other: and this remissness will point out the necessity of establishing some form of government to supply the defect of moral virtue.

Some convenient tree will afford them a State House, under the branches of which the whole Colony may assemble to deliberate on public matters. It is more than probable that their first laws will have the title only of Regulations and be enforced by no other penalty than public disesteem. In this first parliament every man by natural right will have a seat.

But as the Colony encreases, the public concerns will encrease likewise, and the distance at which the members may be separated, will render it too inconvenient for all of them to meet on every occasion as at first, when their number was small, their habitations near, and the public concerns few and trifling. This will point out the convenience of their consenting to leave the legislative part to be managed by a select number chosen from the whole body, who are supposed to have the same concerns at stake which those have who appointed them, and who will act in the same manner as the whole body would act were they present. If the colony continues encreasing, it will become necessary to augment the number of the representatives, and that the interest of every part of the colony may be attended to, it will be found best to divide the whole into convenient parts, each part sending its proper number: and that the *elected* might never form to themselves an interest separate from the electors, prudence will point out the propriety of having elections often: because as the elected might by that means return and mix again with the general body of the electors in a few months, their fidelity to the public will be secured by the prudent reflection of not making a rod for themselves. And as this frequent interchange will establish a common interest with every part of the community, they will mutually and naturally support each other, and on this (not on the unmeaning name of king) depends the *strength of government and the happiness of the governed.*

Here then is the origin and rise of government; namely, a mode rendered necessary by the inability of moral virtue to govern the world; here too is the design and end of government, viz., Freedom and security. And however our eyes may be dazzled with show, or our ears deceived by sound; however prejudice may warp our wills, or interest darken our understanding, the simple voice of nature and of reason will say, 'tis right.

I draw my idea of the form in government from a principle in nature which no art can overturn, viz., That the more simple any thing is, the less liable it is to be disordered, and the easier repaired when disordered; and with this maxim in view I offer a few remarks on the so much boasted constitution of England. That it was noble for the dark and slavish times in which it was erected, is granted. When the world was overrun with tyranny the least remove therefrom was a glorious rescue. But that it is imperfect, subject to convulsions, and incapable of producing what it seems to promise is easily demonstrated.

Absolute governments, (tho' the disgrace of human nature) have this advantage with them, that they are simple; if the people suffer, they know the head from which their suffering springs; know likewise the remedy; and are not bewildered by a variety of causes and cures. But the constitution of England is so exceedingly complex, that the nation may suffer for years together without being able to discover in which part the fault lies, some will say in one and some in another, and every political physician will advise a different medicine.

I know it is difficult to get over local or long standing prejudices, yet if we will suffer ourselves to examine the component parts of the English constitution, we shall find them to be the base remains of two ancient tyrannies, compounded with some new Republican materials.

First.—The remains of Monarchical tyranny in the person of the King.

Secondly.—The remains of Aristocratical tyranny in the persons of the Peers.

Thirdly.—The new Republican materials, in the persons of the Commons, on whose virtue depends the freedom of England.

The two first by being hereditary are independant of the People; wherefore in a *constitutional sense* they contribute nothing towards the freedom of the State.

To say that the constitution of England is an *union* of three powers reciprocally *checking* each other, is farcical, either the words have no meaning, or they are flat contradictions.

To say that the Commons are a check upon the King, presupposes two things.

First.—That the King is not to be trusted without being looked after; or in other words, that a thirst for absolute power is the natural disease of Monarchy.

Secondly.—That the Commons by being appointed for that purpose, are either wiser or more worthy of confidence than the Crown.

But as the same constitution which gives the Commons a power to check the King by with-holding the supplies, gives afterwards the King a power to check the Commons by empowering him to reject their other bills; it again supposes that the King is wiser than those, whom it has already supposed to be wiser than him. A meer absurdity!

There is something exceedingly ridiculous in the composition of Monarchy; it first excludes a man from the means of information, yet empowers him to act in cases where the highest judgment is required. The state of a king shuts him from the World, yet the business of a king requires him to know it thoroughly; wherefore the different parts, by unnaturally opposing and destroying each other, prove the whole character to be absurd and useless.

Some writers have explained the English constitution thus: the King, say they, is one, the people another; the Peers are an house in behalf of the King; the commons in behalf of the people; but this hath all the distinctions of an house divided against itself; and though the expressions be pleasantly arranged, yet when examined they appear idle and ambiguous; and it will always happen, that the nicest construction that words are capable of, when applied to the description of something which either cannot exist, or is too incomprehensible to be within the compass of description, will be words of sound only, and tho' they may amuse the ear, they cannot inform the mind: for this explanation includes a previous question, viz., *how came the king by a power which the people are afraid to trust and always obliged to check?* Such a power could not be the gift of a wise people, neither can any power, *which needs checking,* be from God; yet the provision, which the constitution makes, supposes such a power to exist.

But the provision is unequal to the task; the means either cannot, or will not accomplish the end, and the whole affair is a *Felo de se;* for as the greater weight will always carry up the less, and as all the wheels of a machine are put in motion by one, it only remains to know which power in the constitution has the most weight, for that will govern: and tho' the others, or a part of them, may clog, or, as the phrase is, check the rapidity of its motion, yet so long as they cannot stop it, their endeavours will be ineffectual. The first moving power will at last have its way, and what it wants in speed is supplied by time.

That the crown is this overbearing part in the English constitution needs not be mentioned, and that it derives its whole consequence merely from being the giver of places and pensions is self evident, wherefore, tho' we have been wise enough to shut and lock a door against absolute Monarchy, we at the same time have been foolish enough to put the Crown in possession of the key.

The prejudice of Englishmen in favour of their own government by King, Lords and Commons, arises as much or more from national pride than reason. Individuals are undoubtedly safer in England than in some other countries: but the will of the King is as much the law of the land in Britain as in France, with this difference, that instead of proceeding directly from his mouth, it is handed to the people under the more formidable shape of an act of parliament. For the fate of Charles the First, hath only made kings more subtle—not more just.

Wherefore, laying aside all national pride and prejudice in favour of modes and forms, the plain truth is, that *it is wholly owing to the constitution of the people, and not to the constitution of the government* that the crown is not as oppressive in England as in Turkey.

An enquiry into the *constitutional errors* in the English form of government, is at this time highly necessary; for as we are never in a proper condition of doing justice to others, while we continue under the influence of some leading partiality, so neither are we capable of doing it to ourselves while we remain fettered by any obstinate prejudice. And as a man who is attached to a prostitute is unfitted to choose or judge of a wife, so any prepossession in favour of a rotten constitution of government will disable us from discerning a good one.

Of MONARCHY *and hereditary succession.*

Mankind being originally equals in the order of creation, the equality could only be destroyed by some subsequent circumstance: the distinctions of rich and poor may in a great measure be accounted for, and that without having recourse to the harsh ill-sounding names of oppression and avarice. Oppression is often the *consequence,* but seldom or never the *means* of riches: and tho' avarice will preserve a man from being necessitously poor, it generally makes him too timorous to be wealthy.

But there is another and greater distinction for which no truly natural or religious reason can be assigned, and that is, the distinction of men into KINGS and SUBJECTS. Male and female are the distinctions of nature, good and bad the distinctions of Heaven; but how a race of men came into the world so exalted above the rest, and distinguished like some new species, is worth enquiring into, and whether they are the means of happiness or of misery to mankind.

In the early ages of the world according to the scripture chronology there were no kings; the consequence of which was, there were no wars; it is the pride of kings which throws mankind into confusion. Holland without a king hath enjoyed more peace for this last century, than any of the monarchical governments in Europe. Antiquity favours the same remark; for the quiet and rural lives of the first Patriarchs hath a happy something in them, which vanishes away when we come to the history of Jewish royalty.

Government by kings was first introduced into the world by the Heathens, from whom the children of Israel copied the custom. It was the most prosperous invention the Devil ever set on foot for the promotion of idolatry. The Heathens paid divine honours to their deceased kings, and the Christian World hath improved on the plan by doing the same to their living ones. How impious is the title of sacred Majesty applied to a worm, who in the midst of his splendor is crumbling into dust.

As the exalting one man so greatly above the rest cannot be justified on the equal rights of nature, so neither can it be defended on the authority of scripture; for the will of the Almighty as declared by Gideon and the Prophet Samuel, expressly disapproves of government by Kings, all anti-monarchical parts of scripture have been very smoothly glossed over in monarchical governments, but they undoubtedly merit the attention of countries which have their governments yet to form. *"Render unto Cæsar the things which are Cæsar's"* is the scripture doctrine of courts, yet it is no support of monarchical government, for the Jews at that time were without a king, and in a state of vassalage to the Romans.

Near three thousand years passed away from the Mosaic account of the creation, till the Jews under a national delusion requested a king. Till then, their form of government, (except in extraordinary cases where the Almighty interposed) was a kind of Republic administered by a judge and the elders of the tribes. Kings they had none, and it was held sinful to acknowledge any Being under that title but the Lord of Hosts. And when a man seriously reflects on the idolatrous homage which is paid to the persons of kings, he need not wonder that the Almighty ever jealous of his honour, should disapprove of a form of government which so impiously invades the prerogative of Heaven.

Monarchy is ranked in scripture as one of the sins of the Jews, for which a curse in reserve is denounced against them. The history of that transaction is worth attending to.

The children of Israel being oppressed by the Midianites, Gideon marched against them with a small army, and victory thro' the Divine interposition decided in his favour. The Jews elate with success, and attributing it to the generalship of Gideon, proposed making him a king; saying, *Rule thou over us, thou and thy son and thy son's son.* Here was temptation in its fullest extent; not a kingdom only, but an hereditary one, but Gideon in the piety of his soul replied, *I will not rule over you, neither shall my son rule over you.* THE LORD SHALL RULE OVER YOU. Words need not be more explicit; Gideon doth not decline the honour, but denieth their right to give it; neither doth he compliment them with invented declarations of his thanks, but in the positive stile of a prophet charges them with disaffection to their proper Sovereign, the King of Heaven.

About one hundred and thirty years after this they fell again into the same error. The hankering which the Jews had for the idolatrous customs of the Heathens, is something exceedingly unaccountable; but so it was, that laying hold of the misconduct of Samuel's two sons who were entrusted with some secular concerns, they came in an abrupt and clamorous manner to Samuel, saying, *behold thou art old, and thy sons walk not in thy ways, now make us a king to judge us like all the other nations.* And here we cannot but observe that their motives were bad, viz. that they might be *like* unto other nations, *i. e.* the Heathens, whereas their true glory laid in being as much *unlike* them as possible. *But the thing displeased Samuel when they said, give us a King to judge us: and Samuel prayed unto the Lord, and the Lord said unto Samuel hearken unto the voice of the people in all that they say unto thee, for they have not rejected thee, but they have rejected me,* THAT I SHOULD NOT REIGN OVER THEM. *According to all the works which they have done since the day that I brought them up out of Egypt even unto this day, wherewith they have forsaken me and served other Gods: so do they also unto thee. Now therefore hearken unto their voice, howbeit, protest solemnly unto them and shew them the manner of the King that shall reign over them,* i.e. not of any particular King, but the general manner of the Kings of the Earth whom Israel was so eagerly copying after. And notwithstanding the great distance of time and difference of manners, the character is still in fashion. *And Samuel told all the words of the Lord unto the people, that asked of him a King. And he said this shall be the manner of the King that shall reign over you. He will take your sons and appoint them for himself for his chariots and to be his horse-men, and some shall run before his chariots.* (This description agrees with the present mode of impressing men) *and he will appoint him captains over thousands and captains over fifties, will set them to ear his ground and to reap his harvest, and to make his instruments of war, and instruments of his chariots. And he will take your daughters to be confectionaries, and to be cooks, and to be bakers.* (This describes the expence and luxury as well as the oppression of Kings) *and he will take your fields and your vineyards, and your olive yards, even the best of them, and give them to his servants. And he will take the tenth of your seed, and of your vineyards, and give them to his officers and to his servants.* (By which we see that bribery, corruption, and favouritism, are the standing vices of Kings.) *And he will take the tenth of your men servants, and your maid servants, and your goodliest young men and your asses, and put them to his work: and he will take the tenth of your sheep, and ye shall be his servants, and ye shall cry out in that day because of your king which ye shall have chosen,* AND THE LORD WILL NOT HEAR YOU IN THAT DAY. This accounts for the continuation of Monarchy; neither do the characters of the few good kings which have lived since, either sanctify the title, or blot out the sinfulness of the origin; the high encomium given of David takes no notice of him *officially as a King,* but only as a *Man* after God's own heart. *Nevertheless the people refused to obey the voice of Samuel, and they said nay but we will have a king over us, that we may be like all the nations, and that our king may judge us, and go out before us and fight our battles.* Samuel continued to reason with them but to no purpose, he set before them their ingratitude but all would not avail, and seeing them fully bent on their folly, he cried out, *I will call unto the Lord and he shall send thunder and rain* (which then was a punishment being in the time of wheat harvest) *that ye may perceive and see that your wickedness is great which ye have done in the sight of the Lord,* IN ASKING YOU A KING. *So Samuel called unto the Lord, and the Lord sent thunder and rain that day, and all the people greatly feared the Lord and Samuel. And all the people said unto Samuel, pray for thy servants unto the Lord thy God that we die not, for* WE HAVE ADDED UNTO OUR SINS THIS EVIL, TO ASK A KING. These portions of scripture are direct and positive. They admit of no equivocal construction. That the Almighty hath here entered his protest against monarchical government is true, or the scripture is false. And a man hath good reason to believe that there is as much of king-craft, as priest-craft, in withholding the scripture from the public in popish countries. For monarchy in every instance is the popery of government.

To the evil of monarchy we have added that of hereditary succession; and as the first is a degradation and lessening of ourselves, so the second, claimed as a matter of right, is an insult and an imposition on posterity. For all men being originally equals, no one by birth could have a right to set up his own family in perpetual preference to all others for ever, and tho' himself might deserve some decent degree of honours of his cotemporaries, yet his descendants might be far too unworthy to inherit them. One of the strongest natural proofs of the folly of hereditary right in kings, is, that nature disapproves it, otherwise she would not so frequently turn it into ridicule by giving mankind an *ass for a lion.*

Secondly, as no man at first could possess any other public honours than were bestowed upon him, so the givers of those honours could have no power to give away the right of posterity, and though they might say "we choose you for our head" they could not without manifest injustice to their children say "that your children and your children's children shall reign over ours forever." Because such an unwise, unjust, unnatural compact might (perhaps) in the next succession put them under the government of a rogue or a fool. Most wise men in their private sentiments have ever treated hereditary right with contempt; yet it is one of those evils, which when once established is not easily removed: many submit from fear, others from superstition, and the more powerful part shares with the king the plunder of the rest.

This is supposing the present race of kings in the world to have had an honorable origin: whereas it is more than probable, that could we take off the dark covering of antiquity and trace them to their first rise, that we should find the first of them nothing better than the principal ruffian of some restless gang, whose savage manners or pre-eminence in subtilty obtained him the title of chief among plunderers: and who by increasing in power and extending his depredations, overawed the quiet and defenceless to purchase their safety by frequent contributions. Yet his electors could have no idea of giving hereditary right to his descendants, because such a perpetual exclusion of themselves was incompatible with the free and unrestrained principles they professed to live by. Wherefore, hereditary succession in the early ages of monarchy could not take place as a matter of claim, but as something casual or complimental; but as few or no records were extant in those days, and traditionary history stuff'd with fables, it was very easy after the lapse of a few generations, to trump up some superstitious tale conveniently timed, Mahomet like, to cram hereditary right down the throats of the vulgar. Perhaps the disorders which threatened, or seemed to threaten, on the decease of a leader and the choice of a new one (for elections among ruffians could not be very orderly) induced many at first to favour hereditary pretensions; by which means it happened, as it hath happened since, that what at first was submitted to as a convenience was afterwards claimed as a right.

England since the conquest hath known some few good monarchs, but groaned beneath a much larger number of bad ones: yet no man in his senses can say that their claim under William the Conqueror is a very honourable one. A French Bastard landing with an armed Banditti and establishing himself king of England against the consent of the natives, is in plain terms a very paltry rascally original. It certainly hath no divinity in it. However it is needless to spend much time in exposing the folly of hereditary right, if there are any so weak as to believe it, let them promiscuously worship the Ass and Lion and welcome. I shall neither copy their humility nor disturb their devotion.

Yet I should be glad to ask how they suppose kings came at first? the question admits but of three answers, viz. either by lot, by election or by usurpation. If the first king was taken by lot, it establishes a precedent for the next, which excludes hereditary succession. Saul was by lot yet the succession was not hereditary, neither does it appear from that transaction there was any intention it ever should. If the first king of any country was by election that likewise establishes a precedent for the next; for to say that the right of all future generations is taken away by the act of the first electors in their choice not only of a king, but of a family of kings for ever, hath no parallel in or out of scripture but the doctrine of original sin, which supposes the free-will of all men lost in Adam: and from such comparison, and it will admit of no other, hereditary succession can derive no glory. For as in Adam all sinned, and as in the first electors all men obeyed; as in the one all mankind were subjected to Satan, and in the other to sovereignty; as our innocence was lost in the first, and our authority in the last; and as both disable us from reassuming some former state and privilege, it unanswerably follows that original sin and hereditary succession are parallels. Dishonorable rank! inglorious connection! yet the most subtle sophist cannot produce a juster simile.

As to usurpation no man will be so hardy as to defend it; and that William the conquer was an usurper is a fact not to be contradicted. The plain truth is, that the antiquity of English monarchy will not bear looking into.

But it is not so much the absurdity as the evil of hereditary succession which concerns mankind. Did it ensure a race of good and wise men it would have the seal of divine authority, but as it opens a door to the *foolish*, the *wicked*, and the *improper*, it hath in it the nature of oppression. Men who look upon themselves born to reign, and others to obey, soon grew insolent——selected from the rest of mankind their minds are easily poisoned by importance; and the world they act in differs so materially from the world at large, that they have but little opportunity of knowing its true interests, and when they succeed to the government are frequently the most ignorant and unfit of any throughout the dominions.

Another evil which attends hereditary succession, is, that the throne is subject to be possessed by a minor at any age; all which time the regency acting under the cover of a king have every opportunity and inducement to betray their trust. The same national misfortune happens when a king worn out with age and infirmity enters the last stage of human weakness. In both these cases the public becomes a prey to every miscreant who can tamper successfully with the follies either of age or infancy.

The most plausible plea which hath ever been offered in favor of hereditary succession, is, that it preserves a nation from civil wars; and were this true, it would be weighty; whereas it is the most barefaced falsity ever imposed upon mankind. The whole history of England disowns the fact. Thirty kings and two minors have reigned in that distracted kingdom since the conquest, in which time there has been (including the Revolution) no less than eight civil wars and nineteen Rebellions. Wherefore instead of making for peace, it makes against it, and destroys the very foundation it seems to stand on.

The contest for monarchy and succession between the houses

of York and Lancaster, laid England in a scene of blood for many years. Twelve pitched battles besides skirmishes and sieges were fought between Henry and Edward. Twice was Henry prisoner to Edward, who in his turn was prisoner to Henry. And so uncertain is the fate of war and the temper of a nation, when nothing but personal matters are the ground of a quarrel, that Henry was taken in triumph from a prison to a palace, and Edward obliged to fly from a palace to a foreign land: yet as sudden transitions of temper are seldom lasting. Henry in his turn was driven from the throne and Edward recalled to succeed him. The parliament always following the strongest side.

This contest began in the reign of Henry the sixth, and was not entirely extinguished 'till Henry the seventh, in whom the families were united. Including a period of 67 years. viz. from 1422 to 1489.

In short, monarchy and succession have laid (not this or that kingdom only) but the World in blood and ashes. 'Tis a form of government which the word of God bears testimony against, and blood will atend it.

If we enquire into the business of a King, we shall find that in some countries they have none; and after sauntering away their lives without pleasure to themselves or advantage to the nation, withdraw from the scene, and leave their successors to tread the same idle round. In absolute monarchies the whole weight of business civil and military lies on the King; the children of Israel in their request for a King urged this plea, "that he may judge us, and go out before us and fight our battles." But in countries where he is neither a Judge nor a General as in England, a man would be puzzled to know what is his business.

The nearer any government approaches to a Republic the less business there is for a King. It is somewhat difficult to find a proper name for the government of England. Sir William Meredith calls it a Republic; but in its present state it is unworthy of the name, because the corrupt influence of the Crown, by having all the places in its disposal, hath so effectually swallowed up the power, and eaten out the virtue of the House of Commons (the Republican part in the constitution) that the government of England is nearly as monarchical as that of France or Spain. Men fall out with names without understanding them. For 'tis the Republican and not the Monarchical part of the constitution of England which Englishmen glory in, viz. the liberty of choosing an House of Commons from out of their own body—and it is easy to see that when Republican virtue fails, slavery ensues. Why is the constitution of England sickly? but because monarchy hath poisoned the Republic; the Crown hath engrossed the Commons.

In England a King hath little more to do than to make war and give away places; which in plain terms, is to empoverish the nation and set it together by the ears. A pretty business indeed for a man to be allowed eight hundred thousand sterling a year for, and worshipped into the bargain! Of more worth is one honest man to society and in the sight of God, than all the crowned ruffians that ever lived.

THOUGHTS, *on the present* STATE *of* AMERICAN AFFAIRS.

In the following pages I offer nothing more than simple facts, plain arguments, and common sense: and have no other preliminaries to settle with the reader, than that he will divest himself of prejudice and prepossession, and suffer his reason and his feelings to determine for themselves: that he will put on, or rather that he will not put off the true character of a man, and generously enlarge his views beyond the present day.

Volumes have been written on the subject of the struggle between England and America. Men of all ranks have embarked in the controversy, from different motives, and with various designs; but all have been ineffectual, and the period of debate is closed. Arms as the last resource decide the contest; the appeal was the choice of the King, and the Continent has accepted the challenge.

It hath been reported of the late Mr. Pelham (who tho' an able minister was not without his faults) that on his being attacked in the House of Commons on the score that his measures were only of a temporary kind, replied, *"they will last my time."* Should a thought so fatal and unmanly possess the Colonies in the present contest, the name of ancestors will be remembered by future generations with detestation.

The Sun never shined on a cause of greater worth. 'Tis not the affair of a City, a County, a Province or a Kingdom; but of a Continent—of at least one eighth part of the habitable Globe. 'Tis not the concern of a day, a year, or an age; posterity are virtually involved in the contest, and will be more or less affected even to the end of time by the proceedings now. Now is the seed time of Continental union, faith, and honour. The least fracture now, will be like a name engraved with the point of a pin on the tender rind of a young oak; the wound will enlarge with the tree, and posterity read it in full grown characters.

By referring the matter from argument to arms, a new era for politics is struck—a new method of thinking hath arisen. All plans, proposals, &c. prior to the 19th of April, i. e. to the commencement of hostilities, are like the almanacks of the last year; which tho' proper then, are superceded and useless now. Whatever was advanced by the advocates on either side of the question then, terminated in one and the same point, viz. a union with Great-Britain; the only difference between the parties, was the method of effecting it; the one proposing force, the other friendship; but it hath so far happened that the first hath failed, and the second hath withdrawn her influence.

As much hath been said of the advantages of reconciliation, which like an agreeable dream, hath passed away and left us as we were, it is but right, that we should examine the contrary side of the argument, and enquire into some of the many material injuries which these Colonies sustain, and always will sustain, by being connected with and dependant on Great-Britain. To examine that connection and dependance on the principles of nature and common sense, to see what we have to trust to if separated, and what we are to expect if dependant.

I have heard it asserted by some, that as America hath flourished under her former connection with Great-Britain, that the same connection is necessary towards her future happiness and will always have the same effect—Nothing can be more fallacious than this kind of argument:—we may as well assert that because a child hath thrived upon milk, that it is never to have meat, or that the first twenty years of our lives is to become a precedent for the next twenty. But even this is admitting more than is true, for I answer, roundly, that America would have flourished as much, and probably much more had no European power taken any notice of her. The commerce by which she hath enriched herself are the necessaries of life, and will always have a market while eating is the custom of Europe.

But she has protected us say some. That she hath engrossed us is true, and defended the Continent at our expence as well as her own is admitted; and she would have defended Turkey from the same motive viz. the sake of trade and dominion.

Alas! we have been long led away by ancient prejudices and made large sacrifices to superstition. We have boasted the protection of Great Britain, without considering, that her motive was *interest* not *attachment;* that she did not protect us from *our enemies* on *our account,* but from *her enemies* on *her own account,* from those who had no quarrel with us on any *other account,* and who will always be our enemies on the *same account.* Let Britain wave her pretensions to the Continent, or the Continent throw off the dependance, and we should be at peace with France and Spain were they at war with Britain. The miseries of Hanover last war ought to warn us against connections.

It hath lately been asserted in parliament, that the Colonies have no relation to each other but through the Parent Country, *i. e.* that Pennsylvania and the Jerseys and so on for the rest, are sister Colonies by the way of England; this is certainly a very roundabout way of proving relationship, but it is the nearest and only true way of proving enmity (or enemyship, if I may so call it.) France and Spain never were, nor perhaps ever will be our enemies as *Americans* but as our being the *subjects of Great Britain.*

But Britain is the parent country say some. Then the more shame upon her conduct. Even brutes do not devour their young, nor savages make war upon their families; wherefore the assertion if true, turns to her reproach; but it happens not to be true, or only partly so, and the phrase, *parent* or *mother country*, hath been jesuitically adopted by the King and his parasites, with a low papistical design of gaining an unfair bias on the credulous weakness of our minds. Europe and not England is the parent country of America. This new World hath been the asylum for the persecuted lovers of civil and religious liberty from *every part* of Europe. Hither have they fled, not from the tender embraces of the mother, but from the cruelty of the monster; and it is so far true of England, that the same tyranny which drove the first emigrants from home, pursues their descendants still.

In this extensive quarter of the Globe, we forget the narrow limits of three hundred and sixty miles (the extent of England) and carry our friendship on a larger scale; we claim brotherhood with every European Christian, and triumph in the generosity of the sentiment.

It is pleasant to observe by what regular gradations we surmount the force of local prejudice as we enlarge our acquaintance with the World. A man born in any town in England divided into parishes, will naturally associate most with his fellow-parishioners (because their interests in many cases will be common) and distinguish him by the name of *neighbour:* if he meet him but a few miles from home, he drops the narrow idea of a street, and salutes him by the name of *townsman:* if he travel out of the county and meet him in any other, he forgets the minor divisions of street and town and calls him *countryman,* i. e. *county-man:* but if in their foreign excursions they should associate in France, or any other part of *Europe,* their local remembrance would be enlarged into that of *Englishmen.* And by a just parity of reasoning, all Europeans meeting in America, or any other quarter of the Globe, are *countrymen;* for England, Holland, Germany, or Sweden, when compared with the whole, stand in the same places on the larger scale, which the divisions of street, town, and county do on the smaller ones; Distinctions too limited for Continental minds. Not one third of the inhabitants, even of this Province, are of English descent. Wherefore, I reprobate the phrase of Parent or Mother Country applied to England only, as being false, selfish, narrow and ungenerous.

But admitting, that we were all of English descent, what does it amount to? Nothing. Britain being now an open enemy, extinguishes every other name and title: and to say that reconciliation is our duty, is truly farcical. The first king of England, of the present line (William the Conqueror) was a Frenchman, and half of the Peers of England are descendants from the same country; wherefore, by the same method of reasoning, England ought to be governed by France.

Much hath been said of the united strength of Britain and the Colonies, that in conjunction they might bid defiance to the world: But this is mere presumption, the fate of war is uncertain, neither do the expressions mean any thing, for this Continent would never suffer itself to be drained of inhabitants, to support the British Arms in either Asia, Africa, or Europe.

Besides, what have we to do with setting the world at defiance? Our plan is commerce, and that well attended to, will secure us the peace and friendship of all Europe, because it is the interest of all Europe to have America a free port. Her trade will always be a protection, and her barrenness of gold and silver will secure her from invaders.

I challenge the warmest advocate for reconciliation, to shew, a single advantage that this Continent can reap, by being connected with Great Britain. I repeat the challenge, not a single advantage is derived. Our corn will fetch its price in any market in Europe and our imported goods must be paid for buy them where we will.

But the injuries and disadvantages we sustain by that connection, are without number, and our duty to mankind at large, as well as to ourselves, instruct us to renounce the alliance: because any submission to, or dependance on Great Britain, tends directly to involve this Continent in European wars and quarrels. As Europe is our market for trade, we ought to form no political connection with any part of it. 'Tis the true interest of America, to steer clear of European contentions, which she never can do, while by her dependance on Britain, she is made the make-weight in the scale of British politics.

Europe is too thickly planted with Kingdoms, to be long at peace, and whenever a war breaks out between England and any foreign power, the trade of America goes to ruin, *because of her connection with Britain*. The next war may not turn out like the last, and should it not, the advocates for reconciliation now, will be wishing for separation then, because neutrality in that case, would be a safer convoy than a man of war. Every thing that is right or reasonable pleads for separation. The blood of the slain, the weeping voice of nature cries, 'TIS TIME TO PART. Even the distance at which the Almighty hath placed England and America, is a strong and natural proof, that the authority of the one over the other, was never the design of Heaven. The time likewise at which the Continent was discovered, adds weight to the argument, and the manner in which it was peopled encreases the force of it. The Reformation was preceded by the discovery of America as if the Almighty graciously meant to open a sanctuary to the persecuted in future years, when home should afford neither friendship nor safety.

The authority of Great Britain over this Continent is a form of Government which sooner or later must have an end: And a serious mind can draw no true pleasure by looking forward, under the painful and positive conviction, that what he calls "the present constitution," is merely temporary. As parents, we can have no joy, knowing that this government is not sufficiently lasting to ensure any thing which we may bequeath to posterity: And by a plain method of argument, as we are running the next generation into debt, we ought to do the work of it, otherwise we use them meanly and pitifully. In order to discover the line of our duty rightly, we should take our children in our hand, and fix our station a few years farther into life; that eminence will present a prospect, which a few present fears and prejudices conceal from our sight.

Though I would carefully avoid giving unnecessary offence, yet I am inclined to believe, that all those who espouse the doctrine of reconciliation, may be included within the following descriptions. Interested men who are not to be trusted, weak men who cannot see, prejudiced men who will not see, and a certain set of moderate men who think better of the European world than it deserves; and this last class, by an ill-judged deliberation, will be the cause of more calamities to this Continent, than all the other three.

It is the good fortune of many to live distant from the scene of present sorrow; the evil is not sufficiently brought to their doors to make them feel the precariousness with which all American property is possessed. But let our imaginations transport us for a few moments to Boston; that seat of wretchedness will teach us wisdom, and instruct us for ever to renounce a power in whom we can have no trust. The inhabitants of that unfortunate city who but a few months ago were in ease and affluence, have now no other alternative than to stay and starve, or turn out to beg. Endangered by the fire of their friends if they continue within the city, and plundered by government if they leave it. In their present condition they are prisoners without the hope of redemption, and in a general attack for their relief, they would be exposed to the fury of both armies.

Men of passive tempers look somewhat lightly over the offences of Britain, and still hoping for the best, are apt to call out: *Come, come, we shall be friends again for all this.* But examine the passions and feelings of mankind: bring the doctrine of reconciliation to the touchstone of nature, and then tell me, whether you can hereafter love, honour, and faithfully serve the power that hath carried fire and sword into your land? If you cannot do all these, then are you only deceiving yourselves, and by your delay bringing ruin upon posterity. Your future connection with Britain whom you can neither love nor honour, will be forced and unnatural, and being formed only on the plan of present convenience, will in a little time, fall into a relapse more wretched than the first. But if you say, you can still pass the violations over, then I ask, hath your house been burnt? Hath your property been destroyed before your face? Are your wife and children destitute of a bed to lie on, or bread to live on? Have you lost a parent or a child by their hands, and yourself the ruined and wretched survivor? If you have not, then are you not a judge of those who have. But if you have and still can shake hands with the murderers, then are you unworthy the name of husband, father, friend, or lover, and whatever may be your rank or title in life, you have the heart of a coward, and the spirit of a sycophant.

This is not inflaming or exaggerating matters, but trying them by those feelings and affections which nature justifies, and without which, we should be incapable of discharging the social duties of life, or enjoying the felicities of it. I mean not to exhibit horror for the purpose of provoking revenge, but to awaken us from fatal and unmanly slumbers, that we may pursue determinately some fixed object. 'Tis not in the power of England or of Europe to conquer America, if she doth not conquer herself by delay and timidity. The present winter is worth an age if rightly employed, but if lost or neglected, the whole Continent will partake of the misfortune; and there is no punishment which that man doth not deserve, be he who, or what, or where he will, that may be the means of sacrificing a season so precious and useful.

'Tis repugnant to reason, to the universal order of things; to all examples from former ages, to suppose, that this Continent can long remain subject to any external power. The most sanguine in Britain doth not think so. The utmost stretch of human wisdom cannot at this time compass a plan, short of separation, which can promise the Continent even a year's security. Reconciliation is *now* a fallacious dream. Nature hath deserted the connection, and art cannot supply her place. For as Milton wisely expresses "never can true reconcilement grow where wounds of deadly hate have pierced so deep."

Every quiet method for peace hath been ineffectual. Our prayers have been rejected with disdain; and hath tended to convince us that nothing flatters vanity or confirms obstinacy in Kings more than repeated petitioning—and nothing hath contributed more, than that very measure, to make the Kings of Europe absolute. Witness Denmark and Sweden. Wherfore, since nothing but blows will do, for God's sake let us come to a final separation, and not leave the next generation to be cutting throats under the violated unmeaning names of parent and child.

To say they will never attempt it again is idle and visionary, we thought so at the repeal of the stamp-act, yet a year or two undeceived us; as well may we suppose that nations which have been once defeated will never renew the quarrel.

As to government matters 'tis not in the power of Britain to do this Continent justice: the business of it will soon be too weighty and intricate to be managed with any tolerable degree of convenience, by a power so distant from us, and so very ignorant of us; for if they cannot conquer us, they cannot govern us. To be always running three or four thousand miles with a tale or a petition, waiting four or five months for an answer, which when obtained requires five or six more to explain it in, will in a few years be looked upon as folly and childishness—There was a time when it was proper, and there is a proper time for it to cease.

Small islands not capable of protecting themselves are the proper objects for government to take under their care: but there is something very absurd, in supposing a Continent to be perpetually governed by an island. In no instance hath nature made the satellite larger than its primary planet, and as England and America with respect to each other reverse the common order of nature, it is evident they belong to different systems. England to Europe: America to itself.

I am not induced by motives of pride, party or resentment to espouse the doctrine of separation and independance; I am clearly, positively, and conscientiously persuaded that 'tis the true interest of this Continent to be so; that every thing short of that is mere patchwork, that it can afford no lasting felicity,— that it is leaving the sword to our children, and shrinking back at a time, when a little more, a little farther, would have rendered this Continent the glory of the earth.

As Britain hath not manifested the least inclination towards a compromise, we may be assured that no terms can be obtained worthy the acceptance of the Continent, or any ways equal to the expence of blood and treasure we have been already put to.

The object contended for, ought always to bear some just proportion to the expence. The removal of North, or the whole detestable junto, is a matter unworthy the millions we have expended. A temporary stoppage of trade was an inconvenience, which would have sufficiently ballanced the repeal of all the acts complained off, had such repeals been obtained; but if the whole Continent must take up arms, if every man must be a soldier, 'tis scarcely worth our while to fight against a contemptible ministry only. Dearly, dearly, do we pay for the repeal of the acts, if that is all we fight for; for in a just estimation, 'tis as great a folly to pay a Bunker-hill price for law as for land. As I have always considered the independancy of this Continent, as an event which sooner or later must arrive, so from the late rapid progress of the Continent to maturity, the event could not be far off. Wherefore on the breaking out of hostilities, it was not worth the while to have disputed a matter, which time would have finally redressed, unless we meant to be in earnest; otherwise it is like wasting an estate on a suit at law, to regulate the trespasses of a tenant, whose lease is just expiring. No man was a warmer wisher for reconciliation than myself, before the fatal 19th of April 1775, but the moment the event of that day was made known, I rejected the hardened, sullen tempered Pharoah of England for ever; and disdain the wretch, that with the pretended title of FATHER OF HIS PEOPLE can unfeelingly hear of their slaughter, and composedly sleep with their blood upon his soul.

But admitting that matters were now made up, what would be the event? I answer, the ruin of the Continent. And that for several reasons.

First. The powers of governing still remaining in the hands of the King, he will have a negative over the whole legislation of this Continent: and as he hath shewn himself such an inveterate enemy to liberty, and discovered such a thirst for arbitrary power; is he, or is he not, a proper man to say to these Colonies, *You shall make no laws but what I please.* And is there any inhabitant in America so ignorant, as not to know, that according to what is called the *present constitution,* that this Continent can make no laws but what the king gives leave to; and is there any man so unwise, as not to see, that (considering what has happened) he will suffer no laws to be made here, but such as suit his purpose. We may be as effectually enslaved by the want of laws in America, as by submitting to laws made for us in England. After matters are made up (as it is called) can there be any doubt, but the whole power of the crown will be exerted to keep this Continent as low and humble as possible? instead of going forward, we shall go backward, or be perpetually quarrelling or ridiculously petioning.—We are already greater than the King wishes us to be, and will he not hereafter endeavour to make us less. To bring the matter to one point, is the power who is jealous of our prosperity, a proper power to govern us? Whoever says *no* to this question is an *Independant,* for independency means no more than whether we shall make our own laws, or, whether the King, the greatest enemy this Continent hath, or can have, shall tell us, *there shall be no laws but such as I like.*

But the King you will say, has a negative in England; the people there can make no laws without his consent. In point of right and good order, there is something very ridiculous that a youth of twenty-one (which hath often happened) shall say to several millions of people older and wiser than himself, "I forbid this or that act of your's to be law." But in this place I decline this sort of reply, though I will never cease to expose the absurdity of it, and only answer that England being the King's residence, and America not so, makes quite another case. The King's negative here is ten times more dangerous and fatal than it can be in England, for there he will scarcely refuse his consent to a bill for putting England into as strong a state of defence as possible, and in America he would never suffer such a bill to be passed.

America is only a secondary object in the system of British politics. England consults the good of this country, no farther than it answers her own purpose. Wherefore her own interest leads her to suppress the growth of ours in every case which doth not promote her advantage, or in the least interferes with it. A pretty state we should soon be in, under such a second hand government, considering what has happened! Men do not change from enemies to friends by the alteration of a name: And in order to shew that reconciliation now is a dangerous doctrine, I affirm, *that it would be policy in the King, at this time, to repeal the acts for the sake of reinstating himself in the government of the provinces;* In order that HE MAY ACCOMPLISH BY CRAFT AND SUBTILTY, IN THE LONG RUN, WHAT HE CANNOT DO BY FORCE AND VIOLENCE IN THE SHORT ONE. Reconciliation and ruin are nearly related.

Secondly—That as even the best terms which we can expect to obtain, can amount to no more than a temporary expedient, or a kind of government by guardianship, which can last no longer than till the Colonies come of age, so the general face and state of things in the interim will be unsettled and unpromising. Emigrants of property will not choose to come to a country whose form of government hangs but by a thread, and who is every day tottering on the brink of commotion and disturbance. And numbers of the present inhabitants would lay hold of the interval to dispose of their effects, and quit the Continent.

But the most powerful of all arguments is, that nothing but independance i.e. a Continental form of government, can keep the peace of the Continent and preserve it inviolate from civil wars. I dread the event of a reconciliation with Britain now, as it is more than probable, that it will be followed by a revolt some where or other, the consequences of which may be far more fatal than all the malice of Britain.

Thousands are already ruined by British barbarity; (thousands more will probably suffer the same fate.) Those men have other feelings than us who have nothing suffered. All they now possess is liberty, what they before enjoyed is sacrificed to its service, and having nothing more to lose, they disdain submission. Besides, the general temper of the Colonies towards a British government will be like that of a youth, who is nearly out of his time; they will care very little about her: And a government which cannot preserve the peace, is no government at all, and in that case we pay our money for nothing; and pray what is it that Britain can do, whose power will be wholly on paper, should a civil tumult break out the very day after reconciliation? I have heard some men say, many of whom I believe spoke without thinking, that they dreaded an inde-pendance, fearing that it would produce civil wars. It is but seldom that our first thoughts are truly correct, and that is the case here; for there are ten times more to dread from a patched up connection, than from independance. I make the sufferers case my own, and I protest, that were I driven from house and home, my property destroyed, and my circumstances ruined, that as a man sensible of injuries, I could never relish the doctrine of reconciliation, or consider myself bound thereby.

The Colonies hath manifested such a spirit of good order and obedience to Continental government, as is sufficient to make every reasonable person easy and happy on that head. No man can assign the least pretence for his fears, on any other grounds, than such as are truly childish and ridiculous, viz. that one colony will be striving for superiority over another.

Where there are no distinctions, there can be no superiority; perfect equality affords no temptation. The Republics of Europe are all, (and we may say always) in peace. Holland and Swisserland are without wars, foreign or domestic. Monarchical governments, it is true, are never long at rest; the crown itself is a temptation to enterprising ruffians at home; and that degree of pride and insolence ever attendant on regal authority, swells into a rupture with foreign powers in instances, where a repub-lican government by being formed on more natural principles, would negociate the mistake.

If there is any true cause of fear respecting independance, it is because no plan is yet laid down. Men do not see their way out—Wherefore, as an opening into that business I offer the following hints; at the same time modestly affirming, that I have no other opinion of them myself, than that they may be

the means of giving rise to something better. Could the strag-
gling thoughts of individuals be collected, they would frequently form materials for wise and able men to improve into
useful matter.

Let the assemblies be annual with a president only. The representation more equal, their business wholly domestic, and
subject to the authority of a Continental Congress.

Let each Colony be divided into six, eight or ten convenient
districts, each district to send a proper number of Delegates to
Congress, so that each Colony send at least thirty. The whole
number in Congress will be at least 390. Each Congress to
sit ———— and to choose a President by the following method.
When the Delegates are met, let a Colony be taken from the
whole thirteen Colonies by lot, after which let the whole Congress choose (by ballot) a president from out of the Delegates
of that Province. In the next Congress let a Colony be taken by
lot from twelve only, omitting that Colony from which the
president was taken in the former Congress, and so proceeding
on till the whole thirteen shall have had their proper rotation.
And in order that nothing may pass into a law but what is
satisfactorily just, not less than three fifths of the Congress to be
called a majority. He that will promote discord under a government so equally formed as this, would have joined Lucifer in
his revolt.

But as there is a peculiar delicacy from whom, or in what
manner this business must first arise, and as it seems most
agreeable and consistent, that it should come from some inter-
mediate body between the governed and the governors, that is,
between the Congress and the People. Let a Continental Conference be held in the following manner, and for the following
purpose.

A Committee of twenty six members of Congress, viz., Two
for each Colony. Two Members from each House of Assembly,
or Provincial Convention; and five Representatives of the people at large, to be chosen in the capital city or town of each

Province, for, and in behalf of the whole Province, by as many qualified voters as shall think proper to attend from all parts of the Province for that purpose: or if more convenient, the Representatives may be chosen in two or three of the most populous parts thereof. In this conference thus assembled, will be united the two grand principles of business, *knowledge* and *power*. The Members of Congress, Assemblies, or Conventions, by having had experience in national concerns, will be able and useful counsellors, and the whole, by being impowered by the people, will have a truly legal authority.

The conferring members being met, let their business be to frame a Continental Charter, or Charter of the United Colonies; (answering, to what is called the Magna Charta of England) fixing the number and manner of choosing Members of Congress, Members of Assembly, with their date of sitting, and drawing the line of business and jurisdiction between them: Always remembering, that our strength is Continental not Provincial. Securing freedom and property to all men, and above all things, the free exercise of religion, according to the dictates of conscience; with such other matters as is necessary for a charter to contain. Immediately after which, the said conference to dissolve, and the bodies which shall be chosen conformable to the said charter, to be the Legislators and Governors of this Continent, for the time being: Whose peace and happiness, may GOD preserve. AMEN.

Should any body of men be hereafter delegated for this or some similar purpose, I offer them the following extracts from that wise observer on Governments DRAGONETTI. "The Science" says he

of the Politician consists in fixing the true point of happiness and freedom. Those men would deserve the gratitude of ages, who should discover a mode of government that contained the greatest sum of individual happiness, with the least national expence.

DRAGONETTI on Virtues and Rewards.

But where say some is the King of America? I'll tell you friend, he reigns above; and doth not make havoc of mankind like the Royal Brute of Great Britain. Yet that we may not appear to be defective even in earthly honours, let a day be solemnly set a part for proclaiming the Charter; let it be brought forth placed on the Divine Law, the Word of God; let a crown be placed thereon, by which the world may know, that so far as we approve of monarchy, that in America THE LAW IS KING. For as in absolute governments the King is law, so in free countries the law ought to be king; and there ought to be no other. But lest any ill use should afterwards arise, let the Crown at the conclusion of the ceremony be demolished, and scattered among the people whose right it is.

A government of our own is our natural right: and when a man seriously reflects on the precariousness of human affairs, he will become convinced, that it is infinitely wiser and safer, to form a constitution of our own, in a cool deliberate manner, while we have it in our power, than to trust such an interesting event to time and chance. If we omit it now, some [1]Massanello may hereafter arise, who laying hold of popular disquietudes, may collect together the desperate and the discontented, and by assuming to themselves the powers of government, may sweep away the liberties of the Continent like a deluge. Should the government of America return again into the hands of Britain, the tottering situation of things, will be a temptation for some desperate adventurer to try his fortune; and in such a case, what relief can Britain give? Ere she could hear the news, the fatal business might be done; and ourselves suffering like the wretched Britons under the oppression of the Conqueror. Ye that oppose independance now, ye know not what ye do: ye

---

[1] Thomas Annello, otherwise Massanello, a fisherman of Naples, who, after spiriting up his countrymen in the public market place, against the oppression of the Spaniards, to whom the place was then subject, prompted them to revolt, and in the space of a day became King.

are opening a door to eternal tyranny, by keeping vacant the seat of government. There are thousands, and tens of thousands, who would think it glorious to expel from the Continent, that barbarous and hellish power, which have stirred up the Indians and the Negroes to destroy us, the cruelty hath a double guilt, it is dealing brutally by us, and treacherously by them.

To talk of friendship with those in whom our reason forbids us to have faith, and our affections wounded thro' a thousand pores instruct us to detest, is madness and folly. Every day wears out the little remains of kindred between us and them, and can there be any reason to hope, that as the relationship expires, the affection will encrease, or that we shall agree better, when we have ten times more and greater concerns to quarrel over than ever?

Ye that tell us of harmony and reconciliation, can ye restore to us the time that is past? can ye give to prostitution its former innocence? neither can ye reconcile Britain and America. The last cord now is broken, the people of England are presenting addresses against us. There are injuries which nature cannot forgive; she would cease to be nature if she did. As well can the lover forgive the ravisher of his mistress, as the Continent forgive the murders of Britain. The Almighty hath implanted in us these unextinguishable feelings for good and wise purposes. They are the Guardians of his Image in our hearts. They distinguish us from the herd of common animals. The social compact would dissolve, and justice be extirpated from the earth, or have only a casual existence were we callous to the touches of affection. The robber and the murderer would often escape unpunished, did not the injuries which our tempers sustain, provoke us into justice.

O ye that love mankind! Ye that dare oppose not only the tyranny but the tyrant, stand forth! Every spot of the old world is over-run with oppression. Freedom hath been hunted round the Globe. Asia and Africa have long expelled her. Europe regards her like a stranger, and England hath given her warning to depart. O! receive the fugitive, and prepare in time an asylum for mankind.

Of the Present Ability of America, with some miscellaneous reflections.

I have never met a man, either in England or America, who hath not confessed his opinion, that a separation between the countries, would take place one time or other: And there is no instance, in which we have shewn less judgment, than in endeavouring to describe what we call, the ripeness or fitness of the Continent for independance.

As all men allow the measure, and vary only in their opinion of the time, let us in order to remove mistakes, take a general survey of things, and endeavour if possible, to find out the *very* time. But I need not go far, the enquiry ceases at once, for, the *time hath found us.* The general concurrence, the glorious union of all things, prove the fact.

'Tis not in numbers but in unity that our great strength lies: yet our present numbers are sufficient to repel the force of all the world. The Continent hath at this time the largest disciplined army of any power under Heaven: and is just arrived at that pitch of strength, in which no single Colony is able to support itself, and the whole, when united, is able to do any thing. Our land force is more than sufficient, and as to Naval affairs, we cannot be insensible that Britain would never suffer an American man of war to be built, while the Continent remained in her hands. Wherefore, we should be no forwarder an hundred years hence, in that branch than we are now; but the truth is we should be less so, because the timber of the Country is every day diminishing.

Were the Continent crouded with inhabitants, her sufferings under the present circumstances would be intolerable. The more sea port Towns we had, the more should we have both to defend and to lose. Our present numbers are so happily proportioned to our wants, that no man need be idle. The diminution of trade affords an army, and the necessities of an army creates a new trade.

Debts we have none and whatever we may contract on this account will serve as a glorious memento of our virtue. Can we but leave posterity with a settled form of government, an independant constitution of it's own the purchase at any price will be cheap. But to expend millions for the sake of getting a few vile acts repealed, and routing the present ministry only, is unworthy the charge, and is using posterity with the utmost cruelty; because it is leaving them the great work to do and a debt upon their backs from which they derive no advantage. Such a thought is unworthy a man of honour, and is the true characteristic of a narrow heart and a pidling politician.

The debt we may contract doth not deserve our regard if the work be but accomplished. No nation ought to be without a debt. A national debt is a national bond: and when it bears no interest is in no case a grievance. Britain is oppressed with a debt of upwards of one hundred and forty millions sterling, for which she pays upwards of four millions interest. And as a compensation for her debt, she has a large navy; America is without debt, and without a navy; but for the twentieth part of the English national debt, could have a navy as large again. The navy of England is not worth at this time more than three millions and an half sterling.

No country on the globe is so happily situated, or so internally capable of raising a fleet as America. Tar, timber, iron, and cordage are her natural produce. We need go abroad for nothing. Whereas the Dutch, who make large profits by hiring out their ships of war to the Spaniards and Portuguese, are obliged to import most of the materials they use. We ought to view the building a fleet as an article of commerce, it being the natural manufactory of this country. 'Tis the best money we can lay out. A navy when finished is worth more than it cost: And is that nice point in national policy, in which commerce and protection are united. Let us build; if we want them not, we can sell; and by that means replace our paper currency with ready gold and silver.

In point of manning a fleet, people in general run into great errors; it is not necessary that one fourth part should be sailors. The Terrible Privateer, Capt. Death, stood the hottest engagement of any ship last war, yet had not twenty sailors on board, though her complement of men was upwards of two hundred. A few able and social sailors will soon instruct a sufficient number of active landmen in the common work of a ship. Wherefore we never can be more capable to begin on maritime matters than now, while our timber is standing, our fisheries blocked up, and our sailors and shipwrights out of employ. Men of war, of seventy and eighty guns were built forty years ago in New-England, and why not the same now? Ship building is America's greatest pride, and in which, she will in time excel the whole world. The great empires of the east are mostly inland, and consequently excluded from the possibility of rivalling her. Africa is in a state of barbarism; and no power in Europe, hath either such an extent of coast, or such an internal supply of materials. Where nature hath given the one, she has with-held the other; to America only hath she been liberal of both. The vast empire of Russia is almost shut out from the sea; wherefore her boundless forrests, her tar, iron, and cordage are only articles of commerce.

In point of safety, ought we to be without a fleet? We are not the little people now, which we were sixty years ago, at that time we might have trusted our property in the streets, or fields rather, and slept securely without locks or bolts to our doors and windows. The case now is altered, and our methods of defence, ought to improve with our encrease of property. A common pirate, twelve months ago, might have come up the Delaware, and laid the city of Philadelphia under instant contribution for what sum he pleased; and the same might have happened to other places. Nay, any daring fellow in a brig of

14 or 16 guns might have robbed the whole Continent, and carried off half a million of money. These are circumstances which demand our attention and point out the necessity of naval protection.

Some perhaps will say, that after we have made it up with Britain that she will protect us. Can we be so unwise as to mean that she shall keep a navy in our Harbours for that purpose? Common Sense will tell us, that the power which hath endeavoured to subdue us, is of all others, the most improper to defend us. Conquest may be effected under the pretence of friendship; and ourselves, after a long and brave resistance, be at last cheated into slavery. And if her ships are not to be admitted into our harbours, I would ask, how is she to protect us? A navy three or four thousand miles off can be of little use, and on sudden emergencies, none at all. Wherefore if we must hereafter protect ourselves, why not do it for ourselves? why do it for another?

The English list of ships of war, is long and formidable, but not a tenth part of them are at any one time fit for service, numbers of them not in being; yet their names are pompously continued in the list if only a plank is left of the ship: and not a fifth part of such as are fit for service, can be spared on any one station at one time. The East and West Indies, Mediterranean, Africa, and other parts over which Britain extends her claim, make large demands upon her navy. From a mixture of prejudice and inattention, we have contracted a false notion respecting the navy of England, and have talked as if we should have the whole of it to encounter at once, and for that reason, supposed, that we must have one as large; which not being instantly practicable, have been made use of by a set of disguised Tories to discourage our beginning thereon. Nothing can be farther from truth than this, for if America had only a twentieth part of the naval force of Britain, she would be by far an overmatch for her; because as we neither have, nor claim any foreign dominion, our whole force would be employed on our own coast, where we should, in the long run, have two to one the advantage of those who had three or four thousand miles to sail over, before they could attack us, and the same distance to return in order to refit and recruit. And although Britain by her fleet hath a check over our trade to Europe, we have as large a one over her trade to the West Indies, which by laying in the neighbourhood of the Continent lies entirely at its mercy.

Some method might be fallen on to keep up a naval force in time of peace, if we should not judge it necessary to support a constant navy. If premiums were to be given to Merchants to build and employ in their service, ships mounted with 20, 30, 40, or 50 guns (the premiums to be in proportion to the loss of bulk to the merchant) fifty or sixty of those ships, with a few guard ships on constant duty would keep up a sufficient navy, and that without burdening ourselves with the evil so loudly complained of in England, of suffering their fleets in time of peace to lie rotting in the docks. To unite the sinews of commerce and defence is sound policy; for when our strength and our riches, play into each other's hand, we need fear no external enemy.

In almost every article of defence we abound. Hemp flourishes even to rankness, so that we need not want cordage. Our iron is superior to that of other countries. Our small arms equal to any in the world. Cannon we can cast at pleasure. Saltpetre and gun powder we are every day producing. Our knowledge is hourly improving. Resolution is our inherent character, and courage hath never yet forsaken us. Wherefore, what is it that we want? why is it that we hesitate? From Britain we can expect nothing but ruin. If she is once admitted to the government of America again, this Continent will not be worth living in. Jealousies will be always arising; insurrections will be constantly happening; and who will go forth to quell them? who will venture his life to reduce his own countrymen to a foreign obedience? the difference between Pennsylvania and Connecticut, respecting some unlocated lands, shews the insignificance of a British government, and fully proves, that nothing but Continental authority can regulate Continental matters.

Another reason why the present time is preferable to all others, is, that the fewer our numbers are, the more land there is yet unoccupied, which instead of being lavished by the king on his worthless dependants, may be hereafter applied, not only to the discharge of the present debt, but to the constant support of government. No nation under Heaven hath such an advantage as this.

The infant state of the Colonies, as it is called, so far from being against, is an argument in favour of independance. We are sufficiently numerous, and were we more so, we might be less united. 'Tis a matter worthy of observation, that the more a country is peopled, the smaller their armies are. In military numbers the ancients far exceeded the moderns: and the reason is evident, for trade being the consequence of population, men become too much absorbed thereby to attend to any thing else. Commerce diminishes the spirit both of Patriotism and military defence. And history sufficiently informs us that the bravest achievements were always accomplished in the non-age of a nation. With the encrease in commerce, England hath lost its spirit. The city of London, notwithstanding its numbers, submits to continued insults with the patience of a coward. The more men they have to lose, the less willing are they to venture. The rich are in general slaves to fear, and submit to courtly power with the trembling duplicity of a spaniel.

Youth is the seed time of good habits as well in nations as in individuals. It might be difficult, if not impossible to form the Continent into one Government half a century hence. The vast variety of interests occasioned by an increase of trade and population would create confusion. Colony would be against Colony. Each being able would scorn each others assistance: and while the proud and foolish gloried in their little distinctions, the wise would lament that the union had not been formed before. Wherefore, the present time is the true time for establishing it. The intimacy which is contracted in infancy, and the friendship which is formed in misfortune, are of all others, the most lasting and unalterable. Our present union is marked with both these characters: we are young and we have been distressed; but our concord hath withstood our troubles, and fixes a memorable Æra for posterity to glory in.

The present time likewise, is that peculiar time, which never happens to a nation but once, viz. the time of forming itself into a government. Most nations have let slip the opportunity, and by that means have been compelled to receive laws from their conquerors, instead of making laws for themselves. First, they had a king, and then a form of government; whereas the articles or charter of government should be formed first, and men delegated to execute them afterward: but from the errors of other nations, let us learn wisdom, and lay hold of the present opportunity——*To begin government at the right end.*

When William the Conqueror subdued England, he gave them law at the point of the sword; and until we consent that the seat of government in America be legally and authoritatively occupied; we shall be in danger of having it filled by some fortunate ruffian, who may treat us in the same manner, and then, where will be our freedom? where our property.

As to religion, I hold it to be the indispensible duty of government, to protect all conscientious professors thereof, and I know of no other business which government hath to do therewith: let a man throw aside that narrowness of soul, that selfishness of principle, which the niggards of all professions are so unwilling to part with, and he will be delivered of his fears on that head. Suspicion is the companion of mean souls and the bane of all good society. For myself, I fully and conscientiously believe, that it is the will of the Almighty, that there should be diversity of religious opinions among us. It affords a larger field for our Christian kindness: were we all of one way of thinking, our religious dispositions would want matter for probation: and on this liberal principle I look on the various denominations among us, to be like children of the same family differing only in what is called their Christian names.

In page 54[2] I threw out a few thoughts on the propriety of a Continental charter (for I only presume to offer hints, not plans,) and in this place I take the liberty of re-mentioning the subject, by observing, that a charter is to be understood as a bond of solemn obligation, which the whole enters into, to support the right of every separate part, whether of religion, personal freedom, or property. A right reckoning makes long friends.

In a former page, I likewise mentioned the necessity of a large and equal representation; and there is no political matter which more deserves our attention. A small number of electors, or a small number of representatives, are equally dangerous. But if the number of the representatives be not only small, but unequal, the danger is encreased. As an instance of this I mention the following; when the petition of the associators was before the House of Assembly of Pennsylvania, twenty eight members only were present. All the Bucks county members, being eight, voted against it, and had seven of the Chester members done the same, this whole Province had been governed by two counties only, and this danger it is always exposed to. The unwarrantable stretch likewise, which that house made in their last sitting, to gain an undue authority over the Delegates of that Province, ought to warn the people at large, how they trust power out of their own hands. A set of instructions for the Delegates were put together; which in point of sense and business would have dishonoured a school-boy, and after being approved by a few, a

---

[2] Page 433 of this edition. [—ED.]

very few without doors, were carried into the house, and there passed *in behalf of the whole Colony:* whereas did the whole Colony know, with what ill-will that house hath entered on some necessary public measures, they would not hesitate a moment to think them unworthy of such a trust.

Immediate necessity makes many things convenient, which if continued would grow into oppressions. Expedience and right, are different things. When the calamities of America required a consultation, there was no method so ready, or at that time so proper, as to appoint persons from the several houses of Assembly for that purpose; and the wisdom with which they have proceeded hath preserved this Continent from ruin. But as it is more than probable that we shall never be without a CONGRESS, every well wisher to good order, must own, that the mode for choosing members of that body, deserves consideration. And I put it as a question to those, who make a study of mankind, whether representation and election is not too great a power for one and the same body of men to possess? When we are planning for posterity, we ought to remember, that virtue is not hereditary.

It is from our enemies that we often gain excellent maxims, and are frequently surprised into reason by their mistakes. Mr. Cornwall (one of the Lords of the Treasury) treated the petition of the New York Assembly with contempt, because that house he said consisted but of twenty six members, which, trifling number he argued could not with decency be put for the whole. We thank him for his involuntary honesty.[3]

TO CONCLUDE, however strange it may appear to some, or however unwilling they may be to think so, matters not, but

---

[3] Those who would fully understand of what great consequence a large and equal representation is to a State, should read Burgh's Political Disquisitions.

many strong and striking reasons may be given to shew, that nothing can settle our affairs so expeditiously as an open and determined declaration for independence. Some of which are,

First—It is the custom of Nations when any two are at war, for some other powers not engaged in the quarrel, to step in as mediators and bring about the preliminaries of a peace: But while America calls herself the subject of Great Britain, no power however well disposed she may be, can offer her mediation. Wherefore in our present state we may quarrel on for ever.

Secondly—It is unreasonable to suppose, that France or Spain will give us any kind of assistance, if we mean only to make use of that assistance, for the purpose of repairing the breach, and strengthening the connection between Britain and America; because, those powers would be sufferers by the consequences.

Thirdly—While we profess ourselves the subjects of Britain, we must in the eye of foreign nations be considered as Rebels. The precedent is some-what dangerous to their peace, for men to be in arms under the name of subjects: we on the spot can solve the paradox; but to unite resistance and subjection, requires an idea much too refined for common understanding.

Fourthly—Were a manifesto to be published and dispatched to foreign Courts, setting forth the miseries we have endured, and the peaceable methods we have ineffectually used for redress, declaring at the same time, that not being able any longer to live happily or safely, under the cruel disposition of the British Court, we had been driven to the necessity of breaking off all connections with her; at the same time, assuring all such Courts, of our peaceable disposition towards them, and of our desire of entering into trade with them: such a memorial would produce more good effects to this Continent, than if a ship were freighted with petitions to Britain.

Under our present denomination of British Subjects, we can

neither be received nor heard abroad: the custom of all Courts is against us, and will be so, until by an independance we take rank with other nations.

These proceedings may at first appear strange and difficult, but like all other steps which we have already passed over, will in a little time become familiar and agreeable: and until an independance is declared, the Continent will feel itself like a man who continues putting off some unpleasant business from day to day, yet knows it must be done, hates to set about it, wishes it over, and is continually haunted with the thoughts of its necessity.

FINIS.

· 17 ·

Plain Truth

By James Chalmers

The full title is *Plain Truth; Addressed to the Inhabitants of America, Containing, Remarks On a Late Pamphlet, entitled Common Sense.* The first edition was published in Philadelphia on March 13, 1776. On April 17, *Additions to Plain Truth* was published and on May 8 both pamphlets were published together. In London, James Almon brought out four editions of *Common Sense* and *Plain Truth* together during the same year, and an edition was published in Dublin.

Confusion as to the authorship of the pamphlet existed from its publication until only a few years ago. Various men at the time were suspected but no one would admit it, and at least one suspect was attacked by a mob. The Reverend William Smith was thought to be the author for many years. However, Thomas R. Adams, in "The Authorship and Printing of *Plain Truth* by 'Candidus'," *The Papers of the Bibliographical Society of America*, XXXXIX (1955), 230-248, shows that the author was James Chalmers. The confusion concerning the authorship and the complicated printing history

Second edition, Philadelphia, 1776.

of *Plain Truth* is insidious—even the learned Bibliographical Society prints "Authorship of 'Common Sense'" as the running head for Adams' article about *Plain Truth!*

In the following text the numerous typographical errors in the second edition have been corrected, and punctuation has been revised for the sake of clarity.

DEDICATION

TO

JOHN DICKINSON, ESQUIRE,

Although I have not the Honor to be known to You: I am not unacquainted with YOUR native Candor and unbounded Benevolence. As happy as obscure, I am indeed a stranger to the language of Adulation. Flattery I detest; Virtue, I Respect.

BE not offended SIR, if I remark, that YOUR Character, is contemplated with profound Veneration, by the Friends of the Constitution. Those Abilities, which YOU so illustriously displayed in defence of the Constitution, they now supplicate YOU to exert, in saving it from impending ruin, under the Syren form of delusive INDEPENDENCE.

STEP then forth; exert those Talents with which HEAVEN has endowed YOU; and cause the Parent, and her Children to embrace, and be foes no more. Ardous as this extraordinary task may seem, perhaps your Virtue and Talents, may yet effect it. YOUR Endeavors to stop the Effusion of Blood, of Torrents of Blood, is worthy of YOUR acknowledged Humanity. Even the honest attempt upon recollection, will afford you ineffable satisfaction.

MY PRESUMING to inscribe to YOU, the following crude Remarks, is to remind you, SIR, what YOUR distressed Country expects, nay, loudly demands from YOUR extensive Capacity.

I beg you will forgive this temerity; and that you may long

enjoy the fruits of YOUR Exalted Virtue, and remain an Honor to YOUR Country, and to Mankind: Is the ardent wish of

Sir,

Your most Obedient,
and Respectful Servant,

C A N D I D U S.

INTRODUCTION.

If indignant at the Doctrine contained in the Pamphlet, entitled COMMON SENSE: I have expressed myself, in the following Observations, with some ardor; I entreat the Reader to impute my indignation, to honest zeal against the Author's Insidious Tenets. Animated and impelled by every inducement of the Human Heart; I love, and (if I dare so express myself,) I adore my Country. Passionately devoted to true Liberty, I glow with the purest flame of Patriotism. Silver'd with age as I am, if I know myself, my humble Sword shall not be wanting to my Country (if the most Honorable Terms are not tendered by the British Nation) to whose Sacred Cause, I am most fervently devoted. The judicious Reader, will not impute my honest, tho' bold Remarks, to unfriendly designs against my Children——against my Country; but to abhorrence of Independency, which if effected, would inevitably plunge our once pre-eminently envied Country into Ruin, Horror, and Desolation.

PLAIN TRUTH;

CONTAINING,

REMARKS ON A LATE PAMPHLET,

ENTITLED COMMON SENSE.

I have now before me the Pamphlet, entitled COMMON SENSE on which I shall remark with freedom and candour. It may not be improper to remind my reader, that the investigation of my subject, demands the utmost freedom of enquiry. I therefore entreat his indulgence; and that he will carefully remember, that intemperate zeal, is as injurious to liberty, as a manly discussion of facts is friendly to it. "Liberty, says the great MONTESQUIEU, is a right of doing whatever the laws permit; and if a citizen could do what they forbid, he would no longer be possessed of liberty, because all his fellow citizens would have the same power." In the beginning of his pamphlet, the Author asserts, that society in every state is a blessing. This in the sincerity of my heart I deny; for it is supreme misery to be associated with those, who to promote their ambitious purposes, flagitiously pervert the ends of political society. I do not say that our Author is indebted to BURGH's POLITICAL DISQUISITIONS, or to ROUSSEAU's Social Compact for his definition of Government, and his large Tree; although I wish he had favoured his reader with the following extract from that sublime reasoner.

To investigate those conditions of society which may best answer the purpose of nations, would require the abilities of some superior intelligence, who should be witness to all the passions of men, but be subject itself to none, who should have no connections with human nature, but should have a perfect knowledge of it: A Being, in short, whose happiness should be independent of us, and who would nevertheless employ itself about us. It is the province of Gods to make laws for Men.

With the utmost deference to the celebrated ROUSSEAU, I cannot indeed imagine, that laws even so constructed, would materially benefit our imperfect race, unless omniscience deigned previously to exalt our nature. The judicious reader will therefore perceive, that malevolence only, is requisite to declaim against, and arraign the most perfect Governments. Our *Political Quack* avails himself of this trite expedient, to cajole the people into the most abject slavery, under the delusive name of independence. His first indecent attack is against the English constitution; which with all its imperfections, is, and ever will be the pride and envy of mankind. To this panegyric involuntarily our author subscribes, by granting individuals to be safer in England, than in any other part of Europe. He indeed insidiously attributes this pre-eminent excellency, to the constitution of the people, rather than to our excellent constitution. To such contemptible subterfuge is our Author reduced. I would ask him, why did not the constitution of the people afford them superior safety, in the reign of Richard the Third, Henry the Eighth, and other tyrannic princes? Many pages might indeed be filled with encomiums bestowed on our excellent constitution, by illustrious authors of different nations.

This beautiful system (according to MONTESQUIEU) our constitution is a compound of Monarchy, Aristocracy, and Democracy. But it is often said, that the Sovereign, by honours and appointments, influences the Commons. The profound and elegant HUME agitating this question, thinks, to this circumstance, we are in part indebted for our supreme felicity; since without such controul in the Crown, our Constitution would immediately degenerate into Democracy, a Government, which in the sequel, I hope to prove ineligible. Were I asked marks of the best government, and the purpose of political society, I would reply, the encrease, preservation, and prosperity of its members, in no quarter of the Globe, are those marks so certainly to be found, as in Great Britain, and her dependencies. After our Author has employed several pages, to break the mounds of society by debasing Monarchs: He says, "The plain truth is, that the antiquity of English Monarchy will not bear looking into."

HUME treating of the original contract, has the following melancholy, but sensible observation,

Yet reason tells us, that there is no property in durable objects, such as lands, and houses, when carefully examined, in passing from hand to hand, but must in some period, have been founded on fraud and injustice. The necessities of human society, neither in private or public life, will allow of such an accurate enquiry; and there is no virtue or moral duty, but what may, with facility, be refined away, if we indulge a false philosophy, in sifting and scrutinizing, by every captious rule of logic, in every light or position in which it may be placed.

Say ye votaries of honour and truth, can we adduce a stronger proof of our Author's turpitude, than his quoting the anti-philosophical story of the Jews, to debase Monarchy, and the best of Monarchs. Briefly examining the story of this contemptible race, more barbarous than our savages, We find their history a continued succession of miracles, astonishing our imaginations, and exercising our faith. After wandering forty years in horrid desarts, they are chiefly condemned to perish for their perverseness, although under the immediate dominion of the King of Heaven. At length, they arrive in the sterile country of Palestine; which they conquer, by exterminating the inhabitants, and warring like Demons. The inhabitants of the adjoining regions, justly therefore held them in detestation, and the Jews finding themselves constantly abhorred, have ever since hated all mankind. This people, as destitute of arts and industry, as humanity, had not even in their language a word expressive of education. We might indeed remind our Author, who so readily drags in the Old Testament to support his sinister measures, that we could draw from that source, many texts, favourable to Monarchy, were we not conscious, that the Mosaic Law, gives way to the Gospel Dispensation. The reader no doubt will be gratified by the following extract from a most primitive Christian.

Christianity is a spiritual religion, relative only to celestial objects. The Christian's inheritance is not of this world. He performs his duty it is true, but this he does with a profound indifference for the good or ill success of his endeavours: Provided he hath nothing to reproach himself, it is of little consequence to him whether matters go well or ill here below. If the state be in a flourishing condition, he can hardly venture to rejoice in the public felicity, least he should be puffed up, with the inordinate pride of his country's glory. If the state decline, he blesses the hand of GOD, that humbles his people to the dust.

Having defined the best government, I will humbly attempt to describe good Kings by the following unerring rule. The best Princes are constantly calumniated by the envenomed tongues and pens of the most worthless of their subjects. For this melancholy truth do I appeal to the testimony of impartial historians, and long experience. The noble impartial historian Sully, speaking of the almost divine Henry the Fourth of France says,

Thus was this god-like prince represented (by the discontented of these days) almost throughout his whole kingdom, as a furious, and implacable tyrant: They were never without one set of arguments to engage his catholic nobility in a rebellion against him, and another to sow sedition among his protestant officers and gentry.

HUME says, that the cruel unrelenting tyrant, Philip the Second of Spain, with his infernal Inquisition, was not more detested by the people of the Netherlands, than was the humane Charles, with his inoffensive Liturgy, by his mutinous subjects. The many unmerited insults offered to our gracious Sovereign by the unprincipled Wilkes, and others down to this late Author, will forever disgrace humanity. For he says, "that monarchy was the most prosperous invention the Devil ever set on foot for the promotion of idolatry. It is the pride of Kings which throws mankind into confusion: In short, continues this Author, monarchy and succession, have laid not this or that kingdom only, but the world in blood and ashes." How deplorably wretched the condition of mankind, could they believe such execrable flagitious jargon. Unhappily indeed, mankind in every age are susceptible of delusion; but surely our Author's poison carries its antidote with it. Attentive to the spirit of his publication, we fancy ourselves in the barbarous fifteenth century; in which period our Author would have figured with his "Common Sense—and blood will attend it."

After his terrible anathema against our venerable constitution, and monarchy, let us briefly examine a democratical state and see whether or not it is a government less sanguinary. This government is extremely plausible, and indeed flattering to the pride of mankind. The demagogues therefore, to seduce the people into their criminal designs ever hold up democracy to them, although conscious it never did, nor ever will answer in practice. If we believe a great Author, "There never existed, nor ever will exist a real democracy in the World." If we examine the republics of Greece and Rome, we ever find them in a state of war domestic or foreign. Our Author therefore makes no mention of these ancient States.

When Alexander ordered all the exiles, to be restored throughout all the cities, it was found that the whole amounted to twenty thousand, the remains probably of still greater slaughters and massacres. What an astonishing number in so narrow a country as ancient Greece? and what domestic confusion, jealousy, partiality, revenge, heart-burnings must tear those cities, where factions were wrought up to such a degree of fury and despair.

Apian's history of the civil wars of Rome, contains the most frightful picture of massacres, proscriptions, and forfeitures that ever were presented to the world.

The excellent Montesquieu declares,

that a democracy supposes the concurrence of a number of circumstances rarely united. In the first place, it is requisite that the state itself should be of small extent; so that the people might be easily assembled and personally known to each other. Secondly, the simplicity of their manners, should be such as to prevent a multiplicity of affairs, and perplexity in discussing them: And thirdly, there should subsist a great degree of equality between them, in point of right and authority: Lastly, there should be little or no luxury, for luxury must either be the effect of wealth, or it must make it necessary. It corrupts at once, both rich and poor: The one, by the possession, and the other, by the want of it.

To this may be added continues the same Author,

that no government is so subject to CIVIL WARS, and INTESTINE COMMOTIONS, as that of the democratical or popular form; because, no other tends so strongly and so constantly to alter, nor requires so much vigilance, and fortitude to preserve it from alteration. It is indeed, in such a constitution, particularly, that a Citizen should always be armed with fortitude, and constancy; and should every day, in the sincerity of his heart, guard against corruption, arising either from selfishness in himself, or in his compatriots; for if it once enters into public transactions, to root it out afterwards would be miraculous.

Our Author asserts, that Holland and Swisserland are without wars domestic or foreign. About a century ago, Holland was in a few weeks over-run by the arms of France, and almost miraculously saved by the gallantry of her Prince of Orange, so celebrated afterwards by the name of William the Third. Almost from that period, until the treaty of Utrecht, Holland was a principal in wars, the most expensive and bloody, ever waged by human kind. The wounds she then received were unhealed in 1744, when reluctantly roused from her pacific lethargy, she was dragged into war; and losing her impregnable Bergenopzoom, and Maestricht; was again on the brink of becoming a province to France, when happily liberated by the British Nation. In the war of 1756, Holland continually insulted in the capture of her ships, by our cruisers, preserved a humiliating neutrality. If victory indeed had not crowned the British banners, the Dutch indubitably would have assisted their natural Allies, in whatever quarter of the globe attacked: For it is incontestibly true that the existence of Holland, as a State, depends, and invariably will depend, on the prosperity of Great Britain. Since the murder of Barnevelt, and the immortal de Wits, by the deluded furious people, Holland hath too often been convulsed by anarchy, and torn by party. Unfortunately alas! for the cause of humanity, the rugged and incult desarts of Swisserland, preclude not ambi-

456 Tracts of the American Revolution: 1763–1776

tion, sedition, and anarchy. Her bleak and barren mountains do not so effectually secure precarious liberty, as daily vending her sons to the adjoining nations, particularly to France, by whom the thirteen Cantons, could be subjected in as many days, did that court meditate so senseless and delusive an object. Nugatory indeed, if we consider, that France derives more substantial advantage from the present state of Swisserland, than if she exhausted herself, to maintain numerous Battalions, to bridle the Cantons. A moment, let us suppose, that our author's asseverations of Holland and Swisserland, are as real as delusive. His inferences do not flow from his premises; for their superior advantages, do not arise from their popular government, but from circumstances of peculiar local felicity, obliging the princes of Europe, to defend them from the omnipotent land force, if I may so speak of France. After impotently attacking our Sovereign, and the constitution, He contradicts the voice of all mankind, by declaring, that America "would have flourished as much, and probably much more, had no European power taken any notice of her."

If he means, that had this Continent been unexplored, the original inhabitants would have been happier, For once, I agree with him. Previous to the settlement of these Provinces by our Ancestors, the kingdom of France was convulsed by religious phrenzy. This, and Sebastian Cabot's prior discovery, perhaps, happily afforded the people of England, an opportunity of locating these Provinces. At length, peace being restored to France, by her Hero, Henry the Fourth, His nation in turn, were seized with the rage of colonizing. Finding the English claimed the Provinces on the Atlantic, they appropriated the snow banks of Canada, which we dare not suppose, they would have preferred to these fertile provinces, had not the prior occupancy, and power of England interfered. I hope it will not be denied, that the notice taken of us, at this time by an European Power, was rather favourable for us. Certain it is, had not England then taken notice of us, these delectable

Provinces would now appertain to France; and the people of New England, horrid to think, would now be counting their beads. Some years after the Æra in question, the civil wars intervening in England, afforded to the Swedes and Dutch, a footing on this Continent. Charles the Second being restored; England reviving her claim, rendered abortive the Swedish pretensions; and by conquest, and granting Surinam to the Dutch, procured the cession of their usurpation, now New York. I do indeed confess, my incapacity to discern the injury sustained by this second "notice taken of us, by an European Power" in default of which intervention, the Swedes, to this hour, would have retained their settlement, now the famed Pennsylvania; and the Dutch, consequently, had retained theirs. Some time after this period, the people of New England were employed, in framing and executing laws, so intolerant and sanguinary, that to us, they seem adapted for devils, not men.

Indeed it is worthy of note, that the inhabitants of Jamaica, Barbadoes, and Virginia, at that very time, enacted laws, breathing the spirit of humanity, and such as men could bear. Soon after the period in question, arrived the great and good WILLIAM PENN, with his philosophic people called Quakers; together with toleration, industry, and permanent credit. The people of England, encouraged by the extension of their laws and commerce to those colonies, powerfully assisted our merchants and planters, insomuch, that our settlements encreased rapidly, and throve apace. It may be affirmed, that from this period, until the present unhappy hour, no part of human kind, ever experienced more perfect felicity. Voltaire indeed says, that if ever the Golden Age existed, it was in Pennsylvania. France disgusted with the unhappy situation of her American Colonies, had long meditated the conquest of one of our middle provinces. To accomplish this purpose, she extended a line of forts on our frontiers, and actually fortified the place now called Pittsburgh. Justly alarmed by these encroachments in the hour of our distress, we called aloud on Great Britain for assistance, nor was she deaf to our cries. The English ministry, after in vain exhausting all the arts of negociation, declared war against France. After spilling torrents of blood, after expending one hundred and ninety millions of their dollars, and four or five millions of ours, they gloriously reduced the French settlements. Surely it will not be said, that this last NOTICE taken of us by the people of England, was injurious to us. Our enemies indeed alledge, that the last intervention by bloating us with pride, will eventually ruin us, and render the people of Britain objects of derision, for lavishing their blood and treasure, in defence of provinces; "a match not only for Europe, (according to our author,) but for the world." Our author next remarks, "that the commerce by which she hath enriched herself, are the necessaries of life, and will always have a market while eating is the custom of Europe."

I reply, that our exporting grain, is as it were of yesterday, that the recent demand was principally occasioned by the distractions in Poland, and other parts of Europe, and probably will totally or partly fail, soon as the fertile country of Poland, and more fertile Ukraine shall again become cultivated. I believe the Europeans did eat before our merchants exported our grain, and perhaps will eat, when they cease to export it. I deny, that this momentary commerce hath enriched us; and I could adduce numberless melancholy proofs of the contrary. I shall only remark, that in the most fertile and delectable wheat country in America, bounded by Chesopeak-bay, and almost adjoining that of Delaware, a tract of the best wheat land ten years ago, would hardly have exceeded a guinea and a half per acre. Indeed, in 1773, such land covered with wood, would scarcely have sold for four guineas an acre, an undoubted proof of want of PEOPLE, industry, and wealth; particularly so, if we consider that one crop of corn and wheat on such land judiciously cultivated, would actually repay the supposed price. Our author asserts, "that our present numbers are sufficient to repel the force of all the world. That the Continent hath at this time the largest disciplined army of ANY POWER UNDER HEAVEN. That the English navy is only worth three millions and a half sterling," which in effect, would reduce it to thirty-five ships of the line, twenty ships of forty guns, twenty of thirty-six, and eight of twenty guns. "That if America had only a twentieth part of this force, she would be by far an over-match for Britain, that Independence is necessary, because France and Spain cannot assist us, until such an event;" he also affirms "that Great Britain cannot govern us, and that no good can arise from a reconciliation with her."

I shall humbly endeavour to shew, that our author shamefully misrepresents facts, is ignorant of the true state of Great Britain and her Colonies, utterly unqualified for the arduous task, he has presumptuously assumed; and ardently intent on seducing us to that precipice on which himself stands trembling. To elucidate my strictures, I must with fidelity expose the circumstances of Great Britain and her colonies. If therefore, in the energy of description, I unfold certain bold and honest truths with simplicity, the judicious reader will remember, that true knowledge of our situation, is as essential to our safety, as ignorance thereof may endanger it. In the English provinces, exclusive of negroe and other slaves, we have one hundred and sixty thousand, or one hundred and seventy thousand men capable of bearing arms. If we deduct the people called Quakers, Anabaptists, and other religionists averse to arms; a considerable part of the emigrants, and those having a grateful predilection for the ancient constitution and parent state, we shall certainly reduce the first number to sixty or seventy thousand men. Now admitting those equal to the Roman legions, can we suppose them capable of defending against the power of Britain, a country nearly twelve hundred miles extending on the ocean. Suppose our troops assembled in New England, if the Britons see not fit to assail them, they haste to and desolate our other provinces, which eventually would reduce New England. If by dividing our forces, we pretend to defend our provinces, we also are infallibly undone. Our most fertile provinces, filled with unnumbered domestic enemies, slaves, intersected by navigable rivers, every where accessible to the fleets and armies of Britain, can make no defence. If without the medium of passion and prejudice, we view our other provinces, half armed, destitute of money and a navy: We must confess, that no power ever engaged such POTENT ANTAGONISTS, under such peculiar circumstances of infelicity. In the better days of Rome, she permitted no regular troops to defend her. Men destitute of property she admitted not into her militia, (her only army.) I have been extremely concerned at the separation of the Connecticut men from our army. It augur'd not an ardent enthusiasm for liberty and glory. We still have an army before Boston, and I should be extremely happy to hear substantial proofs of their glory. I am still hopeful of great things from our army before Boston, when joined by the regiments now forming, which WANT OF BREAD will probably soon fill. Notwithstanding the predilection I have for my countrymen, I remark with grief, that hitherto our troops have displayed but few marks of Spartan or Roman enthusiasm. In the sincerity of my heart, I adjure the reader to believe, that no person is more sensibly afflicted by hearing the enemies of America remark, that no General ever fell singly and so ingloriously unrevenged before the inauspicious affair of Quebec. I am under no doubt, however, that we shall become as famed for martial courage, as any nation ever the sun beheld. Sanguine as I am, respecting the virtue and courage of my countrymen, depending on the history of mankind, since the Christian Æra, I cannot however imagine, that zeal for liberty will animate to such glorious efforts of heroism, as religious enthusiasm hath often impelled its votaries to perform. If the cruel unrelenting tyrant, Philip the second of Spain, had never attempted to introduce into the Low Countries, the infernal tribunal of the Inquisition, it is most probable, that the present States of Holland, would to this time have remained provinces to Spain, and patiently paid the fiftieth penny, and other grievous exactions. Certain it is, that the fanaticks of Scotland, and people of England, had never armed against the first Charles, if religious enthusiasm had not more powerfully agitated their minds, than zeal for liberty, the operations of which, on the human mind, hath since the Æra in question, ever been more languid, than the former most powerful passion. These hardy assertions, are supported as well by notorious facts, as by the learned HUME, and other judicious historians. I cannot here omit remarking the inconsistency of human nature. The Scotch, the most furious enthusiasts then in Europe, were slaughtered like sheep, by Cromwell at Dunbar, where their formidable army hardly made any resistance, if we except that made by a handful of loyalists, destitute of that passion. Certain it is, that those enthusiasts, were often cut in pieces by their countryman, the gallant Marquis of Montrose, whose troops (Highlanders and other loyalists,) held Presbyterianism in contempt.

With the utmost deference to the honorable Congress, I do not view the most distant gleam of aid from foreign powers. The princes alone, capable of succouring us, are the Sovereigns of France and Spain. If according to our Author, we possess an eighth part of the habitable globe, and actually have a check on the West India commerce of England, the French indigo and other valuable West India commodities, and the Spanish galeons, are in great jeopardy from our power. The French and Spaniards are therefore wretched politicians, if they do not assist England, in reducing her colonies to obedience.——Pleasantry apart! Can we be so deluded, to expect aid from those princes, which inspiring their subjects with a relish for liberty, might eventually shake their arbitrary thrones. Natural avowed enemies to our sacred cause: Will they cherish, will they support the flame of liberty in America? Ardently intent on extinguishing its latent dying sparks in their respective dominions. Can we believe that those princes will offer an example so dangerous to their subjects and colonies, by aiding those provinces to independence? If independent, aggrandized by infinite numbers from every part of Europe, this Continent would rapidly attain power astonishing to imagination. Soon, very soon would we be conditioned to conquer Mexico, and all their West India settlements, which to annoy, or possess, we indeed are most happily situated. Simple and obvious as these truths are, can they be unknown to the people and princes of Europe? Be it however admitted, that those princes unmindful of the fatal policy of RICHLIEU's arming Charles's subjects against him, and the more fatal policy of LEWIS the fourteenth permitting our glorious deliverer to effect the revolution. I say, be it admitted, that those princes regardless of future consequences, and the ineptitude of the times, are really disposed to succour us. Say, ye friends of liberty and mankind, would no danger accrue from an army of French and Spaniards in the bosom of America? Would ye not dread their junction with the Canadians and Savages, and with the numerous Roman catholics, dispersed throughout the Colonies?

Let us now briefly view the pre-eminently envied state of Great Britain. If we regard the power of Britain, unembarressed with Continental connections, and the political balance, we may justly pronounce her what our author does, AMERICA: —"A match for all Europe." Amazing were the efforts of England, in the war of Queen Ann, when little benefited by colony commerce, and e'er she had availed herself of the courage, good sense, and numbers of the people of Scotland and Ireland.

That England then prescribed laws to Europe, will be long remembered. Last war, her glory was, if possible, more eminently exalted; in every quarter of the globe did victory hover round her armies and navies, and her fame re-echoed from pole to pole. At present Great Britain is the umpire of Europe. It is not exaggeration to affirm, that the Russians principally

are indebted for their laurels, to her power, which alone retained France from preventing the ruin of her ancient faithful
ally, the Ottoman Porte. Superfluous it were to enumerate her
powerful alliances, or mention her immense resources. Her
raising the incredible sums of eighteen, nineteen, and twenty-
two millions sterling for the service of the years 1759–60, and
61, was more astonishing to Europe, than the victories of her
fleets and armies. The annual rents of the kingdom of England
only, many years ago, amounted to thirty three millions sterling. Thirty five millions bushels of wheat are annually produced in that kingdom, and perhaps as many bushels of other
grain. Twelve millions of fleeces of wool are there yearly
shorn. In short, the Kingdom is a perfect Bee-hive, in numbers
and industry; and is said to contain more industry, consequently more wealth, than all the rest of Europe. The famed
HUME says, "I should as soon dread, that all our rivers and
springs, should be exhausted, as that money should abandon a
kingdom; where there are people and industry." The British
navy, at the close of last war, consisted of nearly two hundred
ships of the line, one hundred large frigates, and about one
hundred smaller frigates, or other armed vessels. Since the
peace, I believe, the navy has been most vigilantly preserved
by Lord Sandwich, (said to be as equal to that arduous department, as any man in Europe.) Since the war, several capital
ships have annually been built; and it is most certain, that on
six months notice, Great Britain could equip fleets, sufficiently
formidable, to contend with all the naval force, that could,
or would act against her. The immense quantity of naval and
other stores, in the different arsenals, with the royal navy[1] cannot at this time be worth less than twenty millions sterling.
The island of Great Britain, between six and seven hundred
miles in length, and upwards of two thousand miles circum-
ference and being every where indented with harbours, forms

---

[1] Seventeen capital ships were built from 1763 until 1771.

(with other causes) such nurseries of seamen, as the world cannot produce.

Let us now examine our author's account of the navy of Great-Britain. "It is" says he, "worth no more than three millions and an half sterling." This in effect will reduce it to ten second rate ships of war, ten third rate, fifteen fourth rate, ten ships of forty guns, ten of thirty six, and eight of twenty. "If America" says he,

had only a twentieth part of the naval force of Britain, she would be by far an over-match for her, because as we neither have, nor claim any foreign dominion, our whole force would be employed on our own coast; where we should in the long run have two to one the advantage of those who had three or four thousand miles to sail over, before they could attack us; and the same distance to return, in order to refit and recruit. And although Britain by her fleet, hath a check over our trade to Europe, we have as large a one over her trade to the West Indies, which, by laying in the neighbourhood of the Continent, lies entirely at its mercy.

Were it lawful to joke on so serious an occasion, I would remind the reader of our Author's modesty, in saying, "that we claim no foreign dominion." Since we have the most numerous, and best disciplined army under Heaven, and a navy sufficiently strong to combat that of Great Britain. For our present naval armament compose a fleet more than equal to a twentieth part of the British navy, (according to our author's estimation.) Notwithstanding our author's delicacy, relying on the well known utility of melasses, to the New England governments, I hope they will order Admiral Manly to seise Jamaica, and the other West India Islands. The Admiral cannot be at a loss for men; since, according to our author, "a few social sailors, will soon instruct a sufficient number of active landmen, in the common work of a ship." I do indeed confess, that the British ships of war, are constantly equipt altogether with very social sailors; and as constantly drub the French ships, double mann'd, with active landmen, tho' sufficiently instructed by a few social sailors. The reader will perceive, that our author, has humbled the naval power of Britain, with more facility than France and Spain could have done, and, has also expelled her from our ports with happier success, than did Spain, who was compelled to yield her Gibraltar and Portmahon, for the conveniency of her fleets and commerce.

We must indeed allow, that Spain, tho' possessed of Mexico and Peru, cannot maintain the most numerous and best disciplined army under Heaven, nor equip a navy fit to contend with the fleets of Britain. It must also be confessed, that he makes Great Britain, very favourably dispose of her humbled navy, by employing nineteen parts of it in the Mediterranean, Asia, Africa, and I know not where: When he knows we have so great a check on her West India trade, a commerce, of the last importance to her.

I would blush for poor human nature, did I imagine that any man, other than a bigot could believe these ridiculous stories, these arrant gasconades, respecting our numerous and best disciplined army under Heaven, about our navy, and a few social sailors, and that France and Spain will not assist us, (who by-the-bye, according to our author, are able to conquer them,) until playing upon words, we declare ourselves INDEPENDENT. Can a reasonable being for a moment believe that Great Britain, whose political existence depends on our constitutional obedience, who but yesterday made such prodigious efforts to save us from France, will not exert herself as powerfully to preserve us from our frantic schemes of independency. Can we a moment doubt, that the Sovereign of Great Britain and his ministers, whose glory as well as personal safety depends on our obedience, will not exert every nerve of the British power, to save themselves and us from ruin.

"Much" says our author, "has been said of the strength of Britain and the Colonies, that in conjuction they might bid defiance to the world; but this is mere presumption, the fate of war is uncertain."

Excellent reasoning, and truly consistent with our author.

We of ourselves are a match for Europe, nay for the world; but in junction with the most formidable power on earth; why then, the matter is mere presumption. The fate of war is uncertain. It is indeed humiliating to consider, that this author should vamp up a form of government, for a considerable part of mankind; and in case of its succeeding, that he probably would be one of our tyrants, until we prayed some more illustrious tyrant of the army, to spurn him to his primeval obscurity, from all his ill-got honours flung, turned to that dirt from whence he sprung. "A government of our own, is our natural right," says our author.

> "Had right decided, and not fate the cause,
> Rome had preserv'd her Cato and her laws."

Unfortunately for mankind, those are fine sounding words, which seldom or ever influence human affairs. If they did, instead of appropriating the vacant lands to schemes of ambition, we must instantly deputise envoys to the Indians, praying them to re-enter their former possessions, and permit us quietly to depart to the country of our ancestors, where we would be welcome guests. But continues our author,

What have we to do with setting the world at defiance? our plan is commerce, and that well attended to, will secure us the peace and friendship of all Europe; because it is the interest of all Europe to have America a free port, her trade will always be her protection, and her barrenness of gold and silver, will secure her from invaders.

I am perfectly satisfied, that we are in no condition to set the world at defiance, that commerce and the protection of Great Britain will secure us peace, and the friendship of all Europe; but I deny that it is the interest of all Europe to have America a free-port, unless they are desirous of depopulating their dominions. His assertions, that barrenness of gold and silver will secure us from invaders, is indeed highly pleasant. Have we not a much better security from invasions, viz. the most numerous and best disciplined army under heaven; or has our author already disbanded it. Pray how much gold and silver do the mines of Flanders produce? and what country so often has seen its unhappy fields drenched with blood, and fertilised with human gore. The princes of Europe have long dreaded the migration of their subjects to America; and we are sensible, that the king of Prussia is said more than once to have hanged Newlanders, or those who seduced his subjects to emigrate. I also humbly apprehend, that Britain is a part of Europe. Now, *old gentleman,* as you have clearly shewn, that we have a check upon her West India trade, is it her interest to give us a greater check upon it, by permitting America (as you express it,) to become a free port. Can we suppose it to be her interest to lose her valuable commerce to the Colonies, which effectually she would do, by giving up America to become your free port. If therefore it is in the interest of all Europe, to have America a free port, The people of Britain are extremely simple to expend so many millions sterling to prevent it. "It is repugnant to the nature of things, to all examples from former ages, to suppose that this Continent can long remain subject to any external power."

Antiquity affords us no eclarcisement respecting the future government of America. Rome situated in a sterile corner of Italy, long, long, retained the then world in chains, and probably had maintained her dominion longer, had not the cross, removing the empire to Byzantium, weakened the eagles, and in turn, justly been destroyed by the Barbarians. I see no reason to doubt, that Great Britain, may not long retain us in constitutional obedience. Time, the destroyer of human affairs, may indeed, end her political life by a gentle decay. Like Rome, she may be constrained to defend herself from the Huns, and Alaricks of the North. Ingratefully should we endeavour to precipitate her political demise, she will devise every expedient to retain our obedience; and rather than fail, will participate those provinces amongst the potent states of

Europe. "The authority of Great Britain over this Continent, is a form of government which sooner or later must have an end."

This I have granted, and I add, that a million of revolutions may happen on this Continent, for every one of which, I am not indeed so over solicitous, as our Phœnix of Whims, the Author of Common Sense. "The Colonies have manifested such a spirit of good order and obedience to continental government, as is sufficient to make every person happy on that head."

What is this union so highly vaunted of? whence the marching and counter marching through almost every province to disarm those denominated tories? I perfectly agree, that glorious is our union. I execrate those who say, it has been cemented by every species of fraud and violence. Yet notwithstanding I dread its fragility; were an army of Britons in the middle of our country. As the Author of Common Sense is now in the grand monde; and cannot be acquainted with the language of many people in the provinces, I will communicate the general purport of their discourse.—"We, say they, do not see through the wisdom of the present times. We remember with unfeigned gratitude, the many benefits derived through our connections with Great Britain, by whom but yesterday, we were emancipated from slavery and death. We are not indeed unaware, that Great Britain is uniformly reproached with defending us from interested motives. In like manner, however, may every ingrate, reproach his benefactor; since all benefactions may be said to flow from no purer fountain. With predilection, we view our parent state, and wishfully contemplate on our late felicity, almost realizing that state of old, so beautifully feigned by the poets. We venerate the constitution, which with all its imperfections, (too often exaggerated) we apprehend almost approaches as near to perfection, as human kind can bear. We shudder at the idea of arming with more virulence, more unremitting ardour, against the parent state, than against France; by whom our RIGHTS, CIVIL, as well as RE-LIGIOUS, certainly were more imminently endangered. With horror we reflect on the former civil wars, when every crime, odious and baneful to human nature, were alternately perpetrated by the soldiers, particularly by the Independents."

"Every quiet method of peace has been ineffectual; our prayers have been rejected with disdain." I do not indeed agree with the people of England in saying, that those, who so successfully laboured to widen the breach desired nothing less than peace. That they who shortly were to command the most numerous and best disciplined army under Heaven, and a navy fit to contend with the fleets of England, imagining *the time had found us,* disdained to be just. I highly venerate a majority of the Delegates. I have not indeed the honour of knowing all the worthy members; however, I wish the Gentlemen of the Congress, e'er they entered on their important charge, had been better acquainted with the strength of our friends in parliament. I sincerely lament, that the King did not receive the last excellent petition from the Congress; and I as sincerely wish, the Gentlemen of the Congress had not addressed themselves at that juncture, to the people of Ireland.

As to government matters, (continues our Author,) it is not in the power of Britain to do this Continent justice: The business of it will soon be too weighty and intricate to be managed with any tolerable degree of convenience, by a power so very distant from us, and so very ignorant of us; for if they cannot conquer us, they cannot govern us. The difference between Pennsylvania, and Connecticut, respecting some unlocated lands, shews the insignificance of a British government, and fully proves, that nothing but Continental authority can regulate Continental matters.

Until the present unhappy period, Great Britain has afforded to all mankind, the most perfect proof of her wise, lenient, and magnanimous government of the Colonies. The proofs to which we already have alluded, viz. our supreme felicity and amazing increase. Than the affair of the Connecticut invaders, omnipotence only could grant us stronger reasons for praying a continuance of our former beneficent government. Most certainly, every dispassionate person, as well as the plundered Pennsylvanians, must confess, that the Arm of Great Britain alone detained those Free-booters aforesaid, from seising the city of Philadelphia, to which without all doubt, they have as just a claim, as to those fertile regions in Pennsylvania, which they surreptitiously have possessed themselves of. In wrath to mankind, should Heaven permit our Author's new fangled government to exist; I, as a friend to Pennsylvanians, advise them to explore new settlements, and avoid the cruel mortification of being expelled by the *Saints* from their delicious abodes and pleasing fields.—

But (says the Author) the most powerful argument is, that nothing but independence, (that is a Continental form of government) can keep the peace of the Continent, and preserve it inviolate from civil wars. I dread the event of a reconciliation now with Britain, as it is more than probable, that it will be followed by revolt somewhere; the consequences of which may be far more fatal than all the malice of Britain. Thousands are already ruined by British barbarity, thousands more will probably share the same fate. These men have other feelings, than those who have nothing suffered: All they now possess is liberty, what they before enjoyed is sacrificed to its service, and having nothing more to lose, they disdain all submission.

Here we cannot mistake our author's meaning, that if one or more of the middle or southern Colonies reconcile with Great Britain, they will have war to sustain with New England; "the consequences of which may be more detrimental, than all the malice of Britain." This terrible denunciation, fortunately for such Colonies, is as futile as its author. Should Great Britain re-establish her authority in the said Colonies by negociation, surely it is not temerity to add, that the weight of Britain, in the scale of those provinces, would preponderate against the power of New England. If Britain should reduce the Colonies by arms, (which may Heaven avert!) The New England provinces will have as little inclination, as ability, to disturb the peace of their neighbours. I do indeed most sincerely compassionate those unhappy men, who are ruined by our unfortunate distractions. I do fervently pray, that Britain, and the Colonies may most effectually consider their peculiar infelicity. Such attention will do infinite honour to the parent state, who cannot view them as enemies, but as men unhappily irritated by the impolitic measures of Great Britain. "The diminution of trade affords an army, and the necessities of an army, create a new trade." (So says our Author). I am surprised the ministry, so often reproached with ruining the commerce of Britain, never urged, (what was never thought or said before.) Our Author's excellent axiom, "that the diminution, &c." Certain it is, the minority had replied, since the commencement of this century; the diminution of the commerce of France hath afforded her nearly one million of soldiers; but the necessities of this prodigious number of troops, created her so bad a commerce, that she hath twice proved bankrupt since, and more than once experienced the miseries of famine.

"If premiums" (says our Author) "were to be given to Merchants to build and employ in their service, ships mounted with 20, 30, 40, or 50 guns, the premiums to be in proportion to the loss of bulk to the Merchants. Fifty or sixty of those ships, with a few guard ships on constant duty, would keep up a sufficient navy, and that without burdening ourselves with the evil so loudly complained of in England, of suffering their fleets in time of peace to lie rotting in their docks." Yield the palm of ingenuity to our Author, ye DeWits, Colverts, Pelhams, and Pitts. He has outdone ye by constructing a beautiful navy; alas! on paper only. First, no nation in Europe depends on such ships for her defence. Secondly, such ships would be unfit to contend with capital ships. Thirdly, in the hour of danger, these ships on their voyage, on return, would alternately be taken by an active enemy. Lastly, six times as many such ships would be unequally matched with that part of the naval power of Britain, which she actually could spare to combat on our coasts. This cannot be thought exaggeration, if we consider that the British navy, last war, carried about seventeen thousand guns; and upwards of ninety-five thousand social seamen. "No country (says our author) is so happily situated, or internally capable of raising a fleet as America. Tar, timber, iron and cordage are her natural produce." He speaks of forming a fleet, as if he could do it by his Fiat. A third rate ship of the line fitted for sea, is allowed to cost seventy four thousand pounds sterling, which at the present exchange, is about one hundred and twenty nine thousand pounds. Now, as labour, sail cloth, cordage, and other requisites, are dearer than in Europe, we may reasonably suppose the advanced price, at twenty-five per cent. which makes the amount one hundred and fifty four thousand pounds. We must next suppose our navy equal to that of France, which consists of sixty four ships of the line (fifty gun ships inclusive) twenty-five frigates, with ships of inferior force. In case of independence, we cannot admit a smaller naval force. Indeed, when joined to the fleets of France and Spain, the navies so united, and navigated principally with landsmen, instructed by a few social sailors, will be vastly inferior to the squadrons of Britain. The amount therefore of such our navy, will only require the trifling sum of twelve million, six hundred and twenty five thousand pounds currency, which I am very willing to believe we can spare, being scarcely one fourth the value of our property, real and personal. With excellent management, our navy would last eight, nine, or ten years; we therefore would find it extremely convenient to rebuild it constantly at the expiration of that term. Of this there cannot be a doubt, when we remember with our Author, "that ship-building is America's greatest pride. The vast empire of Russia is almost shut out from the sea, wherefore her boundless for-

rests, her tar, iron, and cordage, are only articles of commerce."
I reply, that Russia containing ten times our numbers, is destitute of industry and commerce. She has ports sufficient to build
and contain a navy to subdue the world. Destitute as we have
remarked of industry and commerce, her navy is inconsiderable, and being equipt with landsmen, cannot figure against
ships navigated by social sailors. Who can doubt the ability of
Spain to build a navy? The cargo of two or three of her annual
galeons were sufficient to build a navy as formidable as that
permitted to Great Britain (by the author of Common Sense.)
In her Island of Cuba, possessed of an immensity of fine cedar,
she might construct a navy as formidable as that of Great
Britain, but to what purpose, other than to adorn the triumph
of her enemies; unless she could arm her ships, otherwise than
by active landsmen, instructed by a few social sailors. Our
Author says, "that the Terrible, Capt. Death, stood the hottest
engagement of any ship last war, yet had not twenty sailors
on board," (tho' her compliment of men was upwards of two
hundred.)

We do indeed confess ourselves doubtful on this head, and
therefore wish our Author had produced his authority. We do
apprehend, that naval actions, very generally depend on sea-
man-ship, that is, on dextrously working the ship during the
combat. Now the judicious reader will remember, that ships
of war in engagement cannot be navigated by a few social
sailors, nor even by a bare competency, unless such sailors are
more invulnerable than was the great Achilles.

"Were the Continent (says our Author) crowded with inhabitants, her sufferings under the present circumstances,
would be intolerable, the more sea ports we had, the more we
should have both to defend, and to lose." This is rather incomprehensible; I cannot imagine, that we would be less formidable with ten times our present numbers, if at present we can
defend one sea-port; surely, with ten times as many inhabitants,
we could equally defend ten. If with our present numbers,

we are a match for the world, consequently with ten times as many, we would be a match for ten worlds, which would indeed be prodigious! "The infant state of the Colonies as it is called, so far from being against, is an argument in favor of Independence." This assertion is as absurd, as if he had maintained, that twenty is inferior in number to two. "But the injuries and disadvantages we sustain by that connection, are without number, and our duty to mankind at large, as well as to ourselves, instruct us to renounce the alliance; because any submission to, or dependence upon Great Britain, tends directly to involve this Continent in European wars and quarrels. As Europe is our market for trade, we ought to form no political connection with any part of it." Innumerable are the advantages of our connection with Britain; and a just dependence on her, is a sure way to avoid the horrors and calamities of war. Wars in Europe, will probably than heretofore become less frequent; religious rancour, which formerly animated princes to arms, is succeeded by a spirit of philosophy extremely friendly to peace. The princes of Europe are or ought to be convinced by sad experience, that the objects of conquest, are vastly inadequate to the immense charge of their armaments. Prudential motives, therefore, in future, will often dictate negociation, instead of war. Be it however admitted, that our speculations are nugatory, and that as usual, we are involved in war. In this case we really do not participate a twentieth part of the misery and hardships of war, experienced by the other subjects of the empire. As future wars will probably be carried on by Britain in her proper element, her success will hardly be doubtful, nor can this be thought audacity, if we remember the great things effected by Britain in her naval wars, then secondary objects to her Germanic connections, to which she now politically seens indifferent. Our sailors navigating our vessels to the West Indies during war are exempted from impressment, and if our trade to any part of Europe is then stagnated, it flows with uncommon rapidity in the West Indies, nor is the object of captures inconsiderable.

Our author surely forgets, that when independent, we cannot trade with Europe, without political connections, and that all treaties made by England or other commercial states are, or ought to be, ultimately subservient to their commerce. "But" (says our author,) "admitting that matters were now made up, what would be the event? I answer the ruin of the Continent, and that for several reasons." Reconciliation would conduct us to our former happy state. The happiness of the governed is without doubt the true interest of the governors, and if we aim not at independence, there cannot be a doubt, of receiving every advantage relative to laws and commerce that we can desire. Montesquieu speaking of the people of England, says, "They know better than any people on earth, how to value at the same time these three great advantages, religion, liberty, and commerce." "It is a matter worthy of observation, that the more a country is peopled, the smaller their armies are." This indeed would be worthy of observation, did not daily experience contravert it. The armies of Russia, France, Austria, England, and Prussia, are certainly more numerous than those of Spain, Sweden, Denmark, Portugal, and Sardinia. Now, the first five states contain nearly sixty millions, and the last kingdoms do not contain fourteen millions of people. "In military numbers, the ancients far exceeded the moderns, and the reason is evident, for trade being the consequences of population, men become too much absorbed thereby, to attend to any thing else, commerce diminishes the spirit both of patriotism, and military defence."

Every man of sense, now rejects the fabulous numbers of the army of Xerxes, and other fabled armies of antiquity. The ancient armies, did not exceed in numbers the armies of the moderns. If so, their states had been desolated by the horrid carnage of their battles, arising from the military spirit of defence, from the nature of their arms, and the arrangement of their armies, which permitted the combatants to buckle together, who seldom gave quarter. The Roman armies never exceeded twenty-five legions, which including auxiliaries, did not exceed two hundred and fifty thousand, a number greatly inferior to the armies of France, or perhaps Britain during war. Notwithstanding my ardour for liberty, I do most fervently pray, that we may never exchange the spirit of commerce, for that of military defence, even at the price of augmenting our armies. Let us hear the testimony of Montesquieu in favor of commerce: "Commerce," says he,

is a cure for the most destructive prejudices, for it is almost a general rule, that wherever we find agreeable manners, their commerce flourishes. Let us not be astonished then, if our manners are now less savage than formerly. Commerce has every where diffused a knowledge of all nations, these are compared one with another, and from this comparison arise the greatest advantages. Peace is the natural effect of trade, &c.

The Athenian people, perhaps the most respectable of antiquity, did not long possess a commercial spirit, but were almost continually afflicted by this spirit of military defence. The common people in effect distributed the public revenues amongst themselves, while the rich, were in a state of oppression. According to Lysius the orator and others, it was their custom, when in want of money, to put to death some of the rich citizens, as well as strangers, for the sake of the forfeiture. In short, could we enumerate the infinite train of misfortunes inflicted on mankind, in every clime and age by this self-same spirit of military defence; our readers will surely join us in opinion, that commerce has most happily humanized mankind. I am not unaware, that there are many declamations against commerce, these I have ever regarded as trials of wit, rather than serious productions. Our author's antipathy, and extreme aversion to commerce, is easily accounted for. If his independence takes place, I do aver, that commerce will be as useless, as our searching for the philosopher's stone. "And history (says he,) sufficiently informs us, that the bravest achievements were always accomplished in the non-age of a nation." The Greeks in their early state were pirates, and the Romans robbers, and both warred in character. Their glorious actions were performed, (If I may so express myself) in the manhood of their empire. Carthage, Greece, Asia, Spain, Gaul, and Britain, were not indeed conquered during the non-age of the republic. Agincourt, Cressey, Oudenard Ramillies, Blenheim, Dettingen, and Minden, surely were not fought in the infancy of the English Empire. "With the encrease of commerce, England has lost her spirit." This is really a curious discovery; who is unacquainted, that the English are the lords and factors of the universe, and that Britain joins to the commerce of Tyre, Carthage and Venice, the discipline of Greece, and the fire of old Rome. "The city of London, submits to continued insults, with the patience of a coward. The more men have to lose, the less willing they are to venture, and submit to courtly power with the trembling duplicity of a spaniel." That an inconsiderable part of the people in London, submit to a person not very honorably distinguished in the world is certain, but that the city of London submits to continued insults is certainly a mistake. I suppose our author means, that by submitting to the best laws on earth they submit to continued insults. The rich whom he so very honorably distinguishes, can be at no loss for his meaning. An Agrarian law, would perhaps be convenient for himself and his independents. It may not however be amiss to remind him of that, which in the multiplicity of his projects, he may have forgot, viz. that the richest part of the community will always be an overmatch for the poorest part. "It might be difficult, (says our author,) if not impossible, to form this Continent into a government half a century hence."

Here I humbly apprehend our author's meaning is truly conspicuous. This Continent fifty years hence, infallibly will be richer, and much better peopled than at present; consequently abler to effect a revolution. But alas! e'er that period, our author will forever be forgotten; impelled therefore by his villainous ambition, he would rashly precipitate his country into every species of horror, misery, and desolation, rather than forego his fancied protectorship. "But if you have, (says our author) and still can shake hands with the murderers, then are ye unworthy the name of husband, father, friend, or lover, and whatever may be your rank or title in life, you have the heart of a coward, and the spirit of a sycophant, &c. To talk of friendship with those in whom our reason forbids us to have faith, and our affections wounded through a thousand pores, instructs us to detest is madness and folly."

Ye that are not drunk with fanaticism answer me? Are these words dictated by peace, or base foul revenge, the constant attendant on cowards and sycophants? Does our author so perfectly versed in scripture, mean to conduct us to peace or desolation? or is he fit to legislate for men or devils? Nations after desolating each other, (happily for mankind,) forgive, forget, and reconcile; like individuals who quarrel, reconcile, and become friends. Following the laudable example of the CONGRESS, we lately have most readily shaken hands with our inveterate enemies the Canadians, who have scalped nearly as many of our people as the British troops have done. Why therefore may we not forgive and reconcile—By no means, it blasts our author's ambitious purposes. The English and Scotch, since the first Edward's time, have alternately slaughtered each other, (in the field of Bannockburn, more men fell, than are now in the New-England provinces) to the amount of several hundred thousand. And now view each other as subjects, despising the efforts of certain turbulent spirits, tending to rekindle the ancient animosity. Many of the unhappy men criminally engaged with the Pretender, reconciled by humane treatment to that family against whom they rebelled, served in their armies a few years after. Indeed the conduct of the Canadians to our troops, as effectually illustrates our doctrine, as it reprobates the Anti-christian, diabolical tenets of our author.

The unwarrantable stretch likewise, which that house made in their last sitting, to gain an undue authority over the Delegates of that province, ought to warn the people at large, how they trust POWER

OUT OF THEIR OWN HANDS. A set of instructions for the Delegates were put together, which in point of sense, and business would have dishonored a school-boy, and after being approved by a few, a very few, without doors, were carried into the house, and there passed in behalf of the whole Colony. Whereas, did the whole Colony know, with what ill will that house hath entered on some necessary public measures, they would not hesitate a moment to think them unworthy of such a trust.

This very insidious charge, we cannot read without indignation. If the Pennsylvanians, had happily adhered to their virtuous resolves, it is more than probable, that a constitutional reconciliation had e'er now taken place. Unfortunately, rescinding their opinion, they perhaps adopted the sentiments of *certain persons,* by no means superior in virtue or knowledge. Those not inebriated with independency, will certainly allow, that the instructions to their Delegates, were dictated by the true spirit of peace, justice, and exalted policy. If inspiration had dictated those resolves, obnoxious as they are to independency, our author had reprobated them. How dare the author of Common Sense say, "that they attempted to gain an undue authority over the Delegates of their province?" Who so proper to instruct them, as those chosen by the people; not in the hour of passion, riot and confusion, but in the day of peace and tranquil reflection. The gentleman, whom our author impotently attacks, in this and other innuendos; will be long revered by his grateful countrymen, and the friends of mankind; as well for his true patriotism and extensive abilities, as his unbounded benevolence. Would we profit by the unhappy examples of our ancestors, (which alas! mankind too seldom do,) let us remember the fate of those illustrious patriots, of the first Charles's time. Allied at first with the independents, they did not suspect those execrable hypocrites, of the horrid design of destroying the King and constitution. When they saw through their abominable views, it was too late to save the King and kingdom, for the independents had seized the sovereignty. Soon as they were firmly possessed of power, they persecuted those illustrious patriots, with more unrelenting virulence, than the professed advocates of arbitrary power. Every virtuous Pennsylvanian, must be fired with indignation at the insidious attack made by this independent on the respectable assembly of his province. Indeed, the Assembly of Pennsylvania in this unworthy treatment have a sure earnest of their future expectations. "It is the custom of nations," (says our author) "when any two are at war, for some other powers not engaged in the quarrel, to step in as mediators, and bring about the preliminaries of a peace. But while America calls herself the subject of Britain, no power, however well disposed she may be, can offer her mediation. Wherefore in our present state we may quarrel on forever."

Nations, like individuals, in the hour of passion attend to no mediation. But when heartily drubbed, and tired of war, are very readily reconciled, without the intervention of mediators; by whom, belligerents were never reconciled, until their interests or passions dictated the pacification. If we may use our author's elegant language, mediation is "farsical." I grant however, that the idea of our forcing England by arms to treat with us is brilliant. "It is unreasonable" (continues our author) "to suppose that France and Spain will give us any kind of assistance, if we mean only to make use of that assistance for the purpose of repairing the breach, and strengthening the connection between Britain and America; because those powers would be sufferers by the consequences."

Considering "we have the most numerous, and best disciplined army under Heaven; and a fleet fit to contend with the navy of Britain," we must suppose our Author's brain affected by dwelling constantly on his beloved independency, else he would not have the imbecility to require the assistance of France and Spain. The manner of his prevailing on France and Spain to assist us, is also a strong proof of his insanity. Did those powers hesitate to succour the Scotch rebels in 1745, because they did not declare themselves independent. It then was their interest to create a diversion, alas! too serious in the sequel for the deluded rebels in that kingdom; and were they now interested in aiding us, they undoubtedly would do it in spite of quibbles. In such case, e'er this time, their armies and navies had joined us without interruption: For we must confess, that the efforts of Britain hitherto, would not have precluded the republic of Genoa from aiding us. Suppose our author, had a son or an apprentice eloped to his intimate acquaintance, and desired to enter into his service. If this person replied to the youth: I know your apprenticeship is unexpired, notwithstanding declare yourself a freeman, and I will hire and protect you. I demand, would such odious, ridiculous duplicity, render our supposed person, less criminal in the eyes of our Author, or render the example less dangerous to his own apprentice. "Were a manifesto (says our author) dispatched to foreign courts, &c." This also is a conclusive proof of our author's maniacum delirium. Our author "challenges the warmest advocate for reconciliation to shew a single advantage this Continent can reap by being connected with Great Britain. I repeat the challenge, not a single advantage is derived: Our corn will fetch its price in any market in Europe." Were the author's assertions respecting our power, as real as delusive, a reconciliation on liberal principles with Great Britain, would be most excellent policy. I wave similarity of manners, laws, and customs, most friendly indeed to perpetual alliance. The greatest part of our plank, staves, shingles, hoops, corn, beef, pork, herrings, and many other articles, could find no vent, but in the English Islands. The demand for our flour would also be considerably lessened. The Spaniards have no demand for these articles and the French little or none. Britain would be a principal mart for our lumber, part of our grain, naval stores, tobacco, and many other articles, which perhaps are not generally wanted in any kingdom in Europe. If it is suggested, that the English Islands, impelled by necessity would trade with us. I reply, that it is not uncommon to see English flour for sale in those Islands, as our merchants have more than once found to their cost. Since 1750, flour hath sold in the Islands, at ten and twelve per cent. the price being reduced by flour from England.

Britain is also better calculated to supply us, with woollen goods and other necessary articles, than any kingdom in Europe. Should a separation ensue, Britain will open an extensive commerce to the Baltic, and Russia, for all, or many of the commodities, she now receives from us. The Russians, since their last glorious treaty with the Porte, can now export the commodities of their most fertile Ukraine, through the Mediterranean, until that period, they were constrained to carry their hemp, eight or nine hundred miles to the Baltic, whence by a long and dangerous navigation, it reached the different ports in the Atlantic. I need not inform the reader that such immense land carriage, precluded the subjects of Russia from raising wheat, which generally sold in the Ukraine for ten-pence per bushel, as did rye at five-pence in that extensive region, than which no country on earth is more happily adapted for that grain. The British nation, pre-eminently distinguished for industry and enterprise, will establish factories in the provinces of Russia, and animate those people to emulate our productions, which they will transport by the Mediterranean, to the ports of Europe, and the West-Indies. By these means, and the culture of Poland, our grain would probably be reduced to its pristine price, two shillings and six pence. As our Author is so violently bent against reconciliation, he must either suppose a constant war with the incensed power of England; or admit that he is a proper inhabitant of the domains of Ariosto (the world in the moon.). Now, admitting "we have the most numerous, and best disciplined army under Heaven; and a navy formidable for that of England" pray, what are our resources to pay such considerable armaments? Although I do not wish to mortify my countrymen; I must acknowledge that the neat proceeds of all our produce is inadequate to that end. Our Author allows "that we have a considerable check on the West India commerce of Britain, and that Great Britain has a considerable check upon our European trade."

In case Great Britain insults therefore our European bound ships, we have only to order our admirals to seise their West India-men. Unfortunately, the Algerines, and other piratical states of Africa have no West-India commerce; and not having the clearest distinctions of thine and mine, will be apt to seise our vessels. Our author affirms "that our trade will always be our protection." I therefore crave his pardon, and shall believe, that the sight of our grain, and smell of the New England Codfish, will effectually serve as a Mediterranean pass to the piratical rovers. I do humbly confess my suspicions, least Portugal extremely dependent on Great Britain, may not insult us. When independent, we no doubt will receive strong proofs of friendship from France and Spain. Nevertheless, with the utmost humility I imagine, could we seise Gibraltar or Portmahon, and there station a formidable squadron of capital ships; we might as effectually protect our commerce, as our trade will protect us. The author of Common Sense confidently affirms, "that our trade will always be its protection." I cannot imagine that his purse or watch would effectually protect him on Hounslow, or Blackheath from footpads or highwaymen. Hitherto we have treated of reconciliation on the principles of our being as potent as Great Britain. Let us now consider our army, nearly as I have stated it, and our navy as an object by no means sublunary. It now behoves us well to consider, whether it were better to enter the harbour of peace with Great Britain, or plunge the ship into all the horrors of war.— Of civil war. As peace and a happy extension of commerce, are objects infinitely better for Great Britain, than war and a diminution of her commerce. It therefore is her interest to grant us every species of indulgence, consistent with our constitutional dependence, should war continue, there can be no doubt of the annihilation of our ships, ports and commerce, by Great Britain. The King's ships now in New England, unhappily are more than sufficient to ruin the ports and commerce of these provinces. New York is already secured; and I should be extremely grieved to hear that a small armament were destined against Philadelphia. In the opinion of the best officers of the navy, Philadelphia is accessible to a few forty and fifty gunships, in despite of our temporary expedients to fortify the river Delaware. If such opinion is groundless, the ministry by their imbecillity have befriended us; since by guarding the River Delaware with a few frigates only, they had precluded us from arming our vessels and strengthening the river Delaware. I would remind our author of the constant language, and apparent purport of all ranks in opposition to Great Britain: "We have" (say they) "been the happiest people on earth, and would continue to be so, should Great Britain renounce her claim of taxation. We have no sinister views, we claim not independence; No! Perish the thought." Such I believe also was the tenor of the petitions from the Congress to his Majesty. Now I would ask every man of sentiment, what opinion our friends in Great Britain, nay the whole world will entertain of us, if ingratefully, and madly adopting our author's frantic schemes, we reject reasonable terms of reconciliation? Will they not most assuredly believe, that our popular leaders, have by infinite art, deluded the unwary people into their pre-concerted schemes; on supposition, *that the time had found us?* Those acquainted with Britain must confess, that the minority in parliament, hitherto have been our main prop. Now independency for ever annihilates this our best resource. Let us admit a part of the minority, republicans, or what is more probable, bent on removing the present ministry from their power. Our author's schemes annihilates all their consequence, all their opposition. In case of our independence, should a BARRE, or BURKE, patronise our government; such patrons, would infallibly participate the fate of the great and good DEWITTS; be torn in pieces by the furious People.——If my remarks are founded on truth, it results, *that the time hath not found us;* that independency is inexpedient, ruinous, and impracticable, and that reconciliation with Great Britain on good terms, is our sole resource. 'Tis this alone, will render us respectable; it is this alone, will render us numerous; it is this only, will make us happy.

I shall no longer detain my reader, but conclude with a few remarks on our Author's scheme. The people of those Colonies would do well to consider the character, fortune, and designs of our Author, and his independents; and compare them with those of the most amiable and venerable personages in, and out of the Congress, who abominate such nefarious measures. I would humbly observe, that the specious science of politics, is of all others, the most delusive. Soon after the Revolution, the ablest states-men in England, and other parts of Europe confidently predicted National ruin, infallible ruin, soon as the Public debt exceeded fifty millions sterling. The Nation now indebted nearly thrice that sum, is not arrived at the zenith of her credit and power. It is perhaps possible to form a specious system of government on paper which may seem practicable, and to have the consent of the people; yet it will not answer in practice, nor retain their approbation upon trial. "All plans of government (says HUME) which suppose great reformation in the manners of mankind, are merely imaginary."

The fabricators of Independency have too much influence to be entrusted in such ardous and important concerns. This reason alone, were sufficient at present, to deter us from altering the Constitution. It would be as inconsistent in our leaders in this hour of danger to form a government, as it were for a Colonel forming his battalion in the face of an enemy, to stop to write an essay on war.

This author's Quixotic system, is really an insult to our understanding; it is infinitely inferior to HUME's idea of a perfect Common Wealth, which notwithstanding his acknowleged greatness of genius, is still reprehensible. It is not our business to examine, in what manner this author's associates, acquired their knowledge in national affairs; but we may predict, that his scheme of independency would soon, very soon give way to a government imposed on us, by some Cromwell of our armies. Nor is this sentiment unnatural, if we are attentive to constant experience, and human nature. The sublime MON-TESQUIEU, so aptly quoted by the Congress, unhappily corrob-orates our doctrine,

from (says he) a manner of thinking that prevails amongst man-kind. They set a higher value upon courage than timorousness, on activity than prudence, on strength than counsel. Hence, the army will ever despise a senate, and respect their own officers. They will naturally slight the order sent them by a body of men whom they look upon as cowards, and therefore unworthy to command them, so that as soon as the army depends on the legislative body, it be-comes a military one;

and if the contrary has ever happened, it has been owing to some extraordinary circumstances, such as Holland being able to drown her garrisons, and the Venetians having it in their power to compel their troops to obedience by the vicinity of the European armies, Resources to which we forever must be strangers. If independence takes place, the New England men by their consequence therein, will assume a superiority, im-patiently to be born by the other Colonies.

Notwithstanding our Author's fine words about toleration: Ye sons of peace and true christianity, believe me, it were folly supreme, madness, to expect angelic toleration from New-En-gland, where she has constantly been detested, persecuted and execrated. Even in vain would our Author, or our CROMWELL cherish toleration, for the people of New-England, not yet ar-rived in the seventeenth or eighteeenth century, would repro-bate her.—It is more than probable to suppose, that the New-

England governments would have no objection to an Agrarian law; nor is it unreasonable to suppose, that such division of property would be very agreeable to the soldiers. Indeed their General could not perhaps with safety to his existence as a General, refuse them so reasonable a gratification, particularly, as he will have more than one occasion for their services. Let us however admit that our General and troops, contradicting the experience of ages, do not assume the sovereignty. Released from foreign war, we would probably be plunged into all the misery of anarchy and intestine war. Can we suppose that the people of the south, would submit to have the seat of Empire at Philadelphia, or in New England; or that the people oppressed by a change of government, contrasting their misery with their former happy state, would not invite Britain to re-assume the sovereignty.

A failure of commerce precludes the numerous tribe of planters, farmers and others, from paying their debts contracted on the faith of peace and commerce. They cannot, nor perhaps ought not to pay their debts. A war will ensue between the creditors and their debtors, which will eventually end in a general spunge or abolition of debts, which has more than once happened in other States on occasions similar.

Ye respectable descendants of the planters from Holland and Swisserland; who acknowledge, that your fathers have instructed you to felicitate yourselves in existing under the benign British government. And have taught you to execrate the Government of Holland and other popular states, where the unhappy people unacquainted with trial by jury and other peculiar felicities of British Subjects are, (to use the significant language of your fathers) under the harrow of oppressive Demagogues. Do ye possess the wisdom to continue your happiness by a well regulated connection with Britain?

Volumes were insufficient to describe the horror, misery and desolation, awaiting the people at large in the Syren form of

American independence. In short, I affirm that it would be most excellent policy in those who wish for TRUE LIBERTY to submit by an advantageous reconciliation to the authority of Great Britain; "to accomplish in the long run, what they cannot do by hypocrisy, fraud and force in the short one."

INDEPENDENCE AND SLAVERY
ARE SYNONYMOUS TERMS.

F I N I S

Index

Index

In the following index no entries are provided for such broad topics as "English constitution," "British Empire," "Power of Parliament," or "Colonial rights," since the whole of each of the pamphlets reprinted here could be indexed under any one or all of such entries.

THE AMERICAN HERITAGE SERIES

TOPICAL VOLUMES